Tales from a Charmed Life

Tales from a Charmed Life

A Balinese Painter Reminisces

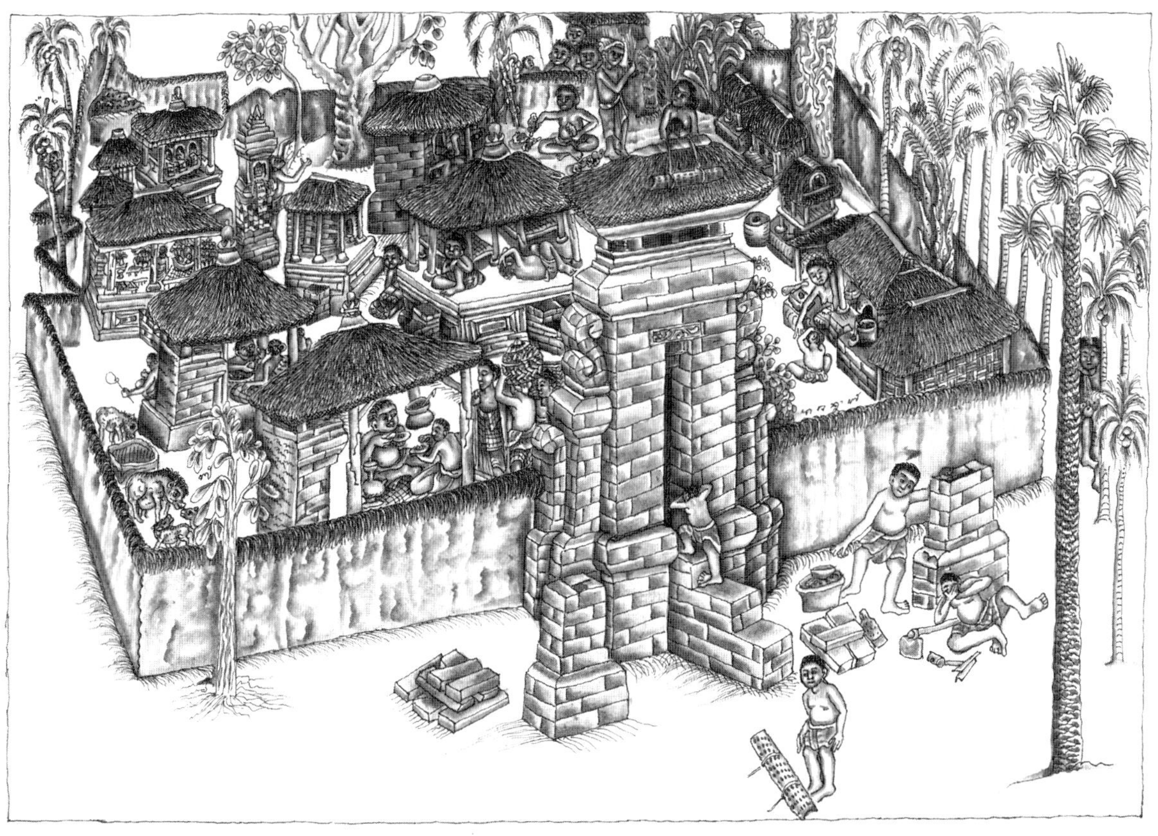

Hildred Geertz and Ida Bagus Madé Togog

HAWAI'I University of Hawai'i Press | Honolulu

Printed in the United States of America
10 09 08 07 06 05 6 5 4 3 2 1

Library of Congress Cataloging-in-Publication Data
Geertz, Hildred.
Tales from a charmed life : a Balinese painter reminisces / Hildred Geertz and Ida Bagus Madé Togog.
p. cm.
Includes bibliographical references and index.
ISBN 0-8248-2822-4 (hardcover : alk. paper)
1. Togog, Ida Bagus Madé, d. 1989—Childhood and youth. 2. Painters—Indonesia—Bali (Province)—Biography. 3. Togog, Ida Bagus Madé, d. 1989—Interviews. 4. Painters—Indonesia—Bali (Province)—Interviews. I. Title.
ND1026.8.T64G44 2005
759.9598—dc22 2004024171

Illustration credits—Figure 1: Tempera on cloth. Photograph by Uwe Hamilton, 1974; Figures 5, 8, 9, 10, 11, 12, 13, 14, 15, 18, 19, 20, 21, 22: Ink on paper, 11½ × 16 in. Geertz Collection; Figure 17: Ink on cloth, 10 × 13½ in., 1984. Geertz Collection; Figures 23, 36, 37, 38: Tempera on cloth, c. 4 × 5 ft. Photographed July 1982, in Peguyungan, Badung; Figure 25: Ink on paper, 28 × 18¼ in., February 21, 1939. Bateson-Mead Collection; Figures 25–34: Ink on paper, 21 × 12 in., 1937–1938. Bateson-Mead Collection; Figures 6, 7, 16, 35. Drawings by Sandra Vitzthum.

University of Hawai'i Press books are printed on acid-free paper and meet the guidelines for permanence and durability of the Council on Library Resources.

Designed by April Leidig-Higgins
Printed by Thomson-Shore, Inc.

Contents

Acknowledgments vii

A Note on Terms, Names, and Spelling ix

Introduction How This Book Came to Be 1

Chapter One Childhood Memories 13

Chapter Two Wanderings, Gambling, Friendships 45

Chapter Three Learning 85

Chapter Four Performing Rituals 119

Chapter Five Family Matters 155

Chapter Six Painting 179

Afterword A Charmed Life 207

Appendix 1 The Dream Pictures (1937–1938) 217

Appendix 2 The Temple Paintings 225

Notes 233

Glossary 237

Bibliography 241

Index 243

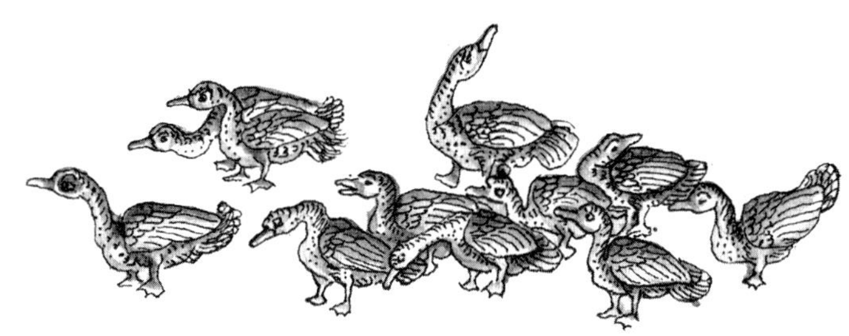

Acknowledgments

I deeply regret that I have taken so long to complete this book, with the consequence that Ida Bagus Madé Togog never had a chance to see it. He died in 1989. I hope that his other children and grandchildren will enjoy looking through it.

My greatest debt, which pervades the whole enterprise, is to Togog's son Ida Bagus Putu Gedé, now named Pedanda Batuan. His patience and understanding, his broad knowledge, and his marvelous ability to teach made it possible to understand what his father told me. Knowing him has been a constant pleasure.

Enabling my research throughout the years has been the friendly and generous support of all those other researchers in Bali, past and present, whose work and friendship has inspired and corrected my far-out guesses and redirected me into more fruitful fields of inquiry. I have named them in my other books, and they know who they are.

A number of people have read various drafts of this book, and I thank them again for their patience and imaginative responses: Adrian Vickers, Karen Gordon, Kenneth George, Eugenia Shanklin, Elizabeth Anne Socolow, Alison Lake, and an anonymous reader for the University of Hawai'i Press. Any mistakes are my own.

My Indonesian institutional sponsors, over the years of field research, were the Indonesian Institute of the Sciences (LIPI) and the University of Udayana in Bali. Funding was given me by the following: the Social Science Research Council; the National Science Foundation (Grant Nos. BNS 81-12418, BNS 84-05549, and BNS 83-14361); the Institute for Intercultural Studies; the Wenner-Gren Foundation; the American Council of Learned Societies; and the Princeton University Committee on Research. I am grateful to all of these institutions.

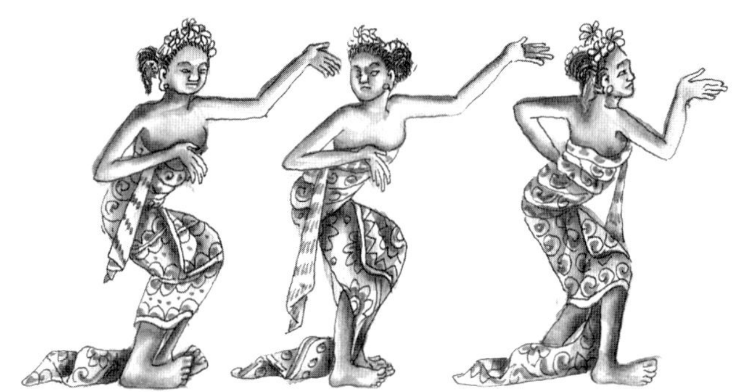

A Note on Terms, Names, and Spelling

There are many variations in pronunciation and spelling of Balinese terms to be found in Bali. I have followed the official dictionary, *Kamus Bali-Indonesia,* for all spelling. All italicized terms are Balinese unless otherwise indicated as Indonesian or Dutch, while Balinese words that are proper nouns are not italicized. For instance, names of gods, names of altars, names of people according to their occupation (e.g, the Pamangku, a particular priest of a certain temple) are not italicized.

Balinese words are built around "roots" with affixes. I try to give the word both with its affix and its root, as in *mecaru* and *caru.* The nasalized prefixes *me-* or *nge-* or *n-* turn a "passive" word into "active" one: for example, *caru,* "an offering that is given to the demons"; *macaru,* "to give an offering to the demons." Adding the prefix *ke-* and the suffix *-an* can convert a concrete term into an abstraction: for example, *sakti,* "spiritual power in the concrete" becomes the abstraction *kasaktian,* "abstract spiritual power."

Balinese words have no plurals (except for doubling when one wants to stress plurality). I usually give them in the singular, relying on context to show that they are plural.

An important meaning-bearing linguistic form in Balinese is the use of social register. An intricate vocabulary for indicating respect or familiarity is employed in nearly every sentence uttered. Such terms carry meanings, not only concerning nuances of the status of the persons to whom one is speaking, but also, importantly, the relative status of persons of whom one speaks.

Honorific titles of people and of gods are required in everyday speech and writing, such as "Ida Bagus" for Brahmana men and "Ida Betara" and "Ida Sanghyang" for gods. I follow Balinese usage here, giving the entire title out of respect for the personages referred to, despite the fact that it adds difficulty for some readers. Some people, in everyday speech, are referred to by a term that would indicate a role—for instance, Pedanda (priest)—so when a role is the subject it is uncapitalized (e.g., *pedanda*) but when used as a proper name (e.g., Pedanda) it is capitalized.

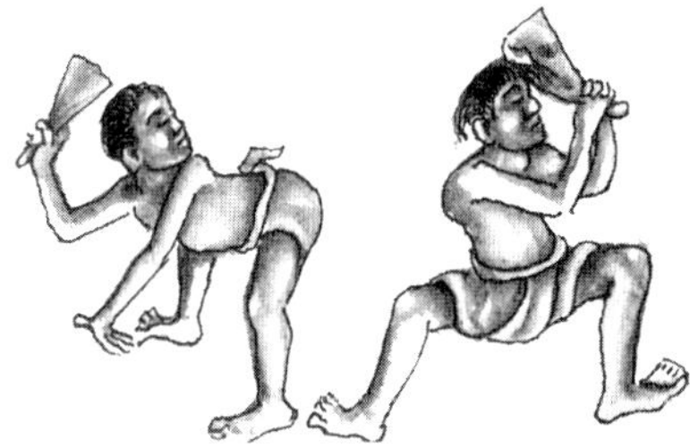

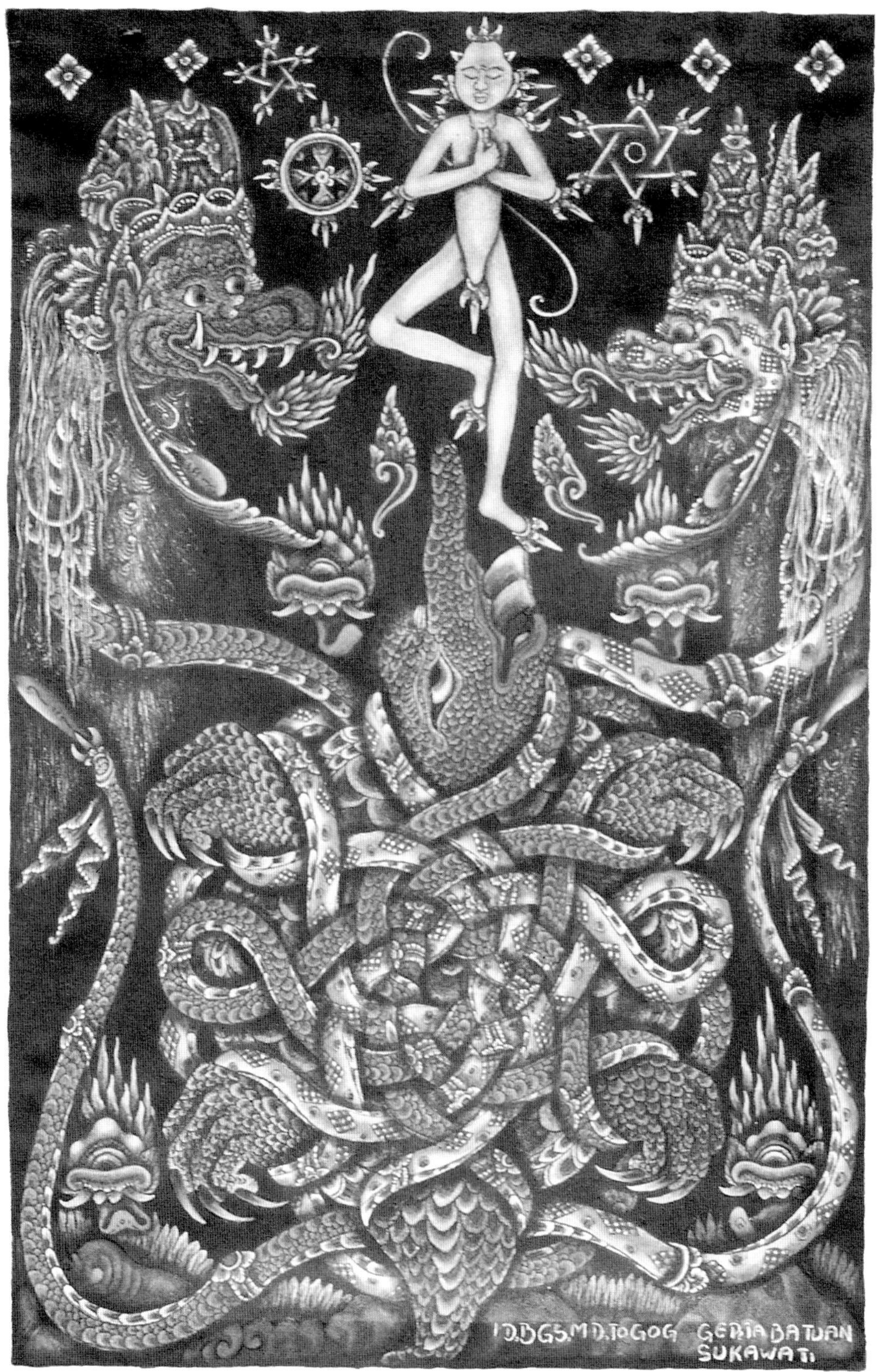

Figure 1. Sanghyang Cintia, the Unknowable Deity. Painting by Ida Bagus Madé Togog, 1974.

Tales from a Charmed Life

Introduction How This Book Came to Be

Ida Bagus Madé Togog was an important innovator in Balinese art in the twentieth century. He was one of the first in his village to attempt the new kind of paintings that foreigners in Bali wished to buy. Landless and needing to support a young wife and infant, when Togog tried his hand at the strange genre, to his own astonishment he was able to earn what he considered an enormous sum of money. That was in 1933. He was then about twenty years old.

With no instruction and with few model pictures to guide them, Togog and his younger kinsmen and neighbors created their own version of the new genre. Other young men were doing likewise in other villages, but because of the relative isolation of villages from one another at that time, each place developed its own forms, styles, and favored pictorial contents. Togog's personal vivid imagination was pivotal to this activity in his own village, Batuan. At first the foreign buyers were a few European artists, wealthy travelers, and Dutch officials in the new colonial government. In the 1970s and 1980s, with the building of a jet airfield and new hotels, a flood of middle-class and hippie tourists came. Most of these were looking for cheap handmade souvenirs, but some wanted high-quality art. Togog came to stand out as an exemplar of "the Batuan style," and foreign cognoscenti often visited his home to purchase his best paintings. Togog's works remained at the top of the market of fine tourist art until his death in 1989.[1]

This book is a compilation of stories Togog told me in 1983 about his early life. They were tape-recorded, and I have tried, in their translation and organization, to preserve his own voice and concerns and to distinguish them clearly from my own. I sought Togog out in the first place because of his position in the history of Balinese painting. I did not choose to study him and his village because I especially admired his paintings, as an art historian might, but because I was curious about the social and cultural events that had produced these artworks and the light that history could throw on the nature of contemporary Balinese society.

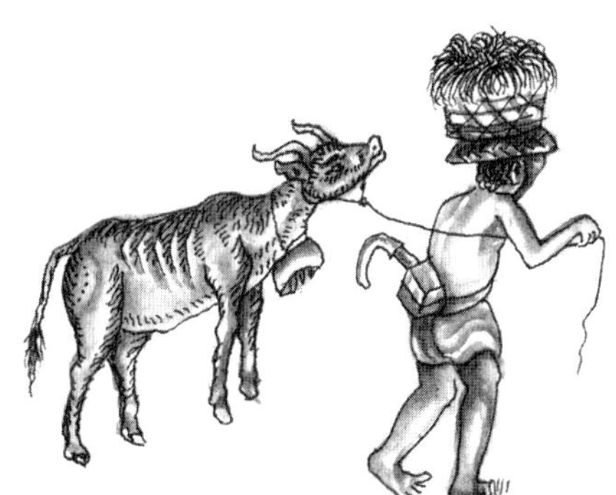

As for Togog's dark and intricate paintings themselves, I wanted to learn how he thought about them, what kinds of meanings he gave the visual forms he produced. I wanted to know in what ways various aspects of his life came together—or did not—in his markings on paper or canvas. I wanted to know how central painting was to his view of himself and his life. Did he see his paintings as commodities, as products of his craftsmanship, as channels for emotional expression, as examples of "Balinese culture" for foreign understanding, or as something else more closely bound into his personal concerns? Principally, I wanted to know if there were deeper meanings to the paintings than might have immediately appeared.

I have found some answers to these questions about painting, but I have learned many other things—about the texture of everyday life in colonial Bali of the 1920s and 1930s, about the activities of a ritual specialist, about wage work on coffee and coconut plantations, about illness and healing, and about gambling. Above all, I gained new insights into the religious foundation of Togog's life, how he made sense of the fears and sufferings he and his family experienced, where the basis of his deep assurance of security resided, and why he felt that his life was protected or "charmed." I learned of these matters not through Togog's explicit teaching, but rather through hearing about specific acts and decisions he made in daily life and in difficult crises. Gradually they became clear to me, as I hope they will to the reader. It was studying these embedded actions—and the ways Togog spoke about them—that transformed my own assumptions and conjectures about the nature of Balinese religious history and profoundly informed the two other books I've written about Balinese art.[2] I explore these issues further in the Afterword.

My First Meetings with Togog

I first learned about Togog while doing a study of a collection of paintings from Bali of the 1930s made by the anthropologists Margaret Mead and Gregory Bateson. In 1936, when Togog was around twenty-five years old and had been painting for about three years, he met Mead and Bateson, who were doing research in Bali at the time. He had heard there were some new *"turis"* at Walter Spies' place, and he had his friends bring them some paintings for sale. Attracted by the expressiveness of these paintings by Togog and his fellows of the village of Batuan, Mead and Bateson decided to study the artists and their works systematically, as part of their investigation of "Balinese character." Over the next three years, they collected 845 paintings and drawings from Togog's village and interviewed each artist about his life and work.

Mead showed me the pictures in 1973. They were still rolled up in the *London Times* of March 1938 in which she and Gregory Bateson had packed them just before leaving Bali at the end of their fieldwork.[3] Some of Togog's larger pictures struck me immediately with their threatening power, even though then I did not then know who he was or what these dark scenes were about.

Bateson and Mead published little on that research.[4] In the 1970s Mead gave me full access to their materials, and I determined to follow up on the work they had begun. My book, *Images of Power: Balinese Paintings Made for Gregory Bateson and Margaret Mead* (1994) presents my interpretations of the meanings of the paintings by the whole Batuan group, set in an understanding of their complex intercultural context.

I arranged to borrow the collection, and in my Princeton office catalogued and displayed some of its pictures. I went to the Library of Congress and read Mead and Bateson's extensive field notes on Bali, largely in Balinese. In 1980 I decided to begin a

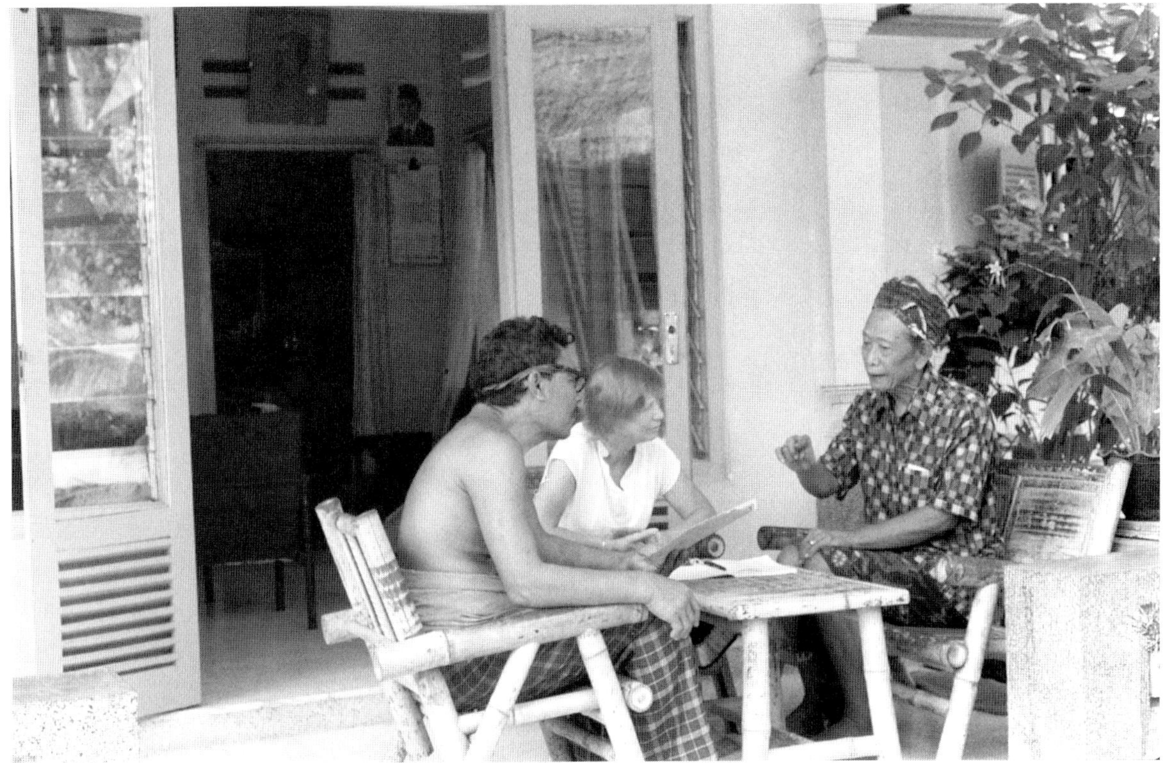

Figure 2. Ida Bagus Madé Togog and Hildred Geertz discussing a picture with Déwa Ketut Baru *(left)*, Batuan, 1982.

long-term field study of the Batuan painters who were now in their seventies, and in 1981 I spent a summer in Bali, started to study Balinese, and arranged for a place to stay in Batuan, a sprawling lowland settlement on the road between Denpasar and Ubud.

In June of 1982 I moved into Batuan, to continue to study Balinese and to begin to get to know some of the older painters. About four weeks after I had settled in, Togog came to see me. Probably he had heard that I was there from my landlord, Déwa Ketut Baru, Togog's old friend, and that I was studying the painters. Although I was fluent in Indonesian, I was still struggling to teach myself Balinese. Togog could speak only marketplace Indonesian and so I stumbled through a few phrases in Balinese, asking haltingly if I could come and talk with him. How about two days later, he asked. I said I would go to his place. He agreed, but then early on the morning of the appointed day, to my surprise, Togog strode into my house, all ready to be interviewed. We had a long and pleasant conversation, with my landlord, Déwa Baru, interpreting into Indonesian as Togog described the main outlines of his life in painting.

In the course of our first long conversation, Togog told me he had once made a couple of paintings for a village temple in Peguyungan near Denpasar. I immediately asked him if we could go to see it, and we arranged to go the very next day. I hired a jitney, and Togog, Baru, and another old friend, a stone-carver who had made the main altar in Togog's family tem-

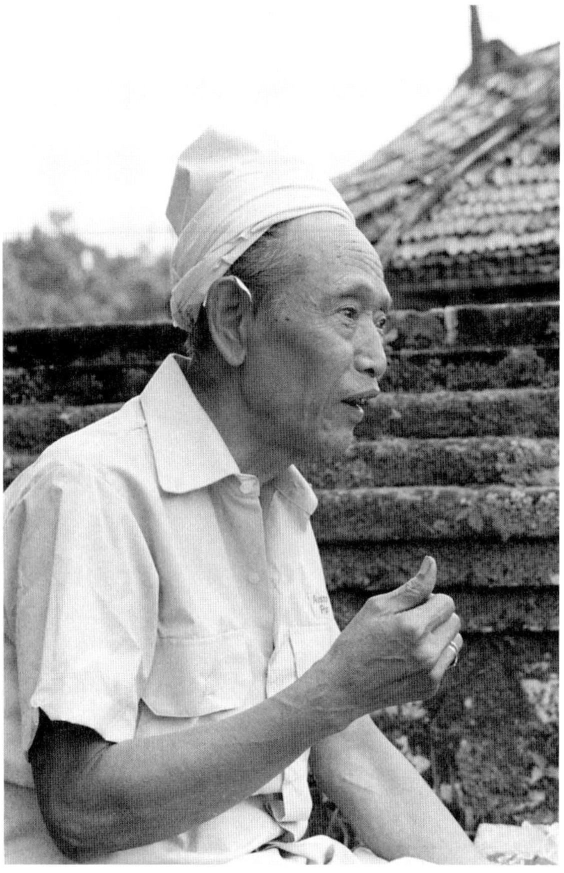

Figure 3. Ida Bagus Madé Togog saying a prayer over a set of offerings, July 1983.

ple, and I piled in. By road it took about an hour to get to the temple. If we had walked on paths across the rice fields it would have been about half the time. The paintings were remarkable (see Chapter 6), but what had greater consequence for me was the trip there and back.

During our pilgrimage to see his temple paintings, Togog turned out to be a jovial, unpretentious, and talkative guide. In the car, with his friends, who were all lower in status than he as a Brahmana, he spoke only the rough, intimate register of Balinese, the one I, as a low foreigner, was never permitted to speak to anyone. Thus while he regaled his friends with many tales of his experiences I could hardly understand him. I believe that one of the stories he told us was about a scary lone trek he took one night from the mountain village of Bayung Gedé, where Mead and Bateson were staying in 1936, home to Batuan—a tale he tells again here, in Chapter 6. Hearing these fragments aroused my curiosity, and I resolved to study harder and try to speak Balinese more, a difficult task in a situation where most people I knew spoke fluent Indonesian.

On my next field trip, the following summer, I asked Togog to tell me his life story, speaking into a tape recorder and starting with his earliest memories. My Balinese was still elementary, but I had arranged with a Balinese student to transcribe the tapes, and I figured I could use them as texts for language practice. I didn't guess how seriously Togog would take my request. He said yes and asked me to come back in two days time, to begin. When I arrived, I saw that he had asked his daughter, Dayu Putu Gambar, to make some offerings. He told me that the offerings were to his ancestors. Only after performing the ritual announcement and presentation did he begin the stories.

In that first recording session Togog focused on his earliest memories, which make up a large part of Chapter 1. He also skipped forward to tell me something of his first attempts at painting, matters on which I had talked with him before. It was clear after more than two hours that there was much more he wanted to tell me, and we arranged to meet again the next day. We went on with nearly daily meetings for more than two weeks. The tape cassettes I gave to my assistant, who took them home to Denpasar and not only carefully transcribed everything Togog and I said, but typed it all up.

It is important to realize that, as he spoke, I never interrupted Togog to ask questions, because at the time my competence in Balinese was still so elementary that I could usually get only the general drift of what he was telling me. I let him decide what to talk about, and did not ask him about omissions, except at the end. The consequence of my passive nonintervention during the interviews, was that the document we produced is almost entirely Togog's own.

After I had been listening to him for more two weeks, Togog said to me that he was nearly finished: "I haven't told you everything. I could fill up fifty cassettes and it wouldn't be enough, but I've told you the important things first." To my puzzlement, he had not yet told me much about his painting career; in particular, he had said nothing about Walter Spies and Rudolph Bonnet and Margaret Mead and Gregory Bateson. So I asked how he had gotten into painting, and he then related much of what is in Chapter 6. This was the only major intervention I made. When Togog finished with that topic, I decided to take careful stock of what he had told me before we made any more tapes, to wait until I had read through all the transcriptions, which by then formed a manuscript of more than three hundred pages.

At the end of August I had to return to Princeton to teach. The day I went to say good-bye until the following summer, I told Togog that I would like to make a book about his life and showed him the typed transcript. Togog's son, Ida Bagus Putu Gedé, who had been sitting nearby painting during our talks, then got up and came over to speak to me. He said that he and his sister had been listening to Togog's recitals to me, and that they were very worried. There is a great difference, said Gedé, between oral accounts and written, published, ones. Telling about experiences in an informal situation, mentioning people in derogatory ways, or laughing about improper sexual acts, are different when they are written down. He and his sister were particularly anxious that no one in Batuan be insulted in print and that Togog's own respectable reputation not be harmed. I was taken aback, and nervously assured him that I would publish nothing they didn't want me to. As a demonstration of my good faith, I gave him the carbon copy of the manuscript to read. Next June, when I come back to Bali, we can talk about it further, I added. When I returned nine months later, they had not read the manuscript, but offered to go over it with me.

The consequence of Ida Bagus Putu Gedé's concern about propriety was that we spent months and months, from 1984 into 1986, going over Togog's words, line by line. The three of us sat together, Togog's son read each sentence aloud, and then we discussed its intent and meaning. Most of our time was spent correcting my translations and interpreting and augmenting what Togog had said, while my tape recorder listened in. Ida Bagus Putu Gedé is an extremely intelligent, lucid, and above all honest man, and he became very interested in the project.

In the end we added much and took out nothing of importance. A few names and several passages describing minor youthful sexual experiments were all that were censored. But what I had gained were two thoughtful teachers of Balinese language and culture, and a heightened sense of the richness of the Balinese language, its specification of nuances of feeling and of status relationships, the complexities of Balinese ritual life, and the expressive depths of Balinese oral storytelling. Without the extensive aid of Ida Bagus Putu Gedé, this book would never have been possible.

Another source of additional materials on Togog's early life was a set of drawings he made for me in 1985, after I had nearly finished a first draft translation. I had had a particularly hard time unraveling the lengthy land dispute Togog had with several people, partly because he didn't like to name people directly, but mainly because he assumed I knew who all the dramatis personae were. After coming to a standstill in interviewing, I tried a different tack. I asked Togog to draw me a map of his neighborhood, houseyard by houseyard, and to indicate on it who was living where, and what relationship everyone had with him. I gave him a pad of drawing paper. When I came back a few days later he had not produced a map, but rather a bird's-eye picture of his childhood houseyard, with little figures among the pavilions that are both shelter and furniture in a Balinese home (see fig. 5).

The next day Togog made another and then another of these complex drawings, finally completing nineteen of them, depicting all the important locales of his earliest memories. Taken together they chart the main places in his childhood Batuan. With my tape recorder listening, Togog spoke about each of these pictures, opening up another wave of reminiscences. I have integrated these drawings and their stories into the first three chapters of this book.

Togog's Presentations of Himself

The form of Togog's text, taken as a whole, is not a "life story" with a plot of crisis and denouement. Nor does it have a main theme of building towards his competence in painting, as my questions might have suggested to him. He also did not choose to cover all the major aspects of "Balinese culture" for the benefit of a foreigner, as was the habit of his son and many other Balinese of the younger generation.

Instead, Togog told me a series of fragmentary anecdotes in much the same way as he had done on the jitney trip to Peguyungan. While he understood that my request for his "life history" (*riwayat hidup* in Indonesian) carried the implication that I wanted him to put his reminiscences in chronological order, he had considerable trouble doing that. Several times he told me that he had been lying awake the night before trying to remember when various things happened and now he had several earlier experiences to tell me. Twice he started a session by asking me to put what he had to tell me on a separate tape and insert it into certain earlier stories. Every tale proved to be independent of the others, and the sequences—despite these efforts to be chronological—were largely according to associations of various sorts, to places, or people, certain activities.

A small number of Togog's accounts, on the other hand, are of a private nature, and concern a sort of experience that he may never before have attempted to put into narrative form. These include the story of his marriage and first child, and the tale of his struggles with close family members over the inheritance of a plot of land; both of these are recorded in Chapter 5.

However, most of Togog's tales bear the marks of frequent tellings to various kinds of audiences, of the sort of performances I witnessed on the way to Peguyungan. For this reason, Togog's tales must be read with an anthropologist's skepticism, a recognition of the ever-present Bakhtinian double-voicing of his words. I have attempted to discern where and how Togog may have tailored his presentation of self and of his world in response, not only to his friends and family's reactions, but also to his perceptions of my expectations as a foreigner. I needed to judge where alteration had occurred, where my own efforts to formulate a coherent sense of him and his world might have been intuited and adopted by him.

After all, I was by no means the first foreigner to come to Togog and ask him about himself and his works. There had been many others, starting with the artists Rudolf Bonnet and Walter Spies in the early 1930s, and then Bateson and Mead, whom he knew over a period of two years. And in the 1970s the Swiss geographer, Albert Leeman, often visited him, buying many of his paintings. In the 1980s the Australian art historian Adrian Vickers interviewed Togog at length in the course of his work on the *gambuh* dance drama and its poetic texts.[5] In fact, I had gone to see Togog twice in 1980 before I moved to Batuan, and although I was at the time just another nameless stranger, Togog and his son greeted me hospitably and answered my questions about how he had started making pictures to sell to tourists and who were his fellow early painters. At that time Togog had easily talked to me how he had started painting, about the contents of his first pictures, about how the European painters, Bonnet and Spies, had paid him for them, had suggested painting scenes of everyday life, had provided him with paper and paints, and so on. (See Chapter 6 for versions of these anecdotes.) Togog was familiar with people like me, and he and his son, Gedé, knew (or thought they knew) what would interest and please us.

Nonetheless, after considerable thought, I have come to the conclusion that Togog did not revise his stories for me, or if he did so at all, only minimally. His demeanor throughout my acquaintance with him and his construction of these stories are marked by personal simplicity, what the Balinese would term *polos*. One day, when I mentioned to one of Togog's friends that I was having trouble figuring out his family relationships, he said that Togog was *belog*. This might be translated as "stupid," but I don't think that was what was meant. He went on to say that Togog isn't interested in anything that is not right in front of him, or *nyata* (Ind. "obvious"). "For myself," the friend said, "I'm always trying to find out things about my family, to figure out what has happened, but he doesn't do that." This bore out my own experience with Togog. He never tried to systematize or generalize his knowledge. He just told me what he himself had experienced in his own terms. He never appeared to be tailoring his talk to me as his listener, to craft his stories for foreign consumption, to fit my imagined taste or my imagined questions, nor for my imagined approval. In short, Togog did not speak "foreigner talk" as most younger Balinese do today. He gave little or no explication of terms or customs to me as an ignorant outsider. This, of course, was one of the reasons I had such difficulty understanding his text as I listened to it along with the transcriptions others had prepared for me. Togog's son, Gedé, on the other hand, experienced in talking with tourists, almost always knew when a term needed explication.

This simplicity, of course, makes the text, especially the Balinese version, invaluable to an anthropologist. Perhaps anthropologists need two kinds of consultants. The first kind, like Turner's Michona the Hornet, organizes his information to give it the generality and coherence that the anthropologist needs to provide an immediate cultural framework. The second kind, into which Togog falls, provides many diverse unprocessed attitudes and conceptions that are open to multiple interpretations. These unelicited remarks, less certainly products of anthropological expectations, are more likely to be expressions of the more fundamental attitudes and conceptions for which a foreign researcher searching.

What Togog Did Not Talk About

The important Balinese institutions of civility—not mentioning trouble, not confronting enemies, not speaking about one's own strengths—create a conventional mode of talking in which much is suggested rather than spoken, leaving the anthropologist, like everyone else in Bali, to infer and guess a great deal. The more experienced one is in living in Bali, the more accurate these guesses.

Togog was silent about many important pieces of information. For instance, there is very little in these narratives about the sometimes tumultuous larger history within which his life spun itself out. For instance, there are only brief mentions of aspects of the colonial presence, and nothing about the Japanese occupation. The struggle for Indonesian independence, during which Togog's close friend, his wife's brother, was imprisoned for guerilla action and later informally exiled from Batuan for some years was never spoken about, although I later heard these stories from the man himself. Also never mentioned were the vicious local killings of "Communists" in 1965, one of whom in Batuan was a distant cousin of Togog.[6]

Togog sometimes omitted key actors in his narratives. For instance he forgot to explain the presence of his father's father, who was a high Brahmana priest (a *pedanda*) and who seems to have been alive until Togog was about five or six years old. Togog says in his first sentence that there were two priests in his household when he was a child, when in fact there must have been three. Perhaps the elderly *pedanda* was ailing. Another silence surrounds Togog's own children, and his second wife. Also, in his account of his painting career Togog did not describe the significant shift in materials and techniques from ink on paper to tempera on cloth, which occurred around 1945 – 1949 with the opening up of Bali to mass tourism after World War II.

Togog's paintings as well as his stories allude, but only tangentially, to the matters that are most important to him. In his conversations Togog said little about his paintings; but underneath all, there is a sense that the pictures were in fact embedded in his life.

The background notes and commentaries I have written fill in some of Togog's omissions. They range from explaining obvious material details to expanding on my own larger interpretive leaps. I have taken these stories to illuminate one another, and have looked to other knowledge I possess about Balinese discourses and events to help the reader build up a more complete picture of life in Bali in the 1930s. I have tried to listen for the larger plots from which the stories derive their life, the taken-for-granted and therefore unmentioned assumptions that give the paintings and the anecdotes the deeper meanings that they might have held for this most idiosyncratic yet ordinary Balinese.

Translation Dilemmas

I have listened to Togog's tapes many times, and each time the sound brings back the quiet houseyard with its flowering trees. There were always roosters crowing in the background, children laughing, the steady chirp of a cricket in the thatch above us, the clink of our glasses of tea, the dog barking when someone came into the courtyard, and the occasional voice of a ritual client coming to see Togog for advice.

Togog, like most Balinese, spoke emphatically, putting strong stress on the main words in each sentence, giving an impression of intensity and a kind of staccato rhythm. He told his stories energetically, stressing important words, and emphasizing events with exclamations, like *"Bah!"* and *"Peh!"* He imitated the sound of the voices of people in his tales, or would go into a whisper when coming to spooky or naughty parts or when uttering the name of someone older than he. He'd laugh, briefly but often, and sometimes break into song. He enjoyed telling me these stories, as clearly he had enjoyed telling others the same stories in the past.

A great distortion was created as soon as I had Togog's words transcribed and typed. The spontaneous flow of speech, as Togog's son pointed out, obeys different rules of propriety and decorum than the printed word. Even listening to tapes blocks out all the visual and social cues that give so much meaning to the bare bones of what has been said. The raw Balinese transcript that Togog, Gedé, and I worked from was difficult to read, for it had been only minimally punctuated, and sketchily organized into sentences and paragraphs. Later, back in Princeton, I always listened to the tapes while reading his words, for the oral record is fuller and therefore more easily understandable.

But an even greater kind of distortion appeared when I translated Togog's tales from Balinese into English, as I rearranged Togog's spoken words so as to make sense to an English reader. I had to ask myself such questions as: Should I reach for English slang terms that match Togog's informal speech patterns? Should I try to keep the strangeness of some Balinese metaphors? Should I clutter the text with notes on how I have altered it—for instance, where I've added a proper name when Togog gave only a vague pronoun? How should I deal with untranslatable words, like *balé* and *balian* and *sakti*—leave them in Balinese or adopt unwieldy, misleading glosses? How could I find equivalents of Balinese "verbs," which do not have the strong tense indications of English?

The answer to most of those questions is that in making my translation I have stayed as close to the literal as is intelligible. I have not tried to find an American equivalent of Togog's very rural provincial dialect (which is special to Gianyar and to members of its older generation—occasionally even Togog's son did not recognize certain words). I have occasionally modified Togog's words to make things clear (usually in identifying persons), and more often have added in square brackets my own interpretations and explications. I have indicated in brackets the original Balinese terms only where there is no simple English gloss, and compiled a brief glossary of major terms at the end of the book.

One of the biggest losses in translating Balinese into English is that of the various language "levels" or registers, the distinct vocabularies that indicate the relative status of speaker and hearer and of the person who is spoken about. Choice of a register—"high," "middle," or "low" speech—may set the general tone of a social encounter, but the details of word choice—especially in pronouns but also in most other words in the sentences—provide indices of nuances of the relationship and of its fleeting momentary circumstances. One may speak usually with a person in the familiar register but vary it with hints of the high register (as, for instance, a man speaking with his father shifts at various times). Talking in the high register is usually felt to be an effort (and for many such a great strain that at this point they slip into Indonesian, which is more egalitarian). Togog used the term *mabasa,* "to put into language," to refer to speaking in the high register, suggesting its strong consciousness of self, other, and the medium of their interaction.

In making my translations I have had to provide parenthetical indications of the register used, because of how much it conveyed about the relational intentions of the speakers. Our English vocabulary does not have enough terms for indicating how one speaks down to inferiors or talks intimately with people of similar age. I use such terms as "familiarly" and "intimately" when the use of low register is mutual. I use "speaking down" or "impolitely" versus "speaking respectfully" or "politely" for the asymmetric situations. It is important not to think of these registers as "languages" or "levels" of speech, since they are more like "speech styles" or "rhetorical strategies."

In addition to register, other important indices of relationships between persons are status titles and kin terms, which are placed before the name. Personal names are almost always avoided in address, as are pronouns such as "you" or "I," as they may indicate intimacy or inferiority. Freedom from such constraints is felt only in regard to one's children.

Togog's title is Ida Bagus, indicating that he is a Brahmana. To address or even refer to him simply as "Togog" with no title as I do in this book is extremely rude. I follow Western usage in this, even though it is insulting in Bali to do so. This is a good example of Western conventions of writing taking over within the pages of this book, for I would never call him, or even talk about him, as "Togog" in conversation in Bali.

Togog, in his stories, has various people addressing him in different ways, and I give those address names, untranslated, because they reveal much about his relationship to each person. Brahmana men's titles are "Ida Bagus" (or, in Togog's parents' childhoods, "Ida") and the women are called "Dayu." His grandfather addresses Togog as "Agus," from "Bagus," which is very polite, coming from an older man to a child. When he is very little he is sometimes called by fellow Brahmana *"Alit"* or *"Gus Alit"* from *"Ida Bagus Alit,"* a name/title often given to young Brahmana. Non-Brahmana address him as "Ratu" or "Tu" (king), or, after he was the head of a family, as "Ratu Aji." (*Aji* means "father" in the highest register, and here it is a respectful title for someone who has had children.)

Another set of titles distinguishes the children in a family according to birth order. Firstborn Brahmana are called "Putu" or "Kompiang" unless their mother was a commoner, in which case their birth-order title for firstborn is "Wayan." The next three children are called "Madé" "Nyoman" and "Ketut," and the fifth child starts the cycle again with "Wayan." Togog was second-born, and that is why he is called "Madé." Older family members may call him merely "Madé" or its abbreviations "Adé" or "Dé."[7]

Another common usage for identifying people (and the most revelatory of relative status) is the employment of kin terms for non-kin, according to a generational hierarchy of respect.[8] For instance, any older person could be called "mother" or "grandmother" or "aunt." Balinese usage extends terms for immediate nuclear family kin (father, mother, brother, sister, child, grandfather, grandmother) to non-nuclear family members, and even to nonfamily members. However, one's own parent's siblings are not addressed as "mother" or "father" but as "aunt" and "uncle." Cousins are addressed as "brother" and "sister." Children and people younger than the speaker are not addressed by kin terms, but even then personal names are avoided and birth-order terms used instead ("Wayan" or "Ketut," and so on). Older male kinsmen in an "uncle" position (mother's brother or father's brother, or their cousins) Togog addresses as "Po" (which probably is a short form of "Bapa" ("father," in the Gianyar pronunciation). Some Balinese make a distinction between such kin on the father's side, whom they call "Po," as against those on the mother's side, "Wo," but Togog did not.[9]

I have left such terms of address untranslated since they convey so much information. Similarly, I have retained all the many kinds of exclamations that Togog was in the habit of using—*"Bah!" "Beh!" "Aduh!" "Badah!"* and so on—all of which mean something like "Oh!" or "Wow!," "Ouch!" or "Damn!," usually clear from context. And also I have left in Balinese onomatopoeic words for sounds, such as *tek!* ("bang!") and *Remmmmmmm* (a loud growl), for they give a sense of the liveliness of Togog's style, and can be recognized as such by context and the exclamation point.

Togog's narratives depend largely on dialogue, whether he is telling a traditional tale or recalling a personal experience. He presents the dialogues of himself and others in the form of a play script and rarely spells out who the speaker is. In Balinese that is obvious from the register used and also from the terms of address, but in English I have had to name each speaker.

The Organization of This Book

In publishing Togog's words I have struggled to keep close to the vigor of his speech and the liveliness of his anecdotes. At the same time I needed to point out the larger implications, both intended and unintended, of his words. To that end, I have distinguished between his voice and mine through the use of different typefaces. This device allows a reader to read only Togog's words, skipping over mine. It will also point up the never-ending interplay between his frames of reference and mine, and those of the many diverse readers of this volume—dialogues that continue long after the first recordings were made. I have tried not to drown Togog's tales in my comments, or to reduce them to examples for my own arguments, but rather to throw enough light on his words for a reader to see him whole.

For a long time I was committed to publishing Togog's stories in the original order in which he had told them to me so that a reader could follow the lines of his associations. I compiled a complete translation divided only according to the sequence of sessions ("First Day," "Second Day," through "Eighth Day"). But when I started to insert explanatory information and interpretive comments, I found that he had jumped around so much in time and in subject matter that any reader, even the most informed about Balinese culture and society, would be quite rightly confused. The inclusion in this book of Togog's pictures of childhood scenes and his tales about them added further organizational difficulties, since the various events within each picture raise different themes and are from different periods in Togog's life.

Most of Togog's anecdotes illustrate several different themes at once, intertwining friendships, family relationships, courtship and marriage, learning and practicing ritual duties, learning to sing ritual songs, listening to and telling stories, painting. They elude any single framework, sliding easily back and forth in time, and darting from one theme to another. They cast light on many aspects of his life all at once. The anthropological field experience is one in which links are discovered gradually as one becomes more and more involved in people's lives. I hope the reader will have something of the same experience—the aha's of discovery, the maybes of sudden hunches, and the oh yeses of their confirmation—and that a living picture of Togog and his world will gradually emerge.

Togog had neither the training nor the opportunity to revise his spoken narrative for readers, so I have had to do it for him. In doing so I have created two texts, intertwined—his, fairly fluent and fairly easily readable, and mine, in which I provide introductions and discuss all sorts of details, word usage, and customs that he mentioned. In arranging Togog's text into chapters and sections of chapters I kept close to his own words and his organization of each story, but I have slightly changed the order of the stories at times. I have also, in two or three cases, fused together several different versions of the same event that he told me at different times (for example, the land-tenure dispute in Chapter 5).

The resulting order of anecdotes in this book is partially chronological, following Togog's larger sequencing, and partially thematic, following both some of his associations and some of mine. Each chapter groups together anecdotes around a major aspect of Togog's life, but within each of these chapters the stories are arranged roughly according to Togog's probable age at the time of the event recounted, producing in each chapter a sense of growth.

Each chapter is prefaced by a general introduction setting forth some aspects of Balinese life for the aid of readers not very familiar with Bali, and there are lesser introductions and explications within the narratives. The Glossary at the end of the book is intended to enable a temporarily confused reader to refresh or augment his or her memory of specific Balinese words and customs.

I open Chapter 1 with a general description of Togog's immediate family and the clan group within which it was set, as a frame for his earliest experiences, which were mainly in and around his home and neighborhood. The stories range over memories of the man who raised him, whom he called "my grandfather," through his listening to marvelous tales told by an old woman, to his first experience with danger and healing.

Chapter 2 finds Togog, a little older, exploring the region around Batuan as a footloose small boy and daring youth. Its introduction expands to consider some aspects of colonial Bali of the 1920s and 1930s, especially its economic and political institutions. In this chapter Togog tells of his experiences in late childhood when he was free to walk long distances and stay in other villages for several nights or weeks. He speaks in the latter part of the chapter about his adolescent obsession with gambling, about his fishing friendships, and about early responsibilities. A major theme develops in which human life is beset by the constant danger and peril of the ill will of sorcerers, invisible spirits, and even deities.

Chapter 3's tales all involve the learning of the ins and outs of a complex expressive tradition, and tell about acquiring the skills and knowledge involved in telling stories, playing music, dancing, making masks, learning to read the classical literary poems and to sing them, and learning the essentials of ritual work. For Togog, learning stories was intermingled with learning songs, becoming a Brahmana ritual specialist, controlling himself as an adult, moral lessons, and, as well, with learning to draw and paint pictures to sell to tourists.

Chapter 4 groups together all of Togog's anecdotes related to what may have been his most important profession, that of ritual expert; this material shows how he continued to learn new aspects of the practical relationships with the unseen beings with whom he shares his world. It tells of his specialties in determining auspicious and inauspicious days, tooth filing, preparation of the body for burial or cremation, and the construction of mystical layouts for house and temple grounds.

Chapter 5 recounts two major events in Togog's life: the story of his courting and marrying his wife and the birth and death of their first child, and the lengthy dispute among his immediate relatives concerning ownership of one or two plots of rice land. These two issues had direct relevance to his motivation in starting to paint.

Chapter 6 brings together Togog's tales about meeting resident foreigners, learning to paint from them, and selling paintings through them. Some readers, who like me came to Togog through an interest in him as a painter, might want to skip directly to this chapter before going back to read the rest. The various aspects of Togog's life converged in his young adulthood. The history of his learning and practicing the art of painting is bound up with his marriage, his learning of ritual skills, his efforts to provide income for a young family, and his search for meaningful songs and stories. The contexts of these events mutually define one another.

In the Afterword—written entirely in my own voice, although some of Togog's paintings presented there speak for him—I discuss what I learned, as an anthropologist, from my long engagement with Togog and his tales.

Togog's was an uneventful life, but underneath its surface calm it was a dangerous yet charmed life. Glimpses of his perils and his courage can be found among the particularities—and, yes, in the omissions—of Togog's stories. They are set in a complex world and recounted by a person who created his own life within it. The life, the world, and the person are, simultaneously, usual and unique, mundane and occult.

One Childhood Memories

A Small Boy's World • The First Storytelling Session • Early Memories • Togog's Houseyard • Togog's Mother's Family Home • The Noble House of Batuan • The Field Across the Road • Togog's Clan Temple (Pura Penataran Brahmana Buda) • The Village Temple (Pura Désa Batuan) • The Temple of Death (Pura Dalem Jungut) • The Road to Denpasar and the First Foreigner Togog Ever Saw

A Small Boy's World

Togog's village, Batuan, gradually takes form as his tales are told. It is, of course, seen from but one angle—that of an elderly man recalling his childhood—and much is not mentioned. In this first chapter, we get glimpses only of his immediate neighborhood, but in subsequent chapters the lens widens to include the entire region of southern Bali, as he hikes, first to nearby villages, then later up to mountain coffee plantations and over to Karangasem on the far eastern end of Bali.

His home lies on the flat coastal plain, not far from the sea and in sight of the volcanic mountains of Bali, surrounded by rice fields and other villages. Togog was born around 1913, and in the 1920s and 1930s Batuan was a much greener place than it is today, with many open fields and fruit and coconut trees in and around the walled houseyards.

The central settlement of Batuan is made up mainly of nobles, Brahmana and Satria, with a fringe of commoner retainers. Around that core spread five or six large commoner neighborhoods. These are all quite similar physically, and at the time of Togog's childhood and youth, all agricultural. All of these are united into one community by worship in the village temple, the Pura Désa, and by the colonial local administrative setup, which, at the time of Togog's youth, consisted only of several men from Batuan's Satria noble house.

Togog's social world when he was very young was largely confined to the Brahmana clan into which he was born. Brahmana are the highest ritual specialists of Bali (but of course not the only ones). The work of Togog's family and neighbors consisted largely, besides farming and petty commerce in food products, of conducting rituals for others.

The top Brahmana ritual experts are *pedanda.* These are the high priests who, in Bali's lowlands, are needed to sanctify every major ceremony that the commoners hold. Lesser ceremonies are usually conducted by temple priests, the *pamangku,* who are usually commoners. Both types of priests are accompanied in their work by their wives, who serve as ritual assistants, as substitutes, and, when widowed, as priests in their own right.

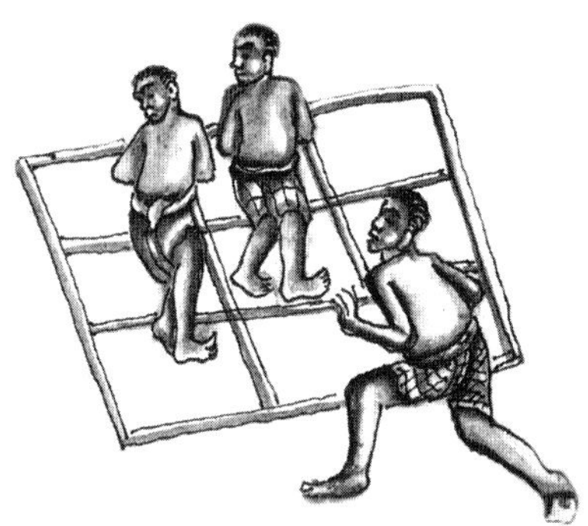

Togog's father's father was a *pedanda,* as were most of his further ancestors in that line. His father's mother was also a *pedanda,* and, after her husband's death when Togog was a toddler, through all of Togog's childhood, she was the head of Togog's household. His father's younger half-brother also became a *pedanda,* his wife's mother was one too, and his own son was later to become one. Togog might have become a *pedanda* had he not made a "wrong" marriage, as recounted in Chapter 5.

Most other Brahmana adults are lesser ritual experts (the men are called *ulaka* and the women, *tukang banten*). Togog was an *ulaka* and traveled around with a *pedanda,* assisting him in his rituals (helping him dress, running errands for him, toting his paraphernalia, carrying home the food that he had earned, etc.). He also made complex offerings and performed simpler rituals, made masks and other artifacts. Togog's wife was also a ritual specialist, a *tukang banten* or offering-maker, who assisted people in their ritual preparations, sometimes staying for a week or more in a client village.

A family with a *pedanda* has the steady economic support of the lower-status clients *(sisia)* who depend on the Brahmana family for their major ritual preparations and performances, and for advice in ceremonial and ethical matters. In return, the *sisia* regularly donate goods and labor for the Brahmana family's domestic needs. Some Brahmana houses have many *sisia,* and these and their descendants usually continue with the family even after the death of their *pedanda,* sometimes for generations, before a new priest is installed in the family. These clients are scattered over a large region, either as individual families or sometimes as whole villages. It is a house's *sisia* who pressure a young Brahmana to train for the priesthood, and it is they who supply most of the material means for him to do so — food, building materials, and labor.

In Batuan there were an especially large number of Brahmana, brought there in the seventeenth or eighteenth centuries by local princes, with a fluctuating number of *pedanda.* In 1937, when Togog was about twenty-five years old, Margaret Mead and Gregory Bateson reported that there were six *pedanda* in Batuan. They were comprised of two sorts: the Brahmana Siwa and Brahmana Buda. Togog was a Brahmana Buda. In Bali, the two are not sects, not doctrinally nor ritually really very different, the distinction between Siwaist and Buddhist theologies and practices having been long since blurred in Bali (as it was in India). Today, while the differences are valued by those involved, in actuality they come down to a division between kinship groups.

The official genealogy of the Brahmana Buda of Batuan shows that they descend from a deity, Ida Betara Gnijaya Mahadewa. This god had three sons, all with the title of Mpu, indicating that they were humans with godlike powers, what I have called masters of *sakti.*[1] One branch of their descendants came to Bali and became the Brahmana Siwa, and another branch became the Brahmana Buda. When the latter migrated to Bali from Java, they settled in Budakling in eastern Bali. The Brahmana Siwa have always been more numerous, having more *pedanda* and hence more *sisia,* and are more widely distributed.

The claim to spiritual efficacy of all Brahmana lies first of all in this genealogical tie to the gods. It is not so much descent or some sort of automatic transmission through genes that makes this claim strong, but rather the notion that contemporary Brahmana individuals are all reincarnations of their mystically powerful forebears: the potent predecessor protects and strengthens his present incarnation. This gift is augmented by the ownership and proximity of inherited talismans *(pusaka),* in the form of jewels, weapons, and ritual paraphernalia such as bells, and sacred books *(lontar).* Training and spiritual practice are important adjuncts to inheritance, and most male Brahmana start out life learning to read and interpret the sacred writings of the *lontar* and also to memorize prayers and spells (mantra) and the rest of the lore necessary for conducting rituals. If a person has both these inherited and acquired attributes, his life might be said to be "charmed," although the English word since the Protestant Reformation has been drained of its medieval meanings and replaced with an alien notion of "lucky."

Although the Brahmana Siwa group in Batuan consists of several clans that settled in Batuan at different historical times from different places, the Brahmana Buda group considers itself to be one clan.[2] The founding ancestor, a *pedanda,* of Togog's clan moved to Batuan from the center of Brahmana Buda in Budakling in Karangasem (where Togog took refuge at one key point in his life). There are branches of the group in, among other places, the village of Banjar in North Bali, in Pliatan near Ubud, and, more recently, in Sukawati, the village just south of Batuan. Togog belongs to the seventh generation after that first Brahmana Buda priest came to Batuan.

Membership in a clan in Bali is reckoned through one's father. Wives move into the houseyard of their husbands and break ties with the gods of their natal home to worship the gods of their husbands' families. Brahmana men may take wives from any stratum of the society, but in practice most marriages are among clan members. Since women usually maintain close social ties with their family of origin, their children too are close to their maternal relatives, even when they are not Brahmana. Brahmana women, however, may marry only Brahmana men, and until the last ten years or so when these rules were loosened, few did otherwise. The result is a disproportionate number of unmarried Brahmana women who stay in the households of their parents.

In Togog's childhood, all the Brahmana of Batuan lived near one another, in three quite distinct neighborhoods, two of Brahmana Siwa and one of Buda. Togog's group, the Brahmana Buda of Batuan, had only one clan temple, called the Pura Panataran Brahmana Buda, while the Brahmana Siwa's organization was more complex, centering on a clan temple in the nearby village of Sukawati.

Houseyards, *karang,* are basic social units of the clan, since each contains a family temple (called *mrajan* for nobles like the Brahmana, and *sanggah* for commoners) that is directly subordinate to the clan temple. Several households, or *kuren,* may live within one houseyard. Each *kuren* is defined by a separate kitchen fire and budget, but not a separate ritual center. When a man has several wives, they each form a separate *kuren* with their children.

A houseyard is, physically, a walled garden. The family temple is in the northeastern corner. Each of the households living in it build small, raised pavilion-like structures *(balé)* for themselves in which they sleep, sit, cook, and eat. A household usually has several *balé,* of different sizes and heights, plus sometimes a rice barn, the lower part of which can be slept on. When a family divides, as for instance when two brothers reach adulthood and bring in wives and raise children, if they do not move out of the houseyard, they form separate *kuren,* build separate kitchen sheds and additional sleeping *balé.* While these pavilions belong to those who built them, the land itself belongs to the clan gods (and, ultimately, the village gods), and the entire clan is its steward, deciding who will live on it, but a houseyard normally goes to the sons of the owner. If there are none, the clan decides to whom from outside the immediate family it will be allocated. Because of the high death rates in Bali until the middle of the twentieth century, houseyards were often reallocated.

From the perspective of a child, one's household is the group who provides you with food, clothing, and shelter for sleep. This was the case for Togog; but as he grew past toddler age, he found his food among other relatives elsewhere, and often slept in other houseyards. When Togog's father took a second wife, she lived outside the family houseyard, in that of a cousin. When Togog's older brother married, his wife could not get along with her mother-in-law's mother, the female *pedanda,* and so the couple stayed in her own father's place, next door. Thus, in practice, living arrangements can be flexible, responding to contingencies such as personal antagonisms.

But still, the main residential pattern is a group of paternally related kin living together, along with their in-marrying wives, in one houseyard, sometimes plus neighboring ones. Togog's houseyard had been, for generations, the sacred center for a long line of priests. His father's father had been the most recent priest in the line, but his father had not had the inclination to become one, and Togog, for reasons to be explained later, could not. However, Togog's father's cousin, a man about ten years older than Togog, living elsewhere, did become a priest, and Togog assisted him in his ritual work throughout his life.

Togog's paternal grandfather, the priest named Pedanda Wayan Jelantik, had two wives, both of whom were priests as well, Pedanda Istri and Pedanda Istri Delod. He died sometime before Togog's fifth year. One widow stayed there as head of the household, while the other moved out, with her three children, to serve as priest to the royal house of Sukawati in the village just to the south (that was why Togog called her "Pedanda Istri Delod," meaning the female priest to the south). The old priest had a brother, Ida Bagus Geria, who was given title to half of their houseyard and some of the family rice land. This was the man, Togog's great-uncle, whom Togog called "my grandfather" and who effectively raised Togog and much later willed him his land and his portion of the houseyard.

The head of Togog's houseyard was Pedanda Istri, the widow of the old priest. She had five sons and two daughters. Two older sons moved next door when they married, since it was expected that the youngest son would inherit the houseyard. That left Togog's father, his younger brother, and a boy of about Togog's age, named Ida Bagus Madé Alit. Togog's father, an itinerant peddler, was ill most of his life, as was his younger brother, who also married and was living in the houseyard during Togog's childhood. By the time the old woman priest died, only Togog was left as heir.

The consequence of this family history was that, during Togog's childhood, there were a lot of people living in his houseyard. The head of the houseyard was a woman priest, Togog's father's mother (whom Togog always called "my grandmother," and others called Pedanda Istri Wayan). Her husband died sometime during Togog's first five or six years.

One of Togog's grandfather's brothers was still alive, the man Togog called "my grandfather" *(kakiang tiangé),* Ida Bagus Madé Gria. As recounted below, this great-uncle was the man who, together with his wife, took the most care of Togog as a boy, and later in his life willed him his land and his portion of the houseyard. He lived at one side of the houseyard together with his wife and young daughter. Togog's calling his great-uncle "grandfather" is in accordance with the Balinese kin-name system in which all kin of the same generation are addressed by the terms used in the immediate family. Thus, all of one's grandfather's siblings and cousins are called "grandfather," all of one's father's and mother's siblings and cousins are called "father" or "mother."[3] I give Togog's great-uncle the title "Grandfather" with a capital G to distinguish him from the other grandfathers who played much lesser roles in Togog's life.

Pedanda Istri Wayan had a co-wife called Pedanda Istri Delod, who after their husband died moved away from Batuan to the nearby village of Sukawati (south of Batuan, hence her nickname "Delod" meaning "to the south"). There she raised her three young chil-

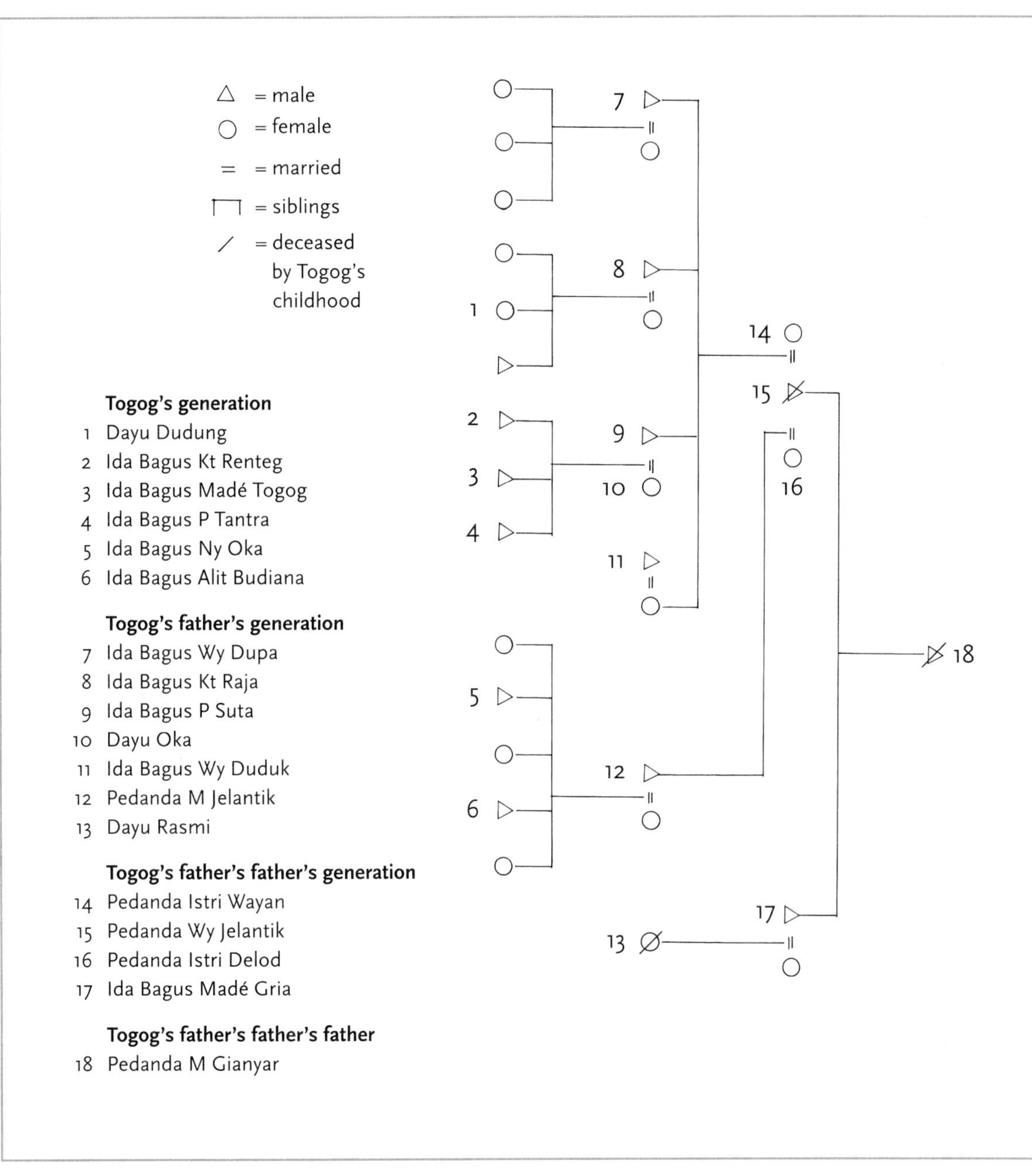

Figure 4. Togog's kin.

dren, one of whom became a priest. This man, Togog's uncle, was only about five years older than Togog, and for many years Togog served as his ritual assistant, referring to him as "my *pedanda.*"

Pedanda Istri Wayan had seven children. Togog's father, Ida Bagus Putu Suta, was the third of these. By the time Togog was born, his two older uncles had married and moved to another houseyard next door, leaving most of the others still there. At least one of his aunts had married and moved nearby; her husband was Ida Bagus Wayan Duduk, who played an important part in various events of Togog's adolescence as a wise advisor. One uncle, Ida Bagus Alit, was a boy of Togog's age, who died as a youth.

Togog's mother and father were virtually penniless —his father an occasional peddler, his mother selling cooked food in the neighborhood. His father and brothers were all sickly men. There was no land to till. His mother had been born in a related Brahmana family just around the corner, and Togog grew close to several maternal uncles. She had three boys of whom Togog was the middle child, and all of whom lived into adulthood.

The First Storytelling Session

When I arrived at Togog's home on the allotted day for the first of our interviews I saw three sets of offerings *(banten)* lying before us on his worktable, which he explained had been made by his daughter, Dayu Gambar. They were about to be proffered to Togog's *leluur,* "those up above," meaning both his gods and his ancestors. By "ancestors" are meant not only one's distant, long-dead kin but also one's recently deceased relatives. The latter may be the most important influences on peoples' lives, judging from reports of spirit mediums *(balian),* whose main job is healing and dealing with other kinds of troubles, such as business and agricultural failure. The medium through her seances enables the living to speak with their dead, who are thereby given the opportunity to inform the family of the causes of their problems and what to do about it. In most cases reported, the ancestors engaged with are the recent dead.[4]

Togog explained to me the nature of the offerings. The first one, he said, was called a *sesantun*—more exactly, a *peras ajengan sesantun.* A *sesantun* (an object that was to play an important part in some of his stories, as it is the main medium for repayment of Brahmana for their services) is a gallon-sized container made of banana leaf, filled with a coconut and uncooked rice and other ingredients, and topped off with palm-leaf decorations and flowers. The second offering before us, somewhat smaller, he said was a *sesariné penuku.* A third one, unnamed, had in it some cloth and a *canang* offering (a simple banana-leaf receptacle containing betel-chewing ingredients), and a wonderful gold ring that he took off his finger. He said that the ring had a great deal of *sakti,* or magical strength. He asked his daughter to bring some "holy water" or *tirta,* and some cooked rice. She had placed white and yellow and red flowers in these offerings, and Togog took out all the red flowers, saying that they were wrong for this offering, as it is not for demonic beings. After a brief prayer, he asked for more offering materials, arranged a small set of offerings on the ground for the demons, and poured some *arak* wine on it.

When everything was ready, Togog signaled me to turn on the tape recorder, and then said another *mantra* and spoke in a quiet voice over the offerings, addressing, in very respectful language, his recently deceased kin and earlier ancestors. He told them about me (whom he called "Nyonya," the respectful title of a foreign woman) and of my request for him to tell me about his life. He said:

I'm going to talk to you who brought me into this world, my ancestors, you who are the reason I am alive. These offerings are to tell you what I am about to do, because if

I say anything wrong in talking with you later they might afflict me. I ask you to come and witness what I say.

Yes, now, I'm going to tell about the way my life has gone. From when I was little up to now. Well, I'm going to tell the bad as well as the good, so please pardon me in advance, please forgive me if I say anything wrong or anything that troubles other people.

When I tell about what it was like when I was a child I hope that you who are listening to me will not get angry at me, will not be made to feel heartsick by what I am about to tell about myself.

What I know about you, my ancestors, is that you came from Majapahit and came down to Bali here. And now here comes from the country of America a woman named Nyonya Hilly, who wants to know about my life. That's why I am going to speak about all of you.

If there are any failings in what I say, I really beg your forgiveness.

And then Togog turned toward me and began, speaking in a different tone of voice and a less elevated language register, to tell me his stories.

Early Memories

Togog's Birth and Naming

When I was very little, just about this big, when I was around ten Balinese years old, there were in my family two female priests *(pedanda istri)*. One lived right here in Gria Gedé. She performed rituals for the royal house of Gianyar. The other wife of my grandfather, also a female priest, lived over there to the east.

Ages, before the schools required statements of age, were not recorded. Based on circumstantial evidence, he was born in 1913. When Togog speaks here of his age, he refers to the Balinese Pawukon year of 210 days, which however are rarely counted after the first three "years." His gesture suggested a child of about five or six.

I was born over there in the east because my father had two wives. [He points to a pavilion nearby.] His younger wife—*ratu!*—was very pretty. He loved *her.* But my own mother, he ignored. I think that my father wasn't very good to my mother, because he had a second, younger wife whom he loved more.

Togog spoke of his houseyard as divided between "the west" (where Togog's father's father lived until he died, and where Togog's father and mother lived) and "the east" (where Togog's father's father's brother—the man he called "my Grandfather"—lived). However there was no wall between them. The whole *karang* had only one family temple and was called Gria Gedé ("the great Brahmana houseyard"). It was said to have been the home of the first Brahmana Buda priest in Batuan.

My mother gave birth to me right over there, in the east, in the *balé* where my Grandfather lived. My Grandfather was named—forgive me for using your name *(tabé pukulun)*—Ida Bagus Madé Gria. [The phrase *tabé pukulun* ("May your lord forgive me") is addressed to his grandfather's deceased spirit.] My Grandfather loved me very much. I was born in his *balé,* and he often told me:

"You were born right here, and your breasts were very large, and my father, the *pedanda,* gave you your name. He said: 'Don't mistreat this little one. After I die I'll come back here [and trouble you if you trouble him]. Give him the name of Togog [*togog* means "statue"]. He will be a man.'" In truth my breasts were like those of a maiden. "Name him I Togog," he said. That's why I never dared to change my name. "He should be born here. That other place to the west [meaning the half of the houseyard where Togog's father was living and Togog lived all his life, and where we were talking] is all in ruins." That's what my Grandfather said. "You were born here. You were named here. I'll provide for you," he said.

Here Togog is telling us how he came to inherit his great-uncle's property, how it was that this man, his Grandfather Gria, having no children of his own, had adopted Togog and took care of him, together with his wife. Later, much later, Grandfather Gria made Togog his heir.

He and his wife loved me very much. Besides, as I remember, they were well off enough to give me things, unlike the people here in this household [meaning that of his own mother and father]. My Grandfather had some rice fields, nearly half a hectare, and he had dry fields as well, and many coconut trees. That's why they could take care of me.

In the morning they sent me to get water, and after I did that they'd give me some food. I often felt exhausted from carrying the water—four coconut shells full at a time is heavy for a small child—but because I was willing to work, to run errands here and there for them, so they loved me a great deal.

My father would go to cockfights far away and come home bringing the chicken [the losing cock, which the winner takes home to eat], and he wouldn't give me any, if I was over there next door. But I never said anything.

Now because my father didn't take care of my mother, she tried peddling, she cooked food and sold it. She built a little stall just east of here. But she always sold the food on credit and no one paid her back, and quickly her money was all gone. She tried again, this time selling cooked snacks, to earn a living for me and my younger brother and my older brother.

My older brother wasn't at home very much. He liked to go hunting with a blowgun.

Young Balinese boys, as will become clear as Togog's stories go on, wander away from home a great deal, sleeping wherever they are welcomed, and picking up food from relatives in other houses.

But I was still at home. And I often fought with my siblings. Until my mother, to punish us, rubbed hot chili in our eyes. She would be just finishing up the cooking. She put the spices on us because we were so very bad. Now when I remember it, it felt like hell.

Whenever I went with my mother to sell food, I always hoped she wouldn't sell it all so that I could have good food to eat. And she failed in that business too.

The Death of Togog's Grandfather's Daughter

My Grandmother and Grandfather [his great-uncle, Ida Bagus Madé Gria, and his wife] were always so sad, so sick at heart, because their only child had died while still a young girl. They had only the one child, named Dayu Rasmi. When she died, she was nearly grown, almost a maiden. [Togog might have been about five years old when his Grandfather's daughter died. They had no other children.]

My Grandfather felt troubled at home all the time, and he would go to the grave where his child lay. He'd go there in the afternoon and he wouldn't come home till late at night. He was very hot in his heart because the path of his only child had led to death. It was the time of the year when the world was in tatters, the period around the Balinese Sixth Month, when they had the sacred *prasutri* dances in the Pura Désa every night.

From the beginning of the Balinese Sixth lunar month (in October or November) through March or April is a period of considerable anxiety. The great demon-sorcerer Ratu Macaling, who lives in an island off the southern coast of Bali, invades Bali, spreading disease and crop failure. In Batuan at this time, for months, propitiary dances (the *prasutri* or *rejang*) are performed every night by all the women and girls of the village (see Chapter 3).[5]

And all the young people went there to dance, and Dayu Rasmi went too. When she fell sick there was no way to help her and she died. She was hardly a maiden and she had been here for just a moment. She had always been very healthy up to that time.

It was the time of the dances every night in the Pura Désa, and she went up there with her cousin, Dayu Belida. They enjoyed talking together so much that they were late coming home. So then the next morning her father asked her, "Last night where were you?" It was because she was his only child.

"Oh I was just visiting on the way home."

He suddenly picked up a broom and beat her on the behind. I saw him do it. He hit and hit her until her mother came. He didn't say a word; he just didn't say anything. And it was only two days later that she fell ill.

Once when I was with my Grandfather, I took a brass tweezers he had and pulled the prongs apart until it broke in two. He kicked me and then, without saying anything, went out.

She was sick for only seven days. He loved her, and he had never scolded her before, because she was his only child. And then that first time he beat her, his anger went right into her. [Here Togog used the term *nyusup,* "went in," a term used to indicate the effect of sorcery on a victim.]

There was no way to cure that sort of sickness and so she died.

When she died they buried her [later to be disinterred and cremated, as is the custom for most deaths]. And every day he went to the graveyard, whether it was night or not. Whenever he thought about his child, he went there. He went there to be with his daughter. When I asked him where he had been, he'd say he'd been somewhere else.

My Grandfather had some birds that he used to lighten his feelings. A little turtledove once flew into his inner room and he was able to catch it alive, and then he used it as a decoy to catch more. He would set up the decoy in a field south of Peninjoan called Dukuh.

I think my Grandfather went to Dukuh to memorize what he had learned from his *lontar* books. . . . Once I went there and peeked at him, and what I saw made me say to myself "this is a clever *(dueg)* man!" [The word *dueg* means "learned," "clever," and "cunning," in the sense having of a sorcerer's abilities, i.e., of being a master of *sakti.*]

Togog told me that once when he asked his Grandfather Gria why he had gone to Dukuh, his Grandfather told him it made him happy to be there because it was very quiet. The plot of land he owned there had once been a cemetery, but during the time of the kingdoms of Negara and Sukawati, the small stream at Dukuh had been the border between the two warring kingdoms, and people from Sukawati would attack Batuan people holding a funeral there. So they abandoned the graveyard and its temple, and moved their rituals to another temple farther from the border, Pura Dalem Jungut. Togog's son said that if you go to Dukuh, to that spot by the stream in the night, you can see lights coming up from the sea, the spirit followers of the demon-king Ratu Gedé Macaling. Togog and his son intended to imply that his Grandfather was a master of *sakti.*

A long time later, when my Grandfather was sick, he said to me, "See that *lontar* there? If sometime you decide to study it, be sure to put a *sesantun* offering next to it. That *lontar,* that one that was bound between wooden boards, was given me by the *pedanda* who came from Karangasem."

This is a reference to the founding ancestor of the local clan of Brahmana Buda, who was very *sakti* and is considered, through his gift of *lontar* books to them, as well as through his possible reincarnation in them, to continue to protect and empower his living descendants.

Then, because he was so sick, my Grandmother said to him, "Eat a little rice," and he answered, "Why should I eat, people eat in order to get well." And it came about as he said and he died.

When he was just about to die, I went to see him. He was asleep and I woke him up: "Grandfather, Grandfather, wake up! Are you sick?" I asked. "Can I get you some medicine? Grandfather, tell me what to get for you!"

"There isn't any medicine that can cure this illness," he said, "There isn't any medicine." So he knew that he was going to be called away. He had a feeling, and it happened. And as he was dying, he didn't move at all, he didn't tremble. I was right beside him and he didn't move. His legs didn't bend up and his arms didn't move. *Adah!*

The fact that Togog's Grandfather knew when he was about to die, and that when he was dying his body didn't twitch and shake in the final throes, are both common signs of a man of *sakti.*

Whatever I wanted my Grandparents gave me and I never thought about it very much. But even today, I like to work. If they told me to chop wood, I was willing to. I never said I didn't want to. In the house next door, to the east, in the morning, they would buy some chicken and cook it with coconut sauce—in the morning they'd eat rice with the sauce, and in the evening they'd eat rice with the chicken. But if they wanted to give me money, they'd give it to me.

But they didn't like to spend money on themselves. If my Grandfather had a *satakan* [string of 200 *képéng* coins], he didn't want to untie and break into it. Only if someone wanted to borrow would they untie it.

When they lent me money, I didn't pay any attention to whether I returned it or not. I stole a little money from them sometimes, but as I remember, never very much—about five *képéng* at a time—because I always wanted to have some money when I went places. I didn't like to ask for money from anyone else but to always have my own ready.

Képéng are iron Chinese coins with square holes in their centers. Large quantities are strung on strings. The word *satakan* means "200." Togog's Grandfather's reluctance to untie such a string is the same as the reluctance to break a large bill.

My Grandfather also liked to raise—uh, those creatures that say "*Rringng*!"—oh yes, crickets. He took me with him out in the night to look for crickets—as far as Tegenungan.

He'd get food that way. My Grandfather did no work in the fields because he had a small amount of land, and he knew how to make do with what he had.

The only work he did was trapping birds. He'd use live birds as decoys to catch others, and then raise them. He'd go to trap birds in the morning and on the way home pick up some dried palm leaves [for thatch]. That was what he did—he didn't really work at all, neither he nor his wife did anything.

Later Togog explained that "not working" in this case meant not only that his Grandfather did not have to work in the fields and could live off the product of his share-cropped land, but also that he didn't have to do wage labor such as working on the coffee plantation, or paint pictures, or sell food. He was able to avoid these kinds of work mainly by living a very simple life with few desires.

So when I went with him to catch crickets in the night, we'd stop to pick a bunch of beans for supper. There were lots of them in the rice fields. And on our way home we'd stop at a deep pool near the rice field where eels were, and we'd catch one or two eels. And then at home we'd cut them up and mix them with coconut meat and vegetable leaves and make *lawar* [a spicy festival dish]. We often did that. It was delicious what we brought home.

Or else sometimes when he won at the cricket fights—he'd gamble near here in Delod Pangkung—if he won three times he'd buy us our dinner. He was a strong gambler.

And also I helped in his house. He'd tell me to go and get the water for them in the morning. Sometimes I felt just completely tired out from all that work. So then, to avoid that work, I'd go visit somewhere else. I'd try anything because I was just a little child, and I'd try any work so that I had something to bring home.

In speaking of the help he gave to his Grandfather, Togog used the term *ayah,* which means "to serve someone you respect highly" and is used to indicate work done not only for someone like his Grandfather, or a king or a priest, but also for the gods and ancestors.

Désak Watin, the Storyteller

There was a woman who lived next door [to the north of Togog's houseyard]. Her name was Désak Watin [by her title, a Satria]. She lived in the home of a woman whom I addressed as "grandmother." Désak Watin was good at telling stories. She and her family had been exiled from Gianyar, but I don't know why.

Désak Watin was a very important woman in Togog's early years, for he loved to listen to her tales. Togog mentioned Désak Watin several times later, usually in connection with particular stories that she had told him. (See also the account of Togog's knowledge of auspicious and unauspicious days in Chapter 3.) Désak Watin's patron, a Brahmana Buda, who was a *balian* capable of counteracting sorcery attacks, plays a role in one of Togog's later stories, in Chapter 2. Togog said that she too was a storyteller, as was Togog's Grandfather.

I often went to her house in the evenings. She knew the whole story of "Koripané ring Daha"—all five parts of it. I'd even cry sometimes when I heard her, because she was so clever a storyteller. Very, very clever! *[dueg]* Désak Watin also told me all about how to know the meanings of the days.

"Koripané ring Daha" is a cycle of stories set in the two kingdoms of Koripan and Daha in ancient Majapahit, Java. Their plots were enacted in the *gambuh* and *arja* dance-dramas. An example of Désak Watin's stories, as retold by Togog, appears summarized in Chapter 3. It is the story of Mantrin Godogan, the Frog Prince who, despite his bizarre appearance, had great *sakti* and was able to win the hand of a beautiful princess.

Désak Watin sold various things to eat, especially a snack made from coconuts, so I would get coconuts to give her. I took them from my Grandfather's [Ida Bagus Gria's] tree in the dark like a thief. I could bring her only two at a time because I was so little.

Once when I was stealing some coconuts from my Grandfather's tree for Désak Watin in the night—I could only take two, one held by its stalk between my teeth, one in my hand, and one hand to hold onto the tree—my Grandfather heard me.

"Who's up there?"

"Me."

"Oh, Agus, you must be taking them to sell them to the north there!" he said. He had thought it was some outsider and went to the bottom of the tree and asked who it was. But when he found out it was me, he didn't mind and said I could sell some more. But he didn't want me to climb up there in the night. So the next morning I went and got two more. He said, "Instead of climbing up there in the night, just ask for the money from your Grandmother." That's what my Grandfather said. He was angry at me because it was dangerous to climb a coconut tree, especially in the night. "If you climb a coconut tree as high as that, you'll fall and break something!" It was because he loved me so much.

Hitting a Girl by Accident with a Rock

Well, there was a mango tree, which was very tall and full of mangos. It leaned over a wall, and I was on the west side of the wall, and the branches of the tree were over the east side. I had no idea that there was someone under the tree on the other side of the wall. Well, I picked up a rock and threw it up into the tree to knock down one of the mangos, and I heard a loud *tok!* The rock had hit someone! It was a girl named I Krondong, a commoner. *Beh!* Was she bloody!

I knew someone was going to come after me, so I ran home. My grandmother the Pedanda was sitting there, and I went inside her *balé* and hid.

And sure enough, in came her grandfather! Kaki Dongkol was his name. Carrying a huge stick! If he had caught me he'd have beaten me.

"Where did Gus Alit go, Ratu Pedanda?" he asked politely.

"What's the matter?" Speaking down.

"Well, it's like this and this and this," he said. "My grandchild was hit by a rock that he threw at her. She said he did it on purpose."

He said I did it on purpose, but I was throwing it at the mango, and I didn't know there was someone under the tree because of the wall between me and the tree. But he accused me of doing it intentionally.

"Ah, don't talk like that." Said my Pedanda, "We older people shouldn't meddle in the affairs of children. She should have some medicine put on her wound. If you don't have anything to put on it, send her here for some." And she added, "Don't make too much of it."

That's what I heard my Pedanda say, and then he left.

A Mysterious Illness

My Grandfather once told me to go and buy some cooked rice, to buy two packages. "Alright," I said, and I went. I bought the rice up near the Pura Désa and then I came home by way of the crossroad and then south. When I was just opposite the Pura Den Pasar and I had to cross the stream in front of it, there was a lot of sand in the stream, all piled up. In those days no one had yet taken the river sand away [for making cement].

I went down into the gully to cross the stream, and I must have fallen, but I didn't know what had happened to me. I tumbled down but I kept the packages of rice high in my hand, somehow. I got sand all over my head, but none on the rice. And when I came to, I wiped the sand off my head. "How could it be that I got sand on my head but not on my hand?" I muttered to myself. So then when I got home, I told my Grandfather how I had tumbled over and over.

"Oh, don't worry about that, maybe you ate something you shouldn't have," he said.

After that I went to sleep in the Balé Dangin.

A *balé dangin* is a kind of pavilion that is larger than the others in a houseyard. *Dangin* means "east" and it normally stands on the eastern side of a houseyard. It is the pavilion in which bodies are laid out preparatory to burial or cremation, and also where the tooth-filing ritual is held, and the place where the highest-status member of the family (usually the oldest male) sleeps. A *balé dangin* may also be referred to as a *balé gedé* or, in the higher register, *balé agung* ("great pavilion") because it is larger and more important than any others in the houseyard. Other people in the family, especially children, may sleep in a *balé dangin,* according to contingencies. When Togog was a small child, he and other children of the family slept there along with the old Pedanda Istri (see fig. 5).

I had just lain down, when all of a sudden I felt as if there was a hole in my side. I began to breathe fast, and it seemed as if the hole was being cut deeper and deeper. With a thud I fell off the platform, and then I turned south and then north, south and north [a common expression for feeling dizzy] feeling very sick. *Peh!* Where was I?

And then my older brother was there asking me what was the matter. I was just a little child, and I was crying, and so he came to see. "What's the matter? What's the matter?" he said. And then he said, "Bah! He needs a *simbuh!* Where's someone chewing betel? Where can we get a *simbuh?*" [A *simbuh* is betel-nut juice mixed with saliva used in a common treatment that requires spitting it onto a person's back; what is important is not the material as such, although betel is closely associated with spirit beings, but the healing power or *sakti* of the person giving it.]

I don't remember where he got it, but they put it on me, and then I came to. I stopped running north and south crying. But my sickness stayed with me, and they couldn't make me well.

So, just as we still do, we went to a healer [a *balian*]

to find out what was the matter. The healer said, "Well, what is it you are looking for, why did you come and talk with me?" And they said, "Well, this little Ida Bagus has all sorts of troubles and his enemies make him go here and go there."

"Where do you sleep? Where you sleep must be the reason you aren't sleeping well." [The *balian* spoke to the Brahmana child in the high register. Togog told him that he had been sleeping on the bench on the *balé dangin* and then the *balian* said that the illness was caused by enemies of the family (i.e., sorcery) but also by the spirits of the *balé*.]

"Don't sleep up high on that bench any more but down below, on the floor." That's what the *balian* said. So then he gave me some holy water *[banyun cokor]* from his own shrine with some medicine in it. It was all because of the place where I slept.

The *balé dangin* in Togog's houseyard had been built for the Pedanda who was Togog's grandfather before Togog was born, perhaps by his client, the prince of the nearby kingdom of Negara when that kingdom still stood, which meant it must have been built before 1891. People had long said that the *balé* was haunted by powerful malevolent spirits *(tenget)*, and no one wanted to sleep there, because if they did they would have all sorts of dreams of frightening beings *(gegodan)*. Later it was discovered that one of the posts supporting the roof had been scarred by burning. The post had been wrapped up with a strip of cloth, but when the wrappings fell off they could see the black portions. While Togog did not say so, this defacing of the post could not have been an accident, but could only have been caused by someone wishing harm to the family, by means of sorcery. See Chapter 4 for an account of the final act, in 1974, of replacing this ensorceled *balé dangin* with a new one.

Togog's Houseyard

When, two years after these interviews, Togog began the series of drawings in response to my request for clarification of the circumstances of his childhood, the first he made was of his own houseyard. As he explained each drawing to me, he launched into the recital of new anecdotes (or new versions of previous ones) which I tape-recorded and present below.

Figure 5 looks at Togog's childhood houseyard from an imaginary high vantage point in the west, where there was a large open field and a small stream that are not shown. Over the north wall, on the left in the picture, was the houseyard where Désak Watin lived. Over the east wall, on the top of the picture, was the home of Togog's cousin and friend, Ida Bagus Wayan Truwi, who grew up to be the village head of Batuan. Over the south wall, to the right, was a road.

The various living structures of the time are not all shown. The house-temple is in the upper left-hand corner (fig. 6, 1). In the center of the houseyard (2) is the *balé dangin,* the eastern *balé* and the largest pavilion where all major personal rituals are held, and where probably the old *pedanda* lived before he died and was laid out before his cremation. In many other houseyards, the *balé dangin* is on the easternmost side, but here it is in the center, as the *balé* of the old *pedanda*'s brother (the man Togog called "my Grandfather,") take up the eastern half of the houseyard, at the top of the drawing. This section is more spacious than it appears. Shown is the Grandfather's main *balé gedong* (8), his kitchen shed (9), and his rice-storage shed (10). The Grandfather's main pavilion is called a *balé gedong* because it has a *gedong* or closed compartment at its rear, where one can sleep or store things. It might also be called a *balé metén.*

On the west side of the houseyard headed by the Pedanda Istri there were two pavilions, a *balé gedong*

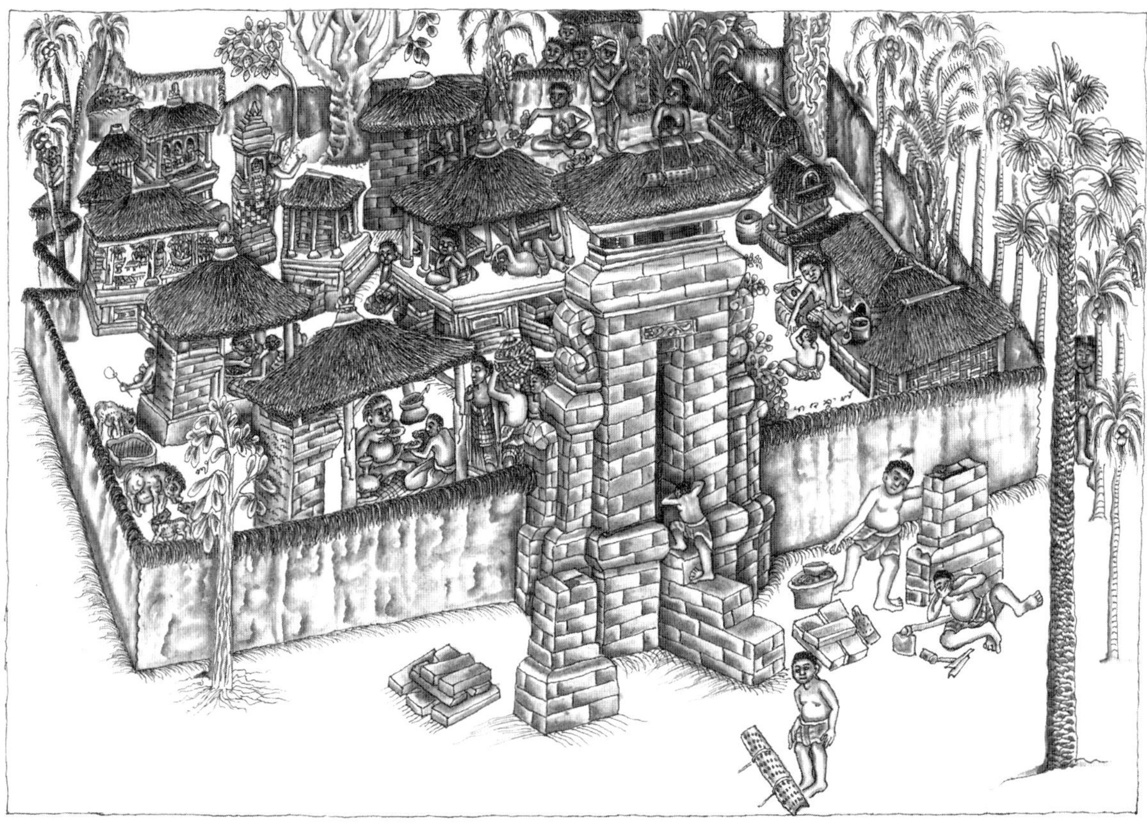

Figure 5. Togog's houseyard in his childhood. Drawing by Ida Bagus Madé Togog, 1986.

(3) and a *balé daoh,* or "western *balé*" (4) where she and her children lived. One of these may have had a closed room on it, but the drawing is not clear. On the right were her kitchen (5) and her rice-storage shed, or *lumbung* (6). Next to the kitchen shed is another small *balé* (7) where a married uncle and his family lived.

As in all of his pictures, Togog represents himself repeatedly, in different parts of the picture, and the anecdotes for each one follow, except for the event depicted in the upper right-hand corner where Togog is seated cross-legged, which is related in Chapter 2.

A Quarrel

Here [in fig. 5, foreground] my older brother was building an altar in front of my gate. [This was an *anglurah* altar, said Togog, a pair of which guard a gate.] He smeared my face with mud, and I cried and went into the yard. There I am [far right] complaining about my brother to my mother. She happened to be mixing spices for dinner and she didn't like us to tell on each other, so she smeared my eyes with those hot spices, and I cried even more. Here I am crying, lying on the floor, and then I fell asleep [on the *balé dangin,* no. 2 in fig. 6]. I slept very soundly.

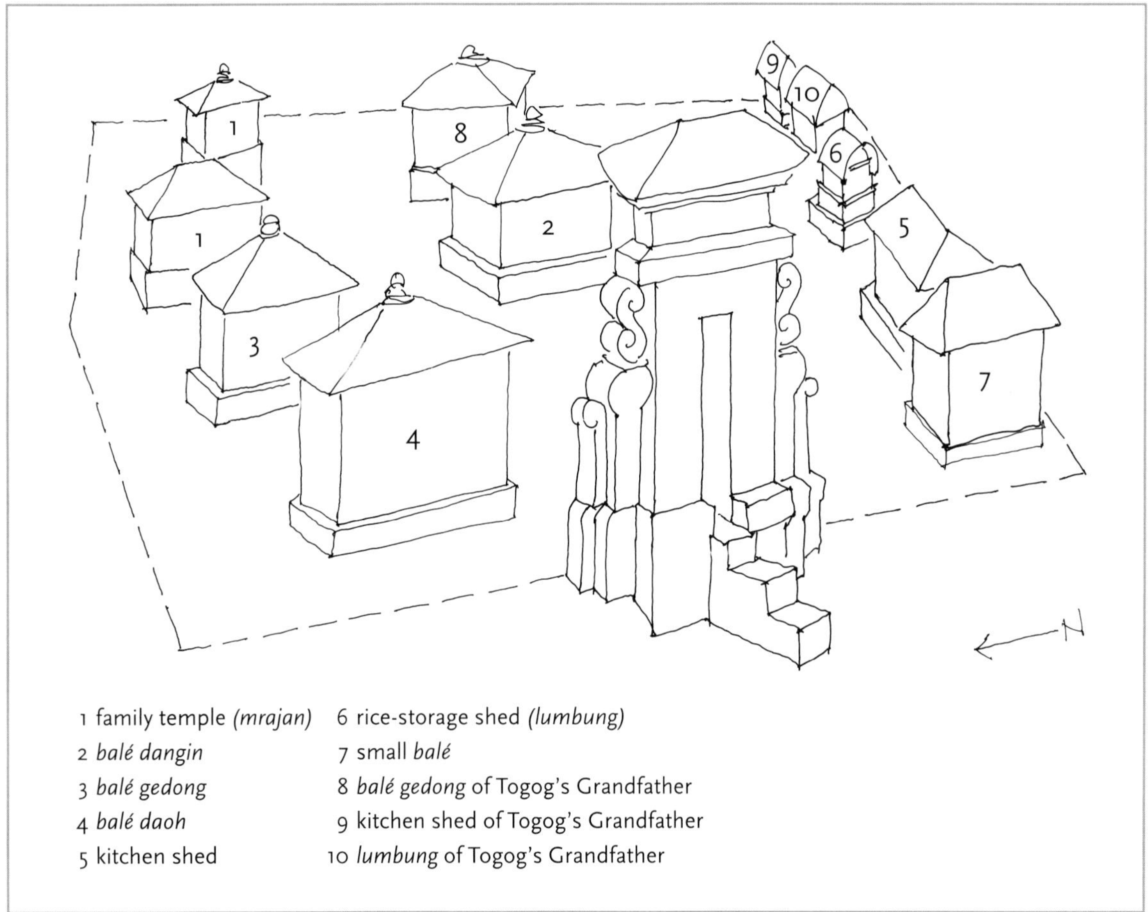

Figure 6. Diagram of figure 5, Togog's houseyard.

And then, later in the afternoon, my grandmother came home from doing a big ritual. Her helper is carrying in the ritual equipment. After she got here she sat in the *balé gedong* [3 in the drawing]. I was over here on the *balé dangin.* And here she is again just coming home, just entering the gate. [This is Togog's father's mother, Pedanda Istri Wayan. The man with a large basket on his head, just inside the gate, walking behind her, is a ritual assistant carrying her liturgical clothing, her bell, and so on.]

I was absolutely certain that they were going to give me some of that food [which they had brought home with them from the ritual as part of their payment], or at least some of the sweets. Or a banana. Here [3 in fig. 6], she has come home first, and she has changed. She is sitting with her youngest child, Ida Bagus Kadé Alit, the youngest brother of my father. He was going to school in Sukawati at the time. [He died young.] He was her assistant. He brought home the offering food.

So here I am sitting across from them, clearing my throat again and again. Only they don't pay any attention to me. Maybe they didn't hear me. It was after dark, and I

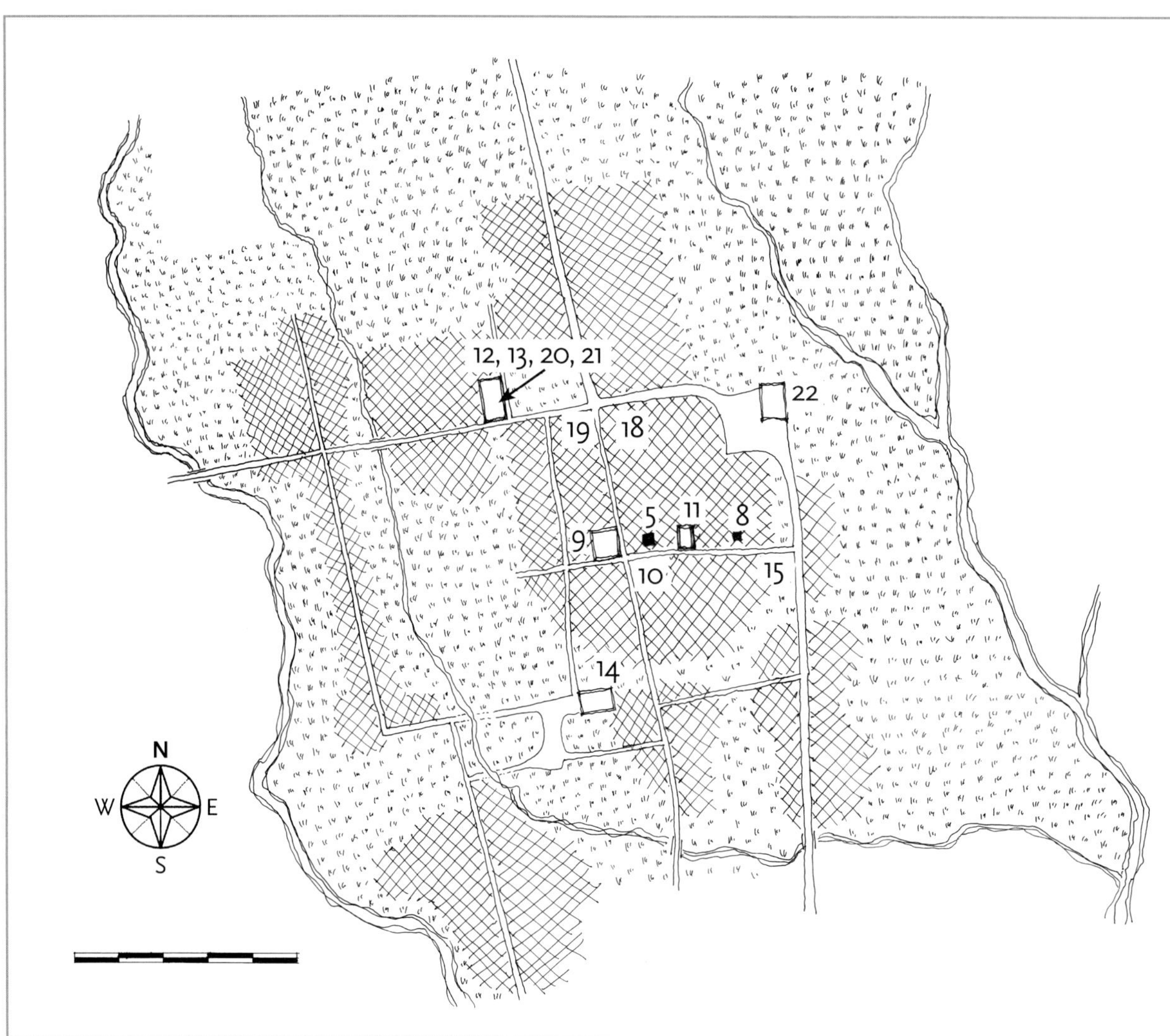

Figure 7. Drawing of Batuan showing the locations of Togog's drawings of his childhood experiences.

still didn't get any food. Here is Ida Bagus Kadé Alit cooking rice in a pot, to put some chicken in. He tore up the chicken and put it in with the rice and some spices. [I'm not certain where this person is.] So the two of them, my grandmother and the son she liked so much, are eating together here.

And no one offered me any. No one offered me anything.

And this [fig. 5 foreground] is when a tile fell off the roof of the gate and almost hit me. I was standing outside the gate and a tile got loose, but it just missed me. The reason it missed me is that I had done no wrong. If it had hit me I'd have been dead. [This is the first of many episodes in which Togog came close to great harm but was saved from it.]

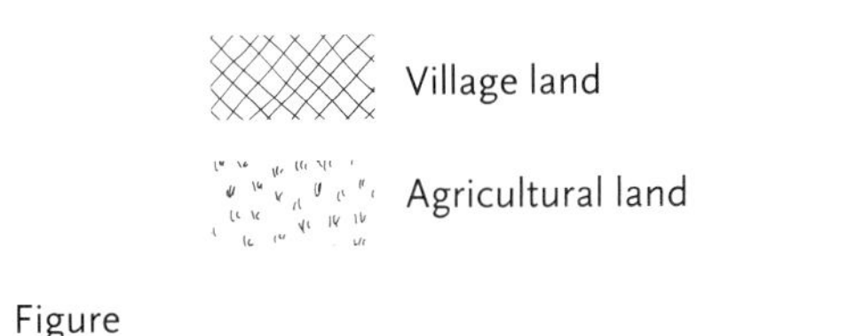

Figure Number in This Book	Location
5	Togog's houseyard in his childhood
8	Togog's mother's family home
9	Noble house of Batuan
10	Field across the road
11	Togog's clan temple: Pura Panataran Brahmana Buda
12	Village temple (Pura Désa Batuan) Inner Courtyard
13	Village temple (Pura Désa Batuan) Outer Gate
14	Temple of Death (Pura Dalam Jungut)
15	Road to Denpasar and the aqueduct
18	Neighborhood of Gria Pacung
19	Neighborhood of Gria Kawan
20	*Prasutri* dance at the Pura Désa
21	Dancing the *gambuh* in the Pura Désa
22	Rebuilding of Pura Dalem Puri

Togog's Grandfather's Home

Over here [fig. 5, top left] is the home of my Grandfather. Here is his kitchen, this is his rice barn. South of the rice barn was a huge *bunut* tree. And along here on the south were lots of banana trees all over the place, very thick. To the north were *jaka* palm trees from which my Grandfather used to make *tuak* wine. Northeast were some *dapdap* trees, very big but without many leaves left because so many people had come and taken their leaves for rituals. And here were some *silik* trees, hung over with the weight of the fruit. Here's where the children played. The fruit would break off and fall and then we'd all go and look for the fruits.

When Togog finished the drawing of his own home at the time of his childhood, he went on to make fourteen more, of sites all over the village. Some were homes of his playmates, some sites of important experiences. Some were temples where he worked and worshiped, his kin-group temple, two temples linked with death, graveyards and cremations, and the main village temple, the Pura Désa. Together the drawings covered almost the whole of central Batuan.

Togog's Mother's Family Home

Togog's mother was also a Brahmana Buda who had grown up just around the corner from the family she married into. Figure 8 shows the cluster of houseyards near Togog's mother's natal houseyard. It is the tiny one in the upper-lefthand corner. During Togog's childhood, her father, mother, and a brother still lived there.

The block of houses is seen from the east, bounded on the left (west) by an irrigation ditch (briefly visible in lower-lefthand corner) and along the bottom of the drawing (the east side) is the road that ran in front of Togog's house.

The episode of frightening his uncle's bull away is pictured at center left. In the top center is a temple, called Pura Ulun Carik, for the rice fields just south of Batuan. The two figures at lower left in the picture are Togog and one of his mother's relatives. Togog has just arrived from harvest work in the mountains, and there was illness in his house, so he was told to go to stay with his mother's family (his uncle's) for a while. That story is told in Chapter 2.

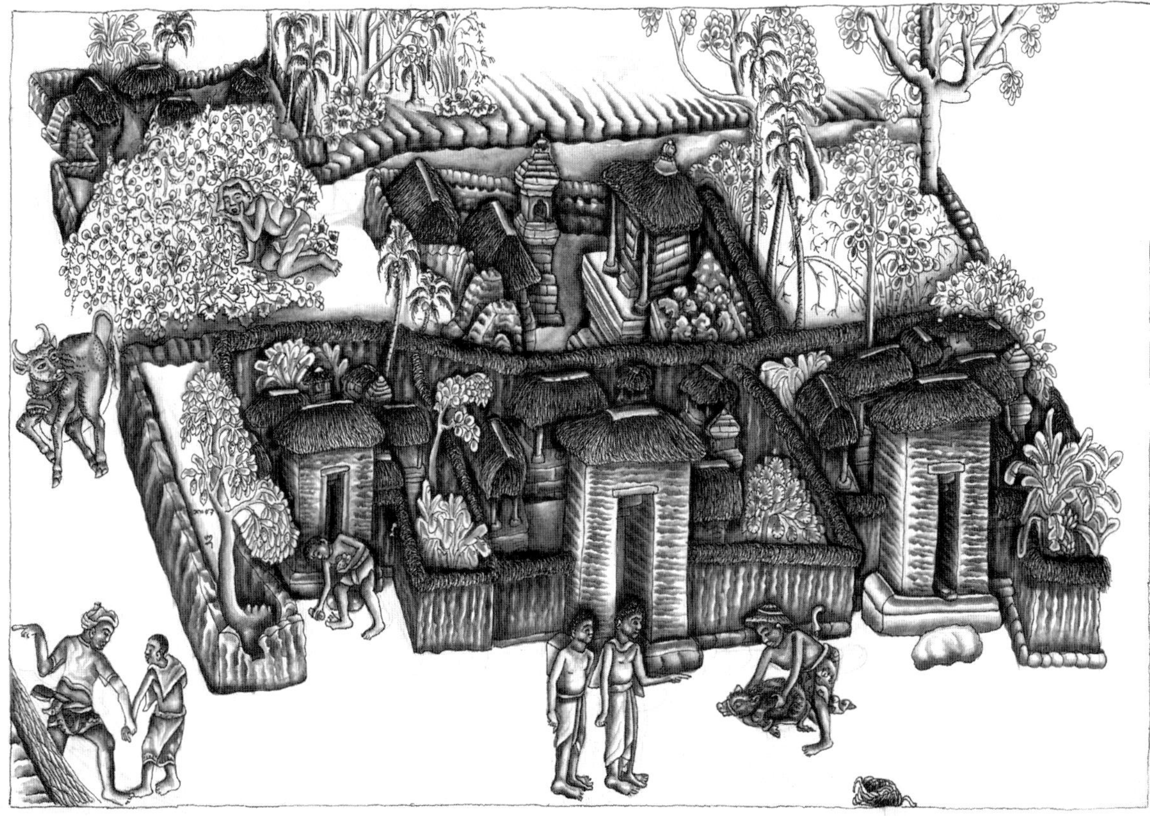

Figure 8. Togog's mother's family home. Drawing by Ida Bagus Madé Togog, 1986.

How Togog Frightened a Bull

The house of my grandfather on my mother's side was just a little ways away, northwest of here [fig. 8]. I liked to go there often when I was little, and my uncle who lived there often took me to work with him in the rice fields.

Once he told me to take care of their bull while he was working in the rice field. It was black and very, very big. And, too, its horns were very sharp. I was supposed to watch over it.

Well, there was a large pool where I would wash the bull, next to the irrigation ditch just alongside the temple there, the Pura Ulun Carik. There were some high bushes right next to the pool, and I was bored with watching the bull.

So I went behind the bushes and I made a very loud growling noise,

"Remmmmmmm!"

Ratu!

The bull jumped up and ran away south, toward the Pura Dalem and past it.

It got far away from me, and there was no one else around. I shouted and shouted that there was a fierce huge bull running loose and that he was mad.

So then my uncle, Po Ketut, ran up behind me and chased after it. And I ran after it too.

The bull ran into an empty paddy field that had only water standing in it.

Chak-chok! Chak-chok! I went right after it.

Bah! Was I muddy chasing that bull!

My uncle—the bull was scared of him, so it stood still. When he shouted, the bull stopped.

But then when it saw me again, even though I was still far away, it began to act crazed some more. It rolled its eyes as if it were about to run away once more.

It was wrong of me to make that growling noise. So then my uncle scolded me a little, "What were you *doing* to that bull?"

I didn't confess that I had growled at it.

I just said: "When I was washing it, all of a sudden it ran away. I don't know why."

I really didn't like taking care of that bull.

An Argument over a Pig

Togog pointed to the man in foreground of fig. 8 holding a pig.

This man here had a house near there. His name was I Teka, he was a commoner *(kaula)*. This other man was Ida Bagus Wayan Truwi—and he was clerk to the village head *(perbekel)*, who was in the noble house.

Togog and Truwi are the two figures standing facing the man with the pig, Teka. The one on the left is Togog as a teenager, and the gesturing one is Ida Bagus Wayan Truwi. Truwi was Togog's cousin. He was five or ten years older than Togog, and had been sent to school for five years. After graduating he worked as secretary to the Dutch-appointed village head, and by 1936 was himself the village head.

Now my mother was taking care of this pig for someone else [Ida Bagus Wayan Truwi's mother, who paid her with some of its piglets]. And she had let it go free, by accident. Well then, this man—I Teka—had been given the order to catch any pigs that were wandering about and keep them until the owners claimed them. He would carry a rope around. To tie up the pigs with. And the one who owned it would have to pay him a hundred coins in fine.

I went to get the pig, but he wouldn't give it to me. So I went to Truwi: "Beli Wayan, Beli Wayan, come and look at your pig, it's all tied up, it'll die." [Togog addressed Truwi, not by his name, but by his birth-order title (Wayan), prefaced by *beli* or "older brother," for he was a cousin.]

It had been tied up since yesterday. The reason that he had kept it tied up from the day before was that a buyer had arrived, and he was going to sell it. And I didn't understand. I saw the pig in the graveyard there, in the bushes, and I wondered what he was going to do.

"*Badah!* that's our pig!"—so I ran home and told my mother, and she told me to go get Beli Wayan, and so then Beli Wayan went to see him.

"Release that animal," he said [speaking down, familiarly, because I Teka was a commoner], "I own that pig." And so then he set it free, and he paid him a hundred.

The Noble House of Batuan

Figure 9 shows the houseyards of Batuan's noble house, the head of the Satria families of Batuan (then called Jero Gedé, "the great house," today, in contemporary terminology called the Puri, "the palace"). The Pura Panataran Satria, the clan temple of the Satria of Batuan, is on the lower right, and is entered by the gateway on the right. In front of the noble house was a broad field with fruit trees and a large, spreading banyan tree, which is shown fallen down at the very bottom of the drawing on the left.

Climbing a Coconut Tree Next to Jero Gedé

[Talking about fig. 9:] This is the *puri,* or *jero gedé* as we called it then. Here is a path between the houses going straight to the west. [He points to the left side of the

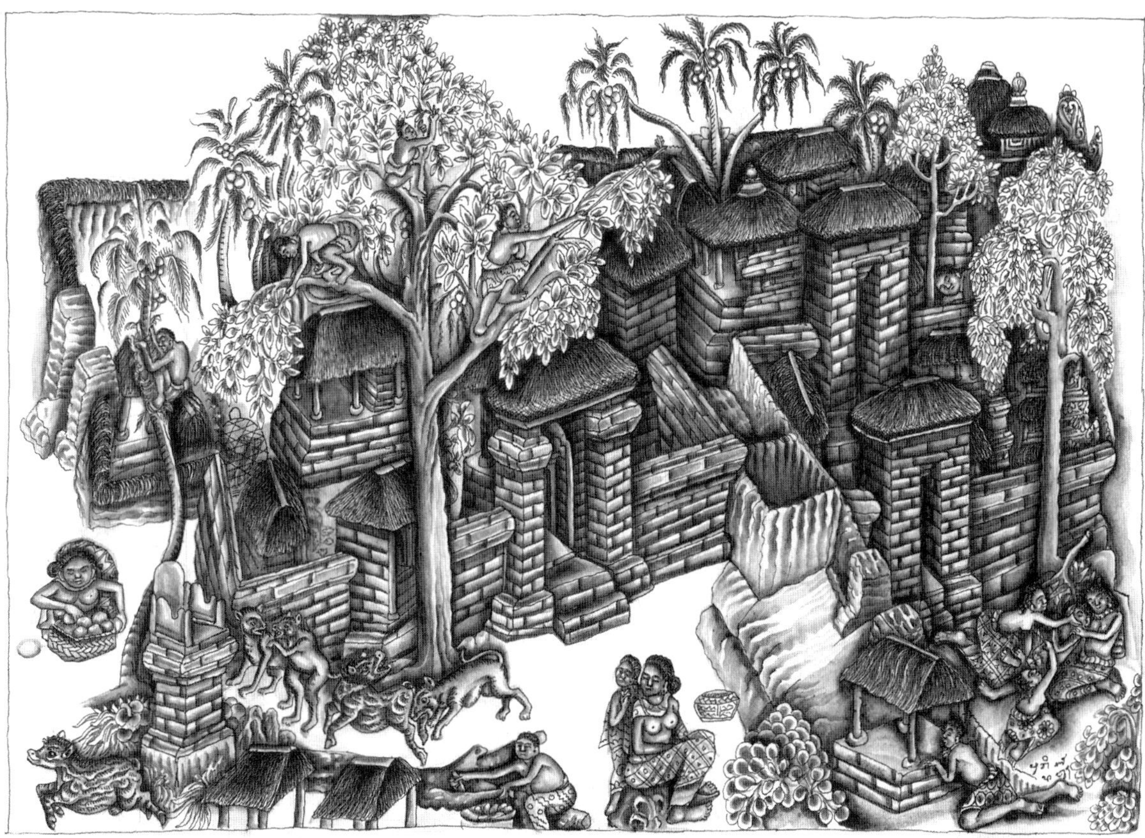

Figure 9. The noble house of Batuan. Drawing by Ida Bagus Madé Togog, 1986.

picture, where a woman is putting coconuts in a basket, and to the figure near her of Togog up in a coconut tree.] This is the way the house was in those days. Now here, she is talking, she says that she owns that coconut tree there. She says: "Do Adé [short for Ida Madé, addressing Togog by his birth-order title, prefaced by Ida—pronounced with the Gianyar–o—his status title as a Brahmana], please help me pick some coconuts and I'll give you one."

At that time they paid seven *képéng* for one.

So I climbed up and threw down about twelve of them. They were growing very thickly. This is just to the west. And you get to this coconut tree where I was picking them.

And then the owner of the coconut tree came and took the coconuts. And she had seen me from inside, from this *balé* just outside the temple, the Pura Penataran Satria, over there on the right. It was far away. So here she is picking up the coconuts, and then she took them all home. I was angry in my stomach, so I jerked open the string that tied the circle of thorns on the trunk to prevent theft and dropped it down. The thorns weren't there any more. And then I went down, *seret!*

She didn't give me one, what! She didn't give me one!

Picking Frangipani Blossoms

Now over here [pointing to the big tree just left of center in fig. 9] is a great *cempaka* tree. Here I am climbing, engrossed in picking the flowers. I'd get eight or seven [coins] for them when I sold them. [*Cempaka*, or frangipangi petals, are used in offerings.]

Now, here [pointing to seated woman, bottom center] is the one who would buy the flowers. She's the Anak Agung Istri [the wife of the head of the Jero Gedé family]. She was fierce watching over her trees. And when she paid, she'd pay short. I just avoided her and climbed the tree. The tree had widely spaced branches, for climbing.

These dogs [at the foot of the tree] are fighting among themselves. There was no one in the *puri* who paid attention to this area and it was all overgrown.

Now these [pointing to the two small black roofs at bottom left] were the sheds for coffee-shops. There were only two. One also sold cooked food and things like ready-made betel quid and nuts. It wasn't very busy.

The Dead Banyan Tree

Now here [in fig. 9, center bottom] there once was a big banyan *(wringin)* tree. It had fallen down, dead. And here am I gathering up the bark. No one from there, no Satria, gathered firewood there.

Togog is the crouching figure at the bottom of the picture, just left of the seated woman with child. Presumably the reason no Satria, that is, no members of the Jero Gedé family, could use wood from their banyan tree was that it would have been dangerous for them, as it had been a tree whose spirit inhabitants had protected them.

Ida Bagus Aji Ketut Sotong bought the wood from the temple group [of Jero Gedé]. He was very fortunate, because just after that they were repairing the paved road. Putting asphalt on it. And they needed firewood. They bought it for good prices.

A Fall from a Tree

[Pointing to lower-righthand corner of fig. 9:] Here, now, just outside the Pura Penataran Satria. It wasn't like it is now. In the area near the temple gate, there was a mango tree. Its trunk was really huge around, at least fifteen armspans. It was very tall too, and its fruit, *beh!* there wasn't just a few of them! Every branch had at least eight or ten mangos on it, all in a row.

There was one branch that I could reach if I jumped up, but it had no fruit on it. At that time the mangos were very ripe, and when I shook the branches as many as eight would fall down all at once. The smaller ones were about so big. They were delicious.

Now once I was up there and there were a lot of girls down below under the tree picking up the fruit. Some of them were from my family, the others from the Jero Gedé family. There weren't any boys. I climbed up, and one of them shouted, "Be careful or you'll fall!"

I answered: "No, I won't fall! And anyway, if someone falls and is knocked out, I'll tell you what to do! If I fall, *blug!* just close up my mouth, close up my nose, close up my ears! I'll come to again!"

That was just empty, silly talk, something I made up. But they believed me and said, "Oh, is that what you do when someone falls?" And I said, "Yes." I was just making up something to say!

So every day I'd climb that tree, and I'd play like a monkey up in the branches.

Suddenly one of them broke and I fell, *glebug!* I had been jumping around out on the middle of the branch, and it broke and I fell!

Six of those girls grabbed me and they tried to close up my mouth, close up my nose, close up my ears! With their hands! I must have been knocked out for a moment, and they were trying to close my mouth and nose and ears, as I had told them to.

"Close his mouth! Close his ears!" they were saying!

I thrashed my arms and legs around. I was all confused

and I rolled over and over several yards. They kept trying to cover my ears and nose and mouth.

Then we were scolded, "Who told you to do that, to close up his mouth, to close up his nose?" Like that. "You shouldn't do that if a person is silent after falling. Don't ever say that again!"

I'd been wrong. If they'd kept on I would have died, smothered. After that I didn't dare tell people false things like that. I just kept quiet.

Another time I was climbing up that big *cempaka* tree out in front of the Puri, and I would climb up and pick the flowers. It stood just to the south of the home of Anak Agung Istri. It was very, very tall. Whenever someone climbed the tree, other people would wait below and get any flowers that he dropped. I carried a long stick to reach the distant flowers and cut them, and the people below would gather them up.

Once I was climbing very high, it was about four o'clock as we say now, and all of a sudden while I was up there, I got sick in my bowels and I couldn't do anything but let them go. The people below just ran away, and a dog came and licked up the feces. And everyone laughed at me for doing something so improper. When I climbed down again, they said: "Why didn't you send a signal that you were going to shit up there in the tree? You could have hit your friends!" I couldn't make a sign, it came so fast. The day before I had been eating peanuts. I ate a whole dishful, by the handful, and I didn't throw them up then, and I thought I was all right. I was a little in the wrong in that I didn't make a sign.

The Field across the Road

Figure 10 shows the block of homes and fields directly across the road from Togog's home. In the foreground was a large field (by the 1980s converted into more houseyards) where the children played. In the center of the picture, on the edge of the field, stood a stone statue. Togog did not mention the statue, perhaps assuming I knew what it was. I had been told that such a statue had been there, partly buried, until the *pamangku* of the nearby Pura Batu Lépang—which was dedicated to the descendants of the early King Batu Lépang whose palace was in Batuan—became possessed and announced that this statue belonged in Pura Batu Lépang. The statue was said to walk around at night. On hearing the words of the statue's spirit speaking through the *pamangku,* the people then dug up the statue and moved it to the temple of Batu Lépang. Most of these homes at that time were of Satria. Out of the picture, at the top, lay the temple called Pura Dalem Jungut, the most dangerously haunted *(tenget)* temple in Batuan, which is the site of the story about hunting bats.

The road along the right side of the block of houseyards went down to Sukawati, the next village to the south. Togog told me that, at that time, when they had a cremation tower coming up from Sukawati to the burning ground in Batuan for the Triwangsa people, they had to bring it up this road, because the main road was blocked off by a low aqueduct to irrigated fields in the east. (See fig. 15, showing the aqueduct over the road.)

At the upper right are two small altars. This is the field called Tegal Lingga, and the altars are those of a small temple called Pura Segara. This Pura, whose name means "Temple of the Sea," is supported by a small group of Satria families, and is also said to be very *tenget.* It is associated with the demon-king Ratu Gedé Mecaling, who seasonally comes up from the sea to bring epidemics of cholera and malaria.

[Speaking about fig. 10:] And here, it was empty, nothing there. Today there are houses there, but then there wasn't anything. [Pointing to figure picking fruit off the ground at lower left], and here was a mango tree. I'd go there to gather mango. I'd dare to go there even in the middle of the night. I wasn't afraid. I'd get as many as

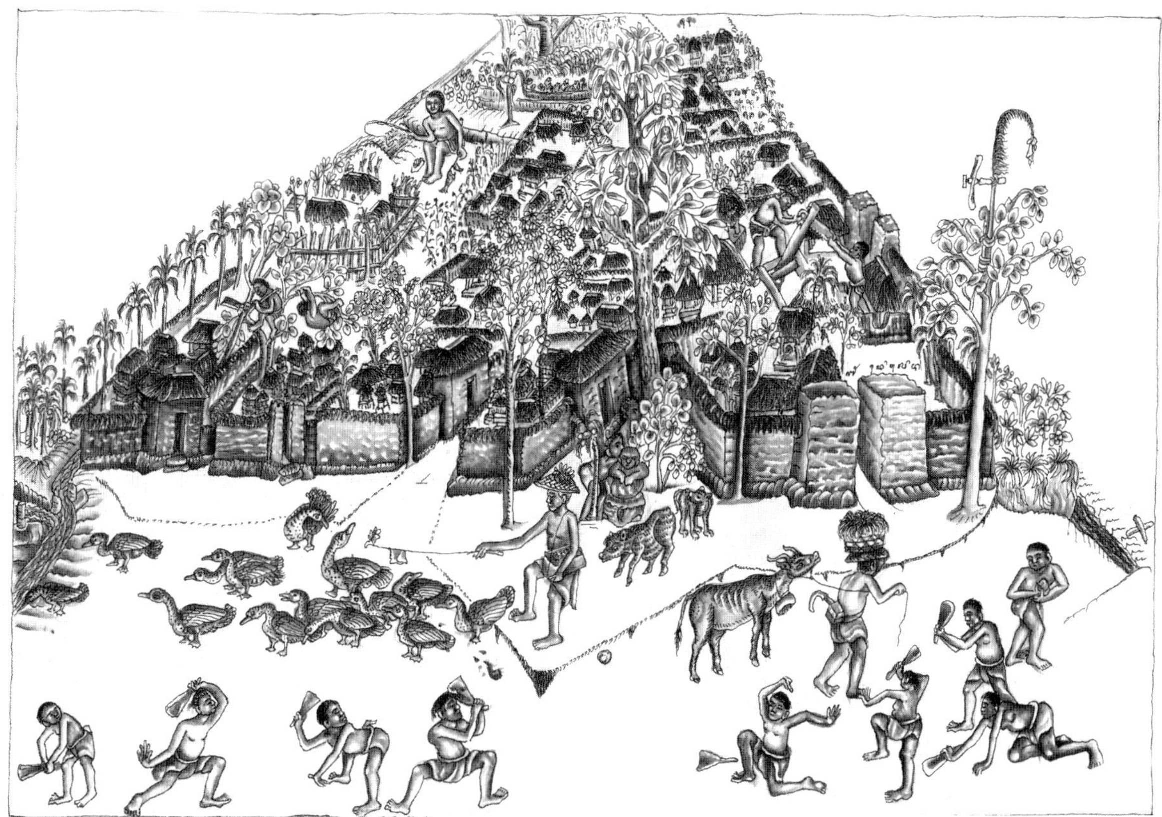

Figure 10. The field across the road. Drawing by Ida Bagus Madé Togog, 1986.

six at a time. I didn't do that just once but many times. It wasn't like today when we buy mango. When they were ripe we'd get them. It was a very quiet place, this one, this field. It just had a broken-down wall. It had collapsed. Not like today. Now it is nice.

This is someone from the house next to the field [the person bending down behind the statue in the center]. She is looking for mango on the ground here. In the middle of the night, I had heard a noise *"blug!"* That was the fruit falling. I heard it from here and then I ran there and found it and ran away. No one saw me.

And now this woman is looking and looking for the fruit. She knew that a fruit had fallen but she can't find it. She's feeling all around. But she didn't know I had taken it. She didn't know. This is in the middle of the night. No one else was out. This kind of mango is very big. Enough for three people.

[Pointing to the boy fishing at upper left:] This is me. And this is me again [pointing to the boy hanging from a branch of a tree at left center]. There was a *dagdag* tree there that fell down. This one was very bent over. Those *dagdag* trees are very weak. So I was told to climb up to the top and pull it down. I was happy to. And here [pointing to the person just to his left] is the one who was cutting the tree. He told me to do it. He didn't know and I didn't know. I liked to climb and it was easy. "Yes, I'll climb it!" And so here I am. And then it broke and I fell. I wasn't hurt at all. But it made the man who told me to

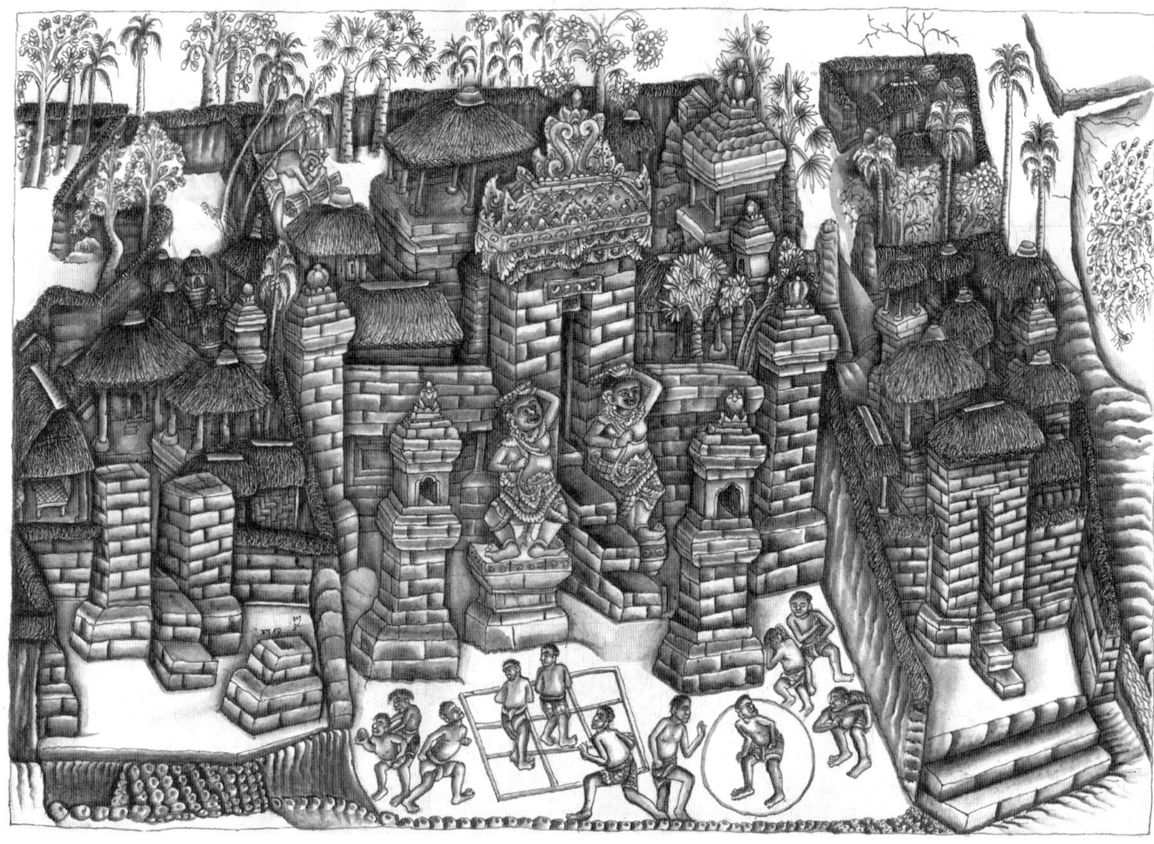

Figure 11. Togog's clan temple (Pura Panataran Brahmana Buda). Drawing by Ida Bagus Madé Togog, 1986.

do it frightened. And he was always nice to me. My hands were very strong holding on. "If anything had happened I would have been very sad," he said.

Togog's Clan Temple (Pura Penataran Brahmana Buda)

Figure 11 centers on the clan temple of all the Brahmana Buda of Batuan, which lay right near Togog's home. On the right of the picture is the houseyard where the family of Togog's friend Ida Bagus Wayan Truwi lived, and later where Gregory Bateson and Margaret Mead stayed during their fieldwork in Batuan (see Chapter 6). Just past it, outside the drawing, was Togog's home. On the left, east of the temple, was the houseyard called Geria Sekangin where lived, during his childhood, another female *pedanda* more distantly related to Togog. Along the bottom of the picture is the narrow road that passes along the side of Togog's home.

In the upper left, the figure tying up a bundle of sticks is Togog as a young adult when he served as *klian* of the Pura Panataran. A *klian* is chosen by the temple group to organize its material activities for a certain period of months. Togog's tasks as *klian* were

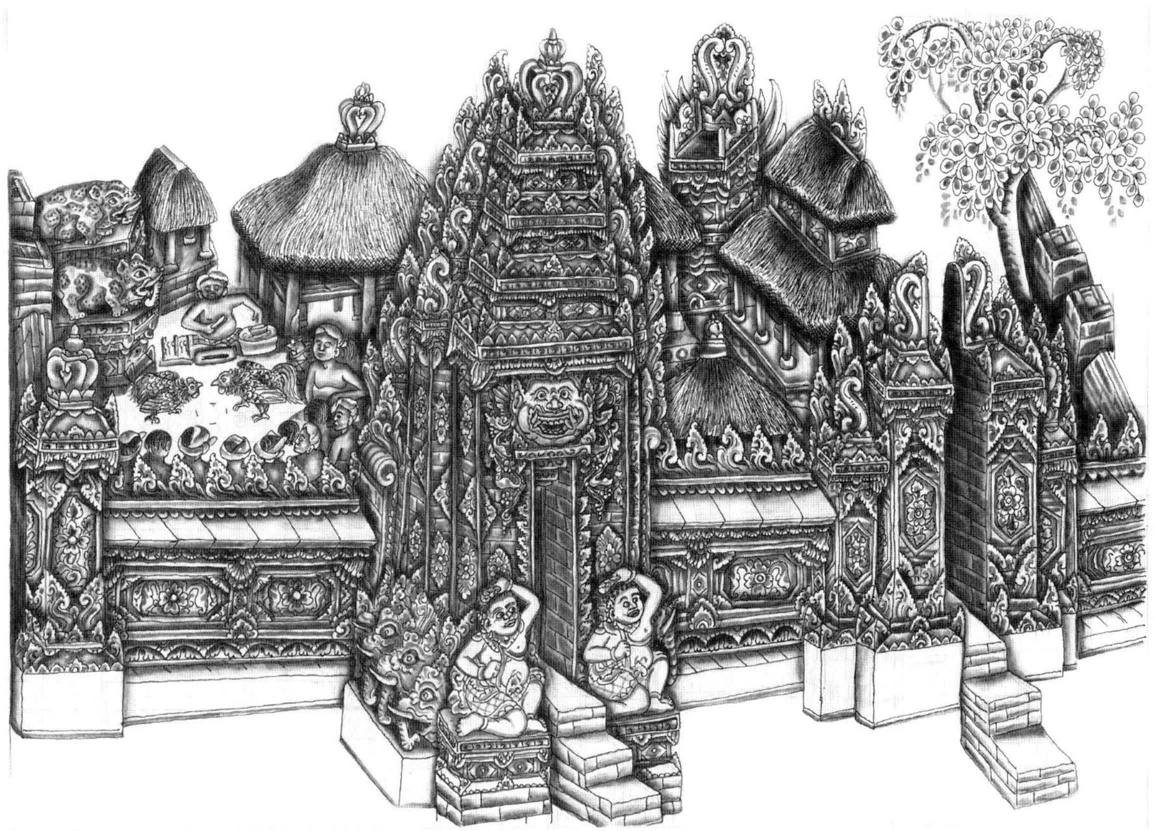

Figure 12. The village temple (Pura Désa Batuan), inner courtyard. Drawing by Ida Bagus Madé Togog, 1986.

to sweep the temple daily, sound the *kulkul* drum as signals to the congregation (to come to rituals, to come to work on the preparations for rituals, or to do minor repairs on the temple). In the picture he has just taken the leaves of a *rontal* tree (which could be used for writing on, in the form of *lontar*—see Chapter 4), and is now turning the rest of the tree into firewood.

Togog is also one of the children playing in the open area in front of the temple. They are playing the games of *"mapincer"* and *"bit nalit."*

The Village Temple (Pura Désa Batuan)

The largest temple in Batuan stands at the upper edge of the village. It is the subject of my book *The Life of a Balinese Temple.* It is attended by the entire community of Batuan, while all of the others have more limited congregations. In 1966, however, almost all of Batuan's nobility were expelled from this temple and forced to build their own Pura Désa, but before that Togog and his family were members. It was in front of the Pura Désa that Togog first learned to play the *gamelan,* performed the *gambuh* dance, and

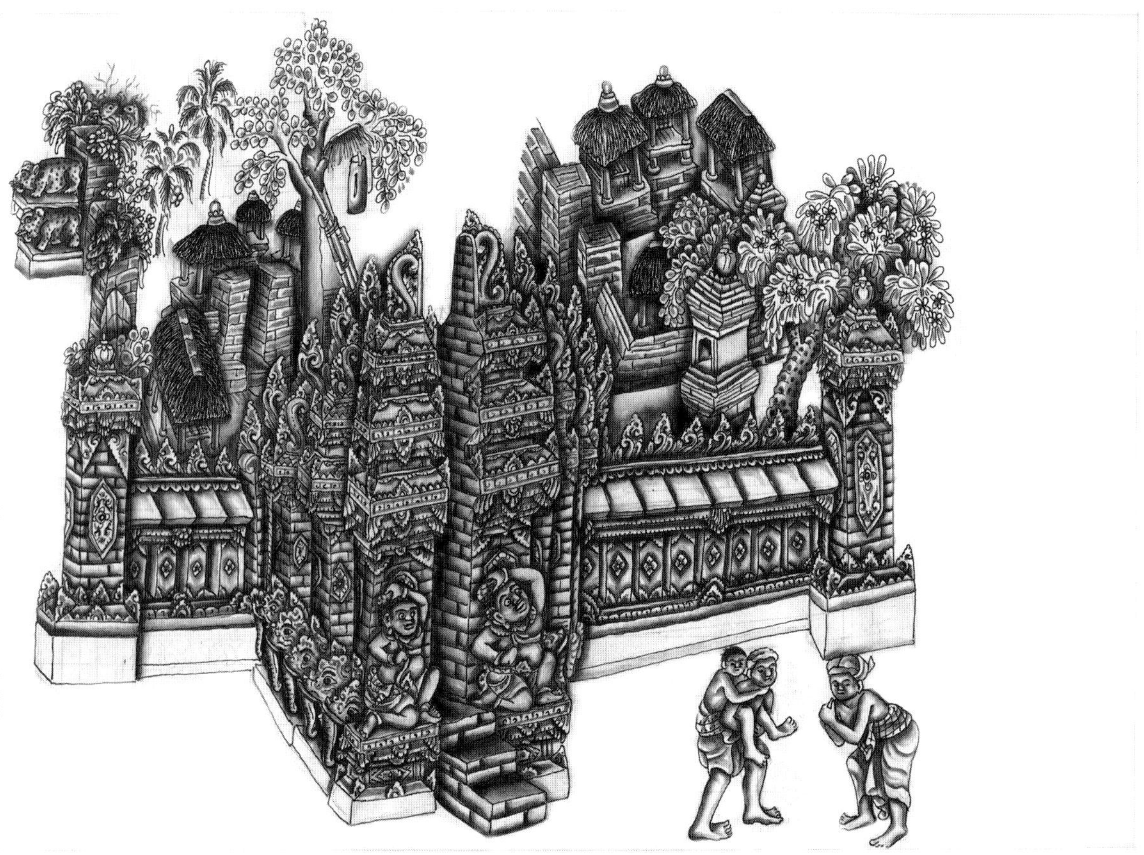

Figure 13. The village temple (Pura Désa Batuan), outer gate. Drawing by Ida Bagus Madé Togog, 1986.

saw many of the *arja* plays that he liked so much (see Chapter 3).

In 1917, soon after Togog's birth, a great earthquake knocked over all the altars, gateways, and buildings of the temple. The villagers rebuilt this part of the temple within ten years, but Togog's image of its carvings is imaginary. Figure 12 shows its innermost courtyard, the visiting place for the highest gods. In it a ritual cockfight is being held, as recounted in the story below. Figure 13 shows the outer courtyard, with altars of various sorts and the main gateway of the temple that opens out onto the road. Inside the courtyard, hanging on a tree, is the long drum made from a tree trunk called a *kulkul,* which calls villagers for meetings and rituals. Later a special tower was built for it.

Stabbed by a Fighting Cock and Healed by a Balian

There was a cockfight going on, inside the Pura Désa. They were having a cockfight in order to ask for rain. There wasn't enough water in the rice fields to plant. So they were asking for rain in the Pura Désa. For the rice fields of Subak Batuan Dauh, and those of Subak Tumpeng. [Tumpeng was the name of the *subak* farthest away from the water source of the whole group of rice fields near Batuan. It was therefore often dry. In the late 1930s the Dutch provided it with extra water, channeled in by special canals from another watershed.]

They put on a cockfight. I was there at the cockfight, because the younger brother of my mother liked cockfights a lot and he often gave me money when I asked for it. He gave me three *képéng*, because he liked me. I never asked my father for money, for he didn't pay attention to me.

Just when I got to the cockfight, I saw one of the cocks running loose with his razor-sharp knife tied on his leg. The cock ran right at me! I jumped away, but it got me right on the thigh! It went very deep—indescribably deep! No blood came out. [Sometimes these steel spurs have been dipped in "poison" *(ubad)* which may be both a lotion made of herbs and a sorcerer's magic potion, put on the spurs so that the opponent's rooster will die instantly. This is why Togog was in serious danger.]

Anak Agung Pekak lifted me up. [This was Déwa Gedé Ukiran, the head of the noble house of Batuan. Togog respectfully calls him "Anak Agung" in the modern style in place of the old-fashioned "Déwa." And instead of using his name, he calls him "Pekak," meaning "grandfather." (See my *The Life of a Balinese Temple,* chap. 5, for a discussion of Déwa Gedé Ukiran.)]

He cried out, "Has anyone been chewing betel nut?" And someone came up and took some chewed betel nut from his mouth and they put it right on the wound.

And then Ida Bagus Madé Tuplen, the curer *(balian)*, said a spell *(mantra)* over me, and so did the grandfather of Déwa Ketut Jero, Déwa Kompiang Krebek [another well-known *balian*]. They stood quietly with hands in prayer position, concentrating for a long time over me. They had enough ability [*saged,* a synonym for *sakti*], all right. They said a spell and then he [Déwa Kompiang Krebek] put a patch over the wound with his betel quid. By the time I got back here at home it was all right. Didn't need any more medicine. I still have the scar on my knee.

Then someone carried me home. It was a commoner from Peninjoan named I Téka. He carried me back to my Grandfather. Still no blood came out. My Grandfather was very sorry for me. So then he had some offerings made and did the ceremony in the family temple, praying for my recovery. After that I didn't need anything else and I got well right away. [Implied is the understanding that being stabbed by a fighting cock is no accident—if any hurt is—and that what is needed for healing is countersorcery.]

The Temple of Death (Pura Dalem Jungut)

Figure 14 shows the main gateway of Pura Dalem Jungut, the temple next to the graveyard and burning ground for the commoners of Batuan. On the other side is the field called Tegal Linggah and the temple called Pura Segara, both of which are very *tenget.* The statue of a mother and children just behind the wall to the left is Men Brayut, to whom many come to pray for help in having children. The term "temple of death" is an inadequate, though brief, translation of "Pura Dalem." Because of the proximity of the graveyard, it is considered to be constantly haunted by spirits of the recently deceased.

Scary Escapades Near the Pura Dalem

Togog told the following story in relation to Figure 14. It must have taken place when Togog was about ten years old. Bat meat is a delicacy, usually cooked, cut-up, and mixed with spices to make *lawar,* a special feast-food.

Now once my older brother was going to catch bats in a net at the Pura Dalem Jungut in the night with a friend. They saw a big shape there, and then they ran away as fast as they could. When they got to this crossroads near my home [on the right in fig. 14], I was standing there with two friends.

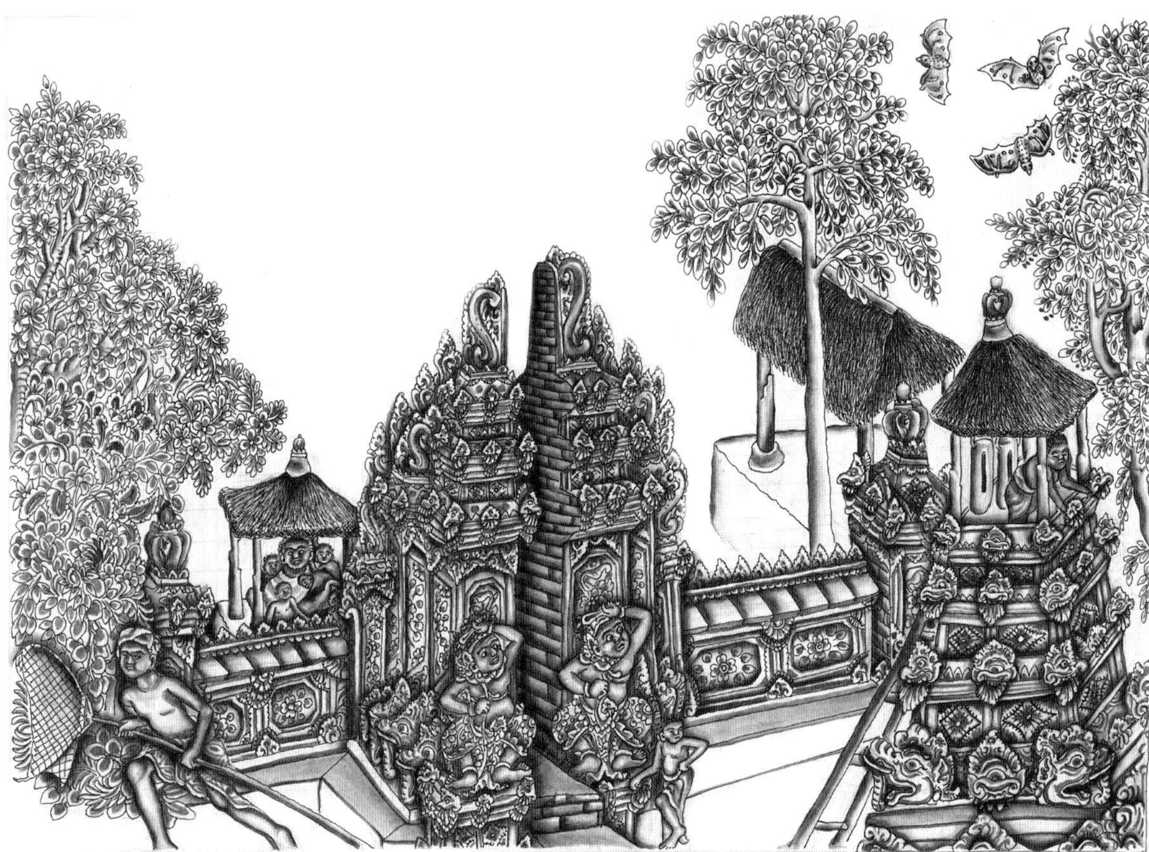

Figure 14. The Temple of Death (Pura Dalam Jungut). Drawing by Ida Bagus Madé Togog, 1986.

"Why are you running?" I said.

"*Bah!* There was a huge being there, two of them, very very tall!" they said. So then I said, "Let's go and look so we can know what they were." So then I went there. "Come on!" I said. Like that. "Come on with me, let's go look at it!" So we went there. And it turned out to be two little trees. When we got there, I said, "There! That's it! Isn't it?" Those trees were very thickly grown, the two of them. The field at Tegal Linggah had these two trees on it. That's what frightened them. That field was very *tenget.*

Once there were people working in the field down there. The crop was ripe—there were pumpkins there, and beans. In the afternoon someone came to buy them. These pumpkin plants grew as tall as a young coconut tree, higher than a house, leaning over. They were very big. And so there were two women who wanted to buy them along with the beans beneath them. They were going to pick them. They came out of the hut there, it was a hut with a door. When they came out they saw something terrifying in shape. They ran over toward the west. The being chased them, and when they got to the Pura Désa, they hid there. It chased them all the way up the road, they said.

And there were other times, when people planted yams and when they harvested them, tied them in bunches, and carried them home, and it would come looking for them and bring them back again.

So then Déwa Kompyang Krébék wanted to plant a crop there, and he put *dapdap* trees at each corner. And he put cotton-cloth strips on them. And then he was going to start to dig up the ground. And his son was often here, his oldest son [Déwa Putu Kebes]. He said that his father put up a temporary altar all piled up with bull dung in the middle of his courtyard. And then he danced in front of it. That's what he did.

Déwa Kompyang Krébék was well known as a man who was so *sakti* that he was not afraid of the *niskala* beings that haunted that field. His son, Déwa Putu Kebes, had the same reputation. I believe that Togog was suggesting that the reason he was not afraid to go down to look at the shapes that had frightened his older brother was not because he didn't believe that scary beings were there, but because he felt confident in his own *sakti* powers to confront them. But Togog never said this to me directly.

Another time someone asked me to go with him to hunt bats, the big ones called *bukal* [flying foxes] and the little ones called *lelawah,* with a big net. We went in the night to the graveyard at the Pura Dalem Jungut where there was a huge banyan tree. We went there and spread out the net halfway up the tree, and I climbed up into the *balé kulkul* [a tower with signal drum made of a log that is beaten with heavy stick]. I sat up there and thought that maybe I'd see a witch transformed into a frightening being. So I grabbed the big stick that they use for beating the *kulkul* drum.

"If something comes down there below I'll beat the *kulkul!*" I thought.

The man with me was Ida Bagus Nyoman Sara. He spread the net out down below, and there were about two thousand bats flying all around, high and low. Suddenly there was a big rustling noise in the bushes, sounded like a big pig leaping through. And that caused the bats to immediately fly away. It was just the rustling of the net.

Well, then my friend below just pulled in his net and ran away!

I chased after him, breathing hard with the fear of being left behind. Well, I was high up in the tree, on the watchtower, and it took long to get down. So I chased after him, panting, and finally caught up with him.

"Why were you running away?" I asked.

"Didn't you see what I saw?"

"What could I see? I was up in the tree!"

"*Beh!* It was a very fierce thing, and I was frightened. I couldn't bear it to get any hotter, so I ran."

"I didn't see anything," I said, laughing. [I asked Togog whether he too was afraid, and he said, " No, I didn't know fear."]

The Road to Denpasar and the First Foreigner Togog Ever Saw

Figure 15 shows the Dutch gravel road that went north past Batuan and south to Denpasar, at the spot where the path running in front of Togog's house goes to it, and the block of houseyards near it. An aqueduct had been built straddling the road, carrying irrigation water for rice fields on the other side. The aqueduct was not very high and tall vehicles could not go under it.

[Togog was explaining fig. 15:] Here's the aqueduct, and down below it is the gravel road. Now it's asphalt; they put that in later. There was a pond here [far right on picture, next to the irrigation ditch] with water for cooking rice, for cooking. For bathing too. And over here [pointing to the aqueduct] you could sit and bathe there too. Here are the iron supports of the water pipe. It was a very good place to bathe. The water was deep, and you could sit either at the west end or the east end.

And here I am carrying a blowpipe. I was taking it over to the rice fields, just fooling around. My father was in the rice fields.

And here is a car, half again higher than the aqueduct. Here is a man carrying a gun. He got out of the car. I

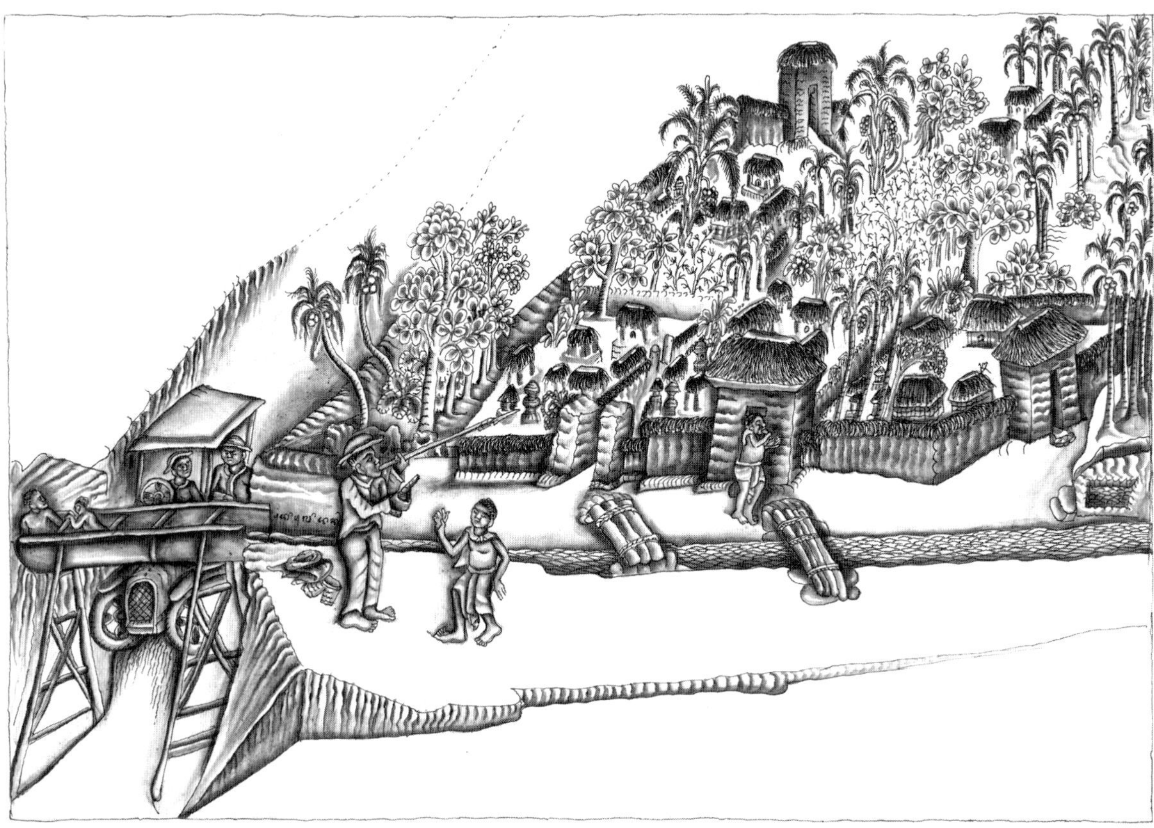

Figure 15. The road to Denpasar and the aqueduct. Drawing by Ida Bagus Madé Togog, 1986.

looked at him. The car had stopped, and it was rare to see a car in those days. The car couldn't go any farther north. I didn't know about that.

So then this man got out. Looking around to see how he could get free from it [to go under the aqueduct]. But he couldn't get free. I was carrying a blowpipe, and he climbed up to where I was and took away my blowpipe.

He said something that I couldn't understand. He was carrying a pistol. And then all of a sudden he made a big noise with the pistol. He wanted to trade the pistol for the blowpipe. I gave him the blowpipe. He said, *"Tukar! Tukar!"* [Indonesian for "Trade!" or "Swap!"].

"*Pah!* He's taking the blowpipe!" I thought. He blew and he blew on it. But the blowpipe wasn't mine, it belonged to someone else. I had borrowed it from Geria Pacung to go shooting.

I just shook my head, "Someone else owns this, someone else!" I said. He wanted to have it. He had it and I couldn't get it back because he was big. The car was black, painted black. He went down to it, and then he climbed up again.

He gave me back the blowpipe, and then I rushed away, I ran away. I didn't dare look back, taking the blowpipe.

I don't know where he was from. He was not a Balinese and not a Dutchman. He was in the car, and the car was too tall. His clothes were all black, and even his skin was black. He sounded his pistol, *nguéng!* and said, "Swap! Swap! Swap!"

This strange man with a black skin and a black automobile was probably from the island of Ambon in the far eastern part of the Dutch East Indies, probably Christian, educated, a civil servant for the Dutch colonial government. Togog's story stresses the incomprehensibility of such an outlandish being, who could come right into his home village and act with the colonial assurance of superiority and privilege over a "native." The man spoke only Malay, the language of the colonial administration, and Togog, able only to interpret the man's gestures, thought quite reasonably that the blowpipe was being grabbed away from him. In the next chapter Togog tells about going on trips away from his village, growing up and getting to know something of the confusing world outside it.

Two Wanderings, Gambling, Friendships

Bali in the Nineteen Twenties and Thirties

Bali in the 1920s and 1930s • Visiting in Nearby Villages • Solitary Trips • Wage-labor and Peddling • Fishing • Gambling • Respect in Language and Gesture • Work and Adult Responsibilities

In this group of stories, Togog tells of his trips away from Batuan. They start in his earliest years, but by the end of this chapter, Togog is a young recently married adult, still wandering. He gradually explored the rest of the world of Bali.

While Togog does not stress it, the underlying condition of his life in those days was one of rural poverty. His family's situation was much like that of the rest of the village, as witnessed in the buildings shown in his drawings, and in the photographs by Gregory Bateson in *Balinese Character.* With the exception of Jero Gedé, the walls were made of mud bricks topped with straw, and most of the *balé* were run-down and had leaky roofs. Togog's son also remembers a childhood of poverty in the 1950s, and even being given rice, corn, and meat in a government dole distributed at the Pura Désa.

Togog and his family, like many others in Batuan, had no direct access to farmland and its products. While Togog's great-grandfather may have owned some rice land, by the time Togog was born the only land in the family was that of his grandfather Gedé. His grandmother, the *pedanda,* had owned at one time several pieces of land, but she had pawned it all away. This was why his mother had to eke out a living by selling cooked food. His older brother was a peddler, carrying baskets of foodstuffs long distances to sell for pittances. Numbers of people from Batuan trekked up to the mountains to plant or harvest in the small plantations of coffee and coconuts for minuscule wages. It was not until the 1970s that tourists started to come to Bali in sufficient numbers to affect the family economy.

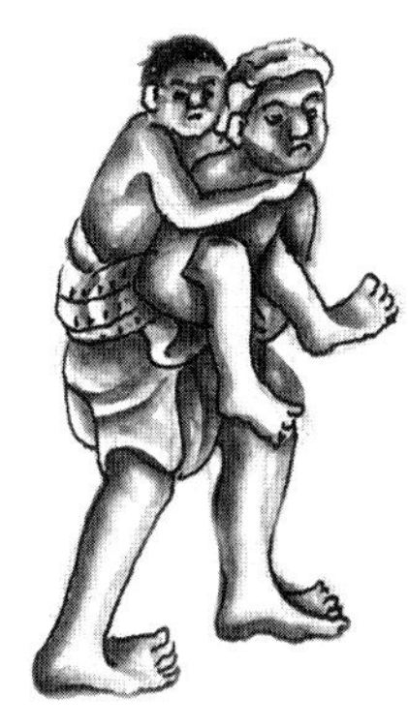

Although no one starved, sickness and early death pervaded everyone's life. Women often died in childbirth, or soon after. Malaria was endemic. During the 1930s some smallpox persisted, but by the middle of the century the colonial government's efforts to eradicate it were finally successful. Periodic epidemics of cholera still raged.

There were major inequities, especially in landownership, but even the wealthiest Balinese, the officials, lived at a standard much like Togog's. For the poorest landless laborers, it was gleaning rights, kinsmen's compassion, or wage work in harvesting or in upland plantations of coffee and coconuts, that kept them alive. For some of Togog's unemployed fellows, marriage was a solution to survival, for the women, like Togog's mother, worked hard, and a new network of relatives gave access to gardens and fruit trees. Still, many of the stories of his childhood are about hunger and good meals. The allure of fishing can be understood only partially as a kind of playful escape from the dreary burdens of the daily household chores of making a living.

For most Balinese ritual activity was as time- and energy-consuming as getting a living. With frequent ceremonies at the many temples, with almost daily domestic and life-cycle rituals, everyone was busy with preparations, performances, processions, cleansings, burnings, and distributions of cooked food. This, of course, was even more true for Brahmana, who not only had their own religious duties but assisted with those of everyone else. The unmarried girls were kept at home with their mothers to help with cooking, child care, and the making of offerings. Boys, on the other hand, were free to wander as they wished. As Togog points out, there was not much to keep him at home.

Togog had kin scattered over the island, in Pliatan near Ubud, in Denpasar, in Kuta, and in the large village of Budakling in Karangasem. As a member of a *pedanda* family, he also had *sisia,* or ritual clients, in many different places: Jimbaran, Peguyungan, Sukawati, Sidang, Pangsan, and elsewhere. These *sisia* were obliged to assist their Brahmana gurus. When they came to Togog's family for advice and liturgical help, they might sleep overnight there and bring with them cooking oil, turtle meat, pigs, rice, and money. The women of the house would cook for them and feed them, as well as providing them with coffee and cigarettes. Several times the *sisia* built new pavilions for Togog's family. Conversely, when Togog went on some of his wanderings, there were *sisia* everywhere to feed him.

During Togog's childhood, cash was little used except in the tiny amounts spent for snacks and salt, although by the end of his life nearly every aspect of life had been monetized. The colonial government imposed a monetary system and taxes that had to be paid in colonial *rupiah* or Dutch *gulden.* But the commonest currency in the village was still the *képéng,* Chinese coins with holes in their middles that were strung together in long strings. This money had been in circulation long before the Dutch arrived, and remained that which one gave to the gods. A settled exchange rate for *képéng* held for those who had access to the Dutch colonial currency. The colonial *rupiah* had lesser units: the *sen* (cent, one-hundredth of a *rupiah*), the *suku* (50 cents), the *talén* (25 cents), the *ketip* (10 cents), and the *ringgit* (two and a half *rupiah*). This last coin was of heavy silver and was the most desired.

During the course of Togog's life, the currency was revised several times, as the Dutch were replaced by Japanese, who were then replaced by the Republic of Indonesia, and then by the Dutch again, and finally again by the Republic. Even more important was a steady inflation in value. In listening to Togog's accounts, some clues as to their date are given by the money he mentions, but he sometimes spoke anachronistically, using contemporary vocabulary to speak of past times.

Employment in the government offices, the best way out of this economic backwater, which was to become an important occupational sector in the postwar period, was confined to one or two men from the noble house, who as boys had admission to the Malay and Dutch-language schools, and a *pedanda* from Togog's extended family who became a colonial judge.

Togog's enthusiasm for gambling, which lasted throughout his life, might be interpreted at the outset as a response to his directionless economic situation, in which cash was a somewhat strange object. Gambling was a source of monetary windfalls. Painting, at least in the beginning, also had this quality of unpredictable profit (see Chapter 6). The encroachment of colonial institutions and their commercial accompaniments into Togog's life pops up in every chapter. The earliest of these encounters, in Chapter 1, was that with the black driver who jumped out of his car and demanded the child's blowpipe. He was offering an exchange, but the appalled Togog thought, quite reasonably given the circumstances, that he was seizing it.

That sort of misunderstanding—both linguistic and practical—foreshadowed many later intercultural confusions. For Togog, it seems, foreigners were always bafflingly unpredictable and covertly powerful, even the European painters Bonnet and Spies in Ubud who sponsored his painting, and probably even me.

Togog's relationships with government officials are illustrated in tax-collecting episodes in this chapter and the court cases in Chapter 5. These officials were usually nobles who, going by their Satria titles, should address a Brahmana very politely, but because of their power always speak down to Togog. Worries about police capture on the part of an eloping couple and the use of the government telephone in bringing Togog back from Karangasem to marry his pregnant girlfriend are further examples of the penetration of the foreign rulers even into the crevices of private family life.

As Togog gradually matures, he talks more and more with strangers. Speaking politely to someone whose relative status to one is unknown is a constant dilemma for travelers, and Togog mentions it from time to time. A good example is given in this chapter.

How much the "outside world" had penetrated into Balinese life even as early as the 1930s emerges sometimes in the vocabulary that Togog uses in his dialogues. His speech was replete with words borrowed from the Indonesian (called Malay in Togog's youth), the language of the government and of traders. Of course, the words I tape-recorded were those of Togog speaking in the 1980s, but I believe that even in the 1930s, many Malay words had long since lost their aura of foreignness. Togog's world as presented by him is not a "traditional" world. The Western contrast of traditional versus modern was not his conception and is not appropriate here. The world of the twenties and thirties was not slow, unified, integrated, harmonious, and meaningful in contrast to an emerging world of the time of his talks with me as fragmented, fast-moving, discontinuous, and baffling. The tentacles of globalization were already reaching into Togog's life.

The people of importance to Togog as his range of activity broadened now included: Togog's mother's mother, who took him on several long trips; his older brother, Ida Bagus Renteg, who also took him on a trip; Togog's mother's brothers, especially the man whom he called Po Ketut (Ida Bagus Ketut Jelantik); the Brahmana woman who lived next door (the patron of Désak Watin, the storyteller, who was also a well-known *balian*); his boyhood friend from next door, Ida Bagus Wayan Truwi, who became a Dutch-educated and Dutch-appointed village head; and two other older men from the Brahmana Siwa clan who took him fishing, Ida Bagus Sotong and Ida Bagus Cukeng.

Visiting in Nearby Villages

Bah! I remember walking with my mother when I was very little. Going way up north, to Silungan, oh, it was even farther! north of Silungan. To get some seeds for cassava. I cried on the road because it was so far.

Another time, my grandmother [Togog's mother's mother] said to me,

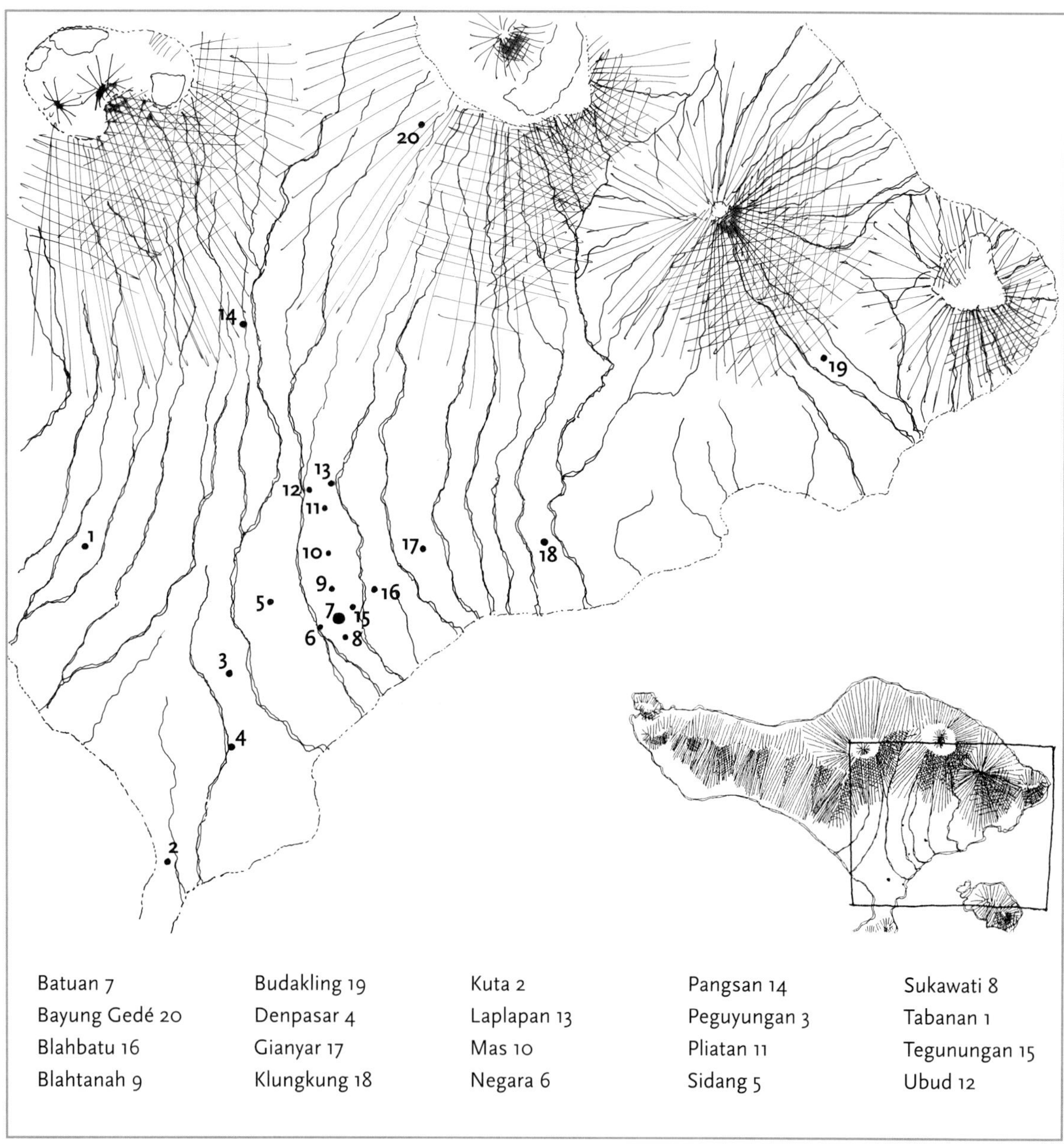

Figure 16. Map of Bali showing some of the places Togog visited. Togog walked to all these places in Bali. In his early youth there were only a few roads (to Ubud, Gianyar, Klungkung, and Karangasem), so one walked on paths, often across rice fields. The rivers were the main barriers in traveling. I could not locate three places Togog mentioned: "Belatungan" where his brother harvested chili peppers, and that seems to be north of Tabanan; "Beléleng," where Togog went to harvest coffee beans, which seems to be in the west-central mountains; and "Jaborana," or Jembrana, where he went to plant in a coconut plantation, somewhere to the west of Tabanan.

"Don't go to the rice field [where Togog had been hired to guard the crops from birds and monkeys] today. Come with me. We'll go visiting." She wanted me to go with her to Laplapan, far from here, northeast of Pliatan. [This was the Brahmana village where she had been born and raised.]

As soon as we got there they gave me a basketful of yams. That area was very poor.

"Just give me a small basketful," I said.

Peh! I had to stop about fifty times on the way back. *Ratu!* It was so heavy!

And it was so far, and it was up hill and down.

Beh! Ratu! I could hardly stand it!

I could hardly stand it, and I said to myself, "I hope I never have to carry yams from there again!"

And the path went up and down, up and down! and the yams were very, very heavy.

And another time my other grandmother [the wife of Togog's Grandfather, Ida Bagus Gria] asked me to go with her.

"Come visiting with me," she said.

We went to Batuh [Blahbatuh] to visit and stayed there a month. In the *puri*. Something happened there: I was accused of being a thief!

Well now, this is the way it was in the *puri* there. They treated me as if I was the ruler. They liked me so much. They gave me really good food. They were very decent. The woman there, named Anak Agung Gria, was a widow, and she needed people to help her. My grandmother went there to ask her friend for some rice and clothes.

It is customary for Brahmana women to earn rice and clothing in return for help in making offerings in their role as *tukang banten*. The name of the royal woman suggests that she had kin ties with the Brahmana families. Togog later explained that they had gone there just to ask for help, but when they arrived found out that there was a big ritual festival in the local Pura Dalem, and Anak Agung Gria asked them to stay and work.

I was carefree. Whatever I wanted I just took! I'd see a piece of cloth and put it right on! And she'd only say to the servants, "Oh, he's just a little boy, don't scold him."

In those days life was really hard. A piece of rough white cotton served for a scarf. And I found one and just took it. But I couldn't know any better, could I? So I took her head-scarf and used it as a sarong. [A sarong is a cloth used to wrap around the lower part of one's body, male or female. A cloth that goes around one's shoulders (a *cerik*) or one's head (an *udeng*) should *never* be placed around the lower part of the body, for this pollutes it.]

I didn't know any better. So she just said, "Ah little Ida Bagus, he's still only little!"

Well, she had a farm manager *(sedahan)*, and I went to his house, too, with my grandmother, and they were nice to me there too.

"Ratu, come and visit me every morning, won't you?" Then he gave me a fighting cock and said, "Ratu, we'll let it have a fight soon. Take care of it for me."

So I took care of it. I plumed it and stroked it, and I fed it, and I thought, "Soon I'll let you have a fight." I felt as if I owned it myself; I thought he had given it to me. I was still very little, you know.

I took it out to the meeting hall and let it have play fights with other cocks. [In these informal play fights the roosters do not have metal spurs on them, nor are bets placed.] And a man from Tegenengan [a village just west of Batuan] saw me and said, "Gus Alit! Gus Alit! Look for a fighting cock for me to enter in a bout in Batuan."

Well, that day I brought the cock back to its owner, but two days later I took it right away. I was going to take it all the way down to Tegenungan to give to that man, but on the way, in Belangsinga, there was a crowd of about forty people who saw me, and they thought I had stolen the cock.

"*Bah!* Thief! Thief!" They thought I was a thief! [Laughs.]

"Go back again! Take it back again! That rooster must belong to someone else!" They said that because I was a child on the road to somewhere else. So I took the chicken back to them.

So after that the rumor came back here in Batuan that I had stolen the cock. Right away, that night, someone from Batuan came for me. I was sleeping up on the high place for preparing offerings next to the family temple. They let me sleep there, and just after I went to sleep the people from Batuan came, and said they had heard that I had been stealing.

I heard the voice of my uncle over in the visitors' house. "Please don't think too badly of him! Forgive him for stealing!"

And the owner answered: "No, it's alright. I *gave* the cock to him to care for it for me. You know how I don't like to groom and train my fighting cocks myself. And besides it gave him some work to do like the other children."

And then he said, "Just go home again." So then my uncle went home.

Later the owner said to me, "Where were you taking the cock?"

"To my 'father' from Tegenungan. He said he was going to put it in a fight and told me to bring it to him there." I said that if he had been at home at the time I would have asked his permission. He wasn't angry at me. After all, he had given me the cock to take care of, to keep with me all the time no matter what. I would take it out of its cage, but later I'd put it back again. I would stroke and preen it and give it practice bouts with the other cocks. He didn't like to take care of his roosters himself. And just because I took back roads to Tegenungan, they thought I was a thief. [Laughs.]

The owner then made fun of me when he thought I was sleeping, and I overheard him say, "He's really such a little little boy!" So right away I wanted to go home. There was a little gap in the wall west of the *balé metén* and west of the family temple. Outside the wall there was cactus, thickly planted, and a ditch all around the place. They were very rich.

I was still very little, and I felt confused and troubled that night. It was about eleven o'clock, and I thought to myself, "I want to go home right now. Why should I stay here?" So I just sneaked out. I jumped right over the cactus. I didn't tell anyone I was going home. I just left.

My grandmother stayed there—she was helping with the offerings for the Pura Dalem. They were going to have a big ceremony. And I went back again to Blahbatuh two days later.

That's how it was, that I was "accused of being a thief" when I was little. They are still today always very good to me there in Blahbatu, in Puri Kelodan as well as in Puri Kajanan. Whenever I go there, they give me good food to eat.

Solitary Trips

I remember once there was a cremation in Ubud, and my Grandfather went up there. I was still very very little. He had been there nine days, and he hadn't come home. So because he hadn't come home in such a long time, I went there myself. I was very little and I had to ask my way many times. "Which is the way to Ubud?" like that.

When I got to Belatanah, I asked, "Which is the way to Ubud?"

"This way, just follow the road!" The road was very bad, all little rocks, not asphalt like today. But finally I got there. I walked all the way.

When I got to Ubud, I saw some people working and I asked, "Where is the Pedanda from Batuan staying?" [Togog's Grandfather must have been serving as ritual assistant to the Pedanda, who must have been the female *pedanda* from Togog's home, his grandmother.]

"Here! Here! Here!" They showed me the Brahmana house *(gria)* next to the noble house *(puri)* in Ubud, and I went there, and when I went in, my Uncle Yan [another ritual specialist from Togog's family] said, "Hey! Who brought you here?

"I brought myself. Because my Grandfather hasn't come home for such a long time."

My Grandfather wasn't angry. "Well, later on you can go home again with me." He wasn't angry, he was moved that such a little boy would come such a long way looking for him. And then, after he finished eating—it was afternoon—he took some meat to bring home with him. It was a great big piece. They were very rich there. While I was there I ran errands for my Grandfather, and then when the ceremony was all over I went home with him.

I went to Pliatan many times. I have a lot of relatives there. [The Pliatan *gria* of Brahmana Buda was the natal home of Togog's mother's mother.] I could always get something to eat there. Even if there were three of us, they'd say, "Come and eat here. Come on!" They were very patient with us. Once I took some coconuts to them there, the ones I had "stolen" from my Grandfather's tree. But it turned out that they already had coconuts there. There was a tree up there by the field in Pliatan that my kinsmen owned, a low one, and I went up and down it gathering coconuts one by one until I had seven. And then I sold them for five *képéng* each.

When I was up in the tree, I heard someone say to my Grandfather, "Where did he get those coconuts?"

"He got them from my field." He said that to his friend, and then he said: "Oh, he's just a child, and he takes only one or two at a time. If he asked me for the money, I'd give it to him, even 25 *képéng*."

When I saw my Grandfather come under the tree, I thought "*Bah!* Here comes the owner of this coconut tree!" But after I heard that from him, I decided to go back home to Batuan. It was clear to me. So I just took coconuts from my Grandfather's tree in Batuan, again one by one. I gave them to get Désak Watin to tell me stories. I valued those stories very much because I was going to use them as subjects for pictures.

Staying in Pangsan

It happened that the wife of my Uncle Ketut [Togog's mother's brother] got pregnant, but it was before they had the marriage ritual *(masakapan)* in the family temple. Now if a child is conceived like that in a Brahmana family, they won't consider it to be kin, so the child has to be sent away. It isn't permitted to raise such an illegitimate child *(astra* or *anak bebinjat)* here. So they took the baby away to Pangsan [to the north of Batuan, nearly in the mountains].

That's how it happened that my Uncle Ketut and his wife were staying there in Pangsan with their baby. I went there to visit them. I didn't take anything with me to eat on the road, and so many times I had to ask the way, *bah!* "Where is that place?" I found it finally.

My Uncle Ketut saw me and said in surprise, "Hello! Look who's come looking for me here! Well, well, who brought you here, little one? I'll sell you for being so naughty, for being so stupid," he scolded me.

"I came because I wanted to know what it's like here."

The man whose house we stayed in was a Gusti. He was the one who raised that illegitimate child, and later when she grew up he made her the wife of his own son.

So I stayed there with them.

Pah! They always gave me really good food! They were all very generous to me there.

While I was in Pangsan, my Uncle Ketut took me out in the fields with him, hoeing and cultivating, because they were preparing the rice fields for planting.

The Gusti said to me, "Tomorrow, Ratu, come with us and help us get the rice field ready for planting. So that when you go back to Batuan you'll know how to do it."

I answered, "Yes, I'd like to."

So I did that, and my Uncle Ketut also went. I thought we were going to work with two cows pulling the plow on one rice field. But there were about nineteen cattle there for the one rice field. [This was an exchange labor party and everyone brought their cattle for the plowing in return for a festive meal.]

In the morning before starting the work the hosts gave the guests, the workers, a feast. It was undescribably delicious —cakes and coffee and tea—as much as you wanted. They killed forty chickens and broiled them. Some of the people were going to hoe, some to rake, and some to plow, cultivating the soil to make ready for the planting of the rice.

So after we had the feast, and we were still sitting on the edge of the rice field, there were two cows there, hitched together for plowing. And he told me, "Come here and hold the ropes," in order to guide the cows. The people made jokes about racing the two of them as they went across each rice field. "The one that loses will be butchered and eaten tomorrow!" It was very jolly, and there were many people watching to see which one would lose.

So then all the teams started to go back and forth. And I too started up, going west then east, west then east, you know. And there was a thick clump of pandanus trees at the western edge of the rice field.

Now, the nose of one of the cows had been hurt, torn by the rope through its nostril, but I didn't know it. The cow suddenly went mad. I kept pulling on the rope. It ran right in among the pandanus trees, nearly to the middle of the clump, trampling them down. I let loose the rope because if I went after them I would have flattened down all the pandanus, and I cried out for help.

The man who owned the cow, who owned the field, cried out, "What's the matter?" [Respectfully] And I said, "Uncle, I was holding the rope and it just ran away" [in the familiar register].

He ran after the cow. They had to cut down the pandanus trees. It took four people to get the cow back, cutting a pathway through the pandanus.

And then when they got to the cow, "*Pah!* That's it! Its nose is all cut by the rope!" said the owner.

I didn't know that. I had never plowed before.

Then he told me, "Go over there and sleep. There, just to the south, is a hut in that coconut field." I was completely worn out. [Laughs]

Togog made Figure 17 showing his experiences in Pangsan in 1984, just after I had left Bali, not in response to a request from me, but stimulated by his telling me these stories. He had it on sale when I returned to Bali in June 1984.

Togog appears in two places in the drawing. The first is just left of center where he is standing in amazement (and perhaps embarrassment) as the cow ran away from him. The second is in the lower right, where he is bending over the water of a stream trying to retrieve a dropped stone chisel. He tells this story below.

It was a nice big hut with six posts holding up the roof, rather than the usual four, and walls of woven bamboo. It was a place for people to guard the coconut trees, and it was empty. While I was sleeping there a woman came with a little child. "Hello!" she said in surprise, "Who are you?"

I told her I was a Brahmana.

"*Aruh!* Wonderful, yes, yes, Ratu!" [Very respectfully] "Say, if you want to—you could stay here and guard my coconut trees until they are ripe. In about ten days they'll fall and you can sell some of them. You'll get some money that way."

There were at least seventy-five trees there. That woman was the one who owned the trees. Her husband was dead and she had a little child. So I stayed, and she went on

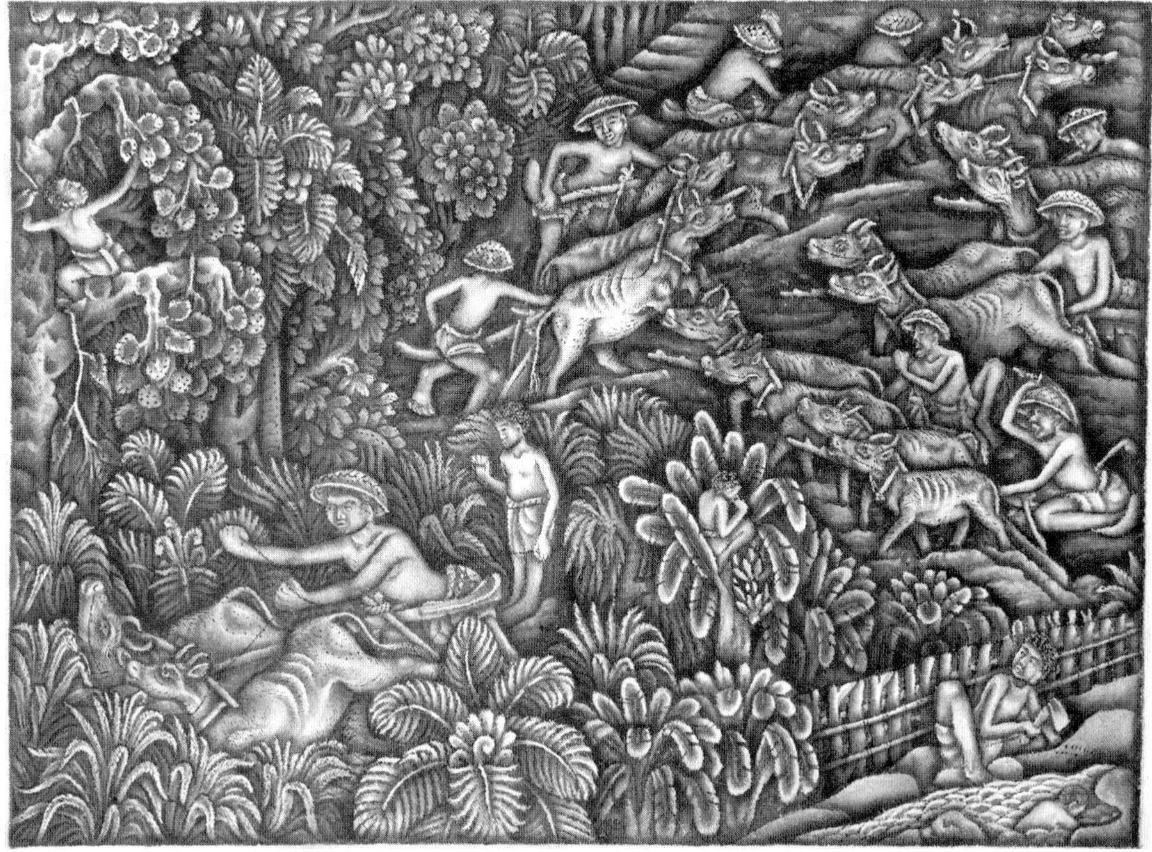

Figure 17. The plowing race at Pangsan. Painting by Ida Bagus Madé Togog, 1984.

home again, but first she said, "Ratu, come again tomorrow, yes?" she said, "You want to make a door for me for this hut?"

I didn't know anything about plaiting bamboo strips or about making a door to close up the hut so one could sleep easily, but I said Yes because I was thoughtless.

So I went there the next morning.

Bah! I was supposed to cut up the bamboo, but there wasn't anything to cut it with. How was I supposed to make a door? I looked around and I realized I was supposed to weave them together. In fact I didn't know how to plait bamboo, but I didn't care at all. I was just thoughtless. *Beh!* The strips of wood were very little and they didn't fit together. And it was getting towards night. I couldn't do it. So the next morning I tried again.

Three days I stayed there. She came three times, with the child, and she brought me my meals from her house. Her house was quite far away. She came with the child and said, "Here, Ratu." Besides that, she had a younger sister. [Whispering] Was she ever pretty! Really pretty!

"*Peh!* Ratu," said the younger sister to me, "I'll keep you company, Ratu, here. These are my coconut trees here, and here's some food for you."

I liked that.

But I was having so much trouble weaving that door. So I left. I just sneaked away, I didn't tell anyone and didn't take anything with me. I couldn't do it. I didn't know how to make that door, and I was just a thoughtless boy, just thoughtless. It was too hard to do.

Some time later in Pangsan I met a man there who said to me, respectfully, "Ratu! If you want to learn how to work, come with me stonecutting!" The man was a very strong man. "Learn how to cut *paras*-stone. Then you can sell the blocks of stone." [*Paras* is the soft volcanic tuff that lines most of Bali's ravines, which is used for much of their stone carving.]

"Okay, let's go, Grandpa *(Kak)!*" I said, in low speech. So we went down into the ravine. There was a huge rock right in the middle of the river and the water next to it was very deep. And leaning over the river right there was a tall banana tree. All its fruit was good and ripe.

"*Tu!* Climb up there and get me a couple of bananas there. I own that tree," he said.

"Really, Grandpa?"

"Yes, really."

I climbed up and up in the tree. I ate one up there. The tree was very tall. Meanwhile he was clearing the rock off so that he could cut off a block. "Grandpa, how many do you want?"

"Two, Ratu." I brought two down to him.

"Tomorrow," he said in high speech, "when we come I'll bring some ground coconut meat to eat with the bananas. That'll taste very good!"

He went on chiseling. *Tek! Tek! Tek!*

All of a sudden his chisel fell in the water.

"*Badah!* Ratu Ida Bagus, my chisel fell in the water!" So he took another chisel, and then it too fell in the water! Both of them fell in the water. I hadn't had a chance yet to learn how to chisel.

So then I went down into the water, to try to find them. But the water was deep, up to my neck. So then I tried with a long stick to feel for them. But the water was full of fine mud, and it was at least a half a meter deep.

"Where is that chisel?" I wondered.

Someone must have been watching over me. I think I was not meant to become a stonecutter. Maybe it's not proper for a Brahmana to be a stonecutter. [Laughs.]

Staying in Sidang

Sidang is about five or six kilometers west from Batuan as the crow flies. The uncle was Togog's father's brother, who lived in the same houseyard with him in Batuan. Their host was a Satria man with the title of *Resi,* indicating that he had studied mystical practice.

Then once I went to stay in Sidang with an uncle. It was this way: my uncle was in love with a girl, but she didn't like him. So, as a ruse to have a chance to be with her so that she'd get to like him, he persuaded the priest to tell her to accompany him to Sidang to help with certain rituals. It was in the home of a man there, a *resi,* who had often come here to study Buda mystical lore *(kabudaan)*. So when my uncle was there with the girl, he took her.

That is, he married her, and they stayed in Sidang for quite a while before returning to Batuan. Togog's son explained to me that in those days an eloping couple was afraid, not only of the anger of the girl's parents but also that they might get the colonial police to arrest the young man, and finally they were afraid of sorcery on the part of someone opposed to the marriage.

So while he was in Sidang I often went there to visit him. Someone was always going down there bringing food to the couple, and I went along. No one told me to go. I was just naughty.

That Resi, he was very good to me. You see, he was very well off. Once he called me to him, "Ratu! Gus Alit!" and he told me to go collect flowers for the rituals. And once he made me a trap to catch birds with a live bird as a decoy. *Peh!* I had to climb very high up to set the trap.

And he also told someone there to teach me how to drive a horse cart. We went here and there on the road to Tingas and then west to Lambing. The Resi had a son there in Lambing living with his former wife. She had left him and returned to her former home with the son, and he went to visit them often, taking me with them to get a meal in Batu Rening.

After I'd been in Sidang quite a long time, a man arrived there from here, from Banjar Tengah in Batuan, named I Remya. He had carved a wooden statue. The Resi had contracted with him to make it, and when I Remya brought him the statue the Resi then took it to Badung to sell. He got five *ringgit* silver for it. It was a very good statue—five *ringgit* coins in silver!

One night when I was fast asleep—they had given me a mattress and a sheet, and it was a thick mattress—I was fast asleep and the Resi woke me up and said, "Gus Alit! Here's the money!"

When I woke up later I thought he had *given* me the money while I was sleeping. *Bah!* Was I happy! I had been there a long time and he'd never given me any money. The Resi wasn't home when I woke up. I thought, "*Bah!* Since I've this money, I'll go to Badung and buy a sarong." So then I went to Badung Denpasar.

While I was in Badung, the man I Remya arrived and asked for his money from the sale. Since I wasn't there, they thought I had *stolen* it. "Bah! Where did Ida Bagus Alit take that money?"

The Resi said to I Remya, "You just go on home now, and if he took the money I'll replace it. Let me worry about it."

In Badung I bought a beautiful checked sarong, exactly what I liked. I was just a stupid little boy, you know! [Laughs.] That cost nearly a *ringgit,* and then I took a horse cart home, used the rest of the *ringgit* to pay for it. When I got home, I changed into my new clothes.

"Hello!" the Resi said to me. "Did you take that man's money?"

"Did that money belong to somebody?" I asked.

"It was I Remya's money, the pay for the carving."

"I thought you gave it to me. I, uh, uh, I still have the rest here."

"Well, how much did you use, Gus?"

"I only spent a *ringgit.*"

"Well, never mind; I'll give him back the rest. I'll tell him I sold it for four *ringgit.*"

That's what he said. But later when I got back to Batuan, they all said again that I had been a thief but that then I had returned four of the coins.

"I thought you had given me the money, as my clothes were all in tatters. That's why I went and bought me some!"

"No I gave it to you just to keep for me!" [Laughs.] "I told you to keep it for me!" Well, I sure didn't feel good in my heart after that. I didn't feel good in my heart.

The business of woodcarving traditional subjects for sale to tourists was established long before painting. Togog must have been around ten when he had this first confusing experience with Dutch money. In the 1920s in Batuan, the extensive rebuilding of the main temple, the Pura Désa, was under way, and I Remya was one of their finest stone carvers. The price of three *ringgit* (7.50 *guilder*) was high, suggesting that Remya had made a particularly large and intricate carving for the foreign trade. The Resi of Pingsan was evidently a commercial middleman in this intercultural trade. Perhaps he had given the money to Togog to carry home with him to Batuan to pay I Remya. See my *The Life of a Balinese Temple* (2004) for examples of I Remya's work.

The next morning at the Resi's house, because they were very busy getting ready for a ceremony, I helped, chopping up and grinding spices for the meat. With my decoy I caught a bird to make a dish called *bé tutu.* I ground up spices from early morning until my hand was nearly broken, and I chopped up the bones of the bird, too. *Bé tutu* is delicious.

Then I was sent to gather flowers for offerings, and I

went to the south where there was a pool with a tree over it. The one who owned the house there—Si Luh was her name—a young girl, asked me, "Tu, are you looking for flowers?"

"Yes," I said.

"Well be careful! Don't trample the little plants in the pool!"

It was a wide pool full of lotus blossoms, and I stepped down into it. I had picked maybe about seventy-five flowers. You know, I'm afraid of leeches, and all of a sudden there was a leech by me as big as my hand.

Bah! I ran out of there and stirred up all the mud and got myself drenched, drenched! My one-and-only sarong was soaking wet. So then I was shivering like a monkey, waiting for my clothes to get dry again. Then after my clothes were dry, the girl Si Luh said to me, "I'll show you how, Ratu, to pick the flowers without walking into the water." She had a long stick with a knife tied onto the end of it. First you cut the flower and then use the long stick to rake it near you.

Wage Labor and Peddling

From his earliest years, when his grandmothers took him on several-hour walking trips, Togog was used to traveling on foot. In the early 1920s, this was the only way to get from place to place, but by the mid-thirties there were trucks and buses crossing Bali, and sometimes the penniless Togog could hitch a ride.

A trek of three hours up to Ubud was nothing to him, nor were the two-day hikes up to the mountains of Tabanan or the coconut plantations of coastal Jembrana. On these trips he learned to pick chili peppers and coffee, to plant coconut trees, about adultery and singing, about malaria and healing, and about sorcerer's poisons.

Going to the Mountains to Harvest Chili Peppers

I wanted to learn how to earn money because I was so spoiled at home with them giving me money whenever I asked for it, and I was afraid I was getting greedy and naughty. I didn't mind wasting even 25 *képéng* on gambling at that time. It made me feel very troubled.

So then I heard that my older brother [Ida Bagus Kompiang Renteg] was planning to go to the mountains, to Belatungan, to pick chilies.

"Beli! Beli! Let me go with you, Beli!"

"Do you know how to pick peppers?" he asked.

"Yes, I can!"

"Okay, you can come," he said.

Bah! It was far! [Laughs.]

We walked the whole way, carrying a basket. We were two days walking to get there. It's rarely that one gets a chance to harvest chilies, and I wanted to learn how to work. Whatever kind of work I could get I liked. So I picked peppers in the forest there, northwest of Bajra, quite near Jembrana.

When we had enough peppers, my older brother brought them down to the market in Tabanan to sell. There was no one in the forest buying them, just people with coffee plantations. He asked the man who owned the coffee plantation, "May I pick peppers here, Uncle?"

"Yes, go ahead," he said. So after my brother sold the peppers in Tabanan market he bought matches and betel-nut leaves and lime to bring as a present to the man who owned the plantation.

Beh! He was happy! We were up there about a month. When we left, my brother didn't give me one *képéng*. *Aduh!* What bad luck! Not one penny! When I asked my brother for some money, he said, "What are you going to buy?" He didn't give me any.

A Trip to Beléleng to Harvest Coffee

One day I heard that some people from the village were going up into the mountains to harvest coffee in Beléleng. I suddenly felt that I really wanted to go along with them.

"*Biang! Biang!* Can I go with you up there?" [He used familiar speech. *Biang* is the high-register term for "mother," used for noblewomen. This woman was Togog's father's younger sister.]

"Yes, in three days." [Also familiarly.]

"Ah, I feel very troubled in my heart because I keep wanting to gamble. I want to stop being a gambler!" I said. "If I'm up there in the mountains who will I gamble with? I'd stop." [It's not clear whether he said this to "Biang" or to himself.]

It was because my Grandfather next door was so good to me, giving me everything. I was becoming arrogant because he loved me so much. Any thing I asked for he gave me. I was a spoiled child.

So three days later I went with them to go and harvest coffee. To pick coffee beans you need to bring a container, but I didn't bring one. I didn't know I had to. I thought that I would climb the tree and just throw the coffee beans down and people down below would take it. [Laughs.] All I brought with me was my shawl, my shirt, my sarong, and a straw hat. When people go to harvest coffee they bring baskets and put the beans in them right away, but I didn't know that. I thought I'd throw them down like mangos and other people would pick them up. [Laughs.]

Well, I went with a woman named Désak Pedit. She knew where to go, in the Batareng woods, northwest of here. It was very far away.

So on the way there, it was getting dark and we were still on the road. She said, "Where's that little path through the woods?" *Beh!* We hurried here and there. Three times we went back again before we found the right path cutting through the woods to the place where Bapan Gembu was, the man who owned the plantation.

Bah! I was so tired I was almost falling over as I walked. We *walked* the whole way, from here to the place west of Tabanan, in Megati!

We finally came to a market at Jampat and we stayed overnight there. Because I was little I was heedless of where I slept. It was in the home of an important person like the village head *(perbekel)* or, as they say today, the *camat* (district head). I went to someone's house, because I didn't want to sleep in the market because there were goats there and we wouldn't have been able to chase them away because we were strangers from far away, just staying there for the night.

In the morning we went on to Beléleng. There were twenty-five of us at least. There were some from Banjar Tengah, in Batuan. One of them was Déwa Kompiang Atih, and many others. Men and women.

Finally we were lucky and found the path through the woods to Bapan Gembu's place, the man who owned the coffee, and we went right there. When we got there, she greeted Bapan Gembu. Désak Pedit spoke with him politely.

There were some people there from Sembung, six of them. They were cutting away the undergrowth under the coffee plants in order to pick the coffee. If they let you work there on the harvest you are very lucky. There was some talk about working together with the people from Sembung. But the people from Sembung went away. I was in the group of Déwa Kompiang Atih, and I asked him, "Kompiang, where are they going, Piang?"

"Oh, they're going to pick coffee to the southwest of here," he answered. I didn't know how large the forest was. In the forest there were little paths, and those people—about forty there were—broke off from here and left. There weren't very many people crossing through there.

When we started, I said, "Piang! Piang! [Kompiang] Can I go with you to pick?"

"Yes, yes, of course. Work over there, but don't leave any berries up on the tree!"

But I didn't bring a container, *beh!* And so I just took my shawl and bundled the berries up in it. Then I put them in a hollow hole in the bottom of a tree, pouring them in over and over with the sound of rattling pebbles.

When the day was over and everyone else brought what they'd gotten back to the owner, he called out to me, "Where're yours?"

"Here it is! Here it is! Take it! I didn't bring anything to put it in."

Then he asked me who I was, and I said I was a Brahmana from Batuan. Then he said, very respectfully: "Ratu! My sun-lord *(surya titiang)*! You're too little and you didn't have anything to work with. Don't try to sell the coffee beans, give them to me and let me sell them for you!"

So he looked for a coffee buyer and said to him, "Over there, Beli, there're some beans to buy from that little Brahmana boy there from Batuan. Buy it from him for the usual price of one *rupiah,* but add a *talén* [one-fourth of a *rupiah*] because he's so little." That's what he said, and he took nothing for himself. So I was given half a *ringgit* [one and a fourth of a *rupiah*]. [Laughs.]

That was the owner, Pan Gembu. He had a wife named I Rumelati. [In a low voice] She was very pretty. Well-shaped body. She had a lover named Si Darma. He lived down in the village, not up in the forest.

So once I Rumelati said to me: "Ratu, Gus Alit, come with me! I'm going home to visit my mother." She did have a mother, but really she was going to meet Si Darma. When she told Pan Gembu she was going home, he must have thought, "She must be going to see her mother." But, in fact, she went to Si Darma's.

I Rumelati had started the love affair with him when she helped Si Darma to court his present wife, helping to arrange the marriage. Because he was a stranger there.

The girl, a cousin of I Rumelati, was working as a servant for I Rumelati, so he had to ask I Rumelati's permission to marry her and her help in his suit. After she had persuaded the girl to marry Si Darma and after they were married, Si Darma and I Rumalati began their affair.

Si Darma was a healer *(balian),* and many people came to him for help and curing. One time when I was there, a couple came to ask for a cure. Si Darma took an earthenware pot, put a string of Chinese coins *(képéng)* around its neck like a necklace, filled it with water, said a spell *(mantra),* and then threw all the coins onto the ground in the courtyard.

"Ratu, you can take that money!" So I did. I got forty coins! Forty! [Once the money has been given to the gods, it no longer has any spiritual value.]

Another time, Pan Gembu said to me, "Ratu, tomorrow help me keep a watch on the butchers who are going to cut up the carabao. Watch out that they don't hide any meat for themselves. Whatever they hide and you find, I'll give you half of." I got a whole basketful of meat from that. There were twelve butchers. That's why I got so much. It was good being with him, I had good work, and he liked me.

From then on whenever they were picking coffee, I wasn't allowed to pick. Instead, I Rumelati would say, "Come with me, Ratu!" Politely. "Here, Ratu, take this little basket of coffee to sell."

It wasn't very much, not more than a canful, but coffee was expensive then. So I carried it to the coffee buyer, but on the way I fell down in some grass, and it all rolled out. I picked it all up again but it was mixed with a lot of dust. I carried the coffee beans and dust to the buyer, and when they were weighed it I got *double* as much money for it! I Remelati gave me a half a *ringgit.* That was my earnings.

I wasn't allowed to pick because I had no basket.

She took me everywhere with her. Her husband! Whenever she came home she brought him a little present, so that he would be happy and not mad at her. In fact, Pan Gembu *never* asked her where she'd been, but when he did she said she went home to visit her mother. But, she *didn't* go there, but went to see Si Darma. *Meh!* She was bad, she was!"

But, *pah!* How Si Rumelati could sing! She was very talented. She'd sing as we went down the mountain, "Sinom." *Meh! Aduh!* She was good!

Now, when I think about her, I wonder how I could have gone around with *that sort* of person!

Then when I went home I had three *rupiah* in silver. I had three *rupiah!* But, when I was almost home, I stopped in Negara [the village just west of Batuan]. It was late afternoon and there was a cockfight going on. So I gambled in the *kobokan* game [laughs], and when I was finished all I had left were three cents *(suku)*. [Laughs.] [A *kobokan* game is a gambling game played with *képéng* coins. Most cockfights also attract people who run gambling games for low stakes, around the outside of the fight.]

So when I arrived home all I had was three cents. But I was very happy. I brought some new clothes I had bought there, a pair of Western pants and a shirt. I didn't have my sarong any more.

The next day after I got home, there was a big ceremony in Peninjoan. I was invited. *Bah!* I was *happy* and I put on my new pants. Now no one had pants in those days. And they all *laughed* at me! I didn't go after all! (Laughs.) They laughed at me because my pants and shirt seemed so strange. *Bah!* The people on the way were roaring with laughter at me.

So I just went right back home, embarrassed at being laughed at, and never got to the festival.

A Trip to Jembrana to a Copra Plantation

So some time after that I heard that a group was going to Jaborana [Jembrana], and I went with them. There were a lot who went from here. The younger brother of my father, named Ida Bagus Madé Tima, that's the father of my second wife, was one of them. There were about eight of us, maybe more. Another was the woman who sells coffee today near the Pura Dalem, Dayu Keben, but at that time she was still unmarried, who later married Ida Bagus Sukawati Klabah. The first to learn about it here was my Po Yan [Ida Bagus Wayan Duduk, who later moved to Sukawati]. That's how we got to go there. They said there was lots of money to be got in Jaborana if you worked really hard.

There was a man named Ida Bagus Jedur [originally from Sukawati], who was the man in charge there. He was very young, but he was in charge. And he was very authoritarian. Late one afternoon he told me to put out a fishing net. The water was so deep it was up to my neck. And the water was foul. It was full of ashes, for they'd been burning the forest up above, and the water seeping into it was full of ashes. It was hard work, and my heart felt very heavy.

We were told to pick insects off the coconut plants before we planted them. We got paid for each insect we got by the Dutchman in charge there, called the cashier *(klesir)* or the boss *(baas)*.

We also planted little coconut shoots. I had only a shawl and a shirt to wear, both in tatters. We were there two months. When we slept, each one by himself, there were bedbugs and huge mosquitoes, and I couldn't sleep very well. We couldn't stand it anymore and we went and asked for mosquito repellant from the boss, but he didn't give us any.

We were put together into a team to work together by the foreman. There were ten of us. He gave the orders.

"Gus Alit!" He said in respectful speech. "Go along with them there! Go to that field and plant coconut shoots. Carry some with you!" The others could carry ten, but I could carry only two coconuts. So I planted my two coconuts.

Our head said, "Go ahead and eat some of the coconut sprouts. The boss isn't here. And then you can plant them anyway." So I dug the holes to put the coconuts in. I was thirsty. I looked carefully around and then I crushed the leaves in my hat and ate them. I drank some milk from a young coconut. I didn't dare drink the water there because it was so full of ashes from upstream.

So then our head, I Guntur, told us to rest. But then the foreman was watching us from above from a distance. I hadn't seen him. He cut our pay because we stopped too often. When you are hoeing, you have to stand up, so every time we squatted down, he cut our pay.

They gave us a calf to butcher and eat, but it was a bad one. Its hooves were all wrong, long and thin. He gave it to us, and we workers butchered it and ate it.

After that everyone got sick. We all got malaria, and everyone started to go home, two or three at a time. But I was left behind there. It was terrible! I cooked some rice gruel for myself. In the morning, before the fever came back, I cooked the gruel. But after it was ready I felt sick again, and the gruel just sat there. I was very thin. I was about half my weight because of the sickness. There was no one to take me to a doctor and get some medicine. All the others were the same.

We weren't without money. When we hoed we got half a *ringgit* for each coconut tree. So I had a lot of money. And the boss had given me a sickle and a hoe with which to work. Everyone was leaving. And I was so sick and I'd lost half my weight. It's amazing I survived! Must be due to the bitterness of my blood.

So then I Guntur from Blusung was sorry for me. He told me to take lessons in the martial art of *pencak*. There was a group of Muslims there, who every Sunday for fun would do *pencak*. I went and watched them. One of them gave me a banana. Their wives brought the students food to eat, various kinds of snacks, and they gave me some. They wanted me to join them, but I couldn't because I felt so weak and sick.

Then a man said to me, "Come with us if you wish to, Ratu, in the morning." In very polite words. "We're going home! You can ride on the horse." He had a red horse, a very good one, and docile.

"*Bah!* That would be very good! I'll go with you."

"Yes, we'll take you to Batuan, Ratu!" He figured like that because I couldn't go home otherwise because I was so sick. I was trembling with fever and chills. *De-deg-deg-deg-deg-deg!*

Well he came the next morning at the first *dauh,* or at about four o'clock, as we say now. [During Togog's childhood, time was measured not by clocks but by a rough system of conventional periods called *dauh.* There were four *dauh* between dawn and noon, and four after it before sundown.] His servant called me, "Ratu, come with us now, we're going home." Respectfully. All their stuff was ready, packed on the horse. My rice porridge still sat there, uneaten. "Yes, I'm coming," I said. I had sold the sickle and hoe. I had half a *ringgit,* money to go home with.

So then I tried to get out of bed, but I couldn't pick up my feet, not one. All my strength had gone, and I couldn't move at all, not even a little. And I just kept on trembling all over. I couldn't go.

"Go along, Yan. Leave me behind. Go along. I can't walk. I can't even put my foot down on the ground," I said. What else could they do! They left me behind.

Well, by six o'clock that morning as we say now, that is in the second *dauh,* suddenly I could get up.

I stood up then, and I said, in a loud, firm voice, respectfully: "Jero! Jero! You who own this forest! You who live here! So that you may grant me my humble wish, I will tell you what is in my heart. I came here, You who own this forest, and I will go away, with no desire to take anything from here. I'm not carrying anything from here home with me to Batuan. I don't lack, at home. Those who came with me here were poor. They didn't have a thing. But now, if you are punishing me, what have I done wrong? It seems as if you have made me sick because you think I am trying to get the wealth of those who live here and carry it home to Batuan. That would be wrong. But in fact I came here to wash away any pollution *(ngelebur dosa),* to beg to be purified *(nunas pengelukatan),* so that my need to gamble would go away. I'm not looking for riches here to take home!"

Togog called this kind of speech to spirits or gods a *darsana*. It is a respectful statement of intent. In it I translate *nglebur dosa* as "to wash away any pollution," but literally it means "to pulverize and dissolve any ritual wrongdoing." He uses another phrase for the same meaning, *nunas pengelukatan,* in which the root *lukat* signifies "to cleanse through ritual." Below he uses another phrase, *mandé ical manah tiangé sané kaon-kaon,* "in order to rid my heart of those things that are bad." *Manah* means both "heart" and "mind" and also, here, "desire." He wants to rid himself of those desires for gambling.

I spoke like that in hatred at being sick.

"Now I am sick like this! What does it mean? I don't think even a healer, a *balian,* could cure this illness! What great evil thing have I done? I came here to beg for your blessing, to erase the badness of my heart *(mangdé ical manah tiangé sané kaon-kaon)!* I'm bad because no one gets angry at me at home, no one scolds me. They give me too much. I have become spoiled. If I was a little bad then, in the future the badness would pile up and pile up until I was really bad. That's why I came here."

Just then, *teg!* my strength took hold again. It was as if I was well again. So I jumped up and left. I left with just a bottle of something to drink and a little package of steamed rice. I told I Guntur, "I take leave of you. I'm going now." And he said, "Here, here's something for you to eat and drink on the way." So I had the one package of rice and the bottle to carry, and off I went.

I felt as if my body was now all right as a result of making that petition *(darsana)*. I felt as if there were no more obstacles.

I got as far as the ravine of the river Leh, and I stopped there. It was hot, exactly noon, and there was no one there. I didn't feel the heat. My body seemed all right. There was a large rock by the stream, and I put my bottle up on the rock. I bathed, and after I bathed, I ate the package of rice.

That's all I remember. I didn't know that the bottle fell off and broke. It did.

Then a man came by, an Ida Bagus from Bajra, from far to the south. He happened to stop there with his little child. His name was Ida Bagus Mantra. He had been working in Jaborana but had stopped for a couple of weeks. They were happy to have the free time and were going home, south. When they stopped there they must have seen me and came up to me. I didn't know it. And they took me to where they were getting some water. That's when I came to again. I sat up and I heard them talking.

And I said to myself, "What's this, where am I? I was down there before, I think." I turned and saw the broken bottle. "Yes, there! That's where I was, to the south. What's going on?" So then he asked me who I was, and I said I was from Batuan, that I was a Brahmana Buda.

"Bah!" he said. "I'll take you. I'll take care of you like my own child." That's what he said, in familiar speech. "Come home with me to my house."

I said "yes," just "yes," because my wits had fled. "Yes, yes," just saying "yes." They were very good and they took me home with then. The road that I was taking to Batuan went on straight to the east from Bajra. It was a long way and the road was bad. But they were going to leave the road and turn south toward the edge of the sea. "Walk this way, with us," they said. It was already late in the day, and if I had tried to find the way home to Batuan I would have had to go twice the distance as far again. So I went with them.

When it was almost night we arrived at his home. The way was good, and it was cool, and I got there all right because Ida Bagus Mantra and his son showed me the way. Now when we got there, his father, a healer, a *balian,* a very good *balian,* said, "Where did you find this little boy, son?"

"I picked him up by the Leh river. I'm going to take him as my child," he said. "Stay here, Dé, Gus Dé!"

"Yes," I said. All my strength and good feelings had gone, and I had been transformed again *(kasiluman)*. [The implication of Togog's use of the term *kasiluman* ("transformed") for a bodily change into weakness is that his sickness was caused by sorcery, and that only a strong *balian* could cure him.]

"Now later, when you want to go home to Batuan, I'll go with you," he said. So the father put me up with him on the *balé dangin*. They had complete set of pavilions: a *balé gedé*, a *balé dauh*, a *balé dangin*, and also the *balé agung*. The *balé* on the west side was a *gedong*, a big one.

See Chapter 1 for a description and illustration of the various kinds of living pavilions or *balé*. *Balé agung* is the high-register term for *balé gedé*. In this house there are two *balé gedé*. The fact that the home of the Ida Bagus had these pavilions meant that he was very prosperous.

His two younger sisters were there. Very pretty girls with nice bodies like my daughter Dayu Tut today.

Then the father told me to take one of their scarfs. All I had with me to put around my shoulders in the night was a head scarf *(udeng)* and it was torn, too. So he gave me a larger scarf *(cerik)* of yellow cotton cloth. "Here, take this scarf, so you won't be cold." So then they made me some good food, served in a fine dish with lots of meat.

"Here, eat here, together with me!" And the father ate too from another dish. I was sitting to his east. But I couldn't eat, even though we were eating together. I could hardly eat three mouthfuls. It was too hard to swallow. So after that he told his son to get a glass of water, and he said a prayer over it, a *mantra*, and gave it to me to drink. "Drink this. It may have some effect. Drink it all up, so that you won't bring your sickness home with you." But his son said, "Don't go home. Stay here with my children, like one of the family. You can help in the kitchen and all," he said. They were rich. All the children thought I was going to be one of the family, that he was adopting me.

So I drank that glassful. Then I slept on the *balé dangin* with Ida Bagus Mantra. I was to the north, and he was to the south with the boy. There was a thick mattress, and it was covered with a fine mat made of soft pandanus leaves.

In the middle of the night I was confused and thought I heard people running, breathing heavily, into the family temple, and I thought I heard them speak, as if they were commoners stealing the coconuts there. I got up and went into the family temple and I bumped into a bamboo offering table. It was the effect of the medicine. I began to get better and that which was causing the illness inside me came out. [Togog used the term *bangket*, "essence of something that is squeezed out," for the word I render as "illness." In fact what came out, the *bangket*, is what has caused the illness.] He had a lot of power, *sakti*. I began to feel lighter *(iing)*, not so heavy *(baat)* as before.

The next morning I could think clearly.

"Ida Aji, Ida Aji, I'm going to go home now," I said.

"What do you mean go home! I thought I was going to adopt you!"

"Well, it is like this. At home there's only my Grandfather, and there is no one else. He has no children. Someday in the future I'll come back and visit you" [respectfully]. [Later Togog added that this was a lie, but he felt that if he hadn't said it the father would not have let him go.]

"Well, if that's how it is, all right. I'll take you to Badung." So then he went and got a motorcar from around there, and we left for Badung. When we arrived, he got out and disappeared, and I didn't know where he went. I didn't know whether I had to pay for the car, but no one asked for the fare. Maybe it was because my face was pale from illness.

When I got home in Batuan, my uncle had died [Togog's father's younger brother]. He came home sick from Jembrana and he died. There were many others who had been with us who were sick, and one in my own house who still was very ill. So when I arrived, they blocked my way and wouldn't let me go into my own home because there was a dead person there, and it might make me sicker because of the grieving. So they put me in the house where Dayu Tut [one of Togog's daughters] now lives, and I stayed there. I didn't dare go and see the dead man because I was so weak and sick. *Beh!* I hurried to that house, for the roads were empty of people because of all the sickness.

I was there about six days, and then I came home to the house next door and helped take care of my Grandfather, who was very sick. Someone else to the east was also very sick, and also, in the end, his life too was crushed out.

Then I had a dream. I was told in the dream to go to a healer, a *balian,* one in Banjar Bedil [nearby, in Sukawati] who had just recently become a *balian.* I was told to have him come and look at me. I told my Grandmother and my Grandfather and they went to get him. So then the healer came. Now, this healer had a feeling that he was going to fail, because he saw how sick I was. So he mixed foreign medicine with the Balinese, added pills to his potion.

When he had made the drink he said to my Grandmother, I overheard him, "Dayu Niang! Dayu Niang!" This *balian* was named I Pekél, from Banjar Bedil, and he said in very polite words: "This little one makes me very worried. It's very difficult for me!" And then he said, "This medicine is going to make him seem crazy." [Togog explained later that the medicine would make the patient act "crazy," and then from what the patient says or does in his craziness the healer would derive a diagnosis.]

"Whatever you say, Wayan [the balian], whatever you say, we'll do. Just make my grandchild better," said my Grandmother in familiar speech. So then he gave me the medicine, and I acted like a lunatic. *Bah!* I *danced* and a lot of people came to watch. I danced and then I put on a play shadow-puppet show! Like, well, you know . . . [Laughs]. [This episode is illustrated in fig. 5, upper right.] And afterwards I felt as if I was all well again inside me. I was acting crazy and all the little children and the grown-ups watched me from next door.

So after that, to make a long story short, I got well. But I was still gripped by the desire to gamble.

Selling Sorcerer's Poison

Once, I picked some candlenuts *(tinkih)* to sell. There was a candlenut tree near my house, a very tall one, owned by my Grandfather. I asked him if I could take the nuts and he let me pick them. I climbed up that tree. Its trunk was as big around as my two hands could reach. So then I took the nuts and peeled them. I planned to sell them in Badung, so that I could learn what it was like in Badung.

There was a man living in Kuta, weaving women's scarfs there, whom I called "uncle," the son of a Brahmana woman here whom I called "grandmother" [the head of the household where Désak Watin lived]. I thought I'd go there and sell the nuts. So when I had about a basketful of them, I carried them to Badung, by crisscross ways. I didn't know where the paved road was. I got to the road at Tainsiap, coming on to it from the rice fields carrying my candlenuts, and someone called to me, "Hey, little boy! (Jero! Nak Alité!) what are you carrying?" [*Jero* is a polite word for "you" used in situations where you don't know the title of the addressee. *Anak alit* means "child" in the high register.]

And I went up to him and he bought some for a penny *(képéng)*. My basket was very heavy, and I didn't ask for much. I took whatever people paid me. Some more people bought some, and that helped. Next to the market in Badung I sold some more. I went on from there to Kuta, where my older brother was staying, buying and selling pigs, as well as my uncle, who made scarfs. I went there all by myself. I had to ask the way, "Jero, where is the road to Kuta?" I had to ask many times.

So then I arrived in Kuta, and I stopped by the market and many people bought my nuts. But I didn't know what price to ask, so when someone said I'll give you two *képéng,* I let him take what he wanted. Some paid six, some paid eight.

Then I asked where the man I called uncle lived, and they said that he lived with I Kamasan and showed me where his house was. When I arrived there and went in, there was my uncle, and he laughed to see me: "*Beh dong!* Who brought you here? You're still so little. So little! Did you come all by yourself?"

"What do you mean! Why should someone come with me? I came alone, of course," I said.

"Well, well, well, well! Come on in and have something to eat!" he said. And he gave me food that was so good it was indescribable, with lots of fish fresh caught in the sea. The sea was right there.

So after that I Kamasan's wife came, and she had been selling spices. She bought the rest of my candlenuts for 60 *képéng*. I figured they were only worth about ten and that she gave me sixty because I was so little and so that I'd have something to get home with.

It was almost nightfall so I stayed overnight there. I Kamasan's wife sat and counted up her earnings. She had made more than ten thousand. I counted up mine too. She wasn't watchful towards me. She didn't act as if she were afraid I'd steal their money. And of course I didn't have anything like that in mind. We piled them up, in stacks of two hundred. In those days, when you put together a string of 200 *képéng*, you always kept back eight from each bunch. When she finished counting she said that she had ten thousand. From selling tobacco and all kinds of spices.

So then she said, "Ratu, stay here because this house is empty!" There were only the two of them there, she and her husband. If I had wanted to I could have stayed there to watch over their house. It was a very nice place, right near the sea, and you could go in the sea to bathe.

Well, in the morning he went out to go gambling at a cockfight, and she went out to go peddling. Just before he went out, someone came in bringing him a gift of a dish of food *(jotan)*. It was a dish of turtle-*anyang*.

A *jotan* is a dish of food sent to neighbors and friends at the time of a family ritual. It can signify an invitation, or merely be a sharing of the feast foods. *Anyang* is a kind of *lawar,* which is a feast dish made of various kinds of minced meats and vegetables and spices.

He put it away for us to eat later. He meant to put it under a large bowl, but in fact he put it on the dish that he himself used to eat off of. He planned to give it to us to eat, to me, my "older brother," and my "uncle." When we came back from the sea, he said, "Ratu, have some dinner! There's some turtle-*anyang* there under that large bowl. That turtle-*anyang* has not been touched by anyone *(sukla)*. Later on I'll buy something for myself to eat."

Sukla means "untouched," as in food not yet begun or not yet offered, and as in clothes that have never been worn. The three guests were Brahmana, while their host, I Kamasan, was a Sudra, their client *(parekan* or *sisia)*. It was taboo for the Brahmana to eat anything that someone else not of their family had eaten, or even that was on a plate from which someone else had eaten. Such leftovers are called *lungsuran*. Such food is polluted for someone of higher spiritual status.

So then he went out, and after a while the three of us were ready to eat. So we looked under the large bowl, but it wasn't there. There were three large bowls, but it wasn't under any of them. We didn't look in his own dish because that wouldn't be proper.

So then we went out to find something else to eat, some fresh fish that had been broiled. We ate our fill of that fish. After a while, he came back, and asked, "Did you eat the turtle-*anyang*?"

"No, Wo, we couldn't find it."

"*Badah!* I forgot and put it over here." And he opened up the cupboard and found it. So then he ate it.

Just a short time later, no longer than it would take to have a betel chew, he felt sick to his stomach! He could hardly move! He was dizzy, swinging back and forth.

So he sent my older brother to go get his wife from the market. His wife came back. She told my older brother to go and get a young coconut. There were some coconut trees right near. And then to get some *jepun* flowers, about twenty. And then she crushed them and mixed them with the fresh coconut milk. And then his wife put some oil in the mixture. And then he drank it. When he had drunk about half of it, he stopped and was quiet for a while. All this time his whole body had been trembling. His whole body had been trembling. So now he was quiet. After a while he sat up.

"What's the matter, Beli?" asked his wife.

"Be quiet for a while!" he said. So after a while, as long as it might take to make *bubur* [rice porridge—about an hour], he came back to his senses, and he said to us: "Ratu! You were very lucky! If you had been hit by that, how awful I would have felt! I Ratu, that was poison!"

Poison! He said it was poison! [The term I translate as "poison" *(racun)* is used by Balinese to designate both material poisons (such as those used to kill rats) and those otherwise harmless substances that have been imbued with death-dealing qualities by a sorcerer.]

"Well, in a little while I'll tell you about it, Ratu," he said.

So after a while, when he really felt better, he went to the cupboard and opened it. There were five bottles there, and a sixth off at the side. They all had white powder in them. He put his finger on the lip of the one, and then touched each of the other ones with it. When the white powder hit that in the others, it was as if the powder in each of them rose up and swarmed around like a swarm of bees, churning around as if it were alive.

"This one here is poison, and it was something like this that hit me," he said. "They put it in the fish."

And then he said: "This is what hit me, and if it had hit you, I Ratu, how would I have felt. Something that was intended for me—it wouldn't have been proper if it hit you. Now if I wanted to get back at the poisoner, I could kill his whole family in a minute, even if there were fifteen people in his family. Those people in Tegal wanted to poison me with their *jotan* gift of their ritual. If, at any time in the future, Ratu, you need some poison, I'll give you some of this. I usually sell it to people."

So then the next day I went home, and he wanted to give me something to take with me for the trip.

I said: "Don't give me anything, Uncle, I already got enough from my sale of the candlenuts. Don't give me any money, Wo." So then I left.

Soon after I got home to Batuan the man from Pangsan came to see me, the one who had taken me with him to cut stone, the one whose chisel fell in the water, the one who was punished for asking a Brahmana to cut stone, so that his chisel was lost. Because it wasn't right *(patut)*.

He came to me and asked me to buy some poison for him.

"Ratu! Gus Alit! Ratu Alit!" he said [respectfully], "find some poison for me, but don't let anyone know you are doing it." Because no one would suspect a little boy.

"But, Kak, that which you want me to get—who are you going to hit with it?" I asked.

"Ratu, do you know that servant woman *(panyeroan)* in the palace at Pangsan, who is lame? She is very *powerful! (sakti)*. Very, very *sakti*. How many times I've tried to get her with different things! I've spent at least 500,000 on these things. But none of them worked. She has the knowledge of a sorcerer and can change herself into a bald-headed demon *(léyak gundul)!*"

Then he said, "Yes, Ratu, I beg of you! I desperately need that magic *(guna)* from *you!* I've tried some from everyone except from a Brahmana. I've tried buying such things from *anak agung*s, from *cokorda*s, from *kaula*s, and none of them worked. Now I humbly request of you, Ratu, to help me. Here is the money."

And he gave me five *ringgit*. *Beh!* I felt as if I was in heaven with so much money. And I thought to myself, "I'll go there [to Kuta] and ask for that poison."

So I said to him [in familiar speech]: "I'll go there tomorrow. I'll go there tomorrow and I'll have it for you at the latest by nightfall." So I promised him.

The man in Kuta had told me, "This one costs five *ringgit*, and that one costs two *ringgit*," Each one had its price. He often sold them.

So then I went to the home of the mother of the man who was staying in Kuta.

"Grandmother! Grandmother! Did your son ever give you some of that stuff from Kuta, that poison?" I was so little, I just said it right out. "Did he ever give you any of that poison?"

"Why, I *have* some!" she said. "He gave me some!" She showed it to me.

"Give it to me, grandmother, please. There's something I want to do with it."

"Here, take it, but don't tell anyone you got it here. It was a present from my son in Kuta." So I took it. She told me to mix it with a dish of *anyang* made from cooked bees, but if there weren't any bees to be found, it could be mixed with honey.

So I brought it there to Pangsan, and when I came into his home, he said, "Hello, my lord arrives!" Then, secretly, we spoke together about it. So then I said to him, "Kak, I didn't ask the person who gave it to me how much this cost, so it was sort of like a present. But you can use it now." [Togog explained that he thought that the price might have been more, but that he settled for the five *ringgit* he'd been given.]

I said, "Don't use it all up in one shot. There's enough here for three people. But it won't take effect for about a month." It was like a white powder in a little bottle.

"Yes, yes, Ratu! Now stay here a little while!" And then he treated me like an honored guest and gave me very good food. And he gave me two more *ringgit*. [Laughs.] When I left I danced like Délem, having all that money!

That was my profit from selling candlenuts!

So then I gave the "grandmother" who gave me the poison a ring that I had found on the ground. She liked it very much, but I thought it wasn't worth much, just the kind of ring you could buy in the market. "Here take this, Niang," I said.

"*Beh!* A ring!" she said.

Now, when I think about it, that stonecutter was doing something wrong. I never found out whether it worked or not, for he never came back.

I went back again to Kuta. I asked again if I could pick some more candlenuts, for the tree was thick with them. I took a small basketful of them and went to the market where there were a lot of candlenut merchants. I went to the one I had sold to before and asked if she would like to buy some candlenuts. "Why should I buy candlenuts?" she said.

"If you order some, I'll bring them to you," I said.

"No, I don't want any. *Bah!* You're too little to carry candlenuts, and if you hadn't been so little I wouldn't have bought any before. I'll buy these you have for just three *képéng*." That's what I got for them.

But I had gotten a profit from selling the other candlenuts.

Fishing

I was hanging around in Gria Pacung to study *kekawin*. [Gria Pacung was a Brahmana house in the Brahmana Siwa clan in Batuan.] I was at Gria Pacung all the time, and things were very good. I was like a family member there. They didn't calculate with me. I was often at the home of Ida Bagus Ketut Sotong. Suddenly he got married to a woman named Ida Ayu Keben, who was a peddler. She still today has a *warung* near the Pura Dalem Puri, near Gria Dalem. Ida Bagus Ketut Sotong made and sold carved wooden statues, but he sold only in his home and never went out. That's why he needed a chance to go out and have fun. So, since I was there, he asked me to go to Badung with him to see a film. Or sometimes he would ask me to go fishing with him. We were good friends, and later on he told his children and family, "In the future, always remember that 'older brother' Madé Delodan [meaning "the Madé who lives south of here," i.e., Togog] was good to your father, and never refuse him whatever he may ask." That's what his instructions were. He told his children about my help to him: "He gave me much help. That's why you all must remember the help that your older brother, Madé Delodan, gave me." And that's why, whenever there is a festival in Gria Pacung, I'm always invited to help in the meat chopping or to do other things.

I liked to go fishing. Once when there was a ceremony in Pura Desa Batuan, I met a Satria man named Déwa Nyoman, who had just lost his wife. She had just died. So that man asked me to go fishing with him to the south [to Sanur], so as to console himself, so that he would not remember his loss. Even now today, his grandchildren remember how their grandfather was good friends with me. They respect me. Every time there is a ceremony here they come and help. They have never turned down a request from me.

After a while I had another friend in Gria Pacung named Ida Bagus Madé Cukeng, the older brother of Ida Bagus Ketut Sotong. His work was buying and selling betel leaves and also making coconut oil. He also had to do work at home every day, husking coconuts, then grating the meat and pressing the oil out of them. Because he did that every day, he felt very tired of it and tried to find a way to get out of his house. So he told me to come and call for him to go fishing with him. So I came to his house and called him, and he came out right away with his fishing rod. And as we went along he murmured to me how he was so very tired now that there was ritual work in the *gria,* so he wanted an excuse to get out and go fishing to relax. So I was a big help, taking him away from the ritual work when I went with him, fishing. Still, even today, his children remember my help.

But when I remember one time we went fishing together I feel afraid. Why do I feel afraid? Because when we were on our way to the fishing place, we crossed a field to get to the river, and in the field were many small sharp stakes [put in to hurt any person or any animal that tried to steal the young plants in the field]. I had jumped into the field, and *aduh!* I was startled to find my foot right next to these stakes. But because I was not doing anything wrong, I didn't land on any of those stakes. He, too, told his children, "In the future don't forget how much he helped me."

I was always looking for good pools of water [to bathe or fish in], and I knew where all the good places were. There was a good one with a waterfall in Tanu, but it was faraway. There was another where a spring came bubbling up quite fast, and after I'd been there to bathe, I'd feel clear in my heart for at least five days. The water was so good. And then there was another northwest of there, called Duma, with a waterfall. There was a large rock there, with water slowly oozing out at its base, and over on the other side a waterfall. That spring was small, the water came out slowly, but I liked it very much. You had to kneel down next to it, and dip the water up with your hands. That was the kind I liked. I'd rank waterfalls third, the spring bubbling up under the rock second, and the small quiet spring number one. When I went there, I'd also look to see if there were fish there. But if I went fishing there, I always said a prayer *(darsana)* like this: "Oh, Sirs! Jero-jero! You who own this river here, don't show me any gold. Don't show me any money. Only *képéng* coins left here in people's offerings, those would be all right for me to take, and I thank you!"

Togog and his son later explained to me that whenever you go to fish in a pool it is best to make a prayer like this. The pool might be owned *(dué)* by a *tonya* spirit, which is the spirit of a dead person who has not been properly cremated, or who drowned in the pool. Because of the spirit's *karma pala,* or fate, he is doomed to stay there in the pool, but he wants to become human again. If he could find a "friend" *(timpal)* he might be freed. A *tonya* tries to entice a human into being his friend by giving him riches, which the human finds by the river in the form of a ring or gold coins. If the human being takes this find home, he will be very rich, but in the future, after his death, all his descendants will have troubles. They will be born deformed, with a cleft palate or a withered arm or the like, or they will be very poor. You can tell that a rich man has a *tonya* friend if he acts oddly and talks to himself. Togog wanted to avoid that, so he spoke to the *tonya* directly.

There might be magic money *(sedana)* there, because that place in the river has very, very powerful bad spirits in it *(tenget)*. The reason I dare to say that place is *tenget* is that many accidents have happened there. So I said that in order not to be disrespectful. After I said that, I could fish there.

Once when we were fishing it was about ten o'clock, as they say now. The pool where we were was very long, and to cross it we had to wade through it, going west. Wo Madé wasn't afraid of bloodsuckers. But I am!

He got down in the water first and said, "Neh! There aren't any bloodsuckers in here!" So, because he said there weren't any, I got in too.

I waded out to the middle of the pool and I thought I felt a bloodsucker on me! It might have been a leaf off a tree. I ran without looking where I was going and fell down in the water up to my neck! All my clothes were soaking wet. When I got out I spread my clothes out to dry, and Madé laughed and laughed a long time. "Ha-ha! Ha-ha!" [Togog laughs in a jeering tone.]

"You were teasing me when you said there were no bloodsuckers!"

"That wasn't any bloodsucker. That was just a leaf under the water! You look startled and wild! If one had gotten on you I would have taken it off!"

So it took a long time to dry my clothes, and he did some fishing while waiting. It was a very large pool, and he didn't catch more than five little *nyalian* fish. [Laughs.]

That place was far from here to the south and east of Batubulan, way out in the middle of the *sawah* where there were no other people.

After that we went home and he said, "I'll come for you again in the morning, okay?"

And so the next morning he came and called for me, and when I came out I asked him: "What's the real reason you always *need* to go fishing? Do you want to leave your home empty? When you catch some fish you don't want to eat them."

"Well, I'll tell you, Dé. If I stay home I have to do all sorts of work! I have to grate coconut meat—twenty coconuts—and then I have to squeeze the milk out of them, and after that I have to boil them up. And then I have to gather food for the pigs and feed them. And by that time it is late afternoon and—*peh!*—I'm all tired out. That's why I ask you to call for me, so that I won't have to grate coconuts." [Laughs.] So he wouldn't have to help around the house. He didn't have a wife, but his younger brother had a wife, and she ordered him around. He sometimes could work for his grandfather in "the Hotel" curio shop.

This was a small shack by the main road where tourist wood carvings were sold, and some of the artisans sat there to work. The sign outside it said "Souvenirs" but Batuan people called it "the Hotel" since, to them, it was just like the Hotel Bali in Denpasar where many of them went to sit on the pavement peddling their wares.

Well, then there was another time when we went fishing again. We went to the rice fields east of Batuan, and then we went down towards the sea along the stream until we came to the bridge just south of Peninjoan. And we had to walk under it. But down around the footing of the bridge, underneath it, there were a lot of *dead dogs* there, twelve of them!

What could I do?! I was too ashamed to turn back again.

There wasn't any water flowing over those corpses [to cleanse them away]. I was looking for some deep, still pools to fish in, deep places where the fish would gather. That's why I just *went on.*

But—*beh!*—my foot went right onto a *dead dog!* There was one dog corpse here and another right over here, and the water was flowing so little over them. Only half of one of them remained, and there were *maggots* all over it, at least two handfuls, and the flies were buzzing and buzzing around. My foot hit another one when I was trying to catch up with him. *Beh!* I couldn't do anything! I couldn't get out of there! I couldn't cry out. So finally I was almost out and then there was another one caught there!

When I finally got out from under the bridge I went straight on west to where he was at a deep, still pool. He had put his line down into it. I was *running* to get away from that awful bad smell! Even though I ran through all those bodies, I stepped on them because there were so many.

The pool was next to a great rock, and only a little water showed. I thought it wasn't very deep. I got a long stick, the center of a palm frond, and I thought to myself, "Is this pool deep or not?" and I shoved it down. I figured that if it was deep I'd put my line down, but if it wasn't how would there be any fish there? And so then I discovered, yes, it was very *deep!* so I put my fishing line down in it. We got four *lélé* fish, as big as this! [a foot and a half long and three fingers wide].

We had gone to all that effort, walking so far—and that was our payment for all that trouble! He gave me his. He didn't like to eat them.

I said, "Here keep one, Madé, of these *lélé* fish, and you can grill them at home with some good spices!" but he didn't want them.

The Story of the *Tonya* in the River West of Negara

All that time when I was home I hung around with Wo Madé and went fishing with him. I knew all sorts of fishing places. Once we went to a fishing hole just west of Negara, south of the big dam. [This is in the River Os, next to Pura Lucuk.]

There is a place there that is like a temple, *pura,* but it isn't a *pura.* I asked Wo Madé about it.

"Madé, Madé! Who worships and takes care of this temple?"

"No one does."

"What do you mean no one does? It's well kept up. It has a good *balé!*"

"When it falls into disrepair *(uug).* maybe the people of the irrigation society *(subak)* nearby fix it up, but there is no one who worships there *(sungsung).*" [A *subak* is both a specific area of irrigated rice land and also the organization of farmers who work together in it to maintain the common irrigation ditches and dams.]

"Don't they have an *odalan* festival here? During all the time we've been coming here there hasn't been one."

"No."

"Well, why isn't there any *odalan* here?"

"Well, this is the story. In the old days, when the kingdom of Negara was in power here, the raja of Negara had a child who was drowned here, in the river on the east side. And the king was angry in his heart. So he sent for two sorcerers, spiritually powerful men [*anak sakti,* a term that could also be translated as "sorcerers"], one from Ketéwél, one from Gianyar, and he told them to avenge him.

[At this point, Togog, who had been telling the story in the intimate register, as told him by his uncle, switched to high language, addressing me.] In that place there was a spirit *(tonya)* who pulled people into the water and drowned them. The two, from Téwél and

Gianyar, wanted to find out if in fact the *tonya* had taken the child, so that they would know, clearly. So the two of them, the one from Téwél and the one from Gianyar, had great offerings made, and they went to the river and dammed it up so that the river was closed off. That's the path of the *tonya.*

So the next night after they had closed it off, the *tonya* came and said to the people who had built the dam, in polite words: "Why have you blocked off my home with a wall of bramble trees? How can I get out?" That's what he said.

And they answered, "'He who destroys will be destroyed!' That was the spell *(pangastawa)* they did it with." [The words the two *anak sakti* recited were *"Né uug, to uug"* Perhaps a more grammatical version might be *"Sané nguug, ento uuga,"* "He who destroys will be destroyed."]

"Pah!" said the *tonya,* "It wasn't me that took the child!"

"We were only doing what the man from Gianyar told us to do," said the people, "and besides what Ida Cokorda from Negara ordered us to do."

And then the *tonya* went to the sorcerer in Gianyar and said: "Why did you close off the way? You've blocked off my house and I can't get out. How can I go out when it is blocked by the spell 'He who destroys will be destroyed!'"

And the sorcerers answered: "*Beh,* please forgive us. We were following the orders of the *raja* of Negara. We'll go and see him tomorrow."

So then the two of them, the one from Téwél and the one from Gianyar, went to speak to the *raja* of Negara, and they said: "It wasn't the *tonya* that took away the child. He told us that. The *tonya* told us: 'Why would I take away a human being? I have no use for one. I already have four children. And my four children are weeping because they can't get out of their house, because the way has been cut off.' That's what the *tonya* told us." They told him that it wasn't the *tonya* that took away the child. They told him that the *tonya* said: "That water there is just the road for the dead, and there's no way to continue his life. Don't wrongly accuse me of taking that child. People who think I pulled the child in wrongly accuse me."

So then Ida Cokorda asked the sorcerers what could he do? And they said he should move the *tonya*'s house. So the king gave the order. When the *tonya* heard what the king said, he was happy. And the king built him that little place that is like a *pura.*

Togog's son explained that the *tonya*'s first house had been in a cave in the rock wall of the ravine, and that when the king had the dam built, the water rose up above the door of the cave. The river originally had two beds right there, parallel, going south. The king in his anger dammed up the western channel, which is still there but has very little water in it. The little temple, the new house for the *tonya,* was built on the flat place between that western channel and the eastern one. The big dam built by the Dutch is north of it. His son added that the people living near the temple keep it up and perform its regular rituals. The *tonya* is still there: a friend of Togog's son was once approached by the children of the *tonya,* who asked him for a kite and some other toys, and when he gave them to them, the children disappeared.

That was the story that Uncle Madé told me while we were fishing, about that temple. He'd often tell me old tales *(satua)* when I asked him to, every time we went.

Gambling

Togog started gambling for *képéng* at an early age, but did not gamble over fighting cocks until much later, probably after he was twenty-five. Cockfighting is a mature man's game, and it involves more money than the card and coin-tossing games that Togog talks about here.

When I was young I loved all kinds of gambling games:

card games, dominoes, coin games. I went often to the homes of the Chinese in Sukawati. That's why even today I have many friends among the Chinese, because I was so used to going to their stores when I was young to hang about and play dominoes.

I played dominoes at the home of a Satria there too. Wherever I was invited, I'd go. Until it got to the point that an Anak Agung from Sukawati [a high noble] told me he was ashamed to see me there day and night.

"Hey! Ida Bagus, you're not lacking anything at home and still you go out and gamble! Looks to me like you're after the girls there! You ought to get married. If you want, I'll speak to one for you."

That's what the Anak Agung said, because he thought it was shameful my being day and night in that house in Sukawati, even eating there. He thought that I must be crazy about a girl there, the daughter of the Satria, whose name was Désak Putu Konoran. She was indeed beautiful, but I went just for the domino games.

One night when I was coming home from Sukawati—in the middle of the night—I got as far as the aqueduct spanning the road at Peninjoan that takes the water to the rice fields on the other side, and there on the road under it, right in my way, was something! It looked like a calf, but it was much bigger, and it had sharp horns, and its coat was shining white.

I didn't dare go near it! My route went right by it under the aqueduct. I didn't dare because it was terrifying. I remembered the old folks' advice: "If you come across something that you think is a witch in animal form, like a monkey or a goat or a horse, crouch down and reach for a stone, and it will run away."

So I squatted down and scratched loudly—*serét-serét!*—on the ground with my hand, but it didn't move away. I shifted nearer, crouching and sidling closer and then back again, but it didn't even turn its head away from me!

"Badah!" I thought, *"Badah!* This isn't a human being! Maybe it is the spirit *(tonya)* of the aqueduct here, of this place here!" So I turned back again towards the south and turned into a little path near the house of a man named I Sukanto and went down that path till I got to the home of one of my relatives whom I call Po Nyoman, and crossed through his yard to the other side. It was the middle of the night, twelve o'clock as we say today, and it was muddy. My feet went *cak-cok, cak-cok* in the mud, and I cleared my throat loudly so they wouldn't think I was a thief, and then, when I came out his front gate I went home. In the morning my Po Nyoman asked me, "Where were you coming from in the middle of last night, all by yourself?" [familiarly].

"Don't worry. Even though I was alone, I was all right," I said [also in familiar words].

So then I went back to Peninjoan. To the home of Pan Muni. He was named after his child, I Muni. Pan Muni was a healer, a *balian,* who would know everyone who knew how to turn themselves into a goat or a monkey. So that morning I visited Pan Muni to ask him about what I had seen the night before.

When I got there, "Hey! Here's Bagus Alit! What do you want, Tu?" he said [respectfully]. He was always good to me like that, and I had often gone there to read his books *(lontar)*. Whatever book I asked for he'd lend me. He had a *lontar* there called the "Oreastro." He showed it to me whenever I visited. It told about the sounds of the letters of the alphabet, about those that take ten and those that take five and those, eight. That's their sounds. I liked to study the "Oreastro," but this time I said, "Uncle, I, uh, I have something I want to ask you about for a moment." I said [speaking down].

"What is it, Tu?" he asked respectfully.

I went into his family temple, and he went too and he said: "Here, which of these *lontar* do you want to read? Just take whichever one you like, Ratu, just take it." Really! Even if he wasn't home, I could go right into his temple and take whichever one I wanted, but there was only one

I really wanted, the "Oreastro." If I asked to borrow it, to take it home, he wouldn't let me, because when he bought it they told him it had been stolen. That's why he wouldn't lend it to me. Any of the other *lontar* he'd give me.

"Last night when I was passing by here under the aqueduct there was something standing there. Could it have been a witch?"

"What?"

"It looked like a calf, but it was very big, very tall, and it had sharp horns, and its hair was white all over. I didn't dare pass under the water pipe near it! I didn't know how to go on toward the north."

"Yes, and then what did you do?"

"I crouched down and it didn't turn its face away from me. I've never seen anything like that. I don't know what it was! It looked like a calf, for it had four feet."

"*Pah!* Ratu, I know! That calf was one of your own guardians *(pajagan)!* Obviously if you had gone on towards the north you would have met with disaster. That's why it blocked your way with its body. That was one of your own ancestors *(lalangitan)* or a spirit *(unén-unén)* from your own temple. It was there to prevent you from going farther north. If, Ratu, you had gone north, you would have met with certain disaster *(sengkala)*." That's what he said.

Later Togog told me he thought he knew who was protecting him that night. The event happened right next to the irrigation aqueduct that crossed over the road (see figure 15). That aqueduct had been built with the aid of a *pedanda,* who placed a guardian spirit there. That *pedanda* was most likely one of Togog's own ancestors.

"Now, I'll tell you the names of all those people whom I have taught the magical lore for transforming themselves into animals, both those from around here and those from up there in Batuan." So he told me all their names, including even the Satria near him. "This Désak So-and-So can become a goat. That Désak So-and-So can become a monkey—if you meet a monkey with a long tail, that's her." He told me all their names, and I knew one of them, who sells food, who I had heard he'd taught how to be a goat. In fact I'd bought food from her. Then he said, "*Beh!* It was a very good thing for you, Ratu, that you gave in and didn't go on to the north!"

So then I went home.

I went there again many other times because I liked to study his *lontar,* about the sounds of the ancient letters, especially the "Oreastro." There were some *lontar* he had had a long time that my grandmother the *pedanda* had sold to him. One of them he didn't dare to keep anymore, and once he said to me: "Ratu, when you go home, take this one with you. It's only this one I don't dare keep. Then you can study it as much as you want. I just want to give it to you!"

That was the *lontar* "Candra Berawa." I took it home with me, and I still have it. I bring it out on every Odalan Saraswati and my daughter puts offerings out for it.

Some time later there was a cockfight in Guang. I went, taking some money with me. When I got there they hadn't started yet, so, since I like all the gambling games—just as I like to sing the old songs *(kidung* and *kekawin)* or sawing wood or carving house posts, whatever anyone asks me to do I'm happy to do it whether I'm paid or not—well, the cockfight hadn't started yet, so I went to play the game of *kobokan.* In that game if you bet one *rupiah,* you can win ten *rupiah.* I got so absorbed in the game that I kept on until I had lost all my money. The cockfight was only half over, but I didn't have a cent left.

But my desire was still strong. In those days I followed wherever my heart led me. Even when gambling brought sorrow to me, the pleasure of winning made me go on. That's called "the pursuit of pleasure." Nowadays it's illegal to pleasure yourself that way. [The Indonesian government has declared gambling in cockfights illegal, but the law was not fully enforced in the 1980s and before.]

People began to offer me money for bets, and to offer

me food to buy, and I thought: "*Badah!* I'm like a tree that stands straight and tall but whose leaves are turning yellow. That's the symptom of its sickness, those withered leaves." I thought they could see by my face that I had no more money.

Well, I was terribly hungry because I hadn't eaten all day. People were offering me food, but I didn't know whether they wanted to lend it to me or give it to me or sell it to me. I kept going over and over in my mind what to do, and just then I remembered that south of there we owned some rice fields that were being worked by one of our sharecroppers.

Sharecroppers in those days had diverse obligations to the landowner for whom they worked. Whenever the landowner had a major domestic ritual, they were obliged to donate goods and labor in return for meals, and to extend help in situations of need. Togog may have assumed that the money he received from these sharecroppers was a loan. The land was probably that owned by Togog's grandfather.

"*Bah!* What about going there? If I go home now owing two hundred I'll feel embarrassed. Instead I'll go to Lémbéng!" Lémbéng is as far from Guang as it is from Batuan to Mas.

So I went there. I didn't meet anyone on the way because everyone was at the cockfight. I just ran as fast as I could, and because I was only thinking about getting the money before the cockfight was over so that I could make up my losses, I wasn't aware of how fast I was going. I saw a man far to the south of me, and later, when I passed him, I was surprised and realized, "Why, I must have been running!" I just kept on, I didn't feel tired, and even though it was high noon, I didn't feel the heat. To make a long story short, I got to the home of the sharecropper. He was also a food seller, and he was about to leave with the cooked rice when I came in.

"Hey! It's Gus Alit here! What's the matter?" he exclaimed respectfully.

"Uh, Man! Nyoman! it's like this! I lost all my money gambling at the cockfight! Even before the cockfight began I lost it all in the *kobokan* game. I didn't realize that it was going to be all gone. What can I do to keep on playing, Nyoman? What do you and your wife think?"

"Well, sit down first!" And then he gave me dinner, and it was very good. "Eat something first, and then we'll talk about it!"

"No, go look for some money for me, so that I can make up my losses," I said.

So then they jumped down from where we were sitting and said, "Wait here, Ratu," and the two of them went out looking for money for me, and then both came back in a moment, each with some money. The rice field we have there is just one plot, about twenty-five *are,* which they work. They gave me the money. And then, after I ate, I left and ran back to the cockfight at Dalem Guang.

Then I had the thought, "I'll divide this in two, so that if I lose, I'll still have three *suku* left for tomorrow." So I wrapped the money up in two knots in my sarong, the one on the right for gambling with now and the one on the left for the future. So then, if I lost again, I would have three *suku* left.

When I got there, someone asked, "Where'd you go just now, to the south?"

"Oh, it was nothing. I had promised to talk with someone about something there." I didn't tell them my money had been all gone. I wasn't shameless enough to. [Laughs.]

So then I played *kobokan* again. It got to be near sunset and I had lost it all, and I had only the three *suku* left. I felt as if I had won those three *suku.*

Nowadays the cockfights are forbidden by the government. If they weren't forbidden, I'd still be gambling. But now, thanks to that, I've given it all up, and I don't even pay any attention to the little ritual cockfights. Now I'm more concerned about how I look to people.

In those days there were many thieves who, when they knew there was to be a cockfight, if they had no money, would go and wait after nightfall among the coconut trees and watch for people going home.

One time there was a cockfight in Tuyang, in the Pura Dalem Tuyang. I didn't know anyone who was going there that morning, so I just went alone. When I got there, it turned out there really was a cockfight. But I stayed with the *kobokan* game. The man who ran the *kobokan* game was a man from Sukawati. So I thought it would be easy to go home with him when he went back to Sukawati. There was not one person there from Batuan.

So then it was late afternoon and I still expected that after the cockfight was over we would go home together. I kept on playing *kobokan* until long past nightfall, and I had won everyone else's money. I had so much money I didn't know where to put it. Both of my hands were full of wads of money, and there were bundles in my sarong. So then one of my friends from the *kobokan* game asked, "Who are you going to go home with?"

"Oh, there's someone here. Where has he gone to?" I said, but in fact there wasn't anyone.

I went to the man who ran the *kobokan* game and asked, "Wayan, aren't you going home now?"

"No, there's a show later on, a Calonarang, and I'm going to set up my *kobokan* game again."

Beh! I felt it seemed as if my soul *(atma)* had left me! Now I had to go home all alone and it was very late at night. So I left there by a zigzag route so that no one would know I was leaving, so that no one would follow me. Carrying all that money, it was certain someone would come and demand it, take it away from me, once I got out into the open country. No one knew that I left, not even the man who had the *kobokan* game. I first went north and then I turned and went east, toward Guang. In Guang I can't tell you how frightened I felt, and then the road west of Guang was pitch-dark. And it was muddy, and at least six times my foot slipped. Once I nearly fell completely into the mud, but I kept my hands free of the mud because I had the money in them. I carried that money carefully so that it wouldn't get muddy or wet. *Beh! Sangsara!* That mud! When I got to Sukawati there was no lamp lit because it was so late. And it was only when I got to Batuan that I slowed down. I had been running as fast as I could, out of fear that someone was going to grab my money and that there would be no one to help me, as it was so late at night.

Two days later there was another cockfight, this time in Mas. I walked up to Mas too, and again I didn't bet in the cockfight because I didn't really know how. I stayed with the *kobokan* game. I lost at first, but towards evening I began to win. But when I was ready to go home there was no one to go with me. I was forced to go home alone again, and this time it was raining very hard. I ran down the main road, quietly, so that no one would know I was there. If those who had been playing with me knew, they might follow me. So I left secretly. I got as far as Blahtanah, and there wasn't a lamp to be seen. It was very late at night. Just as I was leaving Blahtanah I dropped my money in the ditch. I felt around for it and got some but went on even though most of it was left there behind. I dropped it because I was going so fast. *Sengkala,* a calamity, it was.

Once when I was hanging around in Gria Pacung, I played a gambling game with one of my friends there. I had some money but my opponent didn't have any, so we used grains of corn as counters to note losses and gains. If he lost two, then we'd put two grains of corn on my side. When we were finished, he owed me 20 or 25 *képéng.* Since he didn't have any money, he told me to climb one of his coconut trees later that night and "steal" some coconuts. He didn't own the tree, but his wife did, so he was stealing from his own wife. If his wife knew, she'd be mad at him. So I took as many coconuts as equaled the sum of 25 *képéng.* I threw down as many as could be sold for 25 *képéng,* and he said, "Go sell them over there." I did that a number of times. I was just a child.

In those days my older brother was always every day fooling around at the home of the Chinese widow in Negara. In the evenings he'd go to Tegenungan to teach *gamelan.* In Tegenungan there was a *seka jogéd,* and so my older brother went to Tegenungan, and I went with him. They were very good to me there in Tegenungan. [A *seka jogéd* is an organized group of dancers and musicians who specialize in putting on *jogéd* performances. Most of the people of Tegenungan had the title of Déwa, and were *sisia* of Gria Gedé.]

All the girls treated me like their younger brother. They gave me plenty of food. The people of the village were taking turns each day cooking food for my brother. And I was included. My brother and I were teaching them how to play *gamelan.* I gambled there too, in the *ceki* game, even though I didn't have much money. When I was poorest, I'd have at least two *képéng,* and that would be enough to gamble with. At that time I didn't know much about girls, but I knew how to talk to them and flirt with them. Those girls there were very pretty. They asked me to help make their headdresses of flowers and I made a nice one with *lontar* leaves, fanned out in a circle and with cutout patterns. It was very well done, and someone asked, "Who made that?"

"Oh, that was made by Ida Bagus Alit."

"*Bah!* Ratu, I like you. Do you like me?" in very familiar words. That's how they'd talk.

I was a long time there, and then, after I went home again, my older brother seemed to be never at home. I went back up to Gria Pacung and then to Sukawati with friends. I went fishing with friends; I wasn't afraid of anything. But I never asked for anything. The kids today when they go somewhere always ask first for some money for their expenses, but I never did. Even when I was going faraway.

Once when I went to Sukawati for a cockfight, there wasn't any going on, but the food sellers said there were a lot of cockfights in Klungkung. So when the bus from Denpasar to Klungkung came along I got right on it and went to Klungkung.

That's why I went to Klungkung for a cockfight. I stayed overnight there—they were having cockfights every day for twenty-two days. I slept on a *balé* right in the cockfight place, with strangers, wrapped in each other's arms. One stranger left very early before dawn, but he didn't take my money.

They had there what we would call today an exhibition—many people selling different things. That's where I stayed overnight.

This "exhibition" was a *pasar malam* (Malay for "night fair,") and the money he used for gambling Togog had just received from Gregory Bateson for pictures he sold him up in the mountain village of Bayung. When we read over this passage, Togog's son questioned Togog, in an attempt to discover the date of this event. Togog said he took with him 2 *ringgit* and 30 *talén,* that is 5.30 *rupiah,* which he had gotten from a bank in Denpasar. Bateson had paid him for some paintings up in Bayung Gedé with a check, which Togog had to go to the bank in Denpasar to cash. This would place the event in 1936. (See Chapter 6 for further details of Togog's transactions with Bateson.) The *pasar malam* had something to do with a ritual in Besakih. It was held in the central square east of the Klungkung *puri,* an area that is now a soccer field.

Another time, in the Nataran in Klungkung, I won a lot. And then the Déwa Agung had a cockfight that lasted twelve days. I slept overnight right in the middle of the place where the cockfights are held because there was no way to get home. There weren't very many busses in those days. After two days there was a truck, and I went home, but it was carrying a load of charcoal. I figured I'd wash off when I got home, but it rained, hard, and the truck had no roof on it, so we covered our heads with the charcoal bags. Because my head was covered I missed Batuan and was carried all the way to Badung. It was late in the afternoon, and I was all black! My skin was black and my clothes were black, because the cover itself was full of charcoal dust, and when it got wet, black water came down on us. Even my face was black!

There were twelve of us in the truck, and when we got to the Badung market we were put down. We just sat there, but I was lucky! Just then Nyoman Cingkang (a Chinese from Sukawati with a truck) came by. He was there with his truck to pick up some merchandise, so he took me home. I was good friends with Nyoman Cingkang because I often fooled around in Sukawati, gambling at the home of Déwa Putu Konoran, a Satria in Sukawati, playing cards. I'd stay there for a month at a time.

Once I sold the gold handle of a kris to have money to bet with. It belonged to my Grandfather, Ida Bagus Gria, and the gold in it was equivalent to eight dinar. I put it in front of the dealer. No matter how much I lost, I still wanted money to go on playing. I sold it for only twenty silver coins. I didn't know any better because of my desire to bet and was in such a hurry to win some money.

I used up the whole sum of money that I got from that gold kris handle on betting and on food for all of us. That was the way I was then. That's why I wanted to cut off that road of mine. I even sold all the coconuts that I got in pawn from someone—I lent him some money. He had seventy-five trees in his *tegal.* I lent him the money and then twenty-five days later I harvested them, and I got 150 coconuts. And then I bought some gold rings without the stones in Klungkung, four of them, and five precious stones.

A gambler can never get rich [because he spends whatever he has, explained Togog]. My wife asked for one of the rings. I gave her one. Another we used for food. And there is one left that I still have today. Those coconuts were all gone, and I didn't use them to make me rich. That's why I feel very grateful now because they won't allow cockfights anymore. Now they only have cockfights when they need them for the temple festival, and just briefly in the morning. Everyone has to stand, all pressed together, the strong ones getting in front. I can't stand being crowded like that, pushed and shoved, and you can't even see the cocks, much less place your bets. That's why I'm very grateful—it's as if I'd been sick and I'd had a purifying ceremony *(penglukatan)* by a *pedanda* to stop going to cockfights.

When they used to have cockfights, if I didn't have any money, I'd go looking for some, and I'd say to anyone who lent me money, "Truly, I will pay you back tomorrow." But then, if I lost, I wouldn't pay for as long as a month. That's wrong, isn't it? The next day he'd come looking for his money: "Oh, tomorrow, when I win . . ." So I'd go on like that, never paying back. That was stretching it—my heart was sick. It was as if my heart/mind was diseased. So I had all those debts.

These days, my desire to gamble has grown dim. I don't want to go out very much anymore. I know all the kinds of gambling, *kobokan, ceki,* all of them.

Respect in Language and Gesture

During Togog's youthful wanderings, he occasionally met strangers. It is almost impossible for Balinese to speak with anyone before discovering their relative status vis-à-vis one another. If one addresses someone wrongly in terms appropriate to a commoner, he risks not only insulting him but damaging his spiritual state. Status markers in Balinese are scattered throughout every sentence, but the most sensitive ones are the pronouns, as is shown in the following story. To address someone using the pronouns *cang* for "I" and *cai* for "you" is potentially demeaning. (If the addressed person is clearly lower in status than the speaker, such as a commoner addressed by a *pedanda,* it is not thought to be demeaning but appropriate.) It is safer to use *tiang* or *titiang* for "I." For "you," the safest is to replace the pronoun with the person's title, for instance, *Ratu, Ida, Madé* or *Biang* ("mother"), or, if you don't know the title, *Jero.*

I went with one of my "fathers" [a distant cousin of Togog's mother] to Pura Ganggangen [in Cangi, the Pura Desa of Sakah, a village just north of Batuan] to catch bats to make *lawar* to eat. It's up in the rice fields north of here. When we got there it started to rain, and we stopped in a *balé* outside the *pura,* and then a man came who asked: "What are you doing here? What are you looking for here?" [said in low Balinese.]

"I *(cang)* am just sitting here," said my cousin, "I'm just sitting here."

"What do you *(cai)* mean using *cang* to speak to me? I'm going to beat you up!"

"If you hit me, I'll hit you back!" [also speaking low, using the demeaning pronouns *cang* and *cai.*]

That's how they talked, *cang* and *cai,* and I was dizzy. He had just gotten there and they were quarreling. He was standing there, and I said to him: "Hey, wait a minute! Sit down first!" I said that speaking down to the Ida Bagus—but I didn't know that he was an Ida Bagus in the beginning when he first spoke and said, "What are you doing here?"

So then when he sat down I asked, in polite words, "Who are you?"

"I'm Ida Bagus from Sakah," he said politely. Well, he turned out to be a distant cousin from Sakah. [And when Togog told him they were Brahmana too, the stranger gave the two young men some advice.]

"Don't talk like that to people. Whether it is nighttime or daytime, you must not speak like that. The person might be a Brahmana like this 'father' here. If a commoner *(jaba)* spoke to him like that, how would that be? He would be *kasepung* [lowered] by him." That's what he said to him.

That was that. And he didn't say another word, not a word came out. So ever after that scolding, after being told by the Brahmana from Sakah, my "father" always used polite speech.

Kasepung, translated above as "lowered," is a complex idea, which will enter into some of Togog's other stories. The term comes from *sepung,* to be covered with dust, with the *ka-* prefix making it into a form meaning the consequence of a past action. To be *kasepung* means to become polluted *(leteh* or *letuh).* The consequences of a Brahmana being *kasepung* can be so serious as to require the polluted person to be exiled from his ancestral temple, and thereby cut off from the protection of his forebears. To counteract the pollution, it would be necessary to have a large ritual purification performed for the Brahmana victim. It is because of this danger that the stranger gives the advice at the end of the anecdote in which he counsels that no Brahmana speak down to a stranger, for fear of being himself polluted by the stranger's response. Thus, it is not the insulter who is damaged, but the insulted person. In this particular case, since they were all Brahmana, the damage was little, but if one of them had been a commoner, or even a Satria, the Brahmana would have been in serious trouble. (See also the story about the slap in the face, related in Chapter 5.)

Work and Adult Responsibilities

Gleaning Yams

My cousin from east of here, Beli Wayan Truwi, who was nearly the same age, asked me to go with him to pick yams.

Togog said he must have been five or six years old when this happened. Truwi was five or ten years older than he. Togog addressed Truwi as "Beli" ("older brother"). It was the custom at the time for landowners to allow small children and poor people to glean as much of a crop of yams as they could carry, even sometimes before the owner was finished harvesting. Togog's son remarked that only children of about five or six were allowed to do that, or very poor people. He said that today it is never done, that the owner usually reserves the right for himself to do that last gleaning.

We went up to Sakah, carrying little baskets. Right then the yam crop was very plentiful and there were only the two of us gleaning. The owner said, "Take anything you can dig up, Ratu Gus Alit, take as much as you can carry home, Ratu." So he told us to go ahead and dig. As we were digging Beli Wayan had a tricky idea. If we found, say, four yams on a plant, we would take two and cover up the other two, stamp down the earth, leave them there in their bed. I went along with the idea—I didn't really understand that we were going to come and get them the next day. I thought that the man who planted them would be looking for them the next day.

Well then suddenly—*aduh!*—it began to rain. It poured. It roared down! *Kerug! Kerug!* And then when I looked south over the rice fields there was lightning—*blarrr!*—and then —*srrrettt!*—to the north. Up there to the north the lightning struck—*blarrr!*—and *plugggg!* And the thunder made such a loud crash I was startled. It hit a coconut tree, burnt it right up. So I was terrified.

[After the rain] we worked some more. *Beh!* We got enough to fill the space under your bed!

I was with Ida Bagus Truwi, the one who later became Perbekel of Batuan, but he was still young then. He'd pick up a leech with his bare hand—I was so afraid of leeches.

"Here! Here! Take this in your hand, you can turn it inside out," he'd say to me. And when he gave it to me, I dared to touch it, but otherwise I didn't. You could turn it right inside out. He'd play like that to encourage me, but I still was afraid of them, still afraid of them.

Now the next day we went back up there to the field, and the heavy rain had washed off the soil from the yams we had buried there. [Laughs.] *Aduh!* How engrossed we were! *Adah!* We freely picked them out of the dirt and quickly our baskets were filled. We went back there two times to get more.

In those days we were very poor. It was like hell *(neraka)!* We often had only *usam* to eat [little cakes made of coconut meat that is left over after all the oil has been pressed out of it, almost devoid of food value]. And sometimes we'd take cakes of *entip* [the burnt crust left on the bottom of a pot after rice porridge has been made in it, scraped up, and soaked] with us to the rice fields. My body was still very young, and strong like a machine. Whatever I ate, my body would use, like a new automobile.

Guarding the Fields from Monkeys

Another time I was sent out to the fields to guard over the growing cucumbers and rice. There were five sections to the rice field, one had cucumber plants while the other four had rice.

The rice had grown half a meter high, but there were monkeys there that wanted to eat it. The monkeys lived in the bushes down in the ravine next to the rice fields. There were two kinds of monkeys. There were large ones called *bojog candi*—about 40 of them—and smaller ones called *bojog ragang*—about 175 of them. The smaller ones were afraid of the larger ones because they were so big and fierce.

My uncle Po Tut built a little hut in the middle of the rice fields, a nice one with plaited bamboo walls, where you could stay when guarding the rice. And I had, as weapons against the monkeys, a blowpipe and a large club with thorny branches tied to it to hit the monkeys with. And my Uncle Tut made me a kind of clawlike tongs with an ear of corn in it as bait, which could clamp down on a monkey's hand.

While the cucumber plants were still young, I had to pick out all the little bugs on the leaves. After a while, sometimes someone would bring us some food and we would stop and eat it. But sometimes we had nothing to eat all day. But we didn't care about food. We just did what we were told to do.

Now, after a while the rice was ready for harvest, and the monkeys were all over. If there was no one in the rice fields, they would come up out of the ravine and eat it. A gang of them could eat up a whole paddy field of rice at once. That's why there were lots of people around in the fields then.

There was a man who had some sugarcane planted in his fields near where I was on guard, right next to the ravine. His name was I Guna from Lod Pangkung [a nearby neighborhood]. He also had a lot of coconut trees just to the east of the fields.

So he called to me, "Ida Bagus, Bagus Alit!" ["Little Bagus"].

"Yes, Uncle," I said, respectfully.

"Keep the monkeys out of my sugarcane, okay?"

"Alright."

"And then whenever you want you can come and take as much of the sugarcane as you like. Like at Galungan, I'll give you five or ten stalks." [Galungan is a big ritual festival when everyone dresses up in new clothes, goes visiting, and eats festive foods. It occurs every 210 days.]

He had a lot of sugarcane, and after that whenever I'd go to his place, he'd give me some, because I guarded it against the monkeys. That's why—even today—whenever I need sugarcane for a ceremony I only have to go to him and ask for it.

The monkeys were very clever, too, at stealing coconuts. They'd pick them with their hands, throw them down, and then go down and gather them up. They were taking the whole harvest of coconuts.

So once I went there carrying the trap with the corn bait that my uncle had made for me, and there were a lot of monkeys on the ground below the trees. If a person comes, they run and hide, but if there is no one there, they'll eat everything up.

Well now, I caught a baby one in my trap when he tried to pull out the bait, the ear of corn. *"Plak!"* went the trap, and it clamped down on his hand.

So he cried out, "Kuek! Kuek!" and he thrashed this way and that. If I had had someone else with me, I could have captured him, but I was alone, carrying only a blowpipe. And all the monkeys were looking at me. There were fifteen huge monkeys there under the tree. *Beh!* What could I do!

I ran away—up onto the rice fields and one monkey chased after me and he wouldn't stop.

There were some people up above there on the rice fields, and they called out, "Run faster! Run faster!" And the monkey came closer and closer up behind me. It really happened, often, that a monkey bit off someone's finger. There's a man named I Teduh, still alive today, who's missing a finger. Those monkeys are very strong, so I ran as hard as I could. And there were some men there carrying sickles. There were three of them. They stood up and the monkey turned around and ran back.

The baby monkey was still thrashing around, and then he got free by himself. If there had been two of us we would have caught him. It was really like hell there in the rice fields those days.

So then the head of the irrigation association [the *pakaséh*], named I Jana, got an idea how he'd get rid of the monkeys. He'd borrow a gun from a man in Sukawati named Anak Agung Gedé Raka. He let him take the gun. It was named "Sinambur."

It had little bullets that flew out all at once like an umbrella opening up. *"Tas!"* it would shoot them all out. He was going to use that gun to shoot the monkeys.

So he got the gun, and six of them went out there. The irrigation association *(subak)* was paying for it. Each shot cost a silver *ringgit*.

He shot it five times. There were about ten monkeys

there. But he didn't even touch any of them. It was a failure, borrowing that gun.

So then they went around to pray at all the nearby temples, asking to be granted the power to kill the monkeys. Both the group of 175 small ones and the group of 40 big ones.

So after they had made the prayers, the whole *subak* membership came out to kill the monkeys. The signal drum *(kulkul)* was beaten, the one just north of the river. And when the *kulkul* sounded everyone came out carrying weapons. Old-fashioned weapons.

So I got ready to go out too whenever the *kulkul* sounded, going after those monkeys.

If you got one, you would be paid a *suku* coin. At that time, a *suku* coin was worth 400 *képéng* coins and you could get about ten kilos of uncooked rice for 300 *képéng*. I got one monkey. We were out there every day for fifteen days. *Bah!* The monkeys would fall down from above, *"Cebur!"* There were many people after them, for the money.

Nowadays the monkeys are almost gone from there. They say there are only about two there now. All of those 175 plus the 40 are gone. It wasn't easy to guard the rice fields. And I did it from the time I was very small.

Helping with a Cremation by Raising Ducks

The priest here in Gria Gedé, my grandfather, died. They began preparing for his cremation. [This was the cremation of Togog's grandfather, Ida Pedanda Wayan Jelantik, together with Togog's Grandfather Gria's daughter, Dayu Rasmi. Togog might have been about five years old at the time.]

I was given the task of raising ducklings. I had thirty of them to take every day to the *sawah* with Ida Bagus Madé Jata, who was also keeping ducklings.

We'd take them out to the rice fields, the one near here called Tambak, and also up to Sakah. Once there were some people there weeding, and they asked us to help with the weeding: "Ratu, Ida Bagus Alit! If you help with weeding, Ratu, I will give you a *tenah* of rice at the harvest." [This may not have been a real promise. A *tenah* is ten bunches of rice stalks, tied together, really too large a payment.]

"Are there any leeches in there?" I was terribly afraid of leeches, and even still today I'm afraid of them.

"No, there aren't any because the rice field is dry now," they said. "Truly!"

But suddenly I got a leech on my knee! I stamped all around. *Aah!* I couldn't take it off. I trampled down all the young rice plants.

For ten days after that everyone laughed at me, and they had to replant there a space as large as two sleeping mats. When the ducks were grown, we had the cremation. It was very exciting, *ramé*. Any cremation here is always *ramé*.

After that cremation, my grandmother [the Pedanda Istri, wife of Togog's grandfather the Priest] was still alive, and I'd go and ask her for money, for a penny, a *képéng*. She was very busy and sometimes went faraway and I'd go with her, trailing behind her asking for a penny. When she gave me money, even a penny, I could buy a lot with it in those days. I could buy peanuts to eat.

Weeding in a Rice Field

One time I was working in the rice fields in the Subak Batuan Dauh. Several people taught me how to do the weeding, how to get the grass out from among the rice stalks. One of them got down in the rice field with me: "This is how to do it, Tu. These little ones that just show a little, pull them up, and then press them into the mud with your foot so that they are killed."

I was very grateful for that advice.

Now in those days, when I went out to work in the fields, they gave me only a little food to take with me. They never gave me a real meal of cooked rice. But just a crust of leftover dried rice and with it just a little coconut cake and salt. Well, I thought that was just delicious! The elixir of life!

Saved by a Guardian Spirit from Spikes Protecting Coconuts

There was another time when I went to pick coconuts after dark. A man named Ida Bagus Bontok told me that he owned a certain coconut tree and told me to climb up it and pick some for him in the night. He really didn't own the tree at all. The tree had branches tied around its trunk to prevent thieves from climbing up to the top. The tree leaned over a rice field full of water, so if I should fall it wouldn't matter. That's what I thought, and so I was willing to climb it. I climbed it quickly, but near the top the owner had put bamboo spikes on the tree, slanting down. I groped up in the dark, near the spike, but it didn't stab me. So then I knew the spikes were there. When I climbed down I was careful that my foot didn't get stabbed by the spikes. When I got down I saw that all I had gotten was a small scratch.

Surely my *ilon*-spirit was protecting me.

The term *ilon* means "to protect or care for some one." Togog felt that because he didn't know he was stealing coconuts, he was protected from being stabbed by the bamboo spikes. The spikes themselves are not so dangerous as the spell that their maker had placed on them. Who this *ilon*-spirit was, Togog does not say, but I would guess it was one of his ancestors.

This is what one of those spikes looks like. [Draws a little spike, like a sharpened pencil.] They call it a *sungga patok*. It's shaped like this, here, like this. This end is sharpened, so that if this hits you it wounds you. These spikes are very strong. You can't pick the coconuts then, because if your hand hits it, the wound is terrible. See, they point upwards. So if you're stabbed by one of these you are really wounded. Well, I guess that it wasn't meant for me to be stabbed by one of them, so I missed them.

I've seen many such spikes, made from bamboo. Once I nearly jumped right onto a spike like that. In a rice field, in Samapan it was, and I asked, "Who put up these spikes, Yan, in the rice field?" Because they shouldn't put them in the middle of the fields like that.

He said, "There was a crazy man got loose here two days ago, and he came and put them up."

Sawing Planks to Build a House

I also helped build a house. I worked in a sawmill, cutting down logs into square posts. The ones I helped make are still there, in the house of the Satria south of mine, the house where Déwa Kompiang Badung lives now; but at that time he was still very little. It was his father, Déwa Ketut Cenik, who was my boss. Déwa Kompiang Badung and I and Déwa Kompiang Payuk worked together. [The sawing was done with a long, two-man saw, in which one person stands down in a ditch and the other stands up above, on either end of the saw.] We were like a team. We went here and there together, and even slept together.

I liked to do that kind of sawing work, and I also liked to sing the sacred songs, the *kekawin,* and I liked to study philosophy.

With my friends [Déwa Ketut Badung and Déwa Ketut Payuk] we did a lot of sawing. We worked for twenty days together, first sawing those taro trees, then smoothing them down.

Paying Land Taxes

Togog must have been a teenager, not yet married, at the time of the following event.

My older brother wasn't home very much at that time, so I had to take care of our land. He was always in Negara at the home of a Chinese widow, fooling around there [having an affair]. At Galungan the Chinese always sent around gifts of food *(jotan),* a whole bushel of sweets *(jajan)* or *arak*-wine. My older brother was always over there, and he didn't come home even when we were very busy. His wife didn't ever come here to help either. [She was staying in the home of her father, just next-door to the north.] Now at that time, too, my mother didn't pay much attention to me, so I was always there next-door to the east.

The tax came due on the land in front of our front door [a small dry field for growing trees and dry crops]. A man from the Punggawa's office in Pliatan had a big book in which was written how much I had to pay. And he wrote in it that it was all paid.

Now, some time later, everyone was very upset, because they were all told that they were in debt [to the colonial government]. The man from the Punggawa's office came to get me, just as I was about to eat. I had just taken a handful of rice—it was rice mixed with small bits of cassava. He came to me and said they were holding an investigation.

Like the police. He said it was the Punggawa himself who had come, and he was in the Balé Banjar of Banjar Gedé. There were six men with him, with guns. Actually, it wasn't the Punggawa of Pliatan, because he was in Java, they said, but there was a substitute for him.

I believe the substitute tax collector was the Punggawa of more distant Payangan, who did not know the private arrangements that the regular Punggawa had made with various people in Batuan, agreeing to accept various services, as recounted below, in exchange for the taxes. Apparently he had not noted down that he had excused these people from their taxes, and his substitute was now asking for these back taxes.

I was at home, just in the act of taking some rice to eat, when he said, "You have to come to talk to the Punggawa."

"Yes, I'll come in a minute."

"No, you have to go right now!" That's what he said. *Aduh!* He was tough (*keras,* Ind.). Even now, when I think about it, *ah!*

So when I got there, I said I wasn't able to pay.

"If you don't pay you'll be put in prison for seven days!" That's what he said. But everyone here was very poor. We had to pay, if we didn't we'd go to prison.

So I went to my Grandfather and he said, "I'll find you some money." So then he gave me a silver *ringgit* to pay my debt with.

But then, soon after that, they came after my Grandfather to pay *his* back taxes.

"You owe taxes on your land. If you don't pay you'll be put in prison!" But my Grandfather thought that his taxes had already been paid, for the Puri [i.e., the noble house of Batuan, but Togog indicates by the term a particular man, the head of the *gambuh* troupe who was also the head of the house] had promised to pay them for him.

My Grandfather had just been dancing the *gambuh* in Karangasem, nine days in Karangasem. The leader of the *gambuh* troupe was from the Batuan Puri [probably this was the dancer Anak Agung Gedé Raka, the one who went to Paris with the Pliatan group in 1932] and he had said to my Grandfather: "You don't have to pay your tax. I'll take care of it with your pay for these performances. I'll pay the government. You don't have to pay those taxes." That's what the Puri man said.

But it turned out that the Puri man didn't pay them, and they came looking for him to pay his debts.

Well, my Grandfather felt aggrieved. He felt all the more so because the Puri man hadn't helped him the time that the truck broke down and my uncle was sick and unconscious. They went to Puri Gianyar, which was nearby where they broke down and asked for help. But they couldn't get Puri Gianyar to help them because they said that the troupe had gone to Karangasem without asking permission of Puri Gianyar. "You went there without telling us," they said in Gianyar. He was right, because this group is a part of Gianyar's. Gianyar had always given them whatever they needed, such as gold-painted cloth *(prada)* for costumes. So then, when he went to ask for help, he wouldn't help at all. [The royal family of Gianyar are kin of the Batuan Satria. They often financed the Batuan gambuh group. See Chapter 3 for more on the *gambuh*.] And then now came the man from Puri Payangan, asking for payment of back taxes. First I was in debt and now my Grandfather was in debt. He was really a very rough man.

Standing Guard and Doing Other Odd Jobs for the Punggawa of Pliatan

Now I'll tell you about standing guard. I often stood guard at the office of the Punggawa, and I carried letters for him. I was still very little. Today they wouldn't let a child like me carry something like that, stand guard like that. I was very, very bold. I went with another "grandfather," the one who was blind in one eye, the father of the Pedanda of Gria Dalem.

You got paid if you stood guard. You'd get a hundred pieces of money, but instead of paying you cash, he'd excuse you from your taxes. That was your pay. I followed along with him. He was well liked by Puri Peliatan. Whenever he went there they would feed him. I didn't like to be fed by them, so I brought along my own food. But they'd give him all sorts of things. I just went along with him, for better or for worse. When we had good luck we would just have to stand guard at night there, and we could sleep, and we got fed good food by the Punggawa's wife, who was a woman from Batuan. But once we had bad luck, because the people from Payangan got the job of standing guard, and we had to take a horse back to its owner in Sukawati.

"Is Batuan here?"

"Yes, we're here."

"Is Payangan here?"

"Yes."

So he sent the people of Payangan to stand guard and we had first to take a letter to Gianyar and then take the horse back to Palak, near Sukawati. The Puri in Peliatan had borrowed a horse from a Muslim horse trader. He sold other things too, like opium. And Batuan was given the job of taking the horse back. If we had known how to ride it we would have. But we had to lead him along.

The Punggawa of Pliatan had married a girl from the Puri here in Batuan, Anak Agung Buncing, the younger twin sister of Anak Agung Gria. We stayed overnight at their house once, and they said, "Eat here!"

"No, I've already eaten," we said. So they gave my "grandfather" four chickens to take home and raise for them, and when we left for home, they also gave him some corn to feed the chickens with. [This was another odd-job for which Togog was supposed to get release from his taxes.]

The Cremation of Pedanda Istri

This cremation was attended and studied by Bateson and Mead in 1937.

When it was time for the cremation of my grandmother, the *pedanda* (Ida Pedanda Istri Wayan), I only had 80 *rupiah* for it, so I went to my Grandfather and asked for help in the payments for the cremation. He gave me whatever I wanted: "Here, take this," he said in familiar speech, "and if it is too much, keep what's left over for the future [his own cremation]. If it isn't enough I'll give you some more. If what I have is all used up, it's all right. In the future, when I die, put out just a few little offerings for me. If you can't, never mind."

I went looking for pigs for the cremation, borrowing them from my neighbors—we used up six very large pigs. There were many, many guests—from Peguyungan, from Beng, from Samprangan in Gianyar. There were especially a lot of people who came from Samprangan, from the group of Satrias there. The Satrias here in Batuan come from there.

The Satrias from Beng, Samprangan, and Batuan and the commoners from Peguyungan are all *sisia* of Gria Gedé—Togog's house—and so are obliged to give material help to those Brahmana in it, such as gifts of food and building materials and labor, in return for ritual services.

The people from Samprangan put up this *balé* [the one Togog lived in the rest of his life, where we were speaking] as an offering, and the ones from Beng helped too. They slept here in the *balé* that they had given, didn't want to sleep anywhere else. I was just unrolling one straw mat after another, must have been seventeen at least. They remember today this *balé* that they had given us. And when they have a death ceremony, we are always invited there. When I go there to visit they treat me as their own kin. They were especially nice to me. That's true even today. If today I were to go and ask them for 100 kilos of rice, they'd give me it within two days.

Once when I was very little they offered me five *ringgit* plus 100 *képéng* to take home with me. And they all offered to give me rice, but I said no. I said [speaking downwards], "I don't want any now, Kak," to their *pamangku*, Kak Mangku. "We have enough at home, but if I need some in the future, I'll ask for some."

Three Learning

Cultural Performances

Cultural Performances • The Ritual Calendar • Learning Basic Ritual Skills • Gamelan Playing and Dancing • Storytelling • Creating a New *Arja* Drama • Singing • The Philosophic Content of the Songs and Stories

Togog spoke often about his experiences of learning certain highly valued cultural skills—reading Balinese script, making ritual artifacts, playing music and dancing, singing sacred songs, and storytelling—all of which are important elements in rituals. Many of the anecdotes in this chapter, which extend from certain events in Togog's middle childhood to some in his forties, were told to me at one sitting, suggesting that they were classified together by Togog himself.

For Togog, too, singing Balinese poems, playing music, dancing, and storytelling were all intertwined with rituals. The main theme tying them together in his thoughts was how these performances provided him with moral backbone. While telling me about memorizing new songs, he remarked that he studied the *kekawin* songs because he wanted their moral guidance *(indik):*

"I wanted to change myself, to get rid of the bad in my heart. The best for its *indik* is the "Boma" [the *kekawin* Bomantaka]. What was most important to me was the story. I wanted to know that story so that in the future I could make a picture of it, and so that, if asked, I could tell it. I understood that story very well. Those words entered me."

These songs are in the language Togog calls Kawi or what linguists call Old Javanese, Middle Javanese, Javanese-Balinese, and Balinese-Javanese. In fact, the name of the genre *kekawin* indicates that it is composed in Kawi. The words are not understandable to those who speak only modern Balinese.

Reading Kawi texts is usually a collaborative public act in which one person reads the words aloud, selecting a phrase or sentence at a time, while a second person translates those words from the Kawi into modern Balinese. The whole reading/translating/interpreting performance is called *mabasan,* from the word *basa* or "language," thus it is considered an act of "putting into language." The act of reading the text aloud, in a complex chant, is called *maca* (from *baca,* "to read"), while the following act of translation is called *mabasa.* Togog told me that he never learned how to translate, although he had memorized certain translations.

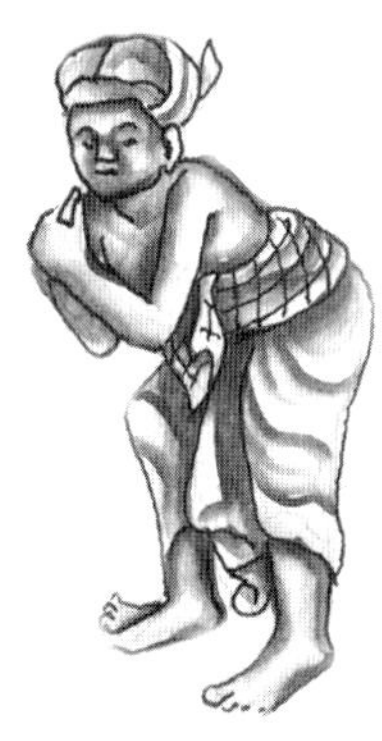

Balinese script is syllabic, a descendant of Indic writing conventions. Much of the Balinese lore for magical and ritual transactions utilizes these syllables—either spoken or written. The student starts with recognition of these syllables. He then moves to writing them on *lontar,* inch-wide strips of dried palm leaf on which the letters are incised with a small sharp knife, then soot is rubbed into the lines to make them legible. Today paper notebooks are used, but when Togog was young he had to learn the difficult art of scratching these small delicate lines. Only when a student is mature and has had several consecration rituals performed over him can he venture into translating and understanding the contents of the writing. Many *lontar* are never read aloud in public because their contents consist of mainly secret *mantra* for sorcery or defense against it. The syllabic letters are important parts of graphic images that are inscribed on many talismans and other ritual artifacts, the making of which is an important Brahmana activity.

Learning to read, like gamelan playing and dance, is taught through apprenticeship, copying closely another's movements, memorization, and repeated practice. Most of these activities can be broken down into component steps, and apprentices are given the simplest of subtasks to do, gradually working up to the most complex.

Learning the ritual skills of a Brahmana is another main subject of this chapter. These activities are reported in more detail in Chapter 4, "Performing Rituals." Brahmana men and women may, if they choose, make careers of ritual preparation and performance, not only as *pedanda,* but also as other ritual specialists. They learn their techniques from their earliest years. While non-Brahmana can and do learn these same skills—reading, singing, making offerings, and even presiding over rituals—Brahmana, because of their ancestry, may bring an added inherited spiritual effectiveness *(sakti)* to such ritual acts.

Togog's apprenticeships—not only in reading but also in the making of ritual offerings, and also, later, in conducting rituals himself—were carried out in a number of different venues. First, of course, was his own household where his Grandfather was a practiced *ulaka,* providing guidance to the many clients of his deceased brother, the *pedanda.* After the death of the *pedanda,* his widow, the *pedanda istri,* continued to perform many of the rituals for their clients, and Togog's Grandfather often served as her assistant.

But most of Togog's early training in reading and ritual skills was, according to him, not among his own group but among the Brahmana Siwa of Batuan. He drew pictures of their two neighborhoods, just to the north of his own, one drawing showing the western portion of Batuan's Brahmana Siwa, called collectively Gria Kawan, and the other, the eastern portion, Gria Pacung (figs. 18 and 19).

The reason Togog went among the Brahmana Siwa for his training was that during his adolescence there happened to be no male *pedanda* among the Brahmana Buda, and it is mainly men who know and teach Balinese writing and literature. During Togog's childhood, the Brahmana Siwa were headed by a well-known and learned *pedanda* priest. He regularly taught the young people of Batuan how to read, starting with teaching them the written alphabet. Togog also learned from various other Brahmana Siwa the painting of masks and cloth for costumes, the making of god-figures, and the drawing of magical images on cloth for funeral shrouds and on pottery for cremations. These last images later proved to be important sources for Togog's paintings.

Togog never learned to read or write Latin letters. Once in the 1980s he had a picture exhibited in the Art Center in Denpasar, and when they told him he couldn't get paid unless he signed for his picture, he had to give them a thumbprint in place of a signature. He signed his pictures with the printed letters of his name, which he had memorized.

Performing—playing the gamelan, dancing in

ritual dramas, and the like—is a part of nearly every Balinese childhood and adolescence, at least in Batuan. These were skills Togog learned but in which he never became accomplished. What interested him most was singing—and the stories the songs told. Togog became a fine singer and a dramatic storyteller, telling both traditional tales and his own experiences with gusto. (Chapters 3 and 4 both start with tales about Togog's childhood and end with ones about his adulthood in postindependence Bali.)

Some of the people important to Togog who are introduced in this chapter are the members of the Brahmana Siwa group called Gria Pacung, most especially the family of Togog's future wife, Dayu Resi—the Pedanda Istri of Gria Pacung (her mother), and Ida Bagus Sanur Tampi and Ida Bagus Madé Diksa (her two brothers); the members of the other Siwa group, Gria Kawan, especially a *pedanda* and two *ulaka,* Ida Bagus Ketut and Ida Bagus Cukeng; Togog's own younger brother, Ida Bagus Tantra; and, lastly, the Pedanda of Gria Kaliungu in Denpasar whom Togog usually called Pedanda Kerta, who is a distant relative. Pedanda Kerta plays an important role in the events recounted in Chapter 5.

The Ritual Calendar

Most Balinese rituals are scheduled according to a complex calendar of propitious and dangerous days. Brahmana are commonly consulted by their clients, and most have memorized its major elements. Each day is understood to be the conjunction of a lunar calender with six other calendars of differing sequences of named days. These weeks contain, respectively, two-, three-, four-, five-, six-, or seven-day cycles, each day with a distinct name.[1] In the boyish fight that Togog recounts below, the issue concerned the propriety of doing farm labor on a certain day that might have been inauspicious. The argument hung on identifying which day of which calendrical cycle it was, in this case based on Togog's knowledge of the names of the three days in the three-day week, and the six days in the six-day week. Togog had been taught these day names at home by the women in his family and by his neighbor Desak Watin.

Once when I was in Gria Kawan, someone asked me, "Dé! Want to work tomorrow in our rice field? Hoeing."

"Okay!" I said. So I went with his son to hoe around the peanut plants. That was the one who recently became the priest, *pamangku,* in the new Pura Desa. He was exactly the same age as me. We went to the fields with some others. There were four of us going to hoe together.

When we got there, the one who was the son of the man who had asked us to work there said, "Ida Bagus Alit!"

"Yes?"

"Uh, Ida Bagus Alit, I'm going to go home" [politely].

"What do you mean, go home?" I asked.

"I have to go home because they are castrating the pigs at home and I have to help. Today is Was." he said. [Was is the name of a day in the 6-day cycle.]

"What do you mean? It's not today, but three days from now, the day for castrating!" I said.

He said, "No, Was is today. It comes every three days!" [in rude speech].

So I answered, because he was already too insolent, "Where did you get that idea, Dé, that Was comes every three days? Was comes every six days!" I said that because I knew how to calculate the days.

"The names of the days are," I said. "Tungléh, Aryang, Urukung, Paniron, Was, Maulu. How can you say it comes every three days, Dé?" [Both boys were named Madé.]

"*Pah!* What kind of knowledge is that?" he said roughly, and he got mad.

We didn't do any hoeing, because we were fighting. Both of us were young and both stubborn, and we didn't think that the other knew the truth.

So that was it. We all went home and didn't get any

work done and argued all the way home. By the time we were just north of the Pura Desa, we were saying really bad things to one another. He said that my speech was like that of a *kokokan* bird, that I had a long neck! He was mad at me and chased me here and caught me in the road and hit me again and again, he was so angry. We didn't get any work done because he got angry.

So the next day when I went there, the father asked me, "Yesterday, what were you fighting about, Dé?"

"He asked to go home, to help with the pig castration. Someone told him that Was came every three days," I said.

And the father said to the son, "Where did you get that idea?"

"Someone told me so. I don't know the calendar *(wariga)*. I just heard that. So-and-so told me."

"No," said his father, "this Madé from the south [referring to Togog, whose home was south of Gria Kawan] is right. Was comes only every six days." Only then did he keep quiet. But he didn't stay angry.

Learning Basic Ritual Skills

Togog started to learn to write Balinese script, as he tells us, not at home but with young friends who were Brahmana Siwa, especially those in the Gria Pacung clan. Among these boys was the brother of the girl he would one day marry. He also learned about the making of offerings, talismans, and masks. These masks were worn in the ritual dance *wayang wong* (or "human puppet play" of Batuan's Pura Désa). The paint on these masks was always put on *(palas)* by Brahmana, thereby imparting some of their mystical efficaciousness, or *sakti,* to the masks that are worn in sacred dances. For the same reason, it was Brahmana who made and painted the little figures or tiny masks that the deities may descend into *(prarahi),* decorated earthenware vessels that hold holy water, and inscribed elaborate images on burial shrouds. The latter images became an important source for some of Togog's first paintings. (See Chapter 6.)

Figure 18 shows the neighborhood of Gria Pacung, looking north. The black-and-white strip along the left side of the drawing is an irrigation ditch. On the other side of that stream is the other Brahmana Siwa neighborhood, Gria Kawan, shown in figure 19. The gravel road at the top of figure 18, which appeared also in figure 15, is a reminder of the commercial and colonial world that surrounded Togog. It had been first laid down around the second decade of the century, going from Denpasar in the south eastward to Gianyar (and to Klungkung and Karangasem beyond it). Soon another branch of the road led to Ubud, where resident expatriate Europeans came to live in the late 1920s, and, after them, the tourists.

Studying in Gria Pacung

Speaking about Figure 18, Togog said:

I went often to Gria Pacung to hang around because I wanted very much to study the sacred literature, *kekawin* and *kidung*. I enjoyed it, that's all. I wanted to teach myself. I didn't want to turn my back on those things. Even today I'm like that—I don't want to turn my back on those matters.

I aimed to build the foundation that I lacked, so that's why I went up there all the time, to Gria Pacung. There I learned painting masks *(pulas)* and also how to write Balinese script.

Someone happened to be doing some writing, and he said to me: "Here is some writing. Let's do it together." The girl I would marry later lived there. I didn't yet think about girls. Whatever anyone told me to do I did it gladly, and I never said, "No, I won't do it."

I worked with my wife's younger brother, in Gria Pacung, the one who is now the *pedanda* in Celuk but at that time was still an *ulaka*.

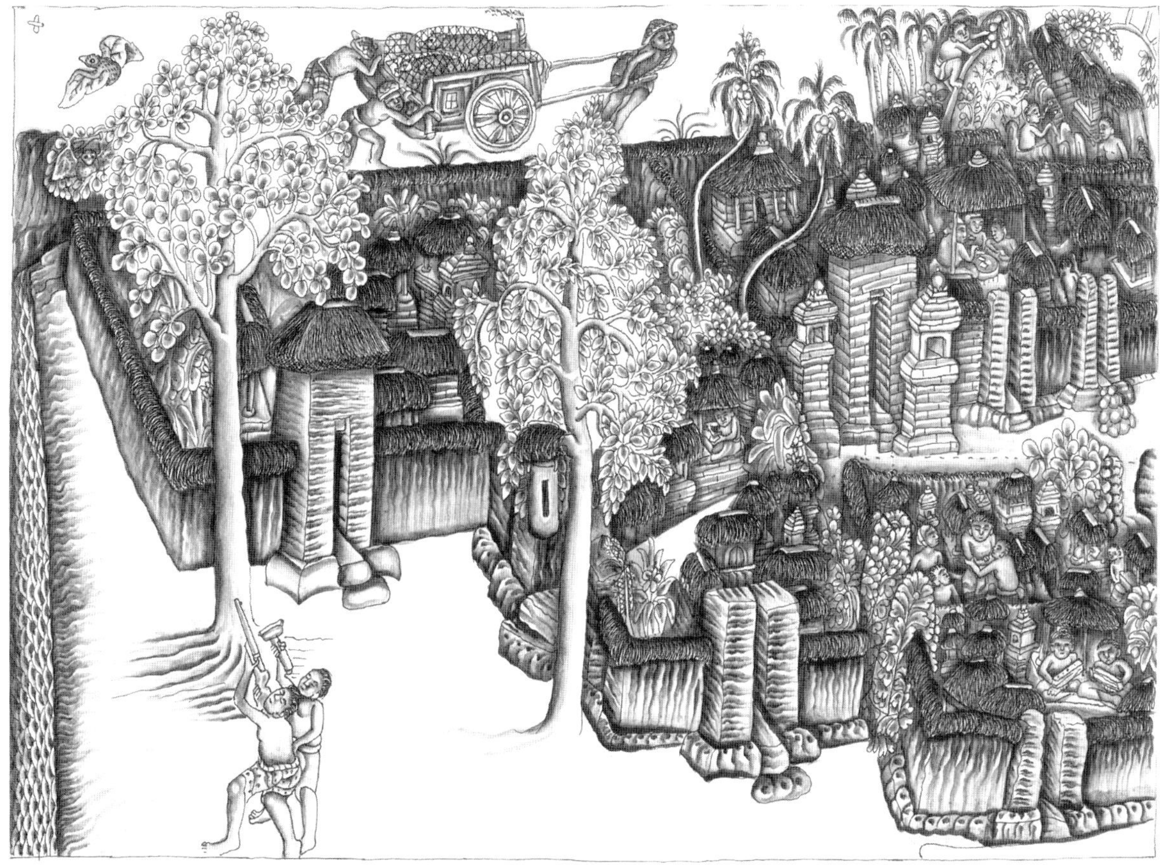

Figure 18. The neighborhood of Gria Pacung. Drawing by Ida Bagus Madé Togog, 1986.

An *ulaka* is any Brahmana who has not become a priest, a *pedanda*. Togog's wife's younger brother was Ida Bagus Sanur Tampi, who, before he became a *pedanda*, was one of the best painters in the Batuan school. (See H. Geertz, *Images of Power* [1994], pp. 110–111.) The making of the mask for the Lémbéng temple must have been done after Togog was an adult.

He knew how to paint masks too, and someone from Lémbéng brought him a set of eleven or fourteen masks to repaint. I painted those, and no one helped me. I did one mask of the sort that you hold between your teeth. You know, the kind with no string around the back. They said it was very magically powerful, *tenget*. It was made from a very fine and flexible wood that would bend when you touched it. That mask I made is still today in Lémbéng. Of course, the priest there [in Gria Pacung] took the responsibility. After all he was the priest.

[Pointing to the figures in lower-righthand corner of fig. 18:] This is Pedanda Nyoman writing down the *lontar* called Kawin Boma [Kekawin Bomantaka]. And when he finished then I took the original, and we are comparing them. And if this one says "east" then that one should too.

We were looking for the mistakes. It took ten days to do it all. [This must have happened later in Togog's life, after he was quite skilled at reading *lontar*.]

[Discussing fig. 18, the small figure carving something alone, about in the center of the picture:] Gria Pacung is the *gria* that was the home *(umah)* of my wife. There I am on the *balé piasan,* in her houseyard. I was working. I was most liked at that time for making *prarai* [god-figures]. The *prarai* were for a cremation. For a male corpse you have writing on it. And you also put on it a picture of a *wayang* figure. I could do it in three days. But I had to have a model. That's very hard. He's called Tastrobayu [Sahastrabahu]. It's a drawing on the edge of a bowl that's used for *tirta.* In the picture I'm making a *prarahi.* This is the model. I did it because my brother-in-law wasn't around very much. And only I was around the *gria* then. That was when the old *anak lingsir* [another word for *pedanda*] was still there. She's since passed away. She was my mother-in-law. [This must have been in 1945 – 1948, after Togog was long married and one of his wife's brothers was out of Batuan for months in the resistance movement against the Dutch.]

[Pointing to the figures above the two readers with *lontar,* one man holding another larger man:] Now here, this is west of the houseyard of the *pedanda.* To the east there was a space. Here there was a wall, but it didn't have a straw covering along its top [to protect the wall from erosion by heavy rains]. They couldn't cover it. Today this is the home of Ida Bagus Putu Blacok. He lives there today, but at that time it was Ida Aji Dé Buteng who lived there. He was acting somewhat crazy, and they sounded the signal drum *(kulkul)* of the neighborhood *(banjar).* I went there when I heard the drum — I was pretty bold. And here is a commoner *(kaula)* named I Teka. From Banjar Peninjoan. From the home where the wood merchant, I Rareng, now lives.

Well he grabbed him, he's very strong, together with the others. They were on the *balé dauh.*

[Pointing to the people playing cards, upper right of fig. 18:] We're playing cards. This is the younger brother of Kompiang Kesiyeh. We were gambling. That day I didn't lose at all. We were using corn for markers. Well, when he lost he owed me 2 *képéng.* Coconuts at that time sold for 7 each. He told me to go and pick a coconut, and to go and sell it. It was more than enough, but he didn't want the rest of the money: "Oh, just take it!"

[Pointing to the person playing an instrument in upper righthand corner of fig. 18:] Here was a big field and next to it the home of I Tongkol. He made *tingklik* instruments. [A *gamelan tingklik* is a small ensemble of instruments made of bamboo tubes suspended in a wooden frame and topped with bamboo keys. It is often used to accompany the *jogéd* dance.] Now I played very well and so he told me to come and play for him every day.

Kaki Tongkol would tell me to come, "Tu, you'll come and play music later this evening, yes?" [respectfully].

"Alright," I'd say [speaking down].

There were eight of us playing together. We'd play here in Batuan, in his house, and he'd walk out, away up north as far as Sakah, so he could hear the sound of the instruments from the distance and tell which instruments were good and which sounded bad. The next day he'd correct their tuning. He bought and sold *tingklik.* When he was tired of our playing, he'd sell them. Then, later, he'd put together another set.

His granddaughter, named I Keronong, was the one I had hit with a rock. She was very very pretty, with pale skin. He told her to learn to dance the *jogéd,* but she didn't want to. That's why he sold the instruments. Then he put together another set and invited me to join in a group *(seka)*, but I didn't want to. I couldn't carry the heavy instruments. The *gandrung* dancer (a female role played by a boy) in the group was I Kakul. He was the *gandrung* because he was very adept at dancing. When he was young he was a *gandrung*. Later, when he wanted to learn other dance moves, it was easy for him.

[Pointing to two figures at bottom left of fig. 18; the one with the gun is Ida Bagus Madé Jatasura from Gria Pacung. This was the painter, about the same age as Togog, who was most admired by Bateson and Mead. See H. Geertz, *Images of Power* (1994) for his pictures.] Here I am with Ida Bagus Madé Jata. He had said to me the day before, "There are a lot of large bats up there." So he asked for a gun from the Jero and they lent it to him.

Here Togog calls the Noble House of Batuan by its earlier name, "the Jero," rather than by its present-day term, "the Puri." The gun had been lent to Ida Bagus Jatasura by Anak Agung Ngurah, the head of the Jero and a clerk in the colonial office in Pliatan. He had borrowed the gun from his office.

The gun belonged to Pliatan. It took size five and a half bullets. Here he's hit a bat, but it's stuck up there, hanging. It's dead but it won't fall. So he used up a lot of bullets but he couldn't move it. It was holding fast by its hand. The next morning he got it. We went there in the night and he said, "You *(Ida)* carry the flashlight. I'll shoot." He was very good at shooting. [Ida Bagus Jatasura addresses Togog respectfully as "Ida" because they are not kin and about the same age.]

Studying in Geria Kawan

[Figure 19 shows the cluster of houseyards called Gria Kawan of Brahmana Siwa, seen from the east. Talking about the man with the mask in his hands, at center right:] This is an old *ulaka*, named Ida Bagus Ketut, painting a mask. I went to Gria Kawan where there were people working on painting masks. I liked that work. With me from home, also helping, was a man I called Po Nyoman [another Brahmana Buda, the younger brother of Togog's mother]. But since I was just watching and learning, no one told me to make an actual mask.

When I got quite skilled, I was asked to work in Sanur and went there with that Ida Bagus Tut [the old *ulaka* from Gria Kawan]. In the Gria in Sanur were a lot of young people, and whenever I went there they treated me just like a family member, saying, in familiar speech, "Come on in! Come right to the kitchen and have something to eat!" [in contrast to a nonfamily guest, who is served food elsewhere, on a *balé*]. They were not formal with me.

I was there a whole month, together with Ida Bagus Nyoman Tantra [Togog's younger brother] from here. He's dead now. When we left, they gave him some money, half a *ringgit*, and they didn't give me even a *suku*. But I didn't care. If someone told me, "Here work on this! Fix this!" I'd do it willingly, because I liked doing it.

[Pointing to the pair at upper-righthand corner of figure 19:] This is the younger brother of the Pedanda of Gria Kawan. I am learning to sing *kekawin;* just like today, I still dare to go anywhere by myself, as long as there is someone who will teach me. His name was Ida Putu Renteh, he taught people. Today there aren't very many who know *kekawin*. I went there often.

Here I'm studying *kekawin*. It's almost twilight, and I've finished painting masks, and then I went here bringing a bottle of *tuak* [palm wine], because people drank *tuak* while they were practicing singing *kekawin*.

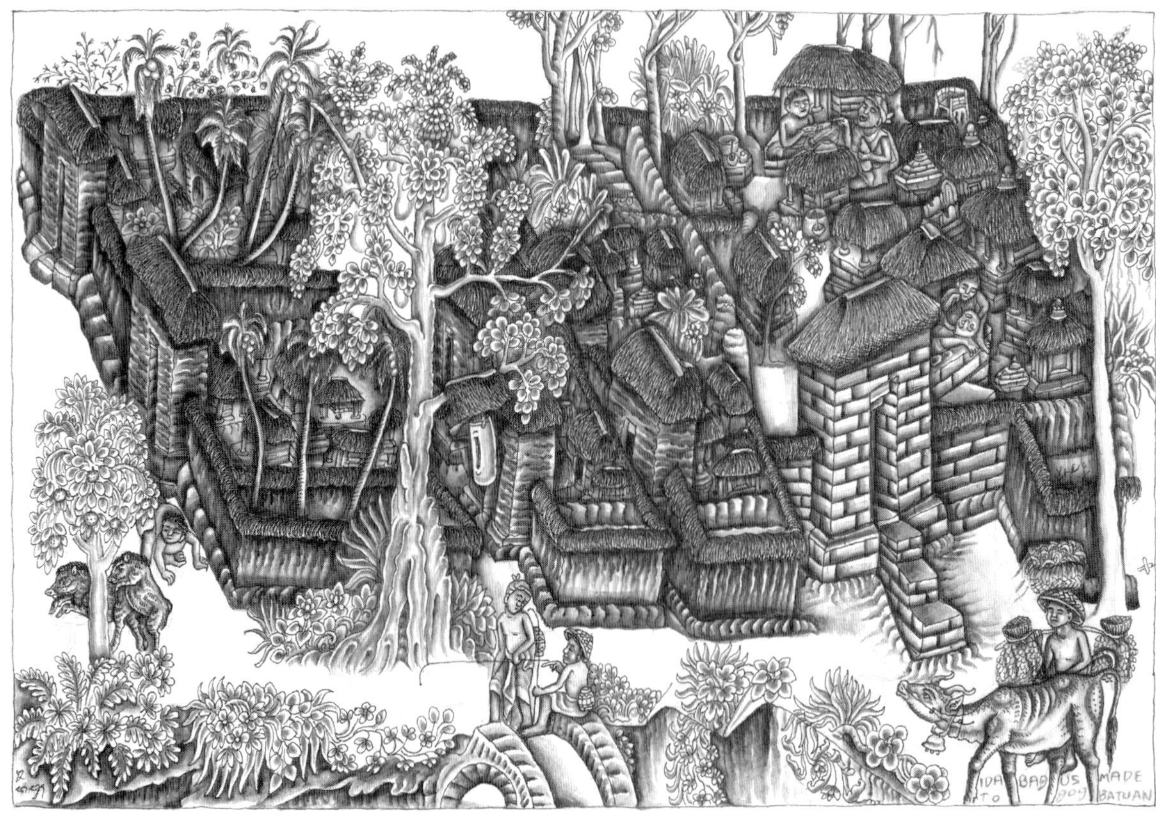

Figure 19. The neighborhood of Gria Kawan. Drawing by Ida Bagus Madé Togog, 1986.

When the old priest of Gria Kawan, I don't know his name, was still alive, I went to visit there. Someone said, "Well, let's go see Ida Aji." He knew how to paint masks, and when I went there, he said [in the low-speech register], "Take this one, and paint it!" So I learned how to paint. You know, in painting masks, you have to put on hundreds of layers, and then it will last and last. Those masks are still good today. I painted one mask there, which is now in the Dentiyis Wayang Wong, a Raksasa Cunguh Lantang, with a long nose and a white face. No one helped me to make it. It's still good today. My Uncle Nyoman worked there too, and he was given a sarong for his work, a very good and expensive one, old style. But I wasn't given anything for it; still I wasn't angry. I didn't put a high price on myself. So I wasn't angry that I wasn't given anything.

The following story, told in relation to figure 19, must be about Togog when he was a very small boy. It concerns the two pigs and the crouching boy on the lowerlefthand side of the picture. It shows Togog returning home late at night from playing the *gamelan* for the Prasutri dance.

Now here, there's a little path between the houses to the north of the *jero* [the Batuan noble house, or *puri*], coming from the west. There was a huge *poh* tree there, which had a lot of fruit, and below it grass. Now here I am, coming along it in the night—I had been at the Pura Désa, it was the time of the Prasutri ritual.

I had gotten tired of playing the gamelan, and so suddenly I just got down from the instrument. Every evening there were many young people there, and so for every instrument there were four people. The older players would let the children play first. Well now I was tired of practicing. Whenever they danced they told me to play, because I knew how to play the music for the Prasutri.

So now I was going home in the night. Now here I was under this tree, and it was very dark. And there were some pigs, bigger than me, who were making a rustling noise. So then I cleared my throat, so that if it [what was making the noise] was a human being it would know I was there. That's what I intended. So I crouched down, and took some leaves, some heavy leaves, and pushed them forward, making a scraping noise. But it just didn't make a sound.

"*Bah!* What's this? Is it the *tonya* [the spirit] of this tree?" I thought. Because it didn't want to leave. So after that I went on my way, but I went through the bushes. And when I came out about a yard, from the west, I heard the sound *"gegek-gegek"*—it was two big pigs, but they didn't make a noise. So then I went off to the east. I didn't dare go near them, so I ran. If they were human beings [that is, sorcerers in animal form], I didn't dare go near them. But I made myself brave and then ran by and away. It was very dark and there were these two figures, big and black, apparently crouching before me. That's all about that.

[Pointing to the two figures with fishing equipment, front center of figure 19:] This is me, waiting for my Uncle Madé Cukeng [from Gria Pacung across the stream]. He was very busy *(tuyuh)* at home, grating coconuts and squeezing out their oil, to feed to the pigs. So then he had told me, "Come and call for me! and then wait for me at the *balé banjar.* I'll come to you." That's what he said.

So then he was at home and he said, "Well, how can I do that work—I've promised I Madé from the south." ["I Madé from the south" is Togog, whose home was to the south of Uncle Madé's. Since Togog was also Brahmana and younger, he is referred to and addressed merely by his birth-order name, Madé. See Chapter 2 for several other stories about going fishing with Cukeng.]

"Well, what can you do, I'll do the grating," said his brother's wife. He didn't have a wife, he was ordered around by his sister-in-law. He was afraid that she was going to give him too much work. So here I am waiting for him. And then he came, and here we are talking about where we will escape to, and I said, "Let's go to the Tanu River, that's faraway." We didn't get back again till late afternoon.

Now over here [at lower right of figure 19] is someone with a bull. He didn't dare come near us because his bull was easily startled, so we left quickly.

Gamelan Playing and Dancing

Batuan had a special unique ritual that was performed almost nightly for four months. It extended from the dark of the moon in October, the Balinese sixth month, to the dark of the moon in March or April, the Balinese ninth month. During this entire period the gamelan was played nearly every night, accompanied by singers called *tandak,* and all the women and girls of the village would dance a slow, stately but erotic dance called the *rejang* or *prasutri.* This ritual dance was intended to divert through seduction the coming of the demon-king Ratu Gedé Macaling, who threatened to inflict epidemic diseases, such as cholera, on the population. All members of the village, young and old, participated. Small boys were encouraged to play and young girls to dance. For many these were their first lessons. Sometimes other performances were put together for the event, and cockfights, which are offerings of fresh blood, were also performed almost daily. (See H. Geertz, *The Life of a Balinese Temple* [2004].) Figure 20 shows the temporary rain shelter for the ritual, Togog playing a gamelan among the adults, the row of village women and girls dancing, and, at the right, the altar to Ratu Gedé Macaling and other spiritual beings.

The *Prasutri* Dance

At the big ritual, the Pura Desa every year beginning in the sixth month, I learned how to play the gamelan. They were playing the gamelan for the ritual *prasutri* dance.

I was very good at playing the music for the *prasutri.* I played the *gendér,* which is placed out in front of the rest of the orchestra. I played the overture before the dancing and then the "Bapang Sisir" music. And then we usually played "Lasem" and "Kuntul." I liked playing up front but I always lost out on the food. They would bring sweets and fruit to the gamelan players, but I wasn't bold enough to smack my lips right up there in front of everyone. *Badah!* Those in back, the *klenang* players, could eat all they wanted and even had more to take home with them.

Dancing the *Gambuh*

The *gambuh* dance is a dance-drama genre that, in Batuan, has been an important element in the rituals in the village temple, Pura Désa Batuan. Traditionally, the Brahmana contribution to those ceremonies has been the performance of the *gambuh,* and it was the Brahmana Buda who were the main participants. When Togog was young, the leaders of the dance aspect were Ida Bagus Kompiang Kuruh, who lived next door to the east of Togog's house, and Togog's Grandfather, Ida Bagus Gria. I Nyoman Kakul, a commoner dancer of great talent and reknown, about ten years older than Togog, danced with the Brahmana and taught many dancers.[2]

Togog never danced more than bit parts, but later in the 1950s and 1960s, when the Brahmana group set up a semiprofessional troupe, with more rehearsals and better costumes, Togog was a member, serving as a source of plots.

The *gambuh* dance in Batuan almost always had a highly amateur quality to it, as to dance in it was considered a required act of respect to the deities.

Figure 21 shows Togog dancing in the *gambuh.* He poses in front of the small structure at the left, a curtained booth out of which each dancer emerges to begin dancing that is flanked by two ritual umbrellas. The two objects in the middle of the performance area are oil lamps, decorated with palm leaves.

When I was young, I Kakul told me to learn the dance of the *prabu* [a princely role in the *gambuh*]. My Grandfather taught me, and I practiced here at home, just outside the yard here. There was at the time a temporary shelter where we practiced dancing. I wanted to learn, but I Kakul didn't want very much to teach me. So I didn't go there to his house to study. I didn't feel like going there. I stayed and practiced with my Grandfather.

He would tell me the stories and the steps right here in the houseyard, "This is the story; and then, when this story is done, do this story—go here, and go there." I learned the Rajasinga cold. My Grandfather was a dancer, but when he was old he wasn't strong enough to dance anymore.

I was glad to spread the knowledge of the stories, because it helped me cover up the confusion in my heart due to what was going on at home because I was so spoiled there. My Grandfather and his wife had a lot of property, gold and other things, and they would not have cared if I used it all up.

I often danced in the *gambuh.* I danced Semar or Turas, in the Pura Désa. And I went with Ketuté to Gianyar to

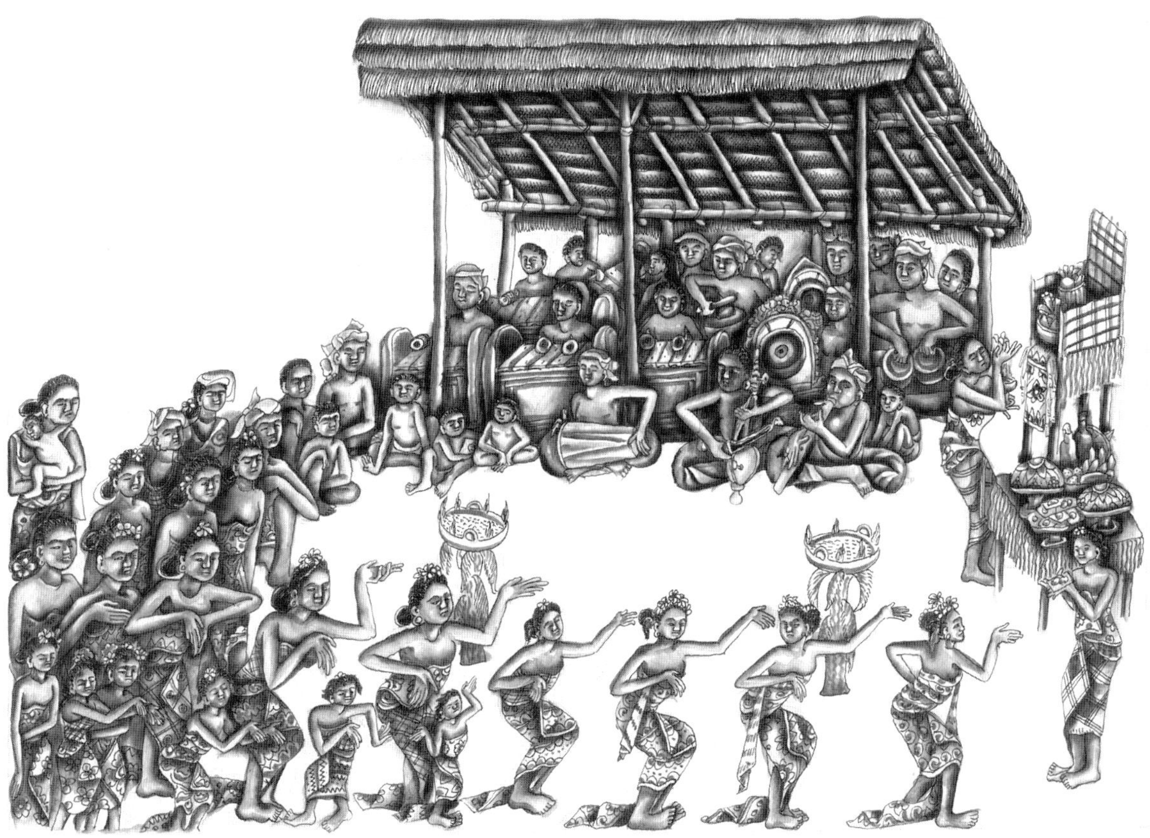

Figure 20. The *prasutri* dance at the Pura Désa. Drawing by Ida Bagus Madé Togog, 1986.

perform. I was the main source for the stories there too. We also went to Pliatan and other distant places.

"Ketuté" was Déwa Ketut Baru who was my landlord (see Introduction) and also a longtime friend of Togog, dancing with him in the *gambuh,* studying *lontar* with him, and for a number of years accompanying Togog when he assisted "his" *pedanda* (Togog's father's half-brother) in rituals (see Chapter 4).

Nowadays there are people who come to me to ask for help with the words of the *gambuh,* or of the *wayang wong,* or the *parwa* [another human shadow play with plots from the Mahabarata] and even the *wayang*—for instance, the story of the Bratayudha.

And also, when it comes to the content *(indik)* of the *gambuh,* it is in the *tandak* songs. I know the *tandak* songs and also the *waséng* songs as well. I taught them to the younger brother of Déwa Ketut Baru [Déwa Putu Beratha], because his voice is very supple *(lemuh),* so that he could sing the *tandak* in the *gambuh.* There are twenty of them. I did that so that the new little shoots would grow.

[Sings:] "The road winds and winds, here is a ravine *(asiluk-siluk marga ana jurang).*" That's one of the songs. I didn't give them to the dancers, because then when they danced you could not tell that they had studied anything. I felt very sad. That's why I went over and over in my heart

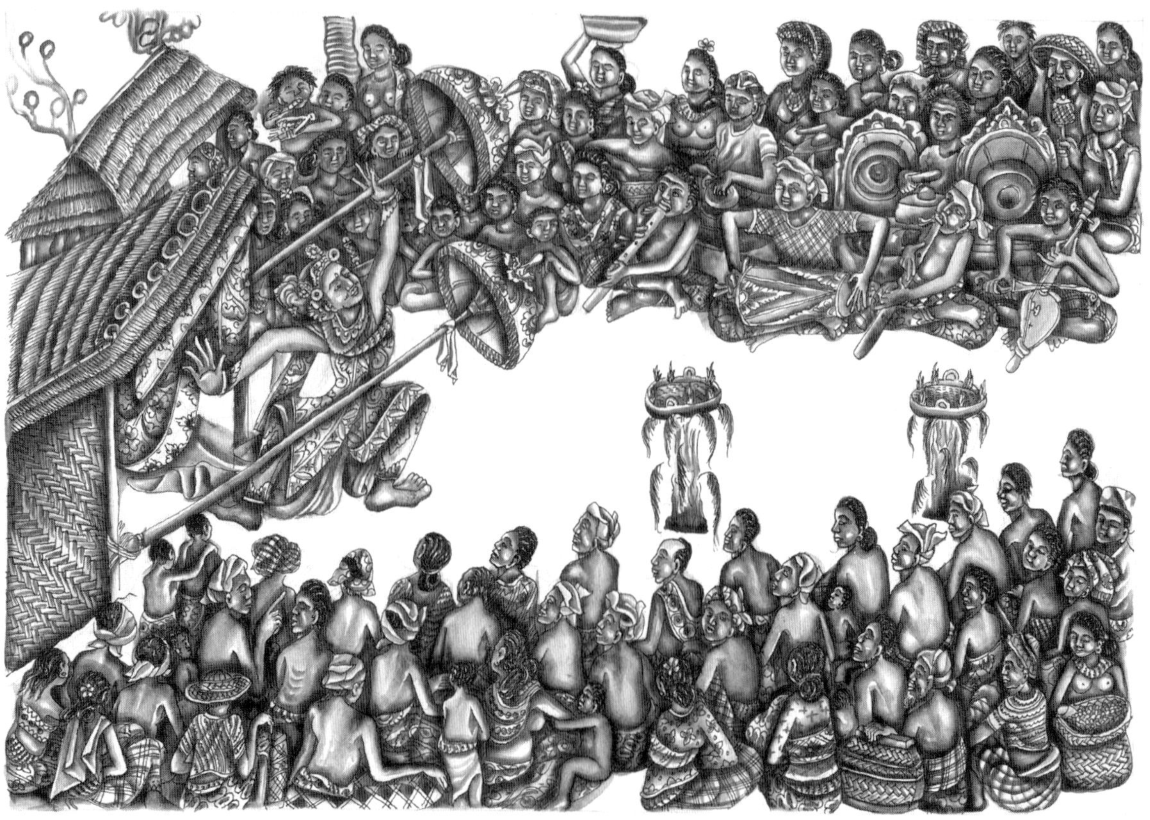

Figure 21. Dancing the *gambuh* in the Pura Désa. Drawing by Ida Bagus Madé Togog, 1986.

thinking I should not dance in the *gambuh* anymore. I also know the speeches of the Ramayana, of the Bratayudha, and also the Wiwa *(Wiwaha)*, and people often ask me for those stories. The same for the *gambuh*, I can give you the stories of the *gambuh*, but forgive me if I make any mistakes.

In the previous year, Togog had been interviewed by Adrian Vickers about the *gambuh* songs and stories. Perhaps this led him to stress them to me. Vickers supplied me with the translation of the line given above.

Now I don't know how to write *(surat)*. I don't know how to write, but I can read *(maca)*. If I'm allowed to read the Parwa I can do it. I've read even in Karangasem once—it was translated by someone from there—and I made no mistakes. Just exactly, exactly *(tet tet tet)*. I could read anything they gave me. I often read from the Parwa there, and it was translated by Ida Kakiang from there [in Karangasem]. Many readers *(juru paca)* have to be corrected: "Well there was something lacking, like this, and something lacking, like that!" I've seen that happen often. But never me. Ask Déwa Ketut Baru. I've gone far away—to Tengenan, to Sawan in Beléleng, and other places, together with Desa Ketut Baru.

Once I danced the *prabu* in the Pura Desa. And when I was in the middle of the floor, dancing, I overheard someone on the side say, "*Peh!* He's a real dancer! I thought he didn't know how!" [Laughs.]

Speaking about figure 21: The *klian* that Togog

mentions below is the man who organizes the *banjar* contribution to rituals at the Pura Désa. Togog told this story interspersed with many long chuckles.

It's the *gambuh* at the end of the *odalan* of Pura Désa Batuan. It was four days long. And my *klian* told me to dance that evening. So I was willing. "Come along with me!" That's what he said. So I followed along. There was a person named I Merano who was learning too.

"If you dance like that, are you brave enough to go out in the middle?" I said [in low words].

"I'd dare to do it, Tu, I'll go along with you, Ratu."

"We'll follow you, the two of us," said the *klian,* "so there will be two of us following you"

"Yes," he said.

And so later, there was another who agreed to dance. I said, "Yes, if I am asked to dance by you, grandfather, I'll do it, so there won't be a lack of followers, I'll go along with you, Ratu."

So there were going to be three followers. [Togog and two other "followers." Beginners usually start with the "followers" role.] Then I put my costume on. I wasn't paying attention to whether the followers were there or not. There were many dancers there, already dancing in the center. And after them, someone called me, "Now, followers!"

But when I went out there, they weren't there! I got out in the center, and they weren't there. We were supposed to do the *tangkilan* [miming making obeisance to a king] dance, but I couldn't do it. There weren't any followers there.

So then here I am dancing. First you usually dance by the umbrellas, and that's what I'm doing here. To touch the umbrellas. After that you go out into the middle and dance. And so here is when they were calling for the followers [to come on stage]. But they weren't there.

Now, I had on makeup made of soot. A big mustache of soot. The one who put it on put a great deal of black on me, and when the sweat ran down, the soot ran with it. I got out into the middle of the floor, right in the *tangkilan* scene, and I just turned and went offstage because I was drenched with sweat and I couldn't stand it. Every time I wiped my face the soot smeared all over. [Laughs.]

He had put too much soot on me! [possibly as a joke]. I was right out in the middle of the dancing floor but I just wanted to quit. So I didn't dance, and walked off quietly. It wasn't that I didn't know the speeches. I knew all the speeches by heart, but I couldn't stand the sweat pouring out like that.

These are the gamelan players. There were a lot of them, all the little children knew how to play. A lot of them, because of the *prasutri* dance. The boys when they came home from taking care of the cows would then play the gamelan.

And these are the people watching. This pair here [indicating the two men in the lower left, talking to one another, one has a long index finger pointing] are two people from Sukawati, and one is saying "Hey, he knows how to dance!"

Dancing in the Calon Arang

The Calon Arang was another dance-drama often presented at the *odalan* of Pura Désa Batuan. It is the story of a powerful witch, or Rangda, named Calon Arang, who is opposed by a *pedanda* named Begawan Kasiapa. The Calon Arang is a particularly *tenget,* or spiritually dangerous, dance, as its performance evokes the presence of human sorcerers. In the performance described below, Togog plays the part of Begawan Kasiapa and a commoner villager plays the part of Punta, one of his servants.

Another time I was told to dance as a *pedanda* in the Calon Arang, as Begawan Kasiapa, who goes up against Rangda Ning Dirah [the queen who transforms herself into Calon Arang, a Rangda]. I had looked up the Calon Arang story. Someone from here had gone to Kedisan to borrow the *lontar* of Calon Arang, and I memorized it as the basis for the dance. I wanted to have it as a pattern for myself that would be full and complete. That's why I borrowed it.

After that I went to talk with a shadow master *(dalang),* a Gusti from Sukawati, from Banjar Tameng. He often performed the Calon Arang in the shadow play, and so I went to him and asked him to explain parts of it, and he told me. That's why I dared to dance with the Rangda. It was a very dangerous *(tenget)* Rangda.

But while I was dancing, the man who danced Punta wanted to make me lose face. His name was I Kontok. In the middle of the performance he said:

> Punta [Kontok]: "I Ratu, please come out and come to the aid of your people!"
>
> Begawan Kasiapa [Togog]: "Yes, I'll try to see what I can do. But I'll study the situation first. If I do well, don't be too pleased, and if I don't do well, don't be too disappointed. Because I'm still learning."
>
> Punta: "Well, which *kanda* do you know? Do you know the *kanda mpat?*"

That's what he asked. He just wanted to defeat me, to show me up as ignorant. So I answered, as the *pedanda,* using very low words like *cai* [for "you"]: "You should not ask a *pedanda* about the *kanda mpat.* If I wanted to, I could tell you about them in thirty *kanda,* but I would not reveal it [my knowledge] here [in front of so many people]!"

The term *kanda* has two unconnected meanings. The main one here is "brother," as in *kanda mpat,* "the four brothers who are godly beings are within each person." These four beings are spiritual guardians of each person. The second meaning of *kanda* is "chapter" or "section," of which there are thirty in the Mahabarata epic. Punta is asking about the *kanda mpat,* but Togog felt that the subject of *kanda mpat* was dangerous esoteric religious knowledge, not to be broadcast publicly.

That got him! He wanted to one-up me, that dancer, but he lost!

I said, "I know thirty *kanda* ["chapters"]. If I didn't, I wouldn't dare come on stage."

He wanted to know about the *kanda mpat,* but I wouldn't tell him. I just kept silent. He didn't get what he wanted because I didn't want to tell him. If I had wanted to I could have told him all about the *kanda,* about the four, the five, the one, and even the one-half *kanda.* I said: "Who the *kanda* are can only be told in the right place. You should not ask a *pedanda* in this place. If you went to a *pedanda* and requested humbly his answers to your questions, he'd tell you, but not in public like this. These matters should be kept secret. If you want to know about them, go to a *gria* and ask there," I said.

He couldn't move! I was amazed that he wanted to match wits right there on the stage, in the dance! That's not good, to raise those matters in public. Even today he's not a popular dancer, not good on stage. Before he comes on, he thinks he's very smart, but when he gets out there in the center of the stage, he isn't. It's very difficult for him.

This anecdote provides a vivid example of how real life and drama fuse in Bali. Togog, a Brahmana playing a Brahmana priest, is challenged by a commoner playing a clown to joke about the *kanda mpat,* a set of powerful *niskala* beings who inhabit each person's body, monitoring their acts and circumstances. Judging that this is a topic too dangerous to laugh about, Togog—both in role and in his own voice—shifts from comedy to sermonizing.

Storytelling

Telling stories to another—an old lady fascinating a circle of neighborhood children in the night, a parent putting a child to sleep, a convivial drinking session in a local *warung,* friends enlivening a long trek through the mountains—was a prized activity in Bali (at least until the recent age of television began). The same stories were circulated in various forms, not only in informal family talk, but also through songs and plays. Many of the songs that Togog treasured were *geguritan,* also called *gending,* popular songs in vernacular Balinese that either tell stories or are sung at key moments in the plots of the Balinese "operetta," the *arja.* The *kidung* and *kekawin* of which Togog has already spoken are more refined songs in the language of *kawi,* which is understood only by a minority, and comes from the *gambuh* dance-drama and the shadow play.

The plots of all of these dramatic productions were recounted orally in many kinds of informal situations. This complex ecology of circulating tales in varied forms in Bali has never been studied in a systematic way. Narratives of all sorts, from the informal to the performed, with their dialogues and foreshadowings and surprises, permeate Balinese life. In Togog's generation, in the absence of the competition of television and books, there was a constant oral dramatization of life experiences in all sorts of contexts.

These stories do not fit most Western generic distinctions, which attempt to classify them by function and epistemological status. They are neither fiction nor fact, never simply "myths" or "folktales" or "children's stories" or "comic anecdotes." As with every other kind of utterance in Bali, any recital of tales has a potentially practical effect. Just to name a character, or to speak about Arjuna or about the *tonya* who lives in a nearby river may have immediate consequences. The story related in Chapter 2 about the *tonya* of the river between Batuan and Negara concerns the real-life danger of drowning in its waters. Another example is the popular plot of *arja* dramas about the brothers Cupak and Grantang, which is too dangerous to dramatize in Batuan, perhaps even to tell, ever since a tree fell on a performance and injured several spectators. Five of the painters of the pictures collected by Mead and Bateson did illustrate the Cupak story—perhaps pictures made for foreigners are exempt from these perils—but none were willing to relate the story to the anthropologists as they did for all the rest of their pictures. The peril of telling the Cupak story lies in the possibility that there might be listeners who are invisible *niskala* beings present at any storytelling session or dramatic performance who might be enraged by some aspect of it. Storytelling is, at least potentially, not mere entertainment, or even merely the construction of moral and cosmological truths, but also an element in the constant negotiation of relationships among listeners and reciters, both human and nonhuman.

The anecdotes that Togog tells about himself greatly resemble the many folktales and drama plots that Togog himself delighted in recounting, in their prevailing form of direct dialogue, their minimal concern with inner states of emotion, and their assumptions about the marvelous nature of human existence.

Learning New Stories from Pedanda Kerta

Pedanda Kerta of Gria Kaliungu in Badung (Denpasar) was a distant kinsman of Togog, a fellow Brahmana Buda who grew up in Batuan, then moved to Denpasar. The Pedanda had been appointed by the colonial authorities to serve as a judge (*kerta*—hence his name), and in consequence had become very rich. Togog remembered when he was a boy that Pedanda Kerta had contributed the major share of materials for the restoration of their clan temple, the Pura Panataran Brahmana Buda.

Togog got to know Pedanda Kerta in Denpasar when, as a youth, he became spiritually polluted and went to him for advice (see Chapter 5). They became friends, and whenever Togog was selling pictures in Denpasar (as recounted in Chapter 6), he'd go there to stay overnight.

Once I went to Gria Kaliungu, the home of Pedanda Kerta—he was a judge in Badung. I went there because I wanted to hear more stories from him, and to make my heart straight. I felt when I went there as if I had just had a purificatory ceremony over me. Good food would not equal it in goodness.

Pedanda Kerta told me stories because he loved me so much at that time. That was because his grandchildren were never at home, so every day the house was empty. And his son—whom it was appropriate for me to call "father" so I addressed him as "Po Ketut" [Uncle Ketut]—was never at home because he was working for the government. And his children were all in school—now, today, they all have high positions in the government.

When I visited him, the Pedanda hardly wanted to sleep because of his pleasure in talking to me. He would tell me the story of how when he came to Badung he was very, very poor, and how it happened that now he did not lack for anything. He owned three hectares of rice land that he got after becoming a judge.

When I came in that night, he said, speaking down, "Hello, what brings you here at such a late hour?" because it was, as we say now, past nine o'clock at night. And I told him about what had just happened to me [see Chapter 6].

"Ah, don't do that! Don't ever sleep in that foreigner's house," he said. "Don't ever sleep there, it is better if you sleep here." He said that because he was strict and good. "When you come here you don't have to bring anything," he said.

And he told me about his life, so that I would be able to imitate it.

"This is the way it was, Madé. When I came here I didn't have anything at all."

And then he told me about the big court case that he had been able to settle. It was a legal dispute that had gone all the way to Java [to the higher court there]. "Even those people in Java couldn't settle it!" Finally, the case came before him as judge. "I was able to settle it, even though the case had been going on long before I became a judge. This is how it was: There was a man who didn't have any children, so he asked someone for a child to adopt. He was a very rich man. And after he had adopted the child, he himself had a child naturally. So then, a long time later, when they had both grown up, the natural son sued the adopted son for the inheritance. But the adopted son wouldn't settle, and they couldn't resolve the case in Bali. Between the son from birth and the son from adoption!"

So then he told me how, when the case came before him as judge, there was also a foreigner there—I forget what they called that foreigner who was the highest authority—and he told the foreigner [speaking down and referring to himself as Kakiang, "grandfather"], "This is easy for me to solve."

And the Pedanda suddenly grabbed the slippers off the feet of the foreigner and put them up on the table.

"Tuan, these are your slippers. If I ask for them and you give them to me, who owns them then?"

"Oh, you would own them then, Pedanda" [speaking respectfully].

Well, it is the same in this case. The one who owns the estate is the adopted son, because he was given it all. The original owner gave it all to the adopted son."

So, long after that, there came a present from Buléléng [where the adopted son lived], a *lontar* and a great deal of rice. I can't tell you how much rice, but it was more than enough.

And then, much later, when the Dutch official over the judge checked up on the judge's salary payments, he found he'd only been getting about 20 *rupiah* a month, when it should have been about 40 or 50. [He discovered that the payments to the judge had been being siphoned off regularly for years by someone else, so that he'd been receiving only half of his due, and the Dutch repaid him for that entire period all at once.]

The Dutch official asked the Pedanda, "Pedanda, how much have you been receiving every month?"

"This much, and this much." And he added it up, and then the foreigner said that the Pedanda should have been getting much more. And then the foreigner said, "Here, take this home." And he gave him a whole can of silver *ringgit* coins.

"He gave me a canful of money, a canful of *ringgit!*" So then he brought all the money home. It was so heavy he had to have a policeman carry it for him.

And then the policeman asked him, "Please give me five *ringgit* to buy some coffee in the future."

"Oh, that's not proper," said the Pedanda. "It's not right for me to give you that money," he said. "I'm going to give you something, Wayan, but in another place, and of another kind."

So, some time after that, the Pedanda invited all the officials and government employees in Badung to a big party (*pésta,* Ind.) in the *gria.* He bought a huge tortoise so everyone had a feast. He took that money and bought food for all, and with what was left over he bought three hectares of rice fields. It was a whole canful of *ringgit*s because he had the right to a payment of 40 or 50, and he had been getting only 15 or 20 every month.

I went there to visit the Pedanda very, very often in my youth, and he told me many other stories, such as the Uncara Karna [Kunjarakarna] that took five visits, I think. And then he also told me the story of Aget and Lacur ["The Poor Man and the Rich Man"; see below]. They were all very important to me, for they all had morals.

The old woman, Désak Watin, had told me many other tales, but the stories the Pedanda told me have stayed with me throughout my life, as guides. I'll tell you one of those stories in a little while.

The Pedanda said to me, "When I came here from my birthplace, I had nothing." He had come from Gunungsari, in Pliatan. Well, now he was very rich, with lots of rice fields. Ever since he became a judge, he bought rice fields, and at the time he was telling me the stories he had a total of two hectares. They were south of the market of Badung, in Sanglah.

Much later on, after the world had changed, during the Japanese time, the Pedanda's son came to me in Batuan and asked me to buy him another piece of rice land. There were some people here who wanted to sell land, and he wanted me to bring them the money. But I thought to myself, "If I do that, I'll have to be in charge of that land myself the rest of the time. I'd have to be his farm manager (*sedahan*)." And I didn't want to be a farm manager.

Later, Togog's son explained to me that managing land brought potential trouble if the land was in pawn to another man who was then working on it as a sharecropper. Togog's job would have been to oversee the harvest to make sure the owner got his share of the crop. Further, if Togog arranged for the new owner to pay off the pawn money, the laborer would then be landless and would hate both Togog and the new owner for it.

"Why should I be his farm manager?" I thought. Since I didn't want to, I went up to Pliatan and found some land there for him, bought it from an Anak Agung in Pliatan. He brought the money, in two whole boxes, two barrelfuls of money. I sent it up to Pliatan, because I didn't want to be his farm manager.

Now I'll get back to the Pedanda's story. He said, "Well, Dé, that's the story of how I came to be rich. Now listen, and in the future when you are grown up, if you go through a time of poverty remember my story."

Now today when I think about it, there was no one in Batuan who could teach me stories of this sort and teach me moral philosophy at the same time.

The Story of the Poor Man and the Rich Man [Pedanda Kerta's story]

There was a very poor man and his wife. The poor man said to his wife: "Yan! Yan! We will prosper if you do the cooking while I work in the rice field!" ["Yan" is short for "Wayan," "firstborn," a polite way of addressing a subordinate.]

"Yes, that is good," said his wife.

"And if you can, Wayan, bring me something to eat in the rice field, for the work makes me hungry."

"Yes, I will. I'll come and look for you!"

So then he went to work. He farmed one field of rice. He prepared the soil, and he planted it, and then when he harvested it he gave half to the owner and he took half home. When he got the rice home, he divided it up into portions for each month, for cooking. He calculated it all out. But there wasn't enough. So then the man said to his wife: "From now on, each day, don't cook more than half a coconut shell *(patan)* of rice."

That's what they used to call them, *patan,* now they call them *kobokan.*

"Don't cook more than this much!" So his wife did that, faithfully.

The next time he cultivated two fields of rice. And after the harvest she took that rice and cooked only one *kobokan* full each day. She had to buy salt and spices, but the other things she took from her garden. And sometimes she would sell things from the garden to buy food for side dishes to eat with the rice. She never sold any rice. But when the end of the time came near, again they ran out of rice.

"Look how little there is! I had thought that we'd have more, enough to buy some clothes for us. Have you been cooking more rice than I told you to?"

"No, I cooked just as much as you told me to, husband."

"Well then, I'll try planting another field." And so this time he planted three fields. And when he had planted the three fields and they harvested the rice and they ate it, it was still just as little as before.

And at the end of the time, even though she had not sold any rice, they still didn't have enough to last them to the next harvest.

"*Badah!* What'll we do? We never have enough!" he said. "*Pah!* This is what we can do! Yan, go and make a *canang* offering, with all the necessary things in it. I don't know how to do those things. I am going to go to the *gria* and ask the *pedanda* for his help."

So she made it and he carried it to the *gria*. The *gria* was in Tanah Legit. When he came into the *gria* he found the *pedanda* seated, reading a *lontar.*

"Hello, why have you come here to see your father?" he said, speaking down. "Why are you bent down with that great load of offerings?"

"Oh, begging your pardon, Ratu, I have a humble request to make."

"Well, sit down there on the step."

So he sat down and then he said, "Oh, Pedanda, I beg your forgiveness for making this request, O Palinggih Pedanda, but I humbly beg for your blessings." That's how he asked for help.

"Well, whatever your request is, I will tell you what I know. I won't be stingy with my knowledge. Whatever I know I give to the world. If I didn't tell people what I know, I would be doing wrong." [This exchange between the poor man and the *pedanda,* and the *pedanda*'s reply, is a standard way of speaking.]

So the poor man explained what his situation was. And after he did so, the *pedanda* said, speaking down (using *cai* for "you"): "Oh, that's how it is. You desire to be no longer poor. Well, if I am to tell you what to do, you must steel yourself. Are you strong enough to do what I will tell you to do?"

"Yes, of course! Whatever I want to do I can do!"

"Now, listen. Tomorrow is Kajeng Kliwon [a day in the calendar when many *niskala* beings are present]," said the *pedanda* from Tanah Legit. "Now, tomorrow make an offering of flowers and betel chew *(canang)* and a small fire offering *(takep api),* and get some holy water and take it to the Balé Ageng, and place it there, and perform the wafting motion of offering *(ngayab)*. The meaning of *ngayab* is to give an offering to whomever it belongs *(dué)* so that he will bestow well-being upon you." [The term *dué* (high register, *druwé;* low register, *ngelah*) means "to own or to belong to." The Balé Ageng that Togog was speaking of was a great shed where cockfights might be held, but quite different from the *balé agung* altar found in the Pura Désa.]

"Go there to put the offerings out together with the fire offering. When that's done, hide yourself, so no one can see you. There are a lot of bushes and trees next to the *balé,* and you can hide in them."

"Thank you, Ratu Pedanda, I am very grateful for your compassionate help." And so he took his leave.

When he arrived home, he told his wife to make the offering with sweets made of golden bananas *(pisang mas)* and of no other sort. Each of these sweets must be divided in two. Those sweets are made of rice that has been soaked until soft, with sugar and bananas added. So she made these and then tied them up with a string.

And then he took the offerings to the great *balé* just before twilight [an hour when many *niskala* beings come out]. It was about what we might call today four o'clock. When he got there it was empty, and no one was on the road. That kind of *balé* was for the festivals of the palace, and usually it would be crowded there. But since it was empty, he went right to the center of the *balé* and placed the offerings there and performed the ritual wafting gesture.

And then he looked for a place to hide. And he said to himself: "If I hide over here, no one can see me. If I am all by myself here, no one can see me." He hid among the *jarak* trees, near some thorn bushes. Only one eye peeked out, so he could see. He hid his face behind leaves. He was eaten up by mosquitoes, but it didn't bother him, because he was so angry about the losses at home.

In the middle of the night, or as we would say now twelve o'clock, a man came in carrying a great purse. And he sat down in front of the offerings. He put down his purse. It was colored black and white *(poléng,* a sign of being *tenget* or *sakti),* and he opened it, and inside it there was a great signal drum *(kulkul),* and also in it there were a lot of *lontar* books with writing on them. He put these next to the offerings, and then he hung up the signal drum and then he beat on it.

The sound of the signal drum was this: *ték-ték-ték-ték-ték!*—like that, not *"tung! . . . tung! . . . tung!"* but *"ték-ték-ték-ték! . . . ték-ték!"* That's how it sounded. And after the drumming stopped, some people came. They came from the south, from the west, from the east. Some came in groups of eleven or ten. They all brought baskets with them—some carried them on their heads, some carried them on shoulder poles. Some even brought the kind of big baskets and shoulder poles that are used for carrying freshly harvested rice. They all gathered around the man sitting there. The ones who came from the south sat on the south. So it was crowded with people sitting there.

When they had all arrived and were all sitting down, he looked at the *lontar* and said to each one, "You go to the house of I Anu and look for . . ." and he told each one what they should go and get. "You four go and get those things." And so four of them went away. He named the owners of the houses they should enter. He said to two of them, "Go to the house of I Adegan, and each of you take two bunches *(tenah)* of rice from there, and take them to the house of I Anu!" [A *tenah* is a measure of newly harvested rice stalks tied in bundles. One *tenah* of rice is enough unthreshed rice to feed a family for a month.]

Well, the man's name was I Adegan. So then they were going to go and steal the man's own rice, and he knew that he had only four bunches left.

Because of that he wanted to go home, but he didn't want those people to know it, because he had heard the man order them to go there to steal his rice. So he tried to slip out of the bushes. And the thorns were going to scratch him, but he didn't feel the thorns because he was so angry. It didn't hurt him.

When he got home, his wife didn't know that her husband had come home. He picked up a big stick and hid himself in the kitchen. But first he took the ladder used to climb into the rice barn and threw it away. He threw it far away. If they wanted to climb up into the rice barn they couldn't, because there wasn't any ladder. He figured that the ones who were ordered to come and take his rice would come but that they wouldn't be able to get it. And he grabbed that big stick, and if they tried to climb up, he planned to spear them with it.

So then, when he was already, two men came in:

"*Peh!* Where is the ladder?" one said. "Where's the ladder? I can't find it. Look for it. Where's the ladder?"

The poor man was holding the big stick up, but he couldn't hit them—it was as if his arms were dead—he couldn't do anything—he couldn't move! So then those people were in the middle of his yard, and then they found the ladder. And then they climbed up and took down the bunches of rice: *blug blug blug!* He still couldn't hit them. So they carried the rice away, two loads. They put the ladder back where they had found it. They had taken the rice away, it was clear.

Later, after the daylight came, his wife woke up, and the man was still standing there unable to move, staring, holding up his big stick.

"What are you doing, husband?" when she saw him.

He told her what had happened, and then he said, "Try and see, climb up and bring some rice down. We won't be able to cook rice today. Yesterday I counted four bunches of rice left, and last night they took four away," he said.

"But where did you put the ladder?"

"Over there! I threw it far away because of what I heard them say last night." She looked for the ladder. He had thrown it really far away. And it wasn't just leaning there, but it was well hidden. If it wasn't fated by the Lord God, they wouldn't have been able to find that ladder.

So she found the ladder, and then she climbed up into the rice barn. When she got up there, the rice was still there! It hadn't disappeared at all!

"Hey, husband, you must have been drunk. You said they took away the rice, but it is all here still."

"Really?" he said. "Really?"

"Really, come and look for yourself." So he did, and there it was.

"*Peh!* It's a good thing I didn't spear them last night, if they were thieves they would have been killed," he said.

"*Peh!* How happy I am, husband! Now I'll go ahead and pound the rice to separate the grains from the straw, I'll pound one bunch *(tenah)*," she said. So she took down one bunch. But there were still four left!

"Beh!" said the husband. "This is what happened to me last night," and he told her all about it. "I went to ask for advice and help from the Pedanda, and he told me what to do. He told me that no matter what happened I should let them do whatever they wanted to do. That's why I felt so weak. I'm going to go back to the Pedanda and ask for an explanation. Whether or not someone came and took the rice, that's what I want to know!"

"Well, husband, if that's how you feel, you'd better go and ask the Pedanda." So then he went to see the Pedanda.

"Hello, look who's come to see me!" said the Pedanda.

"Oh please forgive me, Ratu Pedanda, I came to see you because I would like to tell you what happened last night."

"Well, it happened as I told you it would, didn't it?"

"Yes, Ratu Pedanda, it was terrible, and I'll never forget it as long as I live."

"Well, tell me about it." So he told him what had happened the night before.

"Well now I understand. It's because of the way you are. . . ." And the Pedanda addressed him as "Nyoman," that is, he spoke to him politely. He didn't use *cai* to him, but called him Nyoman. If you call someone Nyoman or Wayan, you are speaking politely *(basa)*.

"Well, this is what it all means, Nyoman. You should

not complain about your misfortune. You bring with you to your birth a certain lot of fortune and misfortune. Now you can understand that the man with the big purse was the person who allocates good and bad fortune to the people. He says to his helpers, 'Here pick this up, and carry it over to the house of I Anu, and carry that stuff here. Take this firewood and put it in the home of that other person.' The being with the *kulkul* drum, he doesn't do that work every day [but only on Kajeng Kliwon]."

But there is another moral to the story: a person's reward for good actions is not always direct. [A person whose rice harvest fails] may be rewarded with fruitful trees, or maybe with a specially thick growth of bananas, which he can pick and sell. That's the moral.

"Nyoman," the Pedanda said, "don't grumble and be sorry for yourself. That's the way life is, as I, your father, know only too well. I also am very poor, but I don't complain. I came into the world poor, but I was granted all this. If your share in this world is only a handful, don't ask for two handfuls." And ever after that the poor man did not bewail his lot.

This story may sound odd to a Western reader. To me the story seems to say that the reason the man was poor was that these mysterious men were taking away his hard-earned rice and distributing it to other people, and that he was able to prevent them from taking it by hiding the ladder. But the *pedanda* in the story—and by implication the *pedanda* telling the story—gave it another interpretation: that the poor man was fated to be poor and there was nothing he could do about it. When, after the event, the stored rice no longer dwindled even when the poor man himself took from it, this was also the operation of fate.

Togog's son, Gedé, in response to my questioning said that the *pedanda*'s interpretation was absolutely correct, and Togog himself agreed. He said he would have used different words and phrases than his father. For instance, the phrase that I translate literally as "the person who allocates good and bad fortune to the people" *(naké né mitehang gumdeparted kekéto),* he said, should be either *Tuhan* (the Indonesian word for the single God) or it should be *sané niskala,* meaning any of the multitudes of invisible beings. I asked Togog's son who the thieves were, and he answered that they were *butakala* or *gamang*—kinds of *niskala* spirits who were carrying out the wishes of Tuhan. The poor man must have done something wrong in an earlier reincarnation, or he may have been being punished for complaining about his poverty. When the thieves came to take his rice away, he was prevented from hitting them, again by a *niskala* being. Togog's son thought that the *pedanda* in the story was trying to get the man to see that everything that happened to him was the will of God and that he shouldn't complain about his life situation.

The belief that punishment is carried over after death into a subsequent reincarnation is called *karma* in Bali. This is an alternative notion to the more prevalent idea that suffering is the consequence of the anger of human sorcerers, ancestors, or local deities.

That's the end of that story. But here is another that he told me.

The Tale of the Poor Man Who Couldn't Give Offerings to His Family God [Pedanda Kerta's story]

There was a poor man. He was so poor that he had nothing with which to make offerings in his family temple. He didn't have any coconuts and none of the other things he needed. And it was the ninth month, the time to go to the sea with offerings.

He was squatting in front of his door, and he saw that the neighbor to his west was about to go to the sea. And the procession escorting all of the gods to the sea came by from the north. Well, he couldn't send anything, even in his own family temple. He felt very sad and so did his wife. They should have made an offering for his ancestors, for a god. His neighbor, a very rich man to the west of him was standing by the road.

Just then there came by a palanquin for the gods *(jempana)*, a yellow palanquin, like gold, with the sound of heavy footsteps, but carried by no one. No one was with it, and there was only one dirty parasol above it. When it passed by the door of the poor man, he didn't know that it carried his own god.

Now the palanquin of his neighbor was accompanied by many people bearing banners, and they all went down to the sea. The poor man just stayed there, coming out of his house at times, because he wanted to see them when they all came back from the sea.

So when they came back again, after having the ceremony by the sea, the palanquin of the rich man returned, and behind it the yellow palanquin with the yellow parasol. The poor man was watching it, and the palanquin turned right into his own house.

"*Peh!* That's the one who made that palanquin," said the rich man.

But the poor man didn't know that it was his, and when he saw it go into his house he said to himself: "*Beh!* Why is that palanquin all by itself going in here? Doesn't it belong to some other clan temple group *(pemaksan)*?"

He went into his house and then came out again, shouting: "Why, this is my own god here! That's what it seems like!" He went again into his house, and there was no one there but his wife.

"Hey! Man, Nyoman," he cried to his wife, "did you see that palanquin come in?"

"No, I've been busy cooking the vegetables here in the kitchen."

"*Peh!* That palanquin came in. That was our god. Don't just stand there. Make some offerings! Make the proper offerings!" So she quickly made some offerings.

Then the rich man came in—he just pretended he was paying a visit—there was no palanquin in his own house.

"*Badah!*" said the rich man. "This is God's act, giving each one his share!"

The poor man was given the palanquin because he had never complained about his poverty.

Yes, those are the stories that Ida Pedanda Kerta of Badung told me. The two stories are about wealth and poverty *(aget lan lacur)*.

Yes, that was the story told me by Ida Pedanda Kerta of Badung. Now, today, I am very grateful, because even today I use that story to guide my actions. Because of that story I was always able to rid my heart of bad feelings. Our share in life is given to us there in heaven. My house and my property here in Batuan—it is as if I am just a visitor here—even though in Batuan other people are rich, I just go along with what I have. I share with others the sorrows and the joys, so that I won't be left alone, so that there will always be someone to help me.

After that I took leave of the Pedanda in Badung. There is more that I could tell you about that time, before it and after it, but right now I'll close off the story about Badung.

The Story of the Greedy Man in Suarga

When I was going over the transcript of Togog's telling of the story of the poor man's offerings with him and his son, Togog said he wanted me to add another story here.

There were two souls in Suarga. Their time in Suarga was over. [The word "soul" is a translation for *atma*. *Suarga* might be translated as "heaven," but it is a place of punishment as well as reward. In some usages it appears as a kind of purgatory where souls stay temporarily until they are finally erased as individuals.]

Now they wanted to leave Suarga and they went to Betara Yama and asked leave to go. One of the souls had brought a lot of riches with him to Suarga, a whole basketful of gold and jewels, and he wanted it back to take to this world with him. The jailor said, all right, your belongings are in that house over there. So he went and opened the door and there were there many baskets of jewels and gold. These were to provide provisions for them when they returned to Bali. One of the two men took many more things than he had brought, because he was a greedy man. The one who stole so many jewels was then reborn as a poor man with nothing at all. But the honest one was reborn into a wealthy family.

That was the point of the story. The bad soul ended up poor like me.

Togog said that this story is in the *lontar* Atmaprasangsa. Togog's son added that this story explains why there are rich and poor in the world, why some people are born crippled, deaf, or dumb and so on. And why we should never complain about our lot in the world, because it was determined by our past actions *(suba-suba karma).*

Creating a New *Arja* Drama

Togog as an adult did not dance but occasionally joined in the planning of *arja* and *gambuh* performances. The following anecdote was told by him in connection with *arja* performances. It is about the performance of an old folktale that Togog had first heard at the knee of the old woman Désak Watin. The *arja* is a popular dance-drama genre that historically derived from the *gambuh* genre, has similar but much simpler dance moves, but in which the language is not *kawi* but everyday Balinese and the songs are from the popular genre of *geguritan. Gambuh* plots are drawn from a variety of sources, probably circulated orally in the main, but all are notionally set in the time of "Majapahit" and concern events that occurred in the competing kingdoms in Southeast Asia of the time, while *arja* plots may come from *gambuh,* but also from elsewhere.

Other people have told me how the old story was first made into an *arja.* They said that at one time in Batuan a crowd of young men who often convivially drank palm wine together once decided to build a huge kite. As they were working on it, they sang a lot of *geguritan,* popular songs that are often part of *arja* performances. It was during one of these sessions that the jovial crowd decided to form an *arja* troupe to perform for pay. One of the plots suggested was the old folktale of the Frog-Prince. One of the older members, a wood-carver named Déwa Putu Kebes, had concocted a new mask of a frog whose big lower jaw would open and close. This inspired them to use it for the Frog Prince story.

The tale of the Frog-Prince concerns the accession to the throne of the kingdom of Koripan. As Togog told it, there was once a prince who was born in the shape of a frog to the king of Koripan, who was horrified to have a son who looked like a frog and immediately exiled him and his mother to a forest. The prince grew up swimming in the pond of his palace in the middle of the forest, and then decided to seek a wife from among the princesses of the king of Daha. When he went to the king and asked for hand of the princess, her father was insulted and ordered him to be killed and chopped up into little pieces. With the help of his ancestral spirits, the Frog-Prince brought himself back to life. This happened twice, and finally the king allowed the marriage to take place. The Frog-Prince then was transformed back into human form, and when his father the king of Koripan came as a guest to the wedding, he recognized the Frog-Prince's mother, his wife, and then accepted his son back as heir to the kingdom.

However, the planners of the Batuan *arja* preferred a version different from Togog's in which it is the mother, not the prince himself, who asks the king for the hand of the princess and is chopped up into little bits, and then is brought back to life by the Frog-Prince. The producers of the *arja* perhaps thought their version more dramatic, or funnier.

The show was a great success. Then, after the war was over and tourists began to come back, a new, much simplified, dance-and-clown version was developed out of the *arja* version, using the same mask. It had simpler music than the *arja*'s *gamelan,* using the simple inexpensive bamboo Jew's harp with which Batuan boys amuse themselves. This tourist version became known in English as "the Frog-Dance."

Whenever they had a *gambuh* performance in those days, I was the only one who knew all the stories. Once they wanted to do the story "The Frog-Prince" in an *arja* performance. I knew the story, for it had been told to me by Désak Watin. I told them that story. There were about six versions, all about the same, but some were better than others.

It was the time when Anak Agung Gria here in the Puri, who liked flying kites, made a big kite at least two-and-a-half arms' span wide. And then he was arranging to put on an *arja* performance. And he asked me, "What would be a good story for the *arja?*"

I told him the story of the Frog-Prince, but he didn't like the story as I told it. He wanted the version in which the mother of the Frog-Prince is killed, but I didn't think that was proper. The proper version is the one in which the Frog-Prince himself gets killed. But they were the ones who were going to do the dance, and they didn't like that.

I said to Anak Agung, "Well if you want to do it that way, Anak Agung, I won't have anything more to do with the *arja.*" And to this day, when they perform the story of the Frog-Prince, they have the mother of the frog killed.

The reason I am against it is because of the moral *(indik)* it gives. If the mother of the Godogan is killed by the king, the king commits a major crime in killing a human being who has done no wrong. But the killing of the Frog-Prince, who is not a human but asks to marry the daughter of the king, is appropriate for a king. So, according to religious rules, the mother of the frog should not be punished. That's what was in my mind, what I was afraid of: "Oh, don't do it that way. It's not right for a dance performance." That was the way I interpreted *(mabak)* it.

When I went over this event with Togog and his son in 1984, Togog's wife's brother, Ida Bagus Diksa, was with us, and the three men had a spirited argument about the moral of the story. Togog's son, in particular, argued that Togog was wrong, that the version in which the mother asks the king for the hand of the princess was the right one. The king was right to have had Godogan's mother killed because she had committed several crimes: first, for suggesting that the princess marry an animal, and second, for suggesting that the princess marry a commoner. Togog, on the other hand, argued that the mother of Godogan had done no wrong and for that reason should not be killed.

Singing

Togog's pleasure in singing was bound up with his pleasure in storytelling, in dance-drama production, and in the performance of rituals. The kinds of songs that Togog loved to sing differed according to the contexts of which they were part: the *gambuh,* the *prasutri,* the *arja,* and convivial drinking sessions. Togog sang enthusiastically songs of all genres, from the classical and serious *kekawin* that he associated with his lessons among the Brahmana Siwa, to the *kidung* that is most often used in ritual accompaniments but also in *gambuh,* to the comical *geguritan* in everyday language that would not be sung in a ceremonial situation. Most of the songs Togog talked about were *kidung,* in which the words are in Literary or Old Balinese and therefore an adult accomplishment.

Another classification that Togog used for the songs is according to the story-cycle to which a song refers. Balinese songs are usually charged encapsulations of narrative moments, and the hearers can supply the framework of story that gives each song part of its sense. The song fills out the mood or the character of the personage portrayed.

Malat Songs

Malat and Waséng songs tell the stories of the adventures of Prince Panji, "the desiring prince" as Vickers has called him, who made amorous conquests in numerous kingdoms at the time of "Majapahit." These songs, in the form called *kidung*, are sung in the *gambuh*.[3]

Togog said that from early childhood he liked the Malat songs, but no one in Batuan knew them all. He'd pick up a verse or two here and there, at a *masangih* (tooth-filing) or at a *nyekah* (memorial ritual), but not at a *mabasan*—they don't do Malat there—and then go home and rehearse them. Then he would go to someone else and ask if they knew any. For instance, there was a *pedanda* in Celuk who knew a lot of Malat. And a man named Sibuh from Sélakarang, who when he found out that Togog wanted to know more about Waséng, told him there was a *lontar* with Waséng songs in Gianyar, and in fact went himself, borrowed it, and lent it to Togog so that he could copy it. There was another *lontar* in the *gria* in Sukawati where Togog was ritual assistant, which Togog borrowed but didn't copy because he could borrow it whenever he wanted.

It was like this: I wanted to change myself so that no one would scold or get angry with me anymore. I was looking for a way to change myself. I was looking for ways to make my heart good in the future.

So a desire to learn the Malat songs bloomed in my heart. Their content *(indik)* can be used for plots in the *gambuh* dances. They had nearly vanished *(putus)* and I was the only one who studied the *lontar*, who learned those stories by heart. Those Malat songs—there was no one else here who studied them as I did. I still know them, but no one wants them sung now.

At one time there was in Delod Pangkung a *gamelan gambang*. Those instruments have the same musical scale *(dong ding)* as the Malat songs. I went to the home of I Mojol, the head of the *gamelan* ensemble, to see if I could learn some more Malat songs. When I came in he said, respectfully, "Oh, what is it brings you here, Ratu?"

"I came to ask for a little help, Uncle." I answered [speaking down].

"What can I do for you, Ratu? Please sit down first." So I sat down there on the *balé dangin*, and then he asked, "What is it exactly you want?"

"I want to know if you know some of the Malat songs, because I'm learning Malat."

But he didn't know any songs. I didn't want to learn to play the *gamelan gambang* and didn't know the do-re-mi scale *(gegrantang)* of the *gamelan gambang*, so my visit was all for nothing!

After that try failed, I still wanted to learn them very much, so I went and asked other people. Those songs *(gending*, a synonym for *geguritan)* are called the Tantri songs, and I went to whoever knew them to learn them. I often went to Ida Bagus Putu Kompiang Awan and Ida Bagus Kompiang Kesiah, his younger brother, to learn new songs, and to Ida Bagus Madé Tupleng [these men were all Brahmana Siwa], who also liked those songs very much. Whenever I met him in the road I'd stop him and ask, "What is the meaning of this, of that?"

Once he told me the story of the coming of our family here to Batuan, from Gianyar. The story was that the Anak Agung of Gianyar had his *puri* first in the village of Beng [just north of Gianyar], but wanted to move to Gianyar.

There was a *gria* in Gianyar with a *pedanda* from my family, and he asked the *pedanda* to move away to Batuan, so that he could build his new palace, Puri Anyar, on the site of the old *gria.* And because of that the Déwa Agung family in Beng helped build this *balé* that we are sitting in now. They are our *sisia.* And in the past, my *pedanda* here was the Bagawanta of the *puri* of Gianyar. It still is today.

Tantri Songs: The Story of the Three Jeleg Fish

The term *tantri* is used by Balinese to refer to almost any animal story, although it derives from the name of the protagonist of the Balinese versions of the Indic Buddhist Jataka tales. Here Togog uses the term to refer to a group of popular songs in the *geguritan* form.

Now, another time, there was to be a visit of a queen to Bali, and they had a big festival *(karya)* in Gianyar. And everyone from all over Bali went. I went too, I was called on to work there, making pictures. They had it in the big square outside the *puri* there. They fixed up a big place for it like they do for the exhibitions *(paméran)* in Badung. I worked there, and they told us that whoever did the best work would get a prize. I went with I Sadeg from Banjar Tengah. He could make *wayang* figures and he brought some unfinished ones. His equipment was heavy.

This event must have taken place in 1935 or 1936 when there was a big exhibition of agricultural and craft products sponsored by the government. Togog said that it was at the time when the head of Gianyar was the father of Anak Agung Gedé Agung, who was called "Anak Agung Méstir" because he had a law degree. Togog's son questioned his father and others about this exhibition, and we found out that it was not the Dutch queen who had visited at that time but someone like a director-general. Togog and Sadeg, and others from other villages—*gamelan* players, shadow puppeteers, and so on—were picked up in a truck. There was to be a contest for the best *gamelan gong,* and the two competing were Tabanan and Pliatan. Pliatan won, Togog said, because Tabanan had too many *céngcéng* (small, high-pitched gongs). When they arrived, someone told Togog where to sit, and instructed him to draw before the audience. He did just black-and-white drawings and had brought his own ink and paper. I Sadeg was told to make shadow puppets for the audience, and his equipment for that was heavier than Togog's. They were given something to drink but no dinner. The *gamelan gong* demonstration was in the afternoon. People had to pay for tickets to get into the fair. Togog said that the organizing group did not want Ngendon to show his pictures because they were too westernized, but they wanted pictures like Togog's. There was also a contest for the best masks, and Togog thought that the best ones there were those made by Déwa Putu Kebes from Batuan, but the prize went to one of his students from Puaya. The main point of Togog's story here, from his own point of view, is that it was then that he learned some new Tantri songs from Sadeg.

They came here and got us and brought us in a truck, but they didn't bring us home. Someone said, politely, "It'll be here in a little while!"

Well, we waited a long time and it was dark and the truck never came. I guess they figured it would be a waste of a car just to bring two of us home. So then I decided.

"Yan, Yan!" I said because I couldn't remember whether Sadeg was Wayan or Madé or what. "Let's not worry too much about it, let's just walk home. We can tell each other stories as we go to keep our spirits up. We won't even know we're tired."

Even if we had waited for a car, none would ever have come. So he was willing, and we set off. We walked by way of Batuh.

He'd sing the *gending,* and he also knew how to translate it *(masanin)* [into ordinary Balinese]. It was the Tantri. I forget it now, but I used to know it by heart. It was the story of the Three Jeleg Fish *(Jeleg Tetiga)*. Two of them wanted to leave home, but one, the littlest one, didn't want to. And he said—this has a philosophical moral—"How can you leave your place of birth? If you do, you'll be destroyed they say!"

Togog told me a brief prose version of the story of the Three Jeleg Fish at another time. It went something like this:

Three *jeleg* fish lived together in a pool. The oldest fish told the others that their water was about to dry up. The middle fish said: "What should we do? Look at the sky. There are no clouds. There won't be any rain. What should we do?" The oldest fish said, "We should all three leave this pool now." But the youngest fish said, "How can you say that, Older Brother? As for myself, I grew up here in this pool. It's my place. Now if you look for a new place to live, where will you put your temple? Certainly harm will come to us if we leave here. If you two want to leave, go ahead. I'll stay here." And so the two left, and they were both caught, killed, and cut up. But the littlest fish stayed loyal to his home. He hid under a rock and he didn't dry up.

This story contains another one embedded within it, for the youngest fish, in making his case for staying, tells his brothers the story of Ida Bagus Batur Taskara. The story of Batur Taskara is one of a criminal priest who is exiled from his home, but tries to return and is killed by the local populace. The youngest fish told the others that if they left the pool, like Ida Bagus Batur Taskara they would never be able to come home again and would be killed. This song about Batur Taskara was sung and danced in Batuan in 1948 as part of a punishment of a group of Batuan Brahmana and commoners who attempted to oppose the power of the royal house of Gianyar. (See H. Geertz, "A Theatre of Cruelty: The Contexts of a Topéng Performance" [1991].)

So we went along like that, telling stories, and when we arrived here in Batuan at the crossroads, Sadeg suddenly realized, "Oh! I forgot where I was, and here we are in Batuan already!"

So then we parted, he went west to his home and I came here. Because he liked listening, and I likewise liked listening in turn, we were able to walk all that way easily.

"*Bah!* That was a very fruitful trip. I learned a lot," I said.

Soon after that there was a ceremony in the *désa* of Negara [adjacent to Batuan]. There was a performance of Cupak there, and my uncle Po Putu from Gria Kaliungu in Badung danced Cupak. I don't remember the story because what I paid attention to were the Tantri songs he sang at the beginning before the story began. They were wonderful to hear. The next day I went to his house because I wanted very much to learn those songs and any other songs Po Putu knew. I went to Badung to learn the Tantri song because in Batuan there was no one who could teach me them. I had just picked up parts here and there. So when I saw Po Putu, he said: "Hey hello! What brings you here without warning?"

"Uncle, I have a request to make. I need your help. There is no one in Batuan who can teach me. I've asked and they don't know the songs. That's why I came here."

"Well, what is it you want?"

"Last night you sang a Tantri song. Please teach it to me so that I'll know how to sing it."

"But how does that song go as they sing it in Batuan?"

So I sang it: *"Sedum titah tan kenéng linésan,"* which means "The lot that the Lord gives us cannot be changed." [The line, *Sedum titah tan kenéng linésan* is from the *gending* of The Three Jeleg Fishes.]

I just sang that much, because I wanted him to finish it. And then he said, "But you can already sing it!"

"That's all I know, and I'm not satisfied."

"*Bah!* That's as much as I know, just enough to use when I dance. I only know bits and pieces. I don't know the whole verse."

Beh! It was just a big loss! My trip there! I went all the way there and asked for the song, and I didn't get it! I wanted to find the complete verse of the song so that I could memorize it. I'd have to look for it elsewhere.

Waséng Songs

I always liked very much to learn new songs. Once I was told by my Pedanda in Sukawati to assist him at a ritual in Pliatan, at the Pura Desa Pliatan. The place where the Pedanda was to sit was very, very high with steps made from concrete.

When the ceremony began, some people started to sing *gending*. The first one they sang was "Wargasari." Then they did a song that I didn't know but I liked very much. No one in Batuan knew it. But when I asked, they told me that the song had *come from* Batuan.

So I told the Bendésa of Pliatan [in words of low respect, for the *bendésa* is a commoner addressed as Wayan, "Yan"].

"Yan! Yan! Go and find me someone who can sing that song for me! Someone who knows it well so I can ask him all about it!"

He answered, "That's Pekak, Ratu. Over there, Tu" [respectfully].

"Tell him to come here and teach it to me!" I said. So then he climbed down slowly from the high place and went to look for him.

"Kak, Kak, that Brahmana wants you to climb up there to see him!" [speaking familiarly].

"Whatever for?" He thought it was the Pedanda who was asking for him, but it wasn't. It was me.

So he climbed up.

"What is it you want, Tu?" [respectfully].

"*Beh!* I want to ask you something, Pekak. What is that song you were singing before? We don't know it at all in Batuan. They say that Batuan is the center of songs, but that one isn't known there. That's why I wanted to ask you for it, Pekak. I really want to learn that song from you, Pekak," I said, speaking down to him.

"Oh that's the 'Waséng.'"

"Oh, then that's the 'Waséng' about the kingdoms of Koripan and Daha. I'll come over for it to your house in two days, Pekak!" I said then.

"All right, Tu. Come to my house and I'll sing it for you—I'll teach you whatever you like as long as I know it." he said. So then, two days later, I didn't have to help the Pedanda, so I went to his house.

When I got there, a shadow puppeteer, a *dalang* from Pliatan, was waiting for me. I Pekak had invited him so that they could sing together. So when I arrived they greeted me respectfully: "Hello, Ida Bagus Aji! Please be seated here! Yes, yes." So then I sat down there. [Ida Bagus Aji is a title given to a man who has children, indicating that Togog was a father by that time.] And so did the *dalang*. First, I Pekak gave us a dinner. I overheard them in the kitchen asking, "What would be the right meat for him?" The food was very good.

And then when we were finished, he asked me this question, very respectfully. "Ratu, Ida Bagus Aji, I seriously request of you with all due respect, grant me the answer to this: in the story about Begawan Kresna Dwipayana, what is the meaning of his name?"

Now because I was going to ask about the song, I didn't put too high a price on my knowledge. "Well, this is how it is, Uncle," I said. "Kresna means 'sea,' Dwipa means 'mountain,' and Yana means 'place.' In the story, Begawan Kresna Dwipayana's parents were married there at Kresna Dwipa and he was born there and that's why he is named that ["the Mountain in the Middle of the Sea"]. That's in the Parwa." *Beh!* He was happy to hear my answer.

Then I Pekak came in. "These *dalang*s shouldn't be asking you these things," he said.

"Yes, it is all right for the *dalang* to ask me. We were speaking about the reason for the name of Begawan Kresna Dwipa Yana and for Begawan Biasa, the two of them, his two names. Biasa means "whatever you want"; that is, whatever he wanted he could get right away. For instance, if he wanted to have a child, right away it would be there." That's what I said.

So then he asked, "What is the reason, when there is

a *wayang lemah,* it has a *dadap* tree? Why do they use a string? What is the meaning of the money? Please tell me." And then he asked, "And what is the meaning of the screen?" [A *wayang lemah* is a performance of *wayang* in the daylight as part of a ritual. It has no light and no screen, but instead a string stretched between two branches of a *dadap* tree stuck in the ground.]

"If a person like me knew that, I'd be a *dalang,*" I answered. "I would like to know." So then he explained it to me. *Bah!* He was very happy.

Then suddenly I Pekak said, "Is it true, I Ratu, that you don't know the *gending* 'Waséng'?" Respectfully.

"No, Kak, please uh . . ." Speaking down to him.

"Yes, I'll teach it to you." He said politely.

He sang it then, but only one verse. And then I sang it along with him. [Singing] *"meh rahina, semu randi, hyang aruna"*—that's the way the song went. [Adrian Vickers translated this above line as "(It's) almost day, a glow of red, the sun . . ."]

"*Beh!* Do you have a *lontar* of this, Pekak?" I asked.

"Yes, I have, Tu!" and he went to get the *lontar.* "Here it is."

"Well, can I borrow it and take it home with me to the south?" I asked.

"Take it, take it!" So then I opened up the *lontar* and read it. It had parts of "Tantri" mixed in, and "Wargasari," too.

"*Badah!* This is all mixed up with other things! It isn't complete either," I said.

"Well, that's what the man in Batuan gave me, I Pageh, your servant *(parekan),* Ratu. He gave me this *lontar,*" he said.

"*Badah!* Really, I don't want this, for it only has part of the 'Waséng,'" I said. "I'll go myself to him and look for it!"

"Yes, go look for it, and if you find it, bring it here."

"Yes, I'll bring one here," I said. Just then some guests of his arrived, and it was almost twelve o'clock, as we say today, and so I said: "Kak! Kak! Kak! I'm going to leave now! I made a promise to a man who had a car to meet him right now," I said. In fact, there wasn't any car. But I didn't want to be given more food.

So then he said, "*Bah!* There is some food just ready to eat!"

"Ah, don't talk like that, Kak. I made a promise to meet a Chinese driver. Right about now he'll be coming from the north," I said.

In fact I walked home. There was no car. In those days there were very few cars. There was one, owned by a Chinese named Man Cingkang, a friend of mine. All the Chinese in Sukawati were my friends. Whatever they wanted I'd make for them if they gave me a model. Once a Chinese said to me, "Ratu, make me a lion. Here's a picture of a lion. I'm going to put it in my temple." I made it for him here, and then later he brought me a present.

So when I was back home again, I went to Silakarang, to an acquaintance named I Sibuh. "Yan, Yan! Yan!" I said.

"Hello, it's Gus Alit come to see me. What is it?"

"Wayan, do you know who has a copy of the *gending* 'Waséng'? Who might lend it to me so that I can learn it?" I asked.

"Yes, I'll look for it for you, Atu! Whatever you want, I'll get you, Ratu! I'll go to Abianbasé to my grandfather there to see if he has it. If I find it, I'll bring it to you in two days."

"Well, if you find it, tell him that I'd like to copy it."

"Yes, Ratu!"

So then two days later he arrived bringing the *lontar.* So I copied it.

I wanted to sing that song everywhere, in tooth-filing rituals and in *nyekah* rituals. [Tooth-filing rituals are performed as a mark of coming of age. *Nyekah* rituals follow cremations as a further severing of the ties between an individual spirit and its former material life.] So I copied it. I know it by heart. There were thirty-five verses. I memorized them all. I also know many of the Tantri stories and the Malat, including its *Pamungkah* [the introduction to a song]. Many, many!

Well! [After I learned all that, a year or so later] my

Pedanda went again to Pliatan, and he told me to assist him. In the home of the Perbekel in Pliatan. He was an Anak Agung. They were having a big tooth-filing ceremony there. *Meh!* it was going to last a long time, because there were nine people having their teeth filed!

So I went with my Pedanda into the household temple. And then the first person for tooth-filing came up. The *gender* started to play and someone to sing. But the first tooth-filing wasn't finished yet, and the singer stopped. He must have been afraid to go on. Maybe he knew more songs but was scared to perform.

So then an Anak Agung from Ubud sang. Very, very well! But he only knew one verse, just one stanza. "That's all I know! There isn't any more." he said, in familiar speech.

So then another person climbed up to have her teeth filed, but there was no one to sing. How 'bout that! And with all those important guests! There were Cokordas and Anak Agungs—lots of them! So then someone must have pointed me out and said: "Well, that Ida Bagus over there, the one who is assisting the Pedanda, from Batuan, he might be willing to. He knows how to sing."

So they came looking for me where I was next to the Pedanda.

"Ratu, I beg of you," the three important people said, very respectfully. "Would you be kind enough to do us a favor? We beg you to us give us the pleasure of singing a little while. Because the *balé dangin* is very empty and silent."

That's how they said it.

"*Pah!* I don't know what to say! I only know a little. And I'm embarrassed to say no because I have to stay and assist the Pedanda. If I wasn't by him, who'd help him?" I said.

"*Pah!* As for that, leave it to me. I'll assist him, Tu!"

"Well, if my Pedanda allows it, Nak Agung! It depends on him. I can't leave him!"

"All right!" said the Pedanda, speaking down to me, "Go on over there and sing! You can sing 'Sampik.' Sing 'Sampik' or 'Sinom!' Just so that there is someone doing the singing! It shouldn't be silent here." ["Sampik" is a very light and popular song from the *arja* that is much easier to sing than the other ritual songs.]

"Yes! If Ratu tells me to do so, I'll do it! I don't know much, but I'll try." I was really very confident because I often sang. I went over there then, and they put a chair up next to where the people lay whose teeth were being filed.

And then I sang. I sang four different songs. First I sang the Pemungkah Malat, and then something else and then another. The "Tantri."

Then the "Waséng." I had only sung one verse of the "Waseng" when in came Pekak.

"Why! There's my sacred one!" [*suryan titiang;* literally, "my sun," but meaning "a man from the Brahmana house to which I have ritual clientship ties"]. "Come here! Ratu, really! Aruh!" he exclaimed respectfully. "I love to hear such good singing. And I wondered who it was singing! That's that very song I taught you!"

So then we sang it together, the two of us.

We sang steadily through all the rest of the ceremony, for all eight of those people having their teeth filed, and I never ran out of new songs. In fact I still knew more. And then when we were finished, I thought to myself: "Why, I'm all ready now! Now, if my Pedanda will allow me, I'll accompany him like this! (Laughs.)

Badah! I would dare to sing as long as he told me to.

Pekak then asked me, "Where did you find that *lontar?*"

"Oh, I'll bring you it sometime," I said, but I never brought it to him.

So after that, whenever there was a reading of the classic books *(papacan parwa),* I would take part. I often went to the home of a certain Gusti, who was having a *nyekah* ceremony, and we read the Putru book.

This event must have taken place about 1960. Togog's son said that he remembered it happening and being talked about at that time. Togog said that when he first told me the story, he thought it had happened much earlier in his life, and that was why he had people calling him "Ida Bagus Alit" which would not have been the case by 1960, after Togog had matured.

Singing in a Procession to the Sea

Then, in Sukawati, the big people liked it very much when I sang the "Malat." I knew it. There was a well-known singer there who said to me: "Oh, why are you memorizing so many? You only need two songs, just two, and you can sing through the tooth-filing of twenty-five people."

"How can you do that, Uncle?" I asked.

"You repeat it again, but softly and slowly, so that the song is unclear, and then for variation you sing it very loudly."

"Well, that's a good way, Uncle," I said, "but I don't like to do that myself."

First I would sing *"Até sedeng,"* and after I sang *"Até sedeng"* I'd sing *"Perihen temen,"* and after *"Perihen temen,"* I'd sing *"Mamuit ngareng,"* which has the same meter *(wirama)*. And after *"Mamuit ngareng"* I'd sing something else.

When I got to the sea, I sang *"Wus manggeh."* I sang about eight there by the sea, eight stanzas *(pada)*, eight stories (*cerita,* Ind.). Then, when we got home again, we had a reading session with the translation done by my relative Ida Bagus Siwa. And with me was Putu Kompiang Awan—we were good friends, and we walked together holding hands as we sang the *kekawin*. When we got back home, they gave us dinner, and we didn't separate.

Many people asked us to sing. Once I was asked to sing for the Pura Désa Batuan. We sang first "Sinom," and after that "Dandang," maybe. There were a lot of people there, and we each sang a verse *(carik)*—a verse of "Sinom" and then "Ginada." I sang the *tembang* "Ginada."

The "Ginada" I liked very much, because within it can be found the basic rules of writing Balinese script, and also I liked the "Sinom," for it tells about Duryadana. I sang *gending* often at that time.

Singing at an Odalan at Pura Désa Batuan

So when they held the Odalan of the Pura Désa, the leaders told me to sing into a microphone. I was telling stories inside the *pura,* and my voice was broadcast outside it. I was often invited to do that during the time when I Pageh was Bendésa. I Pageh Lana, that is. He was the old Bendésa. His house is near yours, south of yours, the one that is abandoned and in ruins. That was I Pageh, the old Bendésa. He was so careful and honest that everyone liked him. He and someone else came to invite me.

This might have occurred in the late 1950s, as is suggested by the mention of a microphone. Togog's son said he remembered it, and he was about five years old at the time. Togog had been asked to *mabasan* with Cokorda Negara Karang (still alive in 1985) and Ida Bagus Tupleng. Just the three of them. But just before they started to read the *lontar,* I Pageh asked them to sing some *gending,* into the microphone, to make things more *ramé.* The *gending* are in *sekar alit* (a metric and rhyme scheme) and much simpler in performance, language, and form than the *kidung* and *kekawin.*

Singing at Pura Dalem Jungut

And then another time I was asked to sing at the Dalem Dlod [Pura Dalem Jungut]. Three people came to get me. I was the only one from here. I sang to greet the visitors from Sanur. People from Sanur often came there to the Pura Dalem Jungut, bringing their dances.

Togog later explained that "the visitors from Sanur" were there because some villages in the Sanur area had Rangda and Barong masks made of wood from trees in the forest of the graveyard next to Pura Dalem Jungut, which are especially *tenget.* They bring these masks up so that the *niskala* beings in them can pay their respects to those in the Pura Dalem at its *odalan.* The *pedanda* from Karangasem was a Brahmana from Gria Kerotok in Budakling, with whom Togog was acquainted. This must have been an especially important *odalan* to have the masks and the *pedanda* visiting from so far away.

I was asked to read together with a *pedanda* from Karangasem who was there to complete their rituals. I knew many of the people from Sanur, both the commoners *(kaula)* and the Ida Bagus.

One of the people from Sanur asked me, speaking down [so the speaker must have been an older Brahmana], "How come you're here? What are you doing here?" Because it was a temple for commoners.

"It's just because I like to be where lots of people are. I like crowds," I answered [in familiar speech]. "Wherever there are lots of people, I go there. If I don't like it there, I just leave."

The Philosophic Content of the Songs and Stories

Now I'll get back to telling you about how I completed my preparations for working as a ritual expert. I went on studying philosophy *(indik)* of the songs because I wanted to change myself, to get rid of the bad in me. And the best for its contents *(indik)* is the Boma, the song Kawin Boma [Bomantaka]. What was most important to me was the story. I wanted to know the story so that in the future I could make a picture of it, and so that, if asked, I could tell it. I understood that story very well. Those words entered me.

After I knew the song of Boma, I learned the Ramayana. I learned the story of the Ramayana, including the story of Wenara, the Kapi Parwa. I also learned the story of the Ramayana about the coming into being of Rawana—I know that too. And after that, I studied a mixture of things, the Uni Yoga, the Udyogaparwa, the Bratayudha, the Wiwa [the Arjuna Wiwaha]. I know the Bratayudha from the beginning, about how Rawana came from Suarga. And then I learned the Wiwa—and in that also I looked especially for the story.

I wanted to learn the story exactly so that it would be easy for me to make pictures of Arjuna so that they would be recognizable.

After that I studied Uncara Karma, which has a lot of stories in it, and then Sutasoma. The ones I learned the most songs from are the Wiwa and the Ramayana. I memorized so much of them that when we went to the sea with the gods, from the graveyard in Batuan all the way to the sea, I sang the whole time without stopping. And then the next month they had a cremation in Gria Pacung. So I went back to study and memorize some more. I wrote one on the wall so I could see it there—four songs *(gending)*. That's why now I know by heart hundreds of songs.

Now, I'll tell you more about the philosophic content *(indik-indik)*. Before I knew much about those matters I ate anything I was given, any kind of meat. If they gave it to me, I ate it. But then my Pedanda taught me: "Don't eat this, and don't eat that. That kind of meat you shouldn't eat. It's called *panca naka* ["five fingernails," or claws] because all the animals that have five fingers are the *panca naka*." One time [recently] some people made *saté* from squirrel meat, but squirrel is one of the *panca naka*. I was given some to eat, but I didn't want to say, "That kind of meat is forbidden food, so I won't eat it," so I just said, "I don't want any."

The other four of the *panca naka* are: monkey and tiger, that's three—isn't it?—three: monkey, tiger, squirrel. Oh, yes, and then there's the black squirrel. That makes four. One more, I can't think of it. There are five of the *panca naka* . . . Ah! Cat! That's the other one, like this cat here. [Laughs.] That food might be delicious but I've never eaten it, not allowed to because it is *panca naka*.

Some other advice that I was given in those days was, "If you take things belonging to someone else without their knowing it, that's stealing. And if you take, for instance, 200 *képéng*, you will feel as if you only had 2 *képéng*"—that will be your punishment for stealing. If someone like me were to steal, the punishment would fall upon all my descendants, my children, my grandchildren,

I Jana was wealthy and could afford the time and money to study the craft of being a *balian*. Later his younger brother became a *balian apun*—a masseur with healing hands—and his grandson became a *balian usada*—a healer whose strength lies in his *lontar*. I Jana is the same man who hired Togog to guard his crops against monkeys.

Once when I was at his place he said: "Ratu, Gus Alit, study hard the sacred literature *(sastra)*, Tu! When you fully understand it, when you really enjoy reading literature, I'll give you one of these *lontar*. There are some books here that once were among your family's sacred possessions. There are ten of them, but one of them, this one, is afflicting me at times. It prevents me from carrying out things that I want to do." [That is, the *lontar* itself is said to have a volition of its own, and it may therefore cause trouble to anyone who owns it illegitimately.]

The books he spoke about came originally from my grandmother the priest. She was as poor as hell. When her husband the priest died, she thought: "What can I do now, my body is very old, and I'm not permitted to carry things on my head. How will I feed myself?" [Most ordinary work of a woman involves carrying things, but since she was a priest, if she carried things on her head she would pollute herself.] So she sold the books to support herself, and these were the ones I Jana had.

I Jana said: "Later, when you understand these matters, I'll return this book to you. It's your sacred heirloom *(pajenengan)*. It will be important to you."

"Yes, if that's what you want to do, Bapa, I'd be glad to take it," I said to him, my servant.

Togog referred here to I Jana as "my servant," *parekan duéné,* perhaps because Togog is of the priestly class and I Jana is a commoner, and also because he has distant maternal ties with Jana and his family. But because I Jana was older and a wise man, he addressed the commoner in respectful language, calling him, also respectfully, "Bapa," which means "father."

Years later, I went back again to I Jana's house. By that time I knew a lot about *sastra*. I had memorized a great deal. He knew the sorcerer's lore *(désti)*. He was rich enough to buy many *lontar*.

I Jana said: "Take this *lontar* home, I give it to you. My older brother doesn't understand *sastra* and now you desire it. I give you this one that used to belong to your grandmother. Take it home."

So I took it home. And always, today, on the day of the Saraswati Odalan, we make offerings to it. My daughter here is very serious about making offerings for the gods.

Now I have long studied those *lontar* ever since and I still don't understand it all. I understand only a little of it. That *lontar* is called Candra Bérawa, and in it is written everything that has happened and that will happen. [Togog added later that it is the story of Begawan Kasiapa and contains *tuturan indik matulung,* "advice on curing."]

I soon received another *lontar,* this one from my Grandfather next door.

He said to me: "Here, take this one home with you, but don't let this book go anywhere else. It is a sacred heirloom of our family, and should stay with you in the future." It was about Begawan Mpu Barada and Begawan Mpu Bahula. [These two are legendary sorcerers who were *pedanda*. Togog said that the *lontar* tells how Mpu Barada meditated *(tapa)* and through that gained *sakti*.] If studied correctly, this *lontar* tells everything that Mpu Barada knew, all of his sorcerer's knowledge *(désti)* that he could use to vanquish his enemies, that he could use to dissolve even their desire to use sorcery against him. So I had just two books then.

Then I received another sacred heirloom. This one was some of the precious articles of clothing a *pedanda* wears when praying *(pamios)*. This is the story of the goings and comings of this heirloom.

My grandmother [the Pedanda] had used these garments as security on a loan—they said she got ten thousand coins—with the things as security. She gave them to a woman named Désak Mongkrég, who put the things away very carefully, high up under the eaves of the *balé metén.* Later Désak Mongkrég got pregnant but after only three months had a miscarriage. She had forgotten the *pedanda*'s clothing was there, and suddenly she realized that it was afflicting her. She said to me, "Now that I know what the matter is and because you understand about *sastra* even though you are still so young, take these home with you."

I said, "Well then, I'll pay you back for them."

"No, Ratu, don't say that," she said. "In holy respect to the old priest, I want to give them to you." So I brought them home too. After all, they were heirlooms from here.

Assisting *Pedanda*

I went to Gria Pacung [of the Brahmana Siwa of Batuan] many times. One time [when Togog was still quite little] the priest there [Pedanda Nyoman] asked me to be his ritual assistant, to go with him.

"Come with me, Dé. We'll go visiting in Tauman." He made me carry a great big basket for keeping *sirih* ingredients in. [These are for betel-nut chewing, which in the case of a *pedanda* is an activity with spiritual consequences as well as pleasant stimulation.] While we were there in Tauman, they gave the Pedanda a whole *centong* of rice and put it in the *sirih* basket, and I had to carry it home.

Peh! I felt as if I wasn't strong enough to carry that much rice! I had to stop at least fifty times on the way. And the priest walked on far ahead of me. *Peh!* And he was very old. And I started to cry, feeling bad because the rice was so heavy, wishing I was home already.

The *pedanda* of the next stories is Ida Pedanda Madé Jelantik of Gria Taman in Sukawati, whom Togog usually refers to as "my *pedanda,*" or "the Pedanda in Sukawati." He was installed as a priest at the age of about twenty-five, when Togog was about twenty. Togog served as his assistant from a very young age through his thirties. This *pedanda* had been born in Batuan, the son of Togog's father's father by a second wife. But he and his mother moved soon to Sukawati, to be groomed there to become a *pedanda.*

After I knew quite a lot of the sacred literature, *sastra,* I often accompanied the Pedanda in Sukawati to help with the ritual. He asked me to go with him, and I stayed with him a long time, for two and a half years (*masa,* or "harvests").

Togog's estimates of time and dates are unreliable. I think he may have started assisting his *pedanda* when he was about sixteen years old, staying with him steadily for about a year, until the events recounted in Chapter 5 drew him away. Togog resumed assisting this *pedanda* some years later, probably in the 1940s or 1950s, together with his friend, Déwa Baru.

I received many gifts because of my knowledge. When we came to a place there would be a group of people *mapacan* and *magending,* and I'd join them. Sometimes I even did small rituals, like a *pamangku.* And I was still learning new things.

Some time later I went together with Déwa Ketut Baru, the one whose house you live in. [Déwa Ketut Baru was my landlord, a *balian.* Baru told me that when he was a young man, he was extremely interested in spiritual matters, and besides studying with various healers, often assisted the Pedanda from Gria Taman in Sukawati. Baru was about fifteen years younger than

Togog.] We were both assisting my Pedanda. We went to Tedung, high in the mountains north and west of here.

To make the story short, when we got there, the Pedanda made ready to do the ceremony. I met a man there from Celuk whom I knew, who was bringing offerings to that temple. But I paid no attention to him. Then after the Pedanda was finished with the ceremony, the hosts gave him four broiled ducks to take home. And he gave them to Ketut and me to take care of.

"Tut, tie them up very carefully, so that when they are carried home they won't fall out." So Ketut went and found some string and wrapped them up very carefully. And then we were ready to go home. I was thinking about how when we got home to the *gria* the Pedanda would give Tut and me two ducks and keep two for the *gria*. How good that would be! So, on the way home the Pedanda was offered a car ride, and we went with him. But the ducks and other things were carried home separately. After we were home, the people carrying the ducks didn't come. I went to look for them in Ketut's house, but they weren't there. Someone said, "Tomorrow they'll bring them to you." But they never did. That was a loss for me and Tut, because that guy just took all the ducks. It must have been that man from Celuk. But neither of us got anything for all our work and for our tying up! That was just a loss. When we got home we didn't have anything.

There was another time when we went to Sawan in Buleleng. Again I went with Ketut Baru. When we got there we were given all our meals there. I just went along with everyone else to get my food. I joined the group from Ubud who were preparing *lawar* for the feast.

But Ketut didn't go with me there. He had much better food to eat because he stayed with the Pedanda and ate what he ate. I felt as if I was being treated like a commoner *(kaula)*. The food they gave me—*peh!*—I couldn't eat much of it because it was so bad.

We were in Sawan a long time, about twelve days, and when we were about to leave I went to the host, an Anak Agung, and asked, "Nak Agung!"—because it was the day before we were to leave I dared to say something—"Nak Agung, why did they give that sort of food to us? In Batuan we aren't given just beans." I said in familiar speech, "What they gave us was mostly coconut meat. There wasn't any real meat!"

"*Beh!* Ida Bagus, don't be angry at me. I gave out the same amount of meat to each cooking group. Two baskets each, and I even weighed them." Each group, from Ubud, from Pliatan, and the group of the Batuan *pedanda,* was placed in a different home, and the owner of each house was given the meat [and he must have taken it for himself], while what I was given wasn't even as good as roasted coconut meat.

I Ketut, though, ate well. He had all sorts of meat dishes because the group he was in had a woman from Batuan in it, and she made sure her cousin got good food.

We were there nine days, and I began to think that it would be better if I went out and bought some food in a *warung* while he was eating all that good food with the Pedanda and I was stuck with the lousy food of the Ubud and Pliatan group. The Ubud people might have liked it but I didn't. It was what you should call hell. But I didn't say anything because I couldn't do anything about it. So when I left they gave me some meat, the whole thigh of a water buffalo, but there wasn't much meat on it. That was how I suffered. For nine days there, when I never got anything good to eat. While Ketut ate well. Just ask Déwa Ketut. It was so in Sawan, Buleleng.

Cremations and Tooth-Filings

Then another day I went with my Pedanda to Pengosekan—but not this time with Ketut. They were doing the *nyekah* ceremonies in Pengosekan. I was asked to make an *ajum* offering, and for that I was given one *santun.*

An *ajum*—or *ngajumé*—offering is used in a cremation or *nyekah* ceremony as a temporary vehicle for the soul. It is a complex concoction, and since it involves making a diagram on a piece of wood inside it, and a *pererai* (face of a god), it is considered the work of Brahmana men, and is always paid for with one *santun*. A *santun* is a unit of payment for many kinds of ritual work, and consists of a tubular basket full of uncooked rice, coconut, fruit, meat, betel nut, and a little money. There are small and large *santun*. A large one contains four coconuts and four eggs—this was the kind Togog was speaking of. A *pedanda* gets four big *santun* for conducting a big ceremony. Another time Togog was paid one *santun* for participating in a *papacan,* or reading of classic literature.

It had in it a meter and a quarter of cotton cloth, and some heavy silver coins in money, but I didn't care very much. After that I was asked to file teeth, and for that I got another *santun*. And after that I made another *ajum,* because there were four different people having the same ceremony. So I made four *ajum,* and I got four *santun,* and each *santun* had four coconuts in it. I was certain to get all that, and four eggs too. It was pretty good.

So then one of the men there named I Gino—he didn't know me . . . Well, he was all ready to start the reading. He was going to read the Putru *lontar* and the Adi Parwa *lontar.* But when they went to do the reading, there was only one other man who could do it, a Déwa from there. An Ida Bagus from Gunungsari was supposed to have come but he hadn't shown up yet. So after my Pedanda had gone up and was ready to do the ritual, they asked me to join the reading. I could do it because the Pedanda gave me permission: "Yes, go over there and do the reading, even if you know only a little. So that their ceremony will be complete." So I climbed down and did the reading. And they gave me another *santun* for doing that. So now I had five. The Pedanda had four. He gets four for one visit.

Just when we finished the reading and I was about to take the *santun,* in came the Ida Bagus from Gunungsari. He'd been in Tegallalang.

He said, speaking familiarly, "*Peh!* What's this? It looks like you've already finished before I got here."

"Well, you were late, and what could we do? If you want that *santun* so much, you can have it," I said, in equally familiar words.

"No, that's not what I meant. I already got one in Tegallalang. I was about to leave when someone grabbed me by the hand and asked me to do a ceremony for his child's first *oton*."

"Well then, since you got one *santun* there, you shouldn't get one here," I said. So he just stood up and left, without saying anything more. That's how I got five *santun*. [It is interesting how often Togog speaks of this ritual work in practical material terms, telling how much he got paid, in meals and in gifts of food to take home and in *santun*. He called these *olih-olihan,* or "gettings."]

Now, there was another time when I went to Pliatan, just west of the Puri. Someone was having a *nyekah* ceremony there also. Now when we got there we found that they had invited only one *juru paca* [reader of the *lontar* scriptures—two people are always needed, one to read the passage aloud, the second to translate it]. Now you have to have two, but there was only one, and they had already prepared offerings for two people. They had prepared a divan for the two people to sit on during the reading right next to the place where the Pedanda does his ritual. And we heard the Anak Agung say: "Who can we get to do this? There's no one here, and it's almost time for the *pedanda* to do the prayers." He asked the one who was giving the ceremony. There was only one *juru paca,* and then he said, "Go and look for another *juru paca*. We need one more." They already had made *banten* for two. He was very troubled because there wasn't a second *juru paca*.

This anecdote shows how important singing is as an aspect of ritual, and how important singing was to Togog himself. Togog appears to assume that a *pedanda*'s ritual should always be accompanied by songs or readings.

So then an Anak Agung from Pliatan said to him, familiarly: "Hey, what's the matter? Ida Bagus Togog here with the Pedanda, he knows how to read the *lontar*." So then they asked me respectfully: "Come down, Tu, and do the reading for us. The Anak Agung has said you must do the reading."

"I can't, I'm helping the Pedanda, and I didn't prepare myself back in the house. I didn't bring my knowledge with me!" I said [in familiar speech], joking.

"Ah, you don't mean that, Ratu!" said the Anak Agung [respectfully].

"Well, ask the Pedanda if he would be willing to let me do the reading. There's no one else to assist the Pedanda."

"I'll assist him, Ratu. I'll assist him," he said.

So then he spoke to the Pedanda, who said to me, "*Beh!* Go on and read a little. Just read a little, since they didn't know they were lacking a reader until just now!" So then I did the reading for them, and I was given a *santun* for it. So now I had six and the Pedanda had five, while I had six. *Peh!* That was to balance off the loss I took when I went with Ketut to Buleleng, and I ended up with more.

Now, my life went on in that way, sometimes good and sometimes bad *(malih aget, malih lacur)*. I often accompanied the Pedanda and with me was Déwa Ketut Baru. Once we went together with the Pedanda to Kapal. There was to be a cremation in three days.

One night the Pedanda from Tegal in Badung was also there. There were two mattresses for the *pedanda* to sleep on, placed in the east-west direction. On the southern one my own Pedanda slept, and the other one was put to the north, up on the *balé piasan*. That's where the Pedanda from Tegal would sleep. And I and Déwa Ketut were going to sleep to the west of them. I don't remember whether it was Déwa Ketut who was with me. There were always two of us from Batuan accompanying the Pedanda from Sukawati, but it might have been a man from Banjar Tengah named Déwa Kompiang Atih.

Togog is here describing a careful placement of sleeping spots according to a sacred hierarchy. The highest-ranking *pedanda*, the one from Tegal, was placed above all the others, and to the north. Their assistants were to be not only lower and southerly, but also to the west of the priests.

So that night in Kapal, after the *pedanda* had eaten, they were going to go to sleep. And I was also going to sleep on the divan to the west, as is proper. My Pedanda was sleeping to the south, and the Pedanda from Tegal to the north. Then the Pedanda from Tegal said to me,

"Hey, child, come and sleep here with me! It's all right! And there are lots of good things to drink here!" I could count twelve different bottles there, the kind you have to buy, sweet drinks.

"How could I dare, Tu Pedanda?"

"It's all right, if I request it!" And he took a pillow and put it lengthwise between us. And then he told me to read with him from the Parwa. I read *(maca)* and he translated *(masanin)*, and it got to be late, as we say nowadays, twelve o'clock.

"Just stay here a moment," he said, and he went out of the house to the crossroads in front. I said to him, "I'll go with you, Tu Pedanda."

"No, no, you may not come with me," he said. So he went out alone. He went out alone in the middle of the silent night.

And then when he came back, and before we started to read again, he told me a story. He told me the story of Lubdaka. That's why I know the story of Lubdaka now. No one in Batuan knows the story of Lubdaka.

So that was the second story I learned from the Badung region; the first was Uncara Karno ["Kunjara Karna"], taught me by the Pedanda of Kaliungu. And now I was learning the story of Lubdaka from the Pedanda from Tegal when I was accompanying my Pedanda to Kapal.

And after we had been reading a while, I asked the Pedanda, "Why did you go out three times in the middle of the night? What were you looking for?" I dared to ask him. "Is that part of the task of a *pedanda,* to go out like that when there is no one there?"

"Oh, no!"

"What was the reason?"

"I'll tell you. I went out to the crossroads."

"Why did you do that?"

"Well, it's like this, my child. I'll tell you. I went out to the crossroads because this is the day of the cremation. I was asked by the Nak Agung here to make sure that the cremation went well. And I went out to the crossroads to find out if any part of the ritual had been omitted. It is there that I can learn whether any offerings have been missed. This day is not entirely propitious. There are inauspicious elements in it. So I need to know what may cause trouble. That's what I went to the crossroads to find out." That's what he said.

Crossroads are always busy with *niskala* beings of all sorts, some of whom may be malevolently inclined towards the holders of the ritual. Usually there is a small altar there, where neighbors place offerings daily. When a burial or cremation procession passes through a crossroads the participants whirl around so as to confuse any such ill-intending beings.

After that we went on reading the *lontar* until dawn. He didn't sleep, and neither did I. It was because he was so dedicated and pious *(yasa)* that he was able to make the *puri*'s ritual good *(yasa)* too. For those three days I was very happy in my heart.

To finish the story, we went home after that, and I did not accompany the Pedanda from Tegal again.

But when we left that day the Pedanda dropped his glasses when we were going home. I had stayed behind to pick up his betel-chewing box, and all the rest had gone on. I saw those glasses there on the ground, and I picked them up and put them in my pocket. So then when my Pedanda came home, by motor car from Badung, he said: "*Badah!* My glasses must have fallen somewhere, and someone must have taken them. What a calamity *(lacur)!*"

"Ah, don't worry," I said. "Are these your glasses?" I hadn't intended to keep them. "Here, Uncle, are these your glasses? [Togog used the slightly familiar "Uncle" *(Wo)* here to address the *pedanda,* who was in fact his uncle.] I thought they were yours, and now that you ask, here they are. You only have to say they're yours; I don't want them."

He was very grateful to get them back. And then the Pedanda said, "Oh, you are very good, and next time we go somewhere together, watch out for me so that I don't lose anything. We'll both watch out carefully."

And then there was the time there was a cremation ceremony in Satria, in Jero Satria, in Badung. They had invited my Pedanda to do the closing ritual *(mutus).* But at the same time there was a ritual in Pengosékan. Pengosékan is far from here. I had to walk to Pengosékan, and I got as far as Belahtanah and there I got a ride in a car. The next day was the cremation in Badung and also on the same day the cremation in Pengosékan. So I had to go first to Pengosékan to bring them their *tirta.* I had to make the holy-water bowls *(payuk)* for it first, and I worked all night on it and didn't go to sleep. I had to do the holy writing on the container and on the paper for the ceremony. I felt pressed from all sides.

There's a lot of writing on the bowl for holy water, a lot of holy writing *(sastra).* But I didn't have to copy. I already knew what to write.

Togog's son explained to me that the marks on the lip of a *payuk* for holding holy water are not really letters but small designs. Nonetheless, Togog refers to making them as *nyurat* (to write). *Payuk* come in pairs, and each pair is called a *tegen*. This term usually refers to the double load that a man can carry hung from a heavy stick across his shoulders, but in this case each *tegen* is very little and light.

The difficulty was that I had both to prepare the vessels for the holy water in Pengosékan and to accompany my Pedanda to Badung. And it was almost dawn and I hadn't finished them yet. There were a lot of people cremating at one time. I didn't know that my Pedanda was about to leave for Badung, and I was waiting for the people to come to Pengosékan for the holy water. So then all of a sudden he said [speaking down, addressing Togog as *waké*]: "I'm leaving for Badung now, but you stay here to give them the holy water. Give them whatever is proper for them, as many *tegen* as they need."

"*Peh,* Ratu, how are you going to go without me? Who will accompany you to Badung?" I said, respectfully.

"*Peh!* If you go with me to Badung, how will they know where to find what they need?" he said. "No, I'll go alone, and when you are finished, come and look for me in Badung. I'll just go on alone to Badung."

So then he went out, carrying his betel-nut box himself. When I went with him, I always carried the betel-chew box. So after he left I worked very hard giving the people their containers and holy water quickly.

Four times the family tried to make me eat something, but I said no. "Not now, later when I'm finished!" But some of the people hadn't come yet, and I waited for them until late in the morning; as we say nowadays, it was already ten o'clock and I still hadn't had anything to eat. They hadn't yet finished with their festival cooking there so they had nothing to give me. I was angry because I was in such a hurry to go on to Badung.

The Pedanda had two ceremonies to do, one in Badung, one in Pengosékan. I was very upset that no one would go with him to Badung. His ritual equipment *(pamios)* was already there—he had two sets of them, one was here and one was sent to Badung. So I goaded the people to hurry and come and get their holy water. It was about ten o'clock, and I decided to let someone else give it to the last few people, and I left.

When I left Pengosékan I hadn't yet eaten anything. I didn't think about eating, because my mind was set on getting it all done. So I set off walking from Pengosékan to Belahtanah. Three times my foot slipped and I almost fell, but I kept on walking, so that I could get quickly to my Pedanda in Badung. Whenever the road was level enough I ran. Well, to make the story short, when I got to Belahtanah, I found a ride on a car. [Belahtanah or Sakah is where the road from Gianyar to Den Pasar meets the road from Pengosékan, which is up near Ubud.] And then I went right on to Badung.

When I got to Badung the car dropped me north of the *puri.* I got out there. The body had not yet been carried to the graveyard, but had just been carried out into the road, and my Pedanda had already gone over to the graveyard. My Uncle Ketut, who lived in Kaliungu, Badung [Ida Bagus Seranta, a son of Ida Pedanda Kerta]—at that time he was a civil servant, a *juru surat*—was assisting the Pedanda. It wasn't proper for my Uncle Ketut to be assisting the Pedanda, because he was dressed in the clothes of a civil servant. I looked for the Pedanda, but I couldn't find him.

Aduh! How crowded it was there in the *puri.* There were twenty soldiers carrying guns to honor the dead man. The coffin was surrounded by people, many to the east of it and many to the west, all wanting to show their solidarity (*mapersatuan,* Ind.) with the deceased, wanting to accompany his coffin.

This funeral was held in Jero Satria, a noble house in Denpasar that had been a center of resistance to the Dutch in the 1940s. The dead man was a member of that resistance, and for the word I translate as "solidarity" Togog used an Indonesian word, *mempersatuan.*

I went into the *puri* to make sure that the Pedanda was not still there. I pushed my way in past all the people, and when I got to the innermost court, the Cokorda said to me, speaking down, "Hey, where are you from?"

"I'm one of the Pedanda's assistants, from Batuan. I'm Ida Bagus Madé Togog," I said politely.

"Why, he's already gone over to the graveyard!" said the other *pedanda,* speaking down.

"Yes, well then, I humbly request leave to go. I'm looking for my Pedanda because there's no one with him from Batuan or Sukawati to help him."

"All right," he said.

"Yes," said I. I took my leave and went to the graveyard. It was true. There he was on the stand for the burning. My uncle Po Ketut was there with him, and when I came, he said, "Hey, just now you get here!" speaking familiarly. And he handed over the job of assisting to me. It wasn't right for him to do that, as he was a civil servant. He said, "Here, take this!" and handed over to me the Pedanda's betel-chew box.

Now by the time I got there I hadn't had anything to eat or drink since the night before. I tried to settle down my feelings, so that I'd be strong and patient inside. I thought of all the moral sayings *(tutur)* that I knew. I was getting sleepier and sleepier. That's how I was able to stand it until that night. I felt good in my heart. No one else can know about that. I'm telling you everything frankly. The good as well as the bad of my experience.

Sometime after that there was a cremation in Puri Kalodan, in Puri Ageng in Pliatan. Now the *pamangku* who was supposed to do the ritual of going to get pure water for the ritual fell sick and he couldn't do it. So then they asked me to go.

"*Pah!* How can I do that? What would I *say* at the spring?" Someone had to go to a spring to ask for *tirta* to use to purify, cleanse, the dead body. The Cokordas and the Anak Agung there begged for my help in doing it. And then my Pedanda told me to do it, saying, speaking down: "Well just go over there and do what you can! You know what to say. Whatever you say [even if it is in ordinary Balinese] will be all right."

The prayer that should be said is like those said in a temple. It's all written up in the *lontar* Usana Déwa.

So I did it. I went to the spring, escorted there by a *gamelan.* There must have been at least four hundred people. It was like the great processions of the gods down to the sea *(makiis).* Only I was dressed in ordinary clothes—though my clothes were all clean. They weren't as fine as those of the other people. The procession went ahead of me, carrying the pitchers for the holy water and the offerings. *Peh!* There were so many offerings there in the river!

So there I was presenting the offerings to the deities. Properly it should have been a *pamangku,* but he couldn't do it. So I was making the ritual motions of wafting the essence of the offerings towards the deities *(ngayabang)* the way we do it here in Bali. I gave the prayer in ordinary Balinese but in the highest words: "Well, whoever it is who has the right to receive these, I offer them to you. I humbly request some holy water *(tirta)* to cleanse the dead person!"

That's all I said because I didn't know the proper prayer *(mantra)* that the *pamangku* knows. "With all respect, we offer you these things. If they are too little or too much, we beg pardon. We beg you respectfully to bestow the holy water on us, O Hyang Tirta, or whoever you are who should bestow it on us."

And then, like a *pamangku,* I sat quietly and meditated. *Bah!* They all smiled, the people behind me, and someone said: "*Bah!* This Ida Bagus is very confident. Whatever he has to do, he just does it. He just knows what to do. He must have practiced this from a very young age."

At this point I asked Togog how old he was at the time. He answered that he must have been about sixteen, but that he was unusually daring.

So, after that, I often went along with the Pedanda. For two years I accompanied him.

Then one time I accompanied the Pedanda to Badung where they were going to do a tooth-filing in the *puri*. When we came in there was a *pepaosan* session going on. I knew what they were reading. It was from the Parwa scriptures.

Now at that time my Pedanda didn't know much about reading *lontar*. This was the Pedanda from Sukawati. And when they asked him to read he broke out into a cold sweat because he didn't know how to read. He was asked something by someone there and *peh*, he didn't know what to say! He was ashamed in his heart.

So then, after we had arrived home again, my Pedanda told me to go and bring down the Parwa *lontar* to study *kekawin*. Because he'd been so confused when asked to join in the discussions with those who were reading. And he invited, as his teacher, old Anak Agung from Puri Kawan Sukawati, called Anak Agung Pekak, to read with him. And I went there too. So from the time we came back from Badung, I studied *mabaosan* with him. And after a while I became very skilled.

Togog's son remarked that many *pedanda* don't really know how to read Kawi, nor do they read much literature. They've memorized only the *wéda*, prayers, they need and no more. If they have had the ceremony in which they are made *pedanda*, the *dwijati* ritual, then they can carry out the ceremonies, whether or not they are fully literate.

Once the Ida Cokorda from Bangli wanted to have a *pedanda buda* go to Bangli to do a ceremony. But he first had to go to the *puri* in Gianyar to ask to have them arrange it. So you see, the Anak Agung in Gianyar "owns" the *pedanda* in Sukawati.

I went with the Pedanda from Sukawati to Bangli, and on the way we stopped at Gianyar. And the Anak Agung said to my Pedanda, in very respectful words, "Won't you please stay a little while here, Pedanda?"

"Yes." We were on our way to a *ngasti* in Bangli the next day and we stopped to visit in Gianyar on the way.

And he spoke very nicely to the Pedanda. Properly. And then the Anak Agung gave the Pedanda a present that he said he had brought back from America—it was a set of buttons. For his clothing.

"Here, please take whichever ones you want, Pedanda." There were six different kinds. And so then he chose the ones he wanted. He took six very nice buttons. He still wears them.

The Anak Agung of Gianyar was probably Anak Agung Gedé Agung, a major figure in national politics from 1945 on. He visited the United States in 1948 as prime minister of Negara Indonesia Timor, and again in about 1956 as Ambassador of the Republic of Indonesia. This suggests that this incident took place some time after 1948.

So I studied there a long time. I liked that sort of work. In fact, I liked to do almost everything. Whatever anyone asked me to do, I did. I never said no. Whether I was given something in return or not, I did it.

Once when I came home from Sukawati, someone here had died, and they asked me to do the ritual cleansing of the corpse *(mresihin)*. He was a *sisia* of our *gria* from Jeléko.

"Yes," I said. But it was more appropriate for my Po Yan to do it, so I asked him, "Po Yan, Po Yan, would you go over there to Jeléko and do that purifying ritual?"

"Yes," he said.

But just then another person came.

"Ratu, Ida Bagus Alit, please come and do the purifying ritual for my dead."

"Yes," I said.

But—*badah!*—here came a *third* one to ask me to do the ritual.

"Alright," I said.

And after him there came, *bah! another one,* a Satria,

asking politely, "I request you, Ratu, to come and do the cleansing ritual."

"Okay."

Bah! Poor me! The first one who came, there was no excuse not to do it, but I couldn't say to the second one that I already had work to do. So I did the last one too. That was the hardest because it was so late. That night I didn't sleep at all.

The first one my Po Yan did, in the daytime, but we didn't know there was going to be another death. So I went right on to the graveyard and did the *pratéka* ceremony, even though it was nighttime. I felt very unfortunate in my heart when I was told to do more work. But finally it was done. "*Bah!* Poor me!" That's what I was thinking.

Another time, much later, I was told by my Pedanda in Sukawati to accompany him to the home of the Prabekel in Pliatan. They were going to do the tooth-filing ritual for nine people. I was helping the Pedanda, so we were sitting up in the temple *(mrajan)*. No one came up there [to bring food for the Pedanda]; no one was paying any attention to us.

"Well, go out there and see what you can find to buy," said the Pedanda to me. I knew that the Pedanda was very hungry, so I went out and bought him a package of steamed rice, one that was very tightly wrapped. I didn't buy anything for myself because I was strong. So I brought that back in, hiding it so that our hosts wouldn't see it, or the guests. The person who was supposed to take care of giving the Pedanda dinner had not been able to come. He had been told, "When the Pedanda comes, serve him this and this." Something had detained him. So when I brought the package of food in, the host saw me and asked, "What's that?"

"It's food for the Pedanda. He hasn't had anything to eat since morning. So I bought him this package of steamed rice," I said. So then the host asked about the man who was supposed to give the Pedanda dinner and found out that he couldn't come because he was sick. To make up for it, the host gave us all sorts of fruits and cakes to take home—a whole basin full of *durian, salak, manggis,* and other things. We three couldn't eat them all up, even in three days.

Now the first of the people climbed up to have the teeth-filing ceremony. There was a man there to sing *kekawin.* I like to listen to the Waséng song, but the singer sang only a little and then stopped. "Why isn't he singing?" I asked myself. I think that he knew a lot of songs by heart but couldn't sing because he was very embarrassed in front of all those important people.

Then a woman sang. They said she came from Ubud. She sang the Tantri from the porch of the *balé gedong.* I knew those songs, and—*ratu!*—what a lovely voice she had. But after she sang only a few of the Tantri songs she stopped. There were still seven more people to have their teeth filed. I knew a lot of songs, and there was a relative of mine from Gunungsari there who knew I could sing.

"Ah, Ratu, Gus Madé from Batuan, invite him to sing, so that the *gamelan* won't be unaccompanied." At least that's what I imagine happened. So then someone came to me in the temple and said, "Gus Dé! Gus Dé! Come down!" That was the servant *(parekané)* of the Anak Agung, whispering very politely, "Would you please come and sing, so that the music will be complete."

"*Peh!* I'm very sorry, but I didn't expect to sing here. And besides, I have to keep the Pedanda company. If I had known when I was at home that I was going to sing, I would have prepared myself," I said.

And then a Dayu, a relative of mine who was working on the offerings, came and said to me [in familiar speech]: "Dé! Dé! Please help. I *(mémé)* beg for your *(ida)* help for him. He will be ashamed to have such a big ceremony but with no singer. Just now the Anak Agung begged me, the Prabekel of Pliatan, asked me if I would be bold and ask you to, just so there'd be someone singing now."

"*Pah!* How can I do that? I have to stay with the Pedanda. I can't leave him alone."

"I'll stay with him," said the Anak Agung. "I'll stay with you, if you will allow him to go," he said to the Pedanda very respectfully.

"Yes, I beg you, Ratu," I said in the highest words to the Pedanda, "to allow me to go and sing there a little while. If you won't command me to sing, I wouldn't dare to leave you," I said to the Pedanda.

"Oh! go ahead! Sing Sinom. Sing whatever you know, just so that there is some singing. If this were a competition you would have had to prepare for at least a month. But what can be done about it?—there has to be someone to sing! It will be good practice for you. Sing Dangdang Gula." That's what the *pedanda* answered [speaking down]. [Dangdang Gula is a name of a melody everyone knows, for which there are many words, rarely sacred.]

"Well, yes, all right. I will do as you command. I'll do what the Dayu here has requested," I said. So then I went up there. There were still seven more people for the tooth-filing ritual. So then they brought a chair up to the *balé dangin* and put it up there with the people having their teeth filed. So there I was seated on a chair. There were many guests there, and they had all sorts of soft drinks for us. There were eight bottles there. I took something to drink right away so that I could sing well. My voice was very bad, very bad, small and tight, because I hadn't been singing much lately.

So then I sang. The first thing I sang was Malat, and after that, Tantri. There were still four more people to do. Then I sang the Waséng. I had only sung one verse of the Waséng when in came Déwa Pekak, the man who had taught me.

"Hello! Here's my Lord! *(betaran tiang) Adah!* I never expected it! Get me a chair right away and put it over there!" he said. They got him a chair and then we sat together and sang. We sang the Waséng. He had only memorized a little of it, but I knew a lot. When it was all finished, I still had more songs that I could have sung. It was very good. I felt like a merchant who goes off and comes back with a big profit.

When the Pedanda of Guang died, they invited me to come and help with *his* cremation. The cremation was about fifteen or twenty days after he died. When that *pedanda* was still alive and I was still a little boy, I went there often to wait on him. He'd send me on errands here and there, but the most important job was going to get his *opium* for him!

In those days opium cost 200 *képéng* for one piece. It was wrapped in tin, and you pressed it and it would come out black. I bought it in Sukawati. Once he asked me to climb up and pick a coconut for him, but I didn't dare because the tree was tall and it leaned over the house *(balé gedong)*, and I was afraid that if I climbed up I'd fall right there on the *balé*. Because he smoked opium, few people came with offerings for him, and he didn't do the prayers.

The old *pedanda* smoked opium in a *cangklong*, a long-stemmed pipe with a small bowl. He would mix the black st uff with wood shavings so that it would burn, and he would inhale the smoke. I asked what 200 *képéng* would buy at that time and Togog said you could buy a kilo of rice for 600 *képéng*. He bought the opium from a Chinese in Sukawati.

So here came the invitation to the cremation because I was a kinsman, and it was proper for all the family from here to go. I went with my uncle on my mother's side, named Ida Bagus Wayan Duduk [the same man who went with Togog to consult about his being expelled from the clan temple (see Chap. 5)], and Ida Bagus Made Datah. The three of us went.

So when it came time to take the body down and bathe it, the head of the *banjar* [a commoner] said: "Whoever is a relative of I Ratu, whoever has the right to touch him, please bathe him now. We don't dare, because he is a *pedanda*." That was his speech [*pidarto,* a word derived from the Indonesian *pidato*].

Besides us, there was a man from Negara, a kinsman

named Ida Bagus Gulem. He was sitting there with his legs crossed on the porch of the *balé gedong*. But he wouldn't get down and help. And the day before he'd taken all the *pedanda*'s clothes and ritual equipment *(alat pamiosané)* back to Negara with him and then come back the next morning. So there he was sitting on the porch, right there, and it was time to bathe the *pedanda*'s body.

So just the two of us did it, by ourselves! I took his back and Po Yan [Duduk] took his head. No one had done anything at all to wash his body for a long time! [The body had been left untouched for nearly three weeks, because his own family had refused to take care of it.] He had been an opium addict [and it had ravaged his body]! And when we picked him up, liquid bubbled up out of his mouth, and from out of his loincloth jumped *maggots!* Wriggling around and falling on our legs!

Ratu! What a terrible smell! I can't tell you how awful it was! So then I sang [the following *kekawin*]:

> O, my older sister! How overjoyed I am to meet with
> you. You come as if commanded.
> Thus is the splendor of the incomparable Manimantaka.
> I must have been here before. It's as if I should have known
> it already, this realm more beautiful than heaven.
> So now that the heaven [of Indra] has been leveled,
> burnt to the ground and all its people fled . . .

This is a verse from the Arjuna Wiwaha, canto 18, stanza 1. The identification and the translation are by Adrian Vickers. Togog's son also translated it for me, and said that it is a famous passage, spoken by Supraba to Ménaka, wife of the ogre-king Manimantaka. Supraba had been sent from Indraloka to the kingdom of the raja Manimantaka, who was threatening to attack and destroy Indraloka. Supraba addresses Ménaka as "older sister" because she is older than he. Supraba is deliberately flattering the woman and is lying by saying that Indraloka has been destroyed.

I sang while I was holding the body so that I would not breathe in that smell that made me want to *vomit!* And the juices kept coming out and falling on me. It was good practice for me [in learning to bear the stench and drippings].

After that, the *klian banjar* told me to climb up on the corpse-carrying tower to throw down coins from above on the way to the cremation ground.

"Don't worry about falling, Ida Bagus, I'll hold your leg, Ratu," said the *klian*. I was afraid of being tipped off it, but there were two people below me [steadying me]. So I kept on singing *kekawin* up there. I could keep on going because I had memorized so many. Everyone else was singing, too, to keep from breathing in the *stink!* If you smelled it you felt like *throwing up!*

So *then,* Ida Bagus Putu Gulem—the man from Negara who wouldn't touch the body before when they took it down to bathe it—the people of the village all went after him! I was up high with the corpse. They pressed around him, pushing and shoving him, and they even took the bamboo platform that had been used for bathing the body and threw it on top of him! Covered him right up with it! They wore him out, and he went home after that.

This was an example of the practice called *ngarap* [see Connor (1979)], in which the people of the *banjar* who have to carry the cremation tower and the corpse attack the relative of the dead man in anger—in this case, for not helping with the ritual. Their acts were intended to defile the deceased, and to insult his family.

They didn't touch me because I was up above. The *klian banjar* was very smart, telling me to climb up on the carrying tower. If I'd stayed down below, I would have had to go and defend my kinsman. That *klian* was very clever!

So I rode on the tower to the graveyard, and then they took the body down and then put it up in the bull figure [for burning]. So when I got down, people ran away from me! Because I stank so disgustingly that no one would come near me! So I went out right away and bathed and washed all my clothes, which were covered with those body juices!

Then there was another time when a *sisia* from my *gria*, Gria Gedé, died. He was a *pamangku* from Jeleka. The people in charge of the ceremony asked me to bathe him. He was a *pamangku* in Pura Dalem Delod Jungut.

When I started to bathe him, an awful stench came out. No one from the village dared to go near him. But I, because I was already used to it after that experience with the rotting dogs when I was fishing, didn't let it bother me. I thought to myself, "This stench is nothing compared with that of the dogs! That was three times worse than this!" That was my thought while I was doing it, and it *freed* me from that smell!

When I had to wash his hair and brush his teeth, my hands were covered with head lice! They were crawling all over! Because he'd been so sick, no one had tried to take the lice out of his hair.

After that we took him to the graveyard to cremate him. No one wanted even to help carry the ceremonial litter! Not one! How was I to do the ritual? Three times I had to shout out to the crowd: "Gentlemen! Gentlemen! If you don't help me hold this sieve [for the holy water], how can I do the ritual? And finally one man stood up and answered, "Yes, I will help!" Because they were all afraid of the smell. But because I was used to it I could do it. It didn't bother me. I did it all the way to the end, and I never worried about it because I had bathed worse-smelling corpses than that, such as that *pedanda* before.

Soon after that there was another big cremation in the *puri*. They held it in the graveyard to the east [next to Pura Dalem Puri]. At the same time those commoners who were having cremations along with the nobles were down in the southern graveyard [Pura Dalem Jungut]. Now the Anak Agung was not in charge of those who were accompanying him, that is, those [commoners] to the south were themselves in charge of their dead. But then I was told to go to the graveyard to the south after I was finished [doing the rituals] in the eastern graveyard.

"There are still more rituals to do down there. They've already gone to the graveyard. Their *kulkul* has already sounded. They must be about to dig up the bones." [This was said in polite language, so it must have been the Anak Agung telling Togog to go and do the rituals in the commoner graveyard.] That meant they were about to do the opening ritual *(ngendag)*. I must have I started to go down there five times, and each time I turned back again because the people whose dead were to be taken care of hadn't directly asked me to come.

I thought to myself, "I'd better go down there anyway, because he told me to." That Anak Agung from here had told me to go and take care of the commoners who were included in with the gentry cremation.

So then I went down there, all alone, no one with me. And there were many people from the village there. When I got there no one paid any attention to me, they all just kept silent. I looked around for a cremation group that was smaller than the rest, and as I passed one of the others someone asked me, respectfully, "Hello, Gus Aji, is there a ritual?"

And I answered, "Oh, no, I'm just looking around." I was embarrassed and didn't want them to know why I had come.

"Have you finished the opening rituals?" I asked, speaking down.

"Yes, we've even finished all the rest. The *pamangku* and I, your subject, have finished it all up, Ratu." she said very respectfully. It was the wife of a man named I Tubah.

"Well, even so, I came to look things over," I said, speaking down.

And then I turned around and went straight home without turning to the right or left to talk to anyone else.

Now, another time, I was asked to go and do the tooth-filing ritual for the daughter of a Cokorda from Pliatan. She had been taken in marriage by one of my kinsmen from Gria Kaliungu [the one in Badung], and since her father was having the ceremony, she went home for it to Puri Pliatan. They wanted me to do the ritual because I was related to her [through marriage].

They sent someone to get me—the man who is now Prabekel in Negara—to ask me to go there to Pliatan. The *punggawa* of Pliatan had a car and I told them I wouldn't walk there, to come and get me with the car. They had to come here anyway to pick up some dancers. So I waited here until they came for me. When it was time to go, I looked for someone to come with me. It was, as they say today, already 9 a.m. When I got there I saw that they were finished with the tooth-filing. Someone said, "Please go over to the *balé dangin* to sit." So I went over there, but no one greeted me, and I just stood there looking around. No one offered me betel nuts or anything. There were many guests there. So then people were whispering about me, "What's he doing there?" because I was standing there. I didn't mind because I'd been told to come by the Cokorda.

"Just stay put," I said to myself, "after all, you were told to come here." The Ida Bagus who had been doing the tooth-filing looked at me, and I looked at him. It was a long time. They were finished with the tooth-filing ritual, and I had been asked to do it. So then the Cokorda came for me, and invited me to eat,

"Come and eat, Ratu!" I had a little child from Batuan with me. Because of him I was willing to eat there, but inside, to my own amazement, I didn't want to eat. If I had followed my own feelings, I would have left for home right then, but I forced myself to act like an ignorant person because of the child. And then we left, the two of us, and walked home. My profit from that trip was only bad feelings in my heart.

Making a Cremation Bull and God-figures

Once my Uncle Kompiang [a relative of Togog's wife from Gria Pacung] said to me, in familiar words: "Ah, go over to Negara! They need someone to start *(endag)* the carving of a cremation bull." [A "cremation bull" is a larger-than-life wood and paper statue of a bull with a hole in its back in which the body is placed to be burnt.] They needed someone to do the ritual first cuts with the chisel.

He said, "I can't do it—and I asked Pa Kompiang Kasieh to go, and even he can't. There are people over there who know how to carve a cremation bull, but they don't dare do it without the hand of a Brahmana on the first cuts."

The phrase Togog used for "the hand" is *tampak tangan*. *Tampak* means "the flat of the hand or foot," and *tangan* means "hand," thus "a handprint." The phrase is used today to mean "a signature," but here the meaning conveyed relates to the belief that any sacred artifact should be at least started *(endag)* by a master of *sakti*, here, by a Brahmana.

"Ah! I'm not afraid. My chisel is ready and sharp. I'll go."

"Good," he said. So I went off to Negara. When I got there they greeted me, respectfully: "Welcome, welcome, Ratu, come over here. Uh, I didn't dare to carve on this wood until it was first cut into by the hand of a person like you, Ratu."

"I was told to come here, but I don't know how to carve, but I do know the ritual. I'll just put my hand on it."

"Yes, that's all right with us."

So first I chipped at the face a little, just hit the chisel three times. And then, they told me to do a little on the stomach and then the feet. When I got to the feet suddenly I had a strange feeling. I felt off all that day. "What's the matter?" I thought in my heart, but I just went along with them.

"Here, do a little more here, a little more there," and I just kept on, because I didn't care.

So when I was finished with the carving, I went back to Batuan and spent the night in the house of the people having the ceremony [Gria Pacung]. When I woke up in the morning, when I got out of bed, I hadn't yet taken two steps when I had a headache—it felt as if I was carrying a load of stinking cow manure on my head!

"*Bah!* What's the matter with me?" I thought, and then I remembered that the day before, when I was starting up the carving of the cremation bull, they hadn't had a *santun* offering there to protect me. That was the mistake! Now I remembered. So I called out to one of the women there in the *gria,* in familiar words: "Dayu, Dayu! Make me up a *santun* offering, and take it to my home."

"Didn't they have a *santun* offering there yesterday?" she asked, also familiarly.

"No, there wasn't any there. The *santun* that was there was for them, not for me."

"*Peh!* You were neglectful. Serves you right! Wo Kompiang here, when he did the first-cut ceremony, he was so sick, throwing up and diarrhea. You can't be careless about that ritual!" she said. And then she made it for me.

So then I met her later and asked "Did you make it?"

"I already took it to your home, Madé."

"Oh, yes, then I won't go home yet, until I'm finished here."

She hadn't gone out of the door when my head suddenly felt clear, my head cleared up because I was no longer in the wrong.

There are proper ways of doing these rituals: if you do an *endag* ritual, you do such and such. If you do a toothfiling, you do such and such. If you do an *endag* ritual in the graveyard, you do such and such. Each one has its own requirements, but they all need a *santun* offering.

In earlier anecdotes it appeared as though Togog valued the *santun* offering primarily for its material worth (a coconut, enough uncooked rice for several meals, and other foods), but here it is clear that it is also an offering to Togog's ancestral beings, who can be angered over missteps and can cause illness.

I've done so many different things. Now I'll tell you about painting *(pulas)* god-figures.

Some people came to me from a village near Singapadu, from the Pura Désa in Sangsi. They had some god-figures [a *prarain déwa* and two *pelinggihan,* one of a lion, the other of a snake, which are used as stand-ins for the deities during a ritual] that had been made and ritually dedicated *(putus)* by a commoner. But their gods had not been pleased and wanted their figures to be made *(tampak)* by a Brahmana, and the gods were causing them trouble, giving them much sickness.

They had gone to a *balian* about the sickness, who had told them the cause of their troubles—that their gods were angry because the figures that the villagers had provided for their descent into the visible world had not been made by Brahmana but by mere commoners. Because of all the sickness in the village, its leaders wanted to mollify their gods by having Togog repair or improve the figures they had made. Often Brahmana merely start *(endag)* or complete *(putus)* a large carving destined for a temple, allowing commoner artisans to do most of the work. Just the fact that a Brahmana has put his hand to it can give a work the requisite *tenget* quality.

The leader of the group from Sangsi came to me and asked me to change their god-figures. They said they'd been made by a commoner, and that they weren't acceptable until they had been made by a Brahmana.

So I went there and worked on them. I didn't change the carving, but I took all the old paint off and put new colors on. The man who had made them in the first place was afraid that they'd be ruined when I went to put on new *prada*-paint, but I already knew how to do it. When you've put all the *prada*-paint on, then you polish it down and put pure shellac over it. He was wrong to worry about it.

Before I began to repaint them, I made some offerings: *tetebasan, sidapurna,* and *panyapu,* for them. [A *tetebasan* offering is a "payment" or "payback" to the gods for wrong-doings or errors. A *sidapurna* offering announces one's intention and asks for success. A *panyapu* serves to sweep away anything that might hinder the success of the work.]

I didn't know whether the people in that temple were *sisia* of my *gria* or not, even though they gave me a small *canang* offering. [Because Togog was still quite young, he was not yet acquainted with all the *sisia,* or ritual clients, of his family.]

I wasn't yet very certain about who our *sisia* were. For instance, when a woman selling food at the cockfights said, in respectful words, "Come here, Tu! Please dine here, Ratu!" I didn't know whether she was offering it to me as a *sisia* [in which case he'd have plenty of chances to repay the favor], or just as a merchant. Wherever I went to cockfights, the women selling food would offer some to me, and I'd only take some if I had the money to pay for it. I didn't like to take from people I didn't know, whom I couldn't repay in some way. From people I knew well, to whom I gave things at times, I didn't mind asking for money.

There was a Chinese man whom I had once given some money to, and he bought me some food. And once, when a group of eight Chinese were walking home together from Guang, I overheard one of them say to the others, "*Wah!* The reason that Ida Bagus gave me some food just before the fight was that I once lent him some money!" That's okay, that's clear.

I asked for money only from my friends, especially those the same age as me. I didn't find out whether that food seller was really my *sisia* until long after that when they came here for a *layu sekar* ceremony when someone there in Lémbéng died.

Rain-dispelling Rituals

Rain-dispelling rituals are needed when a major ceremony is threatened by rain. They are dangerous to perform because it is believed that the rain is brought there by some human sorcerer, using "the lore of the left" *(pengiwa),* who wishes to harm the holder of the ceremony. This means that rain dispelling by a ritual expert is an act of countersorcery, of defense (*penengan,* "the lore of the right"). Both sorcery and countersorcery can backfire on the one who casts the spells. In the following anecdote Togog felt after performing it that his purpose (protecting the paper) was somehow inappropriate, and for that reason he was punished.

Togog told this story in connection with his experiences with the Western artists Spies and Bonnet, recounted in Chapter 6. Here he and his fellow Batuan painter Ida Bagus Madé Wija had been given a great roll of paper a meter and a half in length, which they carried back to Batuan together, and on the way they were nearly overtaken by rain, which would have destroyed the paper.

Ida Bagus Wija was carrying the paper on his head. It was too heavy to carry under your arm—it was like cardboard, as thick as your little finger. I don't know what you call that sort of paper. We were taking turns carrying it.

Well, as we were going along, it became very dark and cloudy. We were already south of Mas and there were rain clouds farther to the south. You couldn't even see the trees because the clouds were so thick. And now there were clouds to the north, to the west. Only on the east was there a little clear place in the clouds.

We got to the long open place south of Mas. Nowadays there are houses and art shops and offices there, but at that time there was nothing there after you left Mas. Gus Madé Wija was walking behind me, and there were some other people coming up behind him, carrying empty baskets—they'd just brought some gifts *(aturang)* to the *puri* in Pliatan and were coming home. Because they had just gone to the *puri* with offerings, they were all dressed up and carrying baskets. When I looked back at them, they were tying up their sarongs very tightly, rolling them up so that when it rained their new clothes wouldn't get wet—rolled up tightly and tied between their legs, like this.

We were way out in the middle of an open field when we heard the rushing sound of the rain—it was already raining where we had just been. So then Ida Bagus Madé Wija said, "Do Adé, Do Adé, don't you know how to do the ritual to keep rain away?"

"*Beh!* How come you're asking me that question? It's the Brahmana Siwa like you who know how to keep rain away! You yourself should know how! I don't know those things as I'm a Brahmana Buda! It would be better if you did the ritual, so as to avoid real trouble!"

Ida Bagus Madé Wija said: "If it rains on this paper, think how much money we'll lose. The *tuan* said that the order came from America!" That's what he said to me. "This heavy paper, if it gets rained on, it can't be used anymore!" [The term *tuan* is the male equivalent of *nyonya,* both meaning "respected foreigner," in Malay and Indonesian.]

And then he swore to me, up and down, that he did not know the ritual for keeping rain away.

"Well, if that's so, Madé," I said to him, "I don't want to request [action against] the one who has sent the rain, I only want to give a prayer to God *(hyangé)*. But, Madé, I'll only ask for the rain to hold off until we get to Belahtanah. There is a brick building *(kantor)*, the home of a Chinese, his shop, where we can take shelter from the rain if it starts raining when we get there."

"All right, Madé, just up to Belahtanah! I beg of you!" he said.

"All right! So that we won't get rained on!" Because by now the rain was very close upon us. We were about to get drenched. We had to do something, he felt.

I was afraid because I didn't have an offering *(canang)* to go with the spell. That's what I was worried about. I knew what to do all right, but I was afraid that in doing it I wouldn't put the things in the correct place. You have to put the magical materials (the *liligundi* and *lalang* plants, mentioned below) right in the middle and not at the side. At the side you need the offerings. That's what I was worried about.

So now, since he had begged me to do it, I said to him, "All right, Madé, look for the topmost twig of a *liligundi* plant, the three topmost twigs, and then get me one blade of *lalang* grass, just the top part, and put it right above my head on the paper."

"But what will happen if I put it there and the wind blows it off?"

"Once it is on there in fact, it doesn't matter if it is blown away. We'll have done it already. Let it blow away," I said. "Just be sure to put it in the right place," I said. "Did you do it yet?"

"Yes, I did," he said.

So he looked for the things, and he put the topmost twigs, three of them, of a *liligundi* tree, there on the paper.

So then, to make the story short, we no longer hurried down the road, just walked ordinarily to show we had faith that we had done what was right. If we hadn't we would indeed be drenched. That's how I felt.

Togog told me later that he had learned the rain-preventing *mantra* through study of a *lontar* in his own library. The particular *lontar* he used was the one that I Jana had given him, which teaches how to do sorcery and countersorcery.

So then we got to Belahtanah, to the shelter of the Chinese man's house, and just as I was going in, the rain came down—indescribably hard. It came from the west, and it came from the north, and the west. And within the time of one betel chew, the road was full of ankle-deep water. The raindrops were as big as your little finger. And then the people carrying the baskets coming up behind us were completely soaked. I turned and saw them. Well, our prayer to Sanghyang Embang had been granted. But the people just to the north of us had been drenched.

Aduh! How dark it was—you couldn't see anything, not

even the trees nearby. You couldn't see to the west, you couldn't see to the south, you couldn't see to the north, but you could see just a little to the east. So after a while, a long time, the rain began to let up, but by then it was very late at night, as we say nowadays, two o'clock. Once I had a watch given me by the *tuan* from Switzerland, and he showed me how to read it. So it was about two o'clock.

"*Peh!* Da Adé, ask again for clear skies till we get home," said Ida Bagus Wija.

"*Badah!* Don't talk like that, Dé. We've already been blessed by the ancestors *(luhur)* greatly. The prayer I sent was not to my own ancestors, but to yours. They were the ones who prevented disaster from overtaking us on the road. Don't complain to your ancestors. In short, I don't know whether it was my ancestors or yours who granted our wish. Now, the rain has stopped. Let's just go home."

So then we went home. We were quite close by then. The next day the clouds were still very dark.

Well, the next morning, the clouds were still very dark. I went to the river to bathe, and I took my fishing pole with me.

When I came to the river—I like to go there in a place just east of the Pura Dalem Puri. There is a banyan tree on an island in the river there, and there is a waterspout that comes from a spring. So when I went there, I'd sometimes say: "Whoever it is who owns this river as well as this spring, don't reveal any pieces of gold to me that I might want to take! And don't show me any jewels! If you showed me them I'd want to take them, so don't show me any!"

If you find Chinese coins in the river, it's all right to take them, for they came there obviously by human means; and I've sometimes found three or four there. That's why I said those things when I went down into the river.

Togog later explained to me that the prayer to "whoever it is who owns this river" is addressed to a *tonya* or a *gamang* (kinds of *niskala* spirit inhabitants of the river). He said that the place in the Besil River where this occurred is well known as an especially *tenget* place.

Togog's son told me another story to explain why it is that it is very dangerous to take found jewels from a river. There were once a *gamang* and a *tonya* who lived in a river. One said to the other, "How can we improve our condition?" And the *tonya* answered, "We can find a poor farmer who wants to get rich easily." So they found one and they put some gold pieces in his irrigation ditch, right above the place where the water goes into the next person's rice field, because that's where he'd be looking carefully. When the farmer found the gold, he took it home. But soon he became sick, and he went to a healer and asked for help. But the healer was a friend of the *tonya* and he told the farmer that the *tonya* was causing his illness, and to mollify him the farmer would have to build a fine temple to the *tonya*. He did that, and got well, and the *gamang* and the *tonya* received many offerings and were raised in status.

So when I got there, I put the bait on the fish-pole and set it in place. It wasn't that I wanted to eat fish so much, but just for something to do while I was bathing.

So I got there, and I took off my clothes. There were some girls just to the south of me. I didn't know their names, but I knew their faces. So then I bathed, pouring water over myself with a coconut shell, and washing my face. And just when I was finished it started to rain again. With lightning and thunder, and one flash came right near me. *Keleppp!*—like that. *Blerrr!* And those girls said: "Ratu, Ida Bagus, you better go home right away, because the sky is getting so dark! Come home with us, Ratu!" They said that in quavering voices, because they were so frightened. I figure that the lightning must have flashed eight times, right there—*Kleppp!*—*Blerr!*

But I just calmly climbed up on top of a big rock and crouched there. I just gave myself up to the rain, just let myself get soaking wet. I knew that I had done wrong the day before, that I had been too bold to do the rain-preventing magic without a *canang* offering. I knew what I should have done—I had known it a long time. It was written right there in the *lontar* I had. So I knew that I had done wrong, and that's why I just gave myself up. As I interpreted it, I couldn't hide from it. So I just let myself get drenched. Let it happen.

Bah! I sat there a long time, crouching on top of that rock. I didn't dare stay under the tree, under that banyan tree, to keep myself dry, because if the lightning were looking for someone, that's where it would look, and that would mean the end of my life, burnt up. That's why I stayed right out in the middle of the river, on a big rock, getting soaked through. Ever since then I've been extra cautious.

It seems as though rain-dispelling rituals incur several kinds of dangers. There are so many ways you can do wrong. One is by asking too often and for too much. Another is by not giving the proper offerings along with saying the spell. If you overstep, the ones to whom you address your request may be angry. In this story, Togog uses the term *luhur*—which can mean both "god" and "ancestor"—for the ones to whom the petition went. He appears to have requested the rain dispelling from Ida Bagus Madé Wija's own ancestors, but it seems to have been Togog's own ancestors who punished him with the rainstorm the next day. They would not have been rained on unless it were magically brought on them by an ill-wishing sorcerer. Togog referred to this human rainmaker as "the one who owned" *(dué)* the rain. To counteract that rain means to counteract that sorcerer, and if the one who performs the ritual is not strong enough *(sakti),* then the sorcerer will be able to hurt him. Togog later tells a story about two *pedanda* who, while performing the rain-preventing ritual, were struck by lightning. The ideas of potential punishment by ancestors or revenge among sorcerers explain the term that Togog uses below when he "challenges" *(adokang)* his friend Déwa Baru to try the rain-dispelling ritual. And also that *lontar* from which he learned the spell, the one he had from I Jana, was in fact, a handbook of countersorcery.

Once when I was going along the beach on my way to Sanur, bringing some things there, it was about to rain, but I just prayed in my heart to my ancestors *(luhur)* that I would be all right.

I said, "If only I can get as far as that boat on the beach ahead"—there was a boat beached up ahead [with a large overhanging bow where he could shelter from the rain]. "If only I can get as far as that boat before it rains," I said. And in fact that's what happened. I had just stepped under it when the rain began. That's why I've never been caught in the rain on a trip.

But that other time, I got rained on because I had done wrong.

There was another time when someone asked me to do the rain-preventing ritual. [This was a man from the Brahmana Siwa group in Batuan.] He asked me to do the prayer over the offerings that he had placed on the altar: "Ida Adé, do the prayer gestures over these offerings up there." He had put the proper offerings there, and he added a special magical material *(srana),* which was a picture of Anoman.

He had done the rain-preventing ritual the day before, but he had been beaten, and it had rained. So now he told me to do the prayer. He had done his ritual with an offering that was filled with all of the different fruits of the market and the magical picture of Anoman. He had prayed to Anoman that he would be strong enough to send the rain clouds away. He had done it over and over, and the rain came anyway. He lost, that's all.

So now it was getting towards twilight, and he asked me [in familiar words]: "Well, what do you think, Dé, can you make the rain go away? Tomorrow is the big cremation. Then they have to make a procession to the sea. Can you stop the rain from coming? Just do the prayer over those offerings."

"Well, I'll only do it if you tell me to, Uncle Kompiang, but you must first allow me to climb up over there!" There was a high altar there, called the *balé surya.* "Let me put my own offerings up there. The ones you put there, you have already given to the gods. I just want to put up one small offering with only one or two pennies. If you let me do that, we can both do the ritual, side by side."

So then I told a child standing there, "Hey, go over there and tell them that Beli Madé would like to have a set of offerings, even a little one with only 25 *képéng*." That's why I said those things when I went down into the river. "Even two or one *képéng* will do."

So they brought me some offerings and some incense. And I climbed high up there on the *balé surya,* and then I looked carefully all around. The rain clouds were to the west, and they were very black and looked as if they were coming this way. And to the north it was also very dark. Now usually when you pray *(ngayabang)* you face towards the east. But now it was as if I were asking for a blessing from the clouds. Where are the clouds coming from, I asked myself. So I turned to the opposite direction from usual when I did the prayer, turning west instead of east. But that's what I had learned from the *lontar,* and that's how I did it. I heard someone down below ask someone else, "What's he doing, facing west like that?" But I didn't pay any attention. I didn't say anything. I was facing west because that's where the clouds were, and I was opposing them. It was like a war, I thought. If I had faced east, the clouds would have come up behind me and hit me in the back, and we would have been drenched.

Well, the end result was that for the next three days there was no rain.

The Ritual Lore of Building

The lore of *sikut* (translated as "measurement" but also "proportions") is a highly complex ritual matter that pertains to laying out buildings and walls, but also to the proper making of daggers and shadow puppets (which may, like buildings, be *tenget* or *sakti*). Any building project must first be visited by a ritual expert to determine the proper proportions among all its dimensions, spatial ratios that have mystical meanings. If these are not followed correctly, the place will be especially vulnerable to sorcerer's attacks. The units of measurements are based on the hand span, arm span, or foot length of the one who owns the plot or building. The prescriptions include not merely measurements but also the proper materials and the proper procedures to be followed in putting the building together. An indispensable element in *sikut* is the follow-up ritual, performed when all is completed, to bring the building (or houseyard, or *kris*) "to life." Knowledge of this lore, referred to below as knowledge of certain *lontar* such as the Asta Kusala (or Kusali), comprises both familiarity with its prescriptions and also the necessary personal *sakti* to make the spells work.

My son, Ida Bagus Ketut Panda, once came to me and said: "Father, come with me tomorrow. There is a man in Tegallinggah who is building a new houseyard gate and needs someone to do the ritual measurements and layout *(sikut karang)*." I had the knowledge but I didn't feel free in my heart. I had often done such measurements, but this one was in a houseyard that was already there. So I thought that I'd look for some help from a friend in Banjar Bedil, Sukawati. We often asked each other questions. Just a short time before he had worked on a building in my own house. His name was Madé Meregan, and he knew all about the *lontar* Asta Kusala and Asta Gumi. And someone said that he even had another *lontar* named Gunung Suméru. I asked to borrow it but I never did. It was still unopened.

Well, this time, I wanted to go and ask him if he'd be willing to help me on this measuring-out job. I already knew the measurements of the yard [in Tegallingah]. The north-south measurements were eleven, and the east-west measurement was eleven [arm spans of the owner]. That much I knew. So I thought to myself, "I'll go and ask him about it, since it's so far [to Tegallingah]." So I was going to go look for him, but my son wouldn't let me. He said that Madé Meregana was working on a cremation tower in Puri Sukawati, and that he'd be there for seven days, working in order to get it done. So my son went to Sukawati to look for him and bring him here. On his Honda motorcycle it only takes a minute. So my son went and got him, and when he arrived here I asked him: "Madé, I'm worried because that place is so faraway. It costs 100 *rupiah* to ride the jitney there, that's how far it is. I'm worried that when I'm there I won't know what to do, and I won't be able to come home and find out, and I'll be embarrassed. Please tell me, Madé, what are the right measurements for that situation?"

So then he calculated. "This much and that much, and if it is less than so much, use this, and if it's more, use that. . . ." He told me three different ways to calculate it and explained them. Then it was all clear in my heart.

Once he and I went to do a measuring job a long way away, northwest of here in Silungen. I liked to go with him because it was so easy for me then. I just sat in the family temple while he climbed down and did all the work. "This . . . this . . . this," he'd say to the owner of the house. I knew he was good; the proof was that we had him do the measurements on my own house. That's why I felt clear in my heart.

So the next day I went off to Tegallinggah. To make the story short, when I got there I looked over the whole plot of land to see what was lacking or what extra it had.

I think I've never seen as good land as that. It was level, and the plants grew richly. Whenever I travel now, I always think of that land as my model to compare with. The leaves were fresh and very green. Whenever you see really green leaves, you know the soil is good. And the bushes, and the yam plants were also very good. The coconut trees were very thick—where elsewhere a coconut leaf might have three branches, these had six. You can tell a dry region by the condition of the coconut leaves. Like my land here in Batuan—whatever tree you plant, half of its leaves turn yellow. Whatever I plant comes up, but it doesn't have much fruit.

So when I got there, they were very hospitable and gave me tea and food. I can't tell you how good it was. I asked them to get some string for me [for making the measurements]. After I had made the measurements, I asked them to get me a brick to bury as the first brick. I did the ritual, burying the right things under the brick and putting out the right offerings.

And when I was finished setting out the *kewangén* offerings with nine coins *(képéng)* in them, eight for each direction, and a ninth one for the middle, then I wrote the letters on the brick. I can't remember now what I wrote, but at that time I knew what to write. And when I was finished with that, I buried the brick and put a little soil on top of it. That was the foundation of the gate. Then the owner of the house filled up the rest of the hole with soil. That's the kind of work a Brahmana does. When I was all done, I went home.

Once, when explaining the drawing of his own houseyard (fig. 5), Togog spoke about a conversation he had with his next-door neighbor over the wall between their houseyards, which was crooked. This conversation must have taken place when they were both adults, when Togog was head of his household but before Truwi left Batuan in 1948.

I was talking with Ida Bagus Wayan Truwi about straightening that wall. There wasn't so much land within the bend in the wall, just about an arm's-breadth.

I said to him, "Beli Wayan, if you want to repair that broken-down wall, it's alright, but you'll have to be the one that keeps it up in the future. [Walls were made of sun-dried blocks of mud, which eroded in the rain; often they were roofed at their top edge with straw, to prevent them from eroding, but even then needed periodic repairing.] If you don't keep it up in the future, I'll be the one who loses, so if you don't want to promise to keep it up, then I won't give you the land. But it would be best if the wall were straightened so that we won't be "hot."

The word Togog used for "hot," *panesan,* also means "vulnerable to sorcery." If there is a large bend in a houseyard wall, it is like an opening through which enemies—usually neighbors—can send sorcery. A wall is sometimes called a *penyengkeran,* from *sengker,* which means "boundary" or "limit," but *penyengkeran* is also a type of *mantra* that draws a boundary around a person that protects them from other people's sorcery.

That's what I said. Walls should be straight and the corners four-square, not curved. That's what's written in the *lontar* Asta Kosala. In a Brahmana's house, it should measure thirteen along the north and south walls, and twelve along the east and west walls. [Togog doesn't give the measuring unit, but it would be based on the arm span of the landowner himself.]

The reason the wall around my houseyard was irregular for so long, they say, is that my ancestor the Pedanda [the one who first built the houseyard] was very *sakti,* and he had a very powerful amulet in his belt. He had sufficient power in himself so that no one would dare to use sorcery against him or his family. A man like that, who is fully prepared [*tetep:* "sure, firm, prepared"] can do anything, even build himself a home in the graveyard. That's called *ketetepang*—it means he has enough protection, and nothing will ever hinder him. [See also the drawing of Togog's Clan Temple (fig. 11), which shows Togog's houseyard on the far left, with his wall bending into the houseyard of Ida Bagus Kompiang Kuruh and his son, Ida Bagus Wayan Truwi.]

The Rebuilding of Pura Dalem Puri

In the early 1950s it was decided to rebuild the Pura Dalem Puri, which was completely in ruins. It was owned and cared for by the nobles of Batuan and Sukawati. It had been left to deteriorate by its stewards for many years, until by 1949 it consisted only of piles of rubble and a few bamboo altars. The regional community of nobles rebuilt it between 1949 and 1956. See H. Geertz, *The Life of a Balinese Temple* (2004), Chapter 8.

My Pedanda was responsible for the laying out of Pura Dalem Puri. After he did it, they put stakes in the ground to show where the walls and gates would be. They had the ceremony for laying the first stone.

I remember going there after that and seeing how they had set out the stakes, and I said to one of the people in charge: "Man, [*Nyoman,* a birth-order title], these distances are not the same as those given us by the Pedanda of Sukawati. They are an arm span longer. Weren't his measurements any good?"

"Oh, when he put the string out, he let it be slack, that's why it looks longer," said one of the two builders *(undagi).*

"Well, you ought to follow his directions. If you don't the temple won't be good for us. I'm not going to be mixed up in this." I said. "I've done many layouts of people's homes and it has to be done right. If it is supposed to be thirteen, then the person who owns the house is not allowed to change it. But you have changed the original measurements a great deal. If anyone here is afflicted with illness in the future, I'm not going to be responsible. I won't have anything more to do with this, since you've made it an arm span longer." I said.

"Well, this is the Durga measurement pattern," said the two builders.

So then I said: "Well, if you use a measurement pattern named Durga, when the god of this temple comes down, you will call her Durga. And if every time the god of this temple comes out, she takes the form of Durga, it will be a very frightening place here in the Pura Dalem." I said, "Even the god of the Mrajapati temple [right next to the Pura Dalem] will take the form of Durga." I was angry because they had not used the measurements that my Pedanda had given them.

Togog's son explained that the god of the Pura Dalem doesn't always take the form of Durga. The god is formless, but takes the form that is expected by the worshipers. So if the worshipers always think that Durga is the only form of the god in the Pura Dalem, then she will always appear that way, and everyone will always be frightened when they are there. He added that because Togog was angry he spoke in an exaggerated way, because of course the name of the measurement wasn't going to have that big an effect on the worshipers.

Once they wanted me to be Klian Dalem but I didn't want to. Because of all the evil spirits there. Since it was given that Durga pattern, whenever I went there I felt it was terrifying. The pattern that my Pedanda of Sukawati had given them was called Déwi Hyang Asih.

I went there at that time, and they were already almost finished with the laying out. And they had changed what he had given them. So whenever the god comes out as Durga, that makes you feel terror. It's like a snake that, even though it doesn't bite you, you think you've been poisoned. Or like that caterpillar with the hairs—if you just accidently brush against it you get a rash, even though it didn't bite you. That's what it was, that's why I give this metaphor.

[Referring to figure 22:] This picture shows the Pura Dalem Puri. This is Gria Dalem.

Gria Dalem is the houseyard with a gateway in the upper-righthand corner of figure 22. It is a houseyard of a family of Brahmana Buda that stands right next to the Pura Dalem, and not far from the graveyard. I estimate that it was built in about the first quarter of this century, when a new Pedanda was established and a home was built for him there. Someone explained to me that a location next to a graveyard is not dangerous to a Brahmana Buda Pedanda of great *sakti.* Some descendants of that Pedanda still live there.

Here, all the nobles are bringing big pieces of *paras* stone from the river to the east.

[Pointing to group with hoes, bottom right.] Here we were digging, and we found a human skull—the teeth were as big as your little finger, very thick. If you hit it, it looked as though it couldn't break—it was very thick. We were leveling the ground outside the temple, where the dancing pavilion is now. And then many people came gathering around. And then we planted it again, very deep. [This find might be of archeological interest. Perhaps the skull was that of a relative of Pithecanthropus Erectus, who was found in nearby East Java.]

And here [pointing to the kiln in the center] we were baking bricks all night. But the fire went out, and we couldn't light it again. So here I am putting my hand inside to see if there is any heat, but there wasn't any. The fire had died down. So when the Pedanda came, he said a prayer over it, and then he told me to go and get some wood remains from a cremation with which to stir up the fire and to burn. The fire had gone out because someone had done sorcery against us *(désti).* It had put the fire out.

I asked why someone would use sorcery to put out a fire like this, and Togog explained that it was a kind of a joke, and that they said it had been done by I Jana (mentioned in Chapter 1), who was just testing his powers of *sakti.* "He might think, 'I'll just try out my skill!' Just for fun. 'I'll just test, see if I'm still *sakti.*'" Togog stressed that although everyone thought that it was I Jana who had caused the fire to go out—his house is very near the graveyard—this was only a guess and no one actually knew he did it. I asked again why I Jana would want to put the fire out, and Togog answered: "Well, it's like this. He was the one who 'knew' *(uning)* the most around here. So people guessed that it was him. No one saw him. But it was because he 'knew' the most, and, besides, he owned a lot of followers *(sisia,* a term usually meaning the clients of a

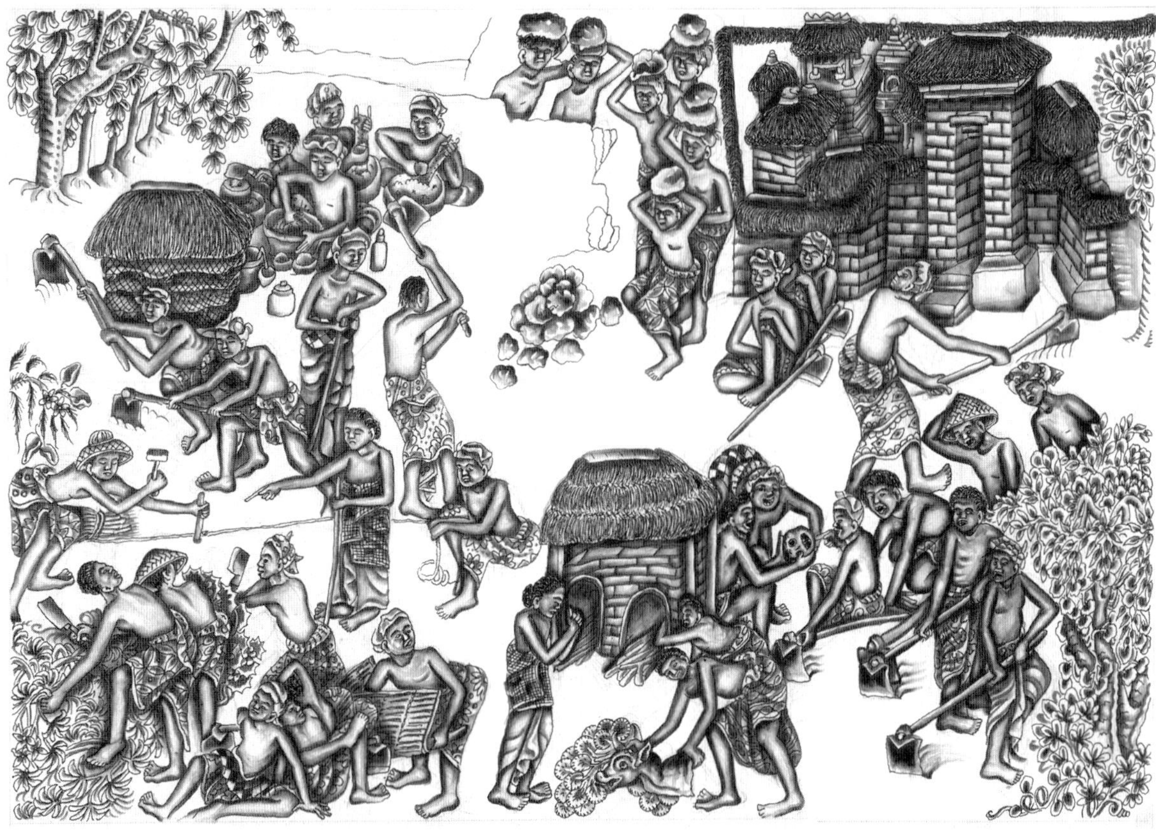

Figure 22. The rebuilding of Pura Dalem Puri. Drawing by Ida Bagus Madé Togog, 1986.

pedanda). He just wanted to see whether he could make trouble. But he couldn't because there were many *pedanda* there. He lost because he was beaten by the *pedanda*." Togog said, "I Jana didn't like *pedanda*—why would he, after all he's a *balian*." (Incidentally, I Jana's descendants, whom I knew, were still somewhat anti-*pedanda,* as they belonged to a Pasek movement that claimed its own priests could perform all rituals.)

So here [points to people working in the lower-lefthand corner], this is the rubbish left over after bathing the corpse, the thing that you bring it to the graveyard in. So there was all this rubbish there, and then the people are burning it, like the leg of the wooden *lembu,* and so on. So they use it to build up the fire.

And here is my Pedanda, saying the spell *(ngelarang)*. And then the fire flared brightly up. After he finished the measuring *(sikut)* he then did the prayer for the dead fire. He was resisting the sorcery. [The word I translate as "resisting" was *ngalangan*. It comes from *alang* or *halang,* which mean to be prevented or thwarted.]

When the fire went out, everyone went looking for firewood, there were about 150 of us. Some were cutting down the grass, because the place was all covered with bushes. Even inside the temple.

Now here [indicating the *pedanda* on the left, who is pointing at two men with stakes and string] my Pedanda is making the ritual measurements. To make the wall around it. [This *sikut* was done before the work began, before the fire was made for the bricks.]

Over here [top left] they are making food for the guests, for the people who are working, and these people are making the food. They made one *balé* [on the left] for the kitchen. People were hungry. There were sixteen who did the cooking. And all those who worked making bricks were fed. Later others came and took their places and they went home. There were a lot of nobles from here and from Sukawati. And some were carrying stones up from the Bisil River.

A Search for a *Sakti* Talisman

The following set of stories Togog told all together. He had been thinking, before we met that day, of telling me about various *tenget* matters, in particular about certain magical coins he had.

He started with a story about an old man who came from a village with a reputation for *tenget*-ness (for sorcery as it turns out), and how he was planning to ask him about these coins. He never got to ask the man, for reasons he explains, but that was the beginning of his quest. These stories, to the end of this chapter, all came together in his mind, with a common thread about a search for a source of *sakti* for himself.

One reason for some obscurities in these anecdotes was Togog's reluctance to tell me exactly what was in his mind that motivated him to go around and ask questions about coins. However, in the process of going over the transcription of the tape with Togog and his son, Togog explained to me that he wanted to find out whether three coins and a kris he had were *sakti*. If they were "alive" in that way, then it would be important to him to "feed" them offerings regularly, he said.

At another time, he remarked that he needed to find out about the kris and coins, not only so that he would be able to eliminate bad impulses in his heart (mostly about gambling), but also to protect himself from the attacks of others.

The kris, he said, he had found *(sambut)*. One of the coins, with a picture of Arjuna on it, he said had been given him by a *pedanda*. The other two coins had been lent to him by a woman named Anak Agung Kalit from the Batuan Puri. These coins had the pictures of Salya and Betara Ratih on them. Anak Agung Kalit had needed some cash and wanted to sell them to Togog, asking five *ringgit pérak* (silver coins of Dutch distribution worth two and a half *rupiah*). But before he bought them, he said, he wanted to find out whether or not they were alive. This was why he went to see the *balian*.

The *balian* took the coins from Togog and kept them overnight. He put his own coin in one dish and the three testing coins in another dish with six others, and filled both dishes with water. The *balian* often healed people with the water in which he had soaked his own *tenget* coin. It wasn't clear to me how this tested Togog's coins, but Togog said that the two borrowed coins failed, while Togog's own coin with the Arjuna on it proved to be alive. So, later, Togog gave the two coins back to Anak Agung Kalit, because they were dead.

Now, there was an old man who told me some stories about mysterious places and happenings. He came from a place that was somewhat *tenget*. The day before he was to have a cremation, he came to my Pedanda to ask him to perform a ritual to prevent rain from falling on his ceremonies.

After the Pedanda had said the spell for rain dispelling, I told Déwa Ketut Baru to do the accompanying ritual with me. It was a ritual to pray to the god who makes it rain. I already knew how to do the ritual, so I challenged Déwa Ketut to do it. [He said later he did that because he felt he didn't need the practice, and Déwa Baru did.]

"Tut! Tut! Tut! Ketut, go help the Pedanda do the rain-dispelling ritual!" and I told Déwa Ketut, "Make a fire here, and don't let it die!" [in familiar words]. And he answered me [respectfully], "Yes, yes, Ratu, go look for some *arak*-wine too."

"Yes, I'll go look for some *arak*."

And quickly I went to the old man and said [speaking down], "Uncle, go and get some *arak* for the *nerang* ritual!"

"Yes, yes, Ratu!" And he brought the *arak*. He brought a full bottle and gave me some, but I didn't like *arak* very much then.

I gave Déwa Baru the *arak* and he did the ceremony, and it worked and the clouds went away.

The reason someone wanted to make it rain on the ceremony might have been because he had felt himself to be made an object of ridicule. When they had the great procession to get pure water *(toya ning)*, there were at least 40 girls and 75 men in it, and they all had fancy kris with carved handles made of gold, and the women had gold flowers in their hair. It must have taken two basketsful of gold. Among those watching them must been a man who knew [how to bring rain] and he must have felt envy. They were all dressed in wonderful clothes, with their sashes trailing on the ground. Someone had gone to Jakarta and brought back beautiful cloth for them. So then someone must have felt—*pah!*—envious, and it was someone who knew how to make rain, I thought. [This is an interpretation on Togog's part of why someone would want to harm someone else by means of sorcery—in this case, because of envy of the fine clothes of a rival kinship group.]

Now I was going to ask that old man who told stories about a kris that I had and about some coins made of silver, but I never got to ask him about it because of that rain-dispelling ceremony.

I heard a story about two people who were killed doing that ritual to stop the rain. They were killed just as they stood there, by the one who knew how to bring the rain. [Togog implied that the killer was a rain-bringing sorcerer.] *Peh!* it's amazing what is in people's hearts. One was a *pedanda* and the other was a Brahmana who was not yet a *pedanda (ulaka)* and they were killed right there as they stood. There was only a small cloud in the sky, as large as a four-posted *balé,* and out from the cloud came a thunderous lightning bolt—*kelep!*—and it struck the two who were trying to prevent the rain and burnt them up as they stood there!

Well, after my Pedanda cleared the clouds away and completed the ceremony, those who had asked him to do it fulfilled their promise to give him some money for it, and so I went out because I didn't want to know about the money, so that I wouldn't desire it. So that's how it happened that I didn't get to ask the old man about the kris handle.

Whenever I went around, everywhere I went I asked about magical coins and kris handles. There was an Anak Agung in Kaba Kaba I asked, but he didn't know anything. I asked him, "Anak Agung, is there anyone around here who buys old, you know, coins?"

"No."

"But do you, Anak Agung, have any coins with names on them?"

Togog described the kinds of coins he was inquiring about as *jinah né madan-adan,* which literally means "money that is named." This term refers to coins with figures such as Arjuna or Salya on them—that is, figures with names. These coins are thought not to have been man-made, but to have appeared miraculously, as for instance in an offering.

"No, no, I've never paid any attention to such matters," he said. So I didn't get any answers.

So then I asked again, "Do you have any old heirlooms *(pajenengan)*—kris or spears—here, Anak Agung?" I dared to ask that.

"No, there aren't any except this one heirloom, which is all rusty. Maybe this one, this is all that I worship *(sungsung)* here." So I didn't get any answers. And then the *pedanda* from Delod Peken in Kaba-Kaba arrived. He, too, asked about the meanings of these things, coins and daggers.

I went once to Kapal too, with my Pedanda, and I still didn't get any answers. There was an old man there, and a *pedanda,* and I asked them, but I got no answer. I did get the story there of Lubdaka. It was told me by the *pedanda* from Tegal, Badung.

After that, we went to Gaji, but I didn't learn much about the coins. I did learn something else in Gaji, about cockfighting. At that time I wanted to reform myself. I had been addicted to gambling, all the different games: *dom, ceki, sampé, toplék, pincer, kobok, cebékéan,* and so on. I liked them all. But someone there told me: "Don't play those gambling games. If you have to play, play the cockfight."

Cockfighting, in Bali, is a form of gambling indulged in largely by men of middle age and older. Togog, like his friends, did not learn its system until middle age. The lore that he wanted to know about gives the gambler insight into which rooster has the mystical potency to win.

"Yes, but I don't know anything about cockfighting, about how to place a bet."

"Well, you do it this way . . . and this way. . . ." And so I went along with his teachings. "It's like this: If someone offers you three-to-two odds, you give him two for his three. So if you win, you get three. That's how it is." So he placed a bet for me, because I still didn't know how to do it. And I won. And then after that I kept on—sometimes winning, sometimes losing. So after that I understood how to bet in a cockfight, and I was hooked.

After that, when I met him, I'd ask other people about cockfighting and someone would say: "This is a good cock; put your bet on it. This is what this kind of cock is called."

I was interested in all that, but not as much as I was in the ways of *tenget* money and weapons.

So a long time later when I was in Pinatih, in Badung, I met a curer *(balian)* who had a *gamang* [a sorcerer's familiar spirit]. I was there for a ceremony at the Pura Desa, and there was an offering-maker, a *tukang banten,* there who told me about him. I was staying overnight there. She told me how she went to the *balian*'s house to get some money from him, 10,000 *képéng.* Now, I have since often visited that *balian*'s house and sat on his sleeping platform. There was no place he could keep money—the ground and the bench were completely bare, and his single pillow was made of wood.

So when the *tukang banten* asked him for the money, he said, "All right. In just a moment, just a moment." So the women went outside, just for a moment, and when she came back in there was the money, all piled up there at the foot of his sleeping mat!

So I asked the *tukang banten,* how could this be?

"Oh, be still, Tu! Whatever he wants he can have right away just by calling his *gamang* and telling him to look for it for him." That's what I would call *sakti,* to have a familiar *(kasihan)* like that.

Well, the *balian*'s son was my friend [so I asked him to help me talk with him], and the son said to me, "Gus Aji, Gus Aji, ask whatever you want of my father!" He was very rich, he was. "Whatever you want, just ask for it."

Later, in going over this section, Togog said that

the *balian* first told him three stories. The first one was about someone who had been trying to kill him. The man sent the *balian* some *arak*-wine with poison in it, but when the *balian* drank it he was not hurt. In retaliation, the *balian* took the poisoned wine to his enemy, and the man drank it and died the next day. The second story was about the *balé* in the temple in Penatih where Togog and his Pedanda had just slept the night before. Next to the *balé,* but lower than it, stands a statue of a *pedanda* sitting cross-legged. If anyone sleeps in that *balé* who is not spiritually strong, he will be afflicted by the spirit of the statue. In fact, two *pedanda* had slept there and died. But Togog and his Pedanda had survived, so the *balian* knew that they were *sakti.* The third story was about a Chinese man who baited anyone who was reputed to be *sakti,* and when the *balian* heard about him, he engaged with him in a testing of their respective powers and defeated the Chinese man.

So, I asked the *balian* [in familiar speech; the *balian* was also a *pamangku,* so he addressed him as "Mangku"]: "Mangku! Mangku! How is it that you are brave enough to fight other *balian* like that? What do you use? Please tell me the truth, I want to learn ."

"Well, it is like this, I have some coins here with eight *wayang* figures on them," he answered [respectfully].

"Yes? How does it work?" said I.

"Well, right now I'm busy. Some other time if you want to know about it *(uning),* come by here again and I'll show it to you, Ratu, so that you can know about it."

So, later, after I brought the Pedanda home and I was free, I went there again on purpose. I wanted to rid my heart of those bad habits [of gambling]. At that time I was making pictures, but I still didn't have a table. I worked on a wooden serving dish that was flat on top. Wherever I went in those days, whether I was assisting the Pedanda or whether I was alone, I always asked about the power of coins and of kris. I had both, and I was trying to find out which was proper for me to use.

I believe that Togog's digression about making pictures but not yet with a table was meant to indicate that he was still young at the time of this anecdote. When Mead and Bateson were in Batuan he did not yet have a table. Perhaps he also meant to point out that he was not yet doing well with the painting, and when he did have money, he was gambling it away.

So I went there to Penatih, and we talked about coins that have a picture of Salya or Arjuna or Betara Ratih on them. So I asked the Mangku: "Uncle Mangku, if you have coins like that, how can you tell whether they are alive *(idup)* [with magical power] or dead *(mati)?* Please tell me a little of what you know." And I asked him straight off: "Uncle Mangku, should I feed those coins? What do you feed them?"

"Well, I'll tell you, Ida Bagus. If the coin is alive, well, it will bring you good fortune, and if it is not alive, it won't bring you anything."

"*Bah,* if that's how it is, Wo Mangku, I'd like to know. I heard that you should feed these coins musk oil from a musk deer's genitals. I have some already, which I bought, and the peddler told me that."

"No, you only do that if you feel that the coins are losing their power."

"Well, that's it. You must know all about it, Mangku."

"I don't really know anything."

"Yes, Mangku, since you really know about it, I ask your help a little. I have a coin. I'll bring it here," I said. At that time I had an Arjuna coin at home here.

"All right, come here again another day, and I'll look at it."

"Well, it is important to me to know that I'm not carrying around something that is as useless as an old river stone. That's why I want to come here, so that I won't be just carrying around an old rock."

"Well, that's very proper. Come here tomorrow morning."

Well, the next day I went there. I walked by way of

Batubulan, where they have the [commercial tourist performance of] *barong* dance now. You go to their *balé banjar* and then you go west. In those days the paths were very narrow, but I didn't dare take anyone with me because that's the kind of knowledge that can't be spread around, that you can't reveal *(ten wéra)* it, that should not be known by many people. So I went there all by myself. *Peh!* It was lonely on the way there, empty, and I had to cross a graveyard. But to make the story short, I got there.

"Oh, you've come, Ratu!"

"Why wouldn't I come? It's so important to me, that which I asked of you, Wo!" I said.

"Yes, yes, well?"

"Here it is!" and I showed him the coin. And he took it and he looked at it, and he put it up to his ear and listened to it. And the coin disappeared. Then he said: "Well, Tu Bagus, leave the money here for a day. Come back tomorrow, Ratu, for it."

"Yes, that's all right; that's well, Mangku," I said.

He had a small turtle in a water jar. At that time I just loved to eat turtle meat, so I looked at that turtle—it had two white feet. A turtle with those markings is called Tri Bulusan. Turtle meat is important for offerings because it is pure *(suci)*. My wife is a *tukang banten,* and she uses them.

"Ah, Wo Mangku, Wo Mangku!"

"Yes, Tu?"

"Wo Mangku, why do you have this? What is this?"

"That's a turtle."

"*Beh!* When you kill these to make *lawar,* Mangku, save a little of the meat aside for me," I said, "and a little of the blood."

"Yes, I'll give you some," he said. "But that turtle, since it was in the form of Tri Bulusan, must have actually been a spirit *(tonya)!* The other day I was going to make *lawar* with it, but I didn't have any oil, so I didn't kill it. I went all around looking for oil, to make the *sambel* [peppery sauce], and I couldn't find any. That's why I haven't killed it yet. Another time I was going to make *lawar,* and I was missing something else from the spices. That's why it is still alive. When I do butcher it, I'll give you some."

"Well, Uncle Mangku, when you do that, keep some aside for me."

"Yes, I'll certainly give you some."

Well, the very next day I went there again, and that turtle had disappeared! There was a large river next to his house, and that's where that turtle must have lived. That was his familiar *(tonya)*. Maybe it was just visiting him, on vacation. That was his familiar *(kasihan),* his friend. So then I asked, "Well, tell me, Mangku, is this coin strong enough to protect me [or does it need something added]?"

"Let's see. It is lacking a little."

"Is it true what the *pedanda* who gave it to me said, that this is a picture of Arjuna, that this is an Arjuna coin?"

"It certainly is, Atu, most certainly. This coin has a different radiance *(téja),* not the kind that comes from polishing it with oil. This is a living coin *(jinah hidup)*." [The word for "radiance" *(téja)* also connotes a quality of *tenget,* as does the term for "living" *(hidup)*.]

And then, when I was about to go, he said: "Ratu, when you carry that coin, knot it into your waist cloth [i.e., not in your sarong], and when you go to shit, don't bring it with you. Put it down somewhere, and after you come back, pick it up again," he said.

"*Beh!*" I said. "Thank you very much!"

When Togog asked the *balian* the basis of his *sakti,* the *balian* told him it was a coin he had, but Togog thought this was not true and that his strength really came from his *gamang* familiar spirit, who was in the turtle, and who had given the *balian* his coin. The *balian*'s talk about cooking the turtle was just a pretense to conceal the turtle's importance. I later asked Togog's son whether he thought that his father had wanted to learn how to have a *gamang* spirit, and he said definitely no.

So after that he told me some of the lore of fighting cocks, especially how to tell a winner. I still carry the coin every day, even though I'm not going to cockfights any more.

So then I went to a cockfight in Klungkung, east of Klungkung, to see if it worked. I went there by myself.

A car pulled up behind me: "Get in, get in, get in! I'll take you there!" So I was taken there, but the charge was double. But I didn't care. I wanted so much to go. I wanted to see the proof [that the coin was strong]. My very first bet I won. But the man who placed the bet with me only wanted to pay half of what he owed me. I had bet four, but he only wanted to pay two.

"I don't want your money," I said. "I didn't bet that. Never mind, Jero, don't pay it. If you bet like that, I don't want to go along. I have a lot more betting to do," I said. I just wanted to go on with the cockfight.

What I have learned about cockfights is that there is a hole in the roof of the cockfight shelter, and that hole is where Begawan Bregu looks through to watch whether the betters are honest or not. "If you aren't going to pay, Jero, don't place any bets. I don't need your money." So after that, I won some and lost some, and then I went home.

Togog later told me about Ida Begawan Bregu, who was very clever at betting at cockfights and never lost a bet. All the other gods always lost. So they went to Betara Indra for advice asking, "Why do we always lose to Begawan Bregu?" Betara Indra told them to make a hole in the roof of the roof so that he, Indra, could watch through the hole to see what Begawan Bregu was doing. He saw that he won all the time. So Betara Indra went down among them when they were about to have a match and the two roosters had their knives tied on them and had been set loose to fight. Betara Indra seized the two cocks and said to Begawan Bregu: "You must stop betting on cocks from now on. But you may have the offerings that are put out before every fight. And you must watch over the betting through the hole to see which people are honest and which are dishonest."

When I had finished working with Togog on the above section, I asked his son whether Togog had sought the power of the coins in order to win at cockfighting. His son then asked his father, "Did you intend to use the coin in order to win in the cockfight?" and Togog answered strongly, "No! It was only so that I would not be afraid!"

Building a New *Balé Dangin*

Now I want to tell about my affection for my son, Ida Bagus Putu Gedé.

I wanted to sell a picture. I priced it at 600 [thousand *rupiah,* probably]. The picture was a story from the Tantri, the story of Paksi Baka, like this one here, about this size in its stretcher. And I had written down the story to go with it. But I hadn't yet found anyone to buy it. So then I priced it at 300, and someone bought it. So then I had the money.

I planned to build our *balé dangin.* I thought that I would change it, because the old one couldn't be used anymore. The old *balé* was magically dangerous *(tenget).*

This is the same *balé dangin* Togog spoke about in Chapter 1 when he said that it was the cause of one of his childhood illnesses. By 1950, according to Togog's son, Gedé, the *balé* had all broken down, and was just a big pile of dirt with small trees growing on it. In about 1960 they cremated Togog's younger brother, Ida Bagus Putu Tantra, and could only afford to erect a temporary *balé dangin* there for the ceremony. Then, in 1974, the time of this account, the new one was built. Perhaps this was when Gedé got married.

A *balé dangin* is the most important pavilion in any courtyard. It is a meeting place of all the kin—past and future—of a family. After a death, an altar is placed under its eaves dedicated to the recently deceased person, and offerings are placed on it at every important ritual, until the cremation. Sometimes it is used for the storage of family heirlooms, such as *lontar.*

I looked for a carpenter from Guang, and he went to find some *tewel* wood for the posts and for the rooftree. He found some great logs that could be cut in two. We needed three like that, for there are six posts.

And, to make the story short, I sent Ida Bagus Putu to buy some bamboo. I told him to go to buy it from Po Madé Meregan [in Banjar Bedil, Sukawati].

[Ida Bagus Putu Gedé:] "Uncle Madé, where can I get what I need?"

"This is what you should do. Go to the mountains to get big bamboo poles, and go to the sea to get coconut-tree trunks." So my son went to Jimbaran [where Togog's family has *sisia*] to get the coconut-tree trunks. There was enough there to make two *balé*—those are our *sisia* there in Jimbaran. He bought them from our own *sisia*, so they were cheaper, unlike buying them from someone on the road.

When he went to look for bamboo, we heard that there was someone with a lot of big bamboo in Bukit Celeng who was a friend of an Ida Bagus in Sukawati. It was he who told my son about it. I forget right now the name of the Ida Bagus.

So then the man from Sukawati, a *balian*, went with my son to Bukit Celeng. That man was certain he could find the bamboo for us. So then we had bamboo from the mountains, posts from Guang, and now we wanted to get the coconut-tree trunks from the sea.

Now that *pamangku* [apparently the one who went with Togog's son to the mountains] often came here. His name is Jero Sumbu [also known as Wayan Rentig]. Now, at that time, I was very concerned to find out about a kris I had that I had found somewhere *(sambut)*.

"Found" *(sambut)* is a cover-term for various ways to come by such objects. Since Togog always also uses the term *pajenengan* for the kris, meaning a sacred heirloom, it stands to reason that he "found" it among his family's treasures. The implication is that it could be inhabited by the spirit of one of his ancestors.

I intended to ask people wherever I went about the action of this kris, about whether or not it would be dangerous to give or lend it to someone else. No one could tell me anything about it except him. I must have asked as many as twenty-five people, some from far away, wherever I traveled to, whether in Badung in the palaces *(puri)* or in the homes of the *pedanda* in Badung. Whomever I met I went up to and asked. Now I wanted to try to see if this *pamangku* could help me: "*Peh,* Mangku, how come you're not afraid to come here in the night alone?" I asked him. "What do you carry with you that gives you the courage to come here? Tell me the truth. Is it some knowledge that you have that protects you so completely? I'd like to learn that. Or is it from an amulet *(jimat),* or a precious stone *(soca),* or something else that you carry concealed, wrapped up? I would like to learn, so that I'll have that kind of courage," I said.

"Ah, if you, Ratu, want to be tough, so that a bullet can't hurt you, I have something at home for you." He said he had something made out of nine kinds of metal, black iron, white, gold.

"No, that's not what I meant. Tell me about something else," I said.

"Well, look at this," and he took off his waistband and pulled out a kris.

"This weapon *(sanjata),* belongs to the god of Besakih.

"*Bah!* If you have that, Mangku Jeroné, you must know about the measurements *(sikut)* of kris!"

"Yes, at home I have a *lontar* all about it," he said.

"*Bah,* if that's so, Jeroné, I'd like to go to your house and consult your *lontar* about this weapon that I found *(sambut).* [Togog later said that when he brought the kris and consulted the *lontar,* it did indeed describe his kris there.]

So then, to make the story short, I brought it to him there.

"Well, what do you think, Mangku?"

He looked at it, and it was exactly like his own.

"*Peh!* This is exactly like mine. It's as if you'd borrowed mine," he said. "There are only six like it, owned by [the god of] Besakih. They were given to us here in Bali. Aside from this one, I know of only four others. If you want to know more about this sacred heirloom *(pajenengan),* you can read about it in the *lontar.* You can use it to protect yourself. First you have to soak it in water. Put some water in a bowl, and put it in the water, and then you can use that water for protection. Whoever is going out, sprinkle them with the water, and they'll be safe on the trip. That's what I have read in the *lontar.* But you also need some important offerings containing a young pig, and other things."

"Well," I said, "whatever you say is needed, Jero, I'll give you. Just tell me what you need. If you need white rice or sticky rice *(ketan),* just tell me how much they will cost, and I'll give you the money to buy them with."

"All right, I'll do it. It is very near to Kajeng Kliwon now, and we can do it then. [Kajeng Kliwon is the calendrical day when many powerful spirits are around, and thus is a suitable time for doing something connected with sorcery.] These are the things you will need, this and this and this. Gather them all together very carefully. You'll need a precious stone that has a mark in it like the footprint of a water buffalo. And you will have to grind that up with a grindstone and break it up into small pieces and then work it down until it is a fine powder. Then, when it is all done, put some of the powder in a banana and give it to everyone in your family to eat." My son here was with me at the time, and he had some, and it happened that my cousin, Ida Bagus Ketut Alit, was there too and he had some, all ground up and eaten in a banana. And some of the powder you rub on the kris. And the water from soaking the *kris* you use at the end of the ritual, to sprinkle everyone. The pig is used in the offerings.

When the ceremony was over, I left the pork and all the rest of the food in the offerings to him. I didn't want to bring them home, all that food that had served as offerings *(lungsuran).* [Togog said this because a Brahmana can't eat the *lungsuran* of other people's ancestors, and the offerings would have been placed in the *pamangku*'s commoner house temple, so they might have been "eaten" by his commoner ancestry.]

And still, today, every time there is Tumpek Landep I do a big ritual for the kris. I bring it out and give it offerings. I made a little box to keep it in, so that the kris would not be touched by various sorts of things [e.g., damaging things sent by a sorcerer]. If that happened, all sorts of troubles would come on me. For instance, a snake might fall down on my bed from above. That's why I was careful not to be overconfident. Twice it actually happened that a snake dropped down into my bed, and I had to look all over for it in my clothes. But even though it bit me, it didn't hurt me, because that kris served to make me immune. That's how it worked. [From my discussing this passage later with Togog and Gedé, they said that an amulet like the kris would provide a sort of tight covering all over one's person, so that nothing like a dagger or a bullet could enter one's body.]

So now I was ready to build the new *balé.* He [Po Madé Meregan from Banjar Bedil] was in charge of it all. The lumber for the big rooftree was ready, and for the pillars. But the rooftree was not good enough for him: "This won't be right, Atu. You should not use two short ones in place of the one long one that you need."

"*Peh!* If that's so, Madé, where can I find a *nangka* tree that's tall enough? If you can find one for me, I'll pay whatever it costs." That's because I had the money from selling that picture.

"Whatever it costs, just tell me, just ask me for the money," I said.

"*Bah!* All right!"

Well, to make the story short, he found one south of here, which was very tall. They picked all the fruits in a basket and gave them to my children in exchange for some wood for pillars. At that time, whatever money was needed I had ready. I didn't have much to do with the building of the *balé,* just discussed it sometimes with Po Madé. Then he came to me and said, "*Bah,* Atu, Atu, find me some *purnama sada* wood to make the wood pegs with." And the lower parts of the *balé* were to be made of teak. The teak was easy to find, but where would I find that *purnama sada* wood?

Purnama sada wood has powerful magical powers. It was to be used to make a small flat strip or wedge *(lait),* about three inches long and one or two inches wide, which is inserted in the joint where the vertical pillar and the horizontal roof girder meet. This wedge is thus a stabilizing element in the building; but several such wedges are also part of a ritual performed in the process of the building. In this case, all of the wedges were to be made of *purnama sada* wood, because this particular *balé dangin* was magically dangerous, *tenget,* and this condition had to be corrected. I couldn't find the term *purnama sada* wood in my dictionaries, but I was assured that it was a very special kind of wood.

The pegs, called *lait,* do more than secure the joints between the larger posts and rafters, in fact they transform any *letuh,* or polluted aspects, of all the building materials, said Gedé. They "pulverize" or "cleanse" the *letuh* away, he said, if any of the wood is *cacad,* or "scarred."

I said, "If you know where that sort of wood can be found, Po Madé, just tell me and I'll go and get it. If I have to go all the way to Jembrana, I will. If you know where it is, just tell me, 'go to the house of so-and-so and get it' and I'll go there! I'll go to Buleleng, even if it takes a week. Just tell me to go there. Or if I have to go to Karangasem, just tell me and I will!"

So he said that we could get that wood in the forest of Seloka, that it grows there. So to make the story short, my brother-in-law has a friend there, in Bukit Badung, the Perbekel. He had often been there, to that Seloka forest at the edge of the sea, to get turtle meat for sale. He had even stayed overnight there two times. And when they didn't have turtle for him, they offered him that wood so that his trip would not be wasted. Now that they knew there was someone who wanted some of that wood, they cut down a tree. Those people there knew how to do it, how to avoid the dangers in the forest, how to recognize the danger signs. If they hadn't known how to prevent trouble, anyone there could have been hurt badly.

So he found some of it and brought it back and gave it to me, saying: "*Pah!* I found some. Your family is fortunate. This is just what you wanted for your *balé*."

This *purnama sada* wood is needed to free the rest of the wood of the *balé* from all impurities, whether in the posts or in the beams. These impurities come about when, for instance, if when you chop down the tree it falls in the wrong direction and gets stuck in the top of another tree. That kind of wood should not be used in a *balé*. When you buy lumber, you don't know whether it is pure or not. It is most important for the posts, which should not be cut down carelessly. There is a special way they must be cut down. There was a tree caught up in another tree when it was cut down in Peninjoan, and someone offered it to me to buy. The top of the tree had been caught up in another tree. It wouldn't fall down, and then it had to be cut in two. That wouldn't be proper for a *balé*. I bought it anyway, but it needed the ritual. So that tree needed to have the purifying ceremony *(lukat)* to rid it of that dirt *(reged)*. *Beh!* [Since I had that special *purnama sada* wood] a lot of carpenters came and asked me for some. I only needed a little [and so could give away the rest]. There must have been twenty-five people who came for some, for a *balé* that was *tenget*. They even came from far away, having heard the news.

You can't sleep in a *balé* that is *tenget* or you'll have fearful dreams and you can't sleep. So that's why they came here to ask for the wood, *purnama sada,* and I gave it to them.

We never slept in our *balé,* and so my son said: "It would be better if we fixed up that *balé*. We can't sleep in it the way it is."

Now, after we'd finished that part, I went to look for some teak. I turned to someone who would know where to get teak. I went to I Wayan Senter [a wealthy art dealer in Batuan].

"Yan, Yan, I hope I'm not troubling you. Do you have any teak here?"

"Yes, I've twenty pieces of teak—take whatever you need, Atu. Whatever you want, big ones or a little one, just carry it away, Atu," he said. So I picked out some big ones, a handsbreadth thick.

So then, to make the story short, the *balé* was completed.

Five Family Matters

Two Intertwining Dramas

Two Intertwining Dramas • The Tale of Togog's Marriage and the Death of His First Child • The Family Dispute over Rice Land

Two chains of anecdotes in this chapter were intricately linked in Togog's mind. The first is the story of the ups and downs of his courtship, marriage, and the birth and death of his first child. The second is about a long and bitter wrangle between two sides of his family, both descendant lines from Togog's father's father, over several plots of rice land. The two narrative streams are not joined by a common concern with immediate family relationships so much as by a longer and deeper involvement with a larger "family" that includes the deceased as well as the living.

The first set, the stories of Togog's marriage and first child, were told to me in the order presented here. Togog included several flashbacks—to his experiences in Karangasem when his girl first refused to marry him, and then another side-story, even earlier, to his adolescence when he was nearly expelled from the temple of the Brahmana Buda group in Batuan for being hit on the head in a gambling quarrel—before finishing the tale with his marriage.

Togog related the second narrative about the dispute over land earlier in the same interview. But he told it in such a confused manner that I couldn't understand it. A large part of the confusion was due to his reluctance to say anything negative about the participants, and in his avoidance of so doing he often referred to people only obliquely, making identification difficult. Two years later I asked Togog's son to tell me the story of the land dispute in greater detail, after I had compiled a genealogical chart of everyone involved at each stage. But he said, no, it would be better for Togog to tell it again himself. Togog said he would in several days. But the very next day he came to my house to ask for a delay of about ten days or so, because there were signs that his ancestors were not happy about his telling it. (It seems that their kitchen had been invaded by a swarm of small worms of some sort.) Finally, when all was ready, we sat down together and Togog gave me the fuller, second version set down below.

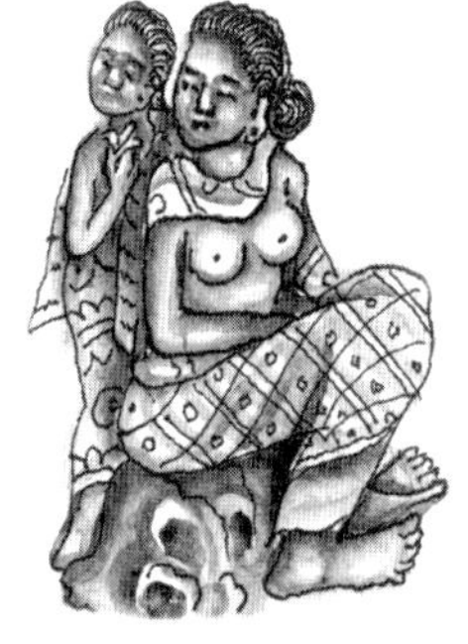

The stories demonstrate that, in Bali, marriage and living arrangements are the affair of a large group of relatives, especially all those with a common houseyard

temple. When a girl marries, the ritual affects not so much the joining of the couple as the severance of the girl from her own ancestors and her shifting of allegiance to those of her husband. All those who live in a houseyard are under the surveillance of the deities of its temple and also that of its recently deceased members, who, until cremation, are nearby and given to interfering in the activities of the living. An undesired marriage may anger any of these, and their anger may affect anyone in the family. Members of the wider circles of kin, those who descend through the father's line, are similarly but less imperilled.

It is such considerations that may have bothered the relatives of Togog's wife-to-be as well as Togog's father's brothers during his youth when Togog was gambling a great deal. Or it may have been more self-interested concerns (of living space or landownership) that motivated them. The "rules" of marriage partners and inheritance were strictly background assumptions, within which the family members maneuvered.

Similarly, inheritance of houseyard land and of rice land is not the affair of one or two people but of many. The customary rule of inheritance of houseyard land in noble families is that it goes to the youngest son, and it is usually observed, but contingencies often require exceptions. Certain plots of rice land are also expected to go to the son who remains in the houseyard, to pay for the continual offerings within the houseyard temple. Other plots of rice land are divided among the siblings and their descendants.

The *banjar*—which usually comes down to the neighbors—must be publicly apprized of every succession and inheritance arrangement, and must approve or disapprove it. The sanctions behind the *banjar*'s interests are the potential punitive acts of the recently dead or the deities of the *banjar* and *désa*. This is not a legalistic system, although it has been in the process of transformation during the whole of the twentieth century, as the colonial government, and after it the republican government, established land registration, land taxes, and a system of judges to enforce them.

In Togog's situation in Batuan, his *banjar* was not only his neighbors, it was also made up solely of members of the Brahmana Buda clan. Their interest was not the maintenance of tax flow, but rather keeping peace among fractious kin, dead as well as living. These were personal rather than legal concerns, much affected by contingencies of early or late death, and of marriage choices.

When studied from the perspective of a single life, it becomes clear that social organization—of kinship or bureaucracy or neighborhood—has a temporal dimension that cannot be ignored. Participants' calculations of future risks, rewards, and satisfactions—both in marriage plans and in access to harvests—and their memories and enduring resentments and affections, are all significant components in how they choose to act. The social arrangements of residence and sustenance are products not of rules as such but of complex successions of choices, some of them compromises.

The various aspects of Togog's life converged in his young adulthood. The history of his learning and practicing the art of painting enters here as well, tightly bound up with his marriage, his learning of ritual skills, his efforts to provide sustenance for a young family, and his search for meaningful songs and stories. The contexts of these ongoing events mutually defined one another.

The Tale of Togog's Marriage and the Death of His First Child

Greatly preferred—especially among the nobility—are clan-endogamous marriages. In this story, Togog's bride-to-be, Dayu Resi, was a Brahmana, but of a different line, the Brahmana Siwa. Her relatives insisted on her marrying a cousin. They felt so strongly about this that they settled for her being the second (and therefor inferior) wife of a not well-off carpenter cousin, and they forced her to go to him. Whether this act was due to antagonism towards Togog (who himself, at the time, was poor with few prospects), to his clan (they may have considered Brahmana Buda lower than Siwa), or to something else, is not clear.

Dayu Resi came from a *pedanda* family. Her mother and father were *pedanda,* and her youngest brother was to become one some years later. As related in Chapter 3, Togog had, throughout his childhood, hung around this family and others closely related to it, learning his Brahmana trade. But Togog too was from a *pedanda* family. It is clear that even Dayu Resi, although she liked him, didn't want to marry Togog either.

When she turned him down, Togog's reaction was to run away from Batuan. He went to the distant village of Budakling in the regency of Karangasem in eastern Bali. His family, many generations ago, had come from there, and his grandfather, Ida Pedanda Jelantik, had gone there for his spiritual training. Since a *pedanda* must periodically return to his spiritual mentor, his *nabé,* to pay his respects, Togog probably had visited Budakling a number of times. In the tale, the Pedanda of Gria Agung of Budakling recognized him and gladly took him in. When Dayu Resi became pregnant with Togog's child, he was told to return and marry her.

To explain about what happened to the baby, Togog interrupted the story of his courtship and marriage to flash back to an event that took place when he was only about twelve years old, when he had been threatened with expulsion from the family temple. Those in the family who were most active in trying to push him out were probably his father's two older brothers. Studying the family genealogy, it is evident that these two uncles could have profited from Togog's expulsion, in that he was also a strong claimant to the family lands formerly owned by their deceased father, the Pedanda. Whatever their motives were, they remained hostile to Togog the rest of their lives, according to him. The daughter of one of these uncles married Togog's older brother and, many years later, became a major contender for the land disputed in this chapter. Togog saw the exclusion from his family of his newborn child as a continuation of that earlier dispute with his uncles.

A person of importance in both these narratives is Pedanda Kerta, the teller of tales in Chapter 3. He was another Brahmana Buda who had moved from Batuan to Denpasar many years earlier to become a religious judge *(kerta)* in the Dutch colonial system. Togog recounts in this chapter how he first came to know Pedanda Kerta during his effort to stay in the family temple group. Later, as a very young man, Togog often went to serve in the Pedanda's household, and later still, when selling pictures in Denpasar hotels, he often stayed overnight at his house. Pedanda Kerta remained a moral guide throughout his life. Togog's Grandfather Gria, his father's father's brother, also plays an important part throughout these events, although he is hardly mentioned.

First Act: The Rejected Suitor

When I was about seventeen years old I wanted to marry my present wife. Of all the girls, only this one was for me. Yes, there were many others, both high- and low-born.

Here Togog showed me a worn photograph of Dayu Resi, Togog's wife, with their daughter, Dayu Putu Gambar (the name means "picture"), at the age of two. The photo had been taken by Gregory Bateson in 1938.

She was by then doing everything a woman should do, all the cooking and so on. Her younger brothers didn't know the classical literature yet, the one here and the other one who is now the Pedanda in Celuk.

The first brother was Ida Bagus Madé Diksa, who was sitting with us listening to Togog's tales, and the second was Ida Bagus Nyoman Tampi Sanur, who was a prolific painter in the 1930s, but later moved with his mother to Celuk, a nearby village, where he became a *pedanda*.

I often went out assisting my wife's mother, the Pedanda Istri of Gria Pacung, at ceremonies. When there was a cremation I would make many of the offerings. If they needed a god-figure *(prarai déwa)* I'd make it for them. And besides I could tell people which were the auspicious days for making cakes for offerings, or for husking rice, or for cutting down trees for the firewood. I already knew all those things.

She was still a maiden, and we were together almost as if we were married, except that we didn't yet make love together. We'd talk together and share things.

So then it happened that there was a big ceremony in Badung, at the Gria of my Pedanda there, Pedanda Kerta, and I was told to go there to help.

The reason I had to go was that my older brother had been asked to help but he didn't want to, so I was sent in his place. I didn't know yet what I was supposed to do there.

When I arrived I discovered a lot of people from here had come too. They told me to make a *gebogan*.

A *gebogan* is a tall offering on a pedestal with a demon face and outstretched hands (a *boma*) at its base, wings behind the hands, and many decorations made of a paste made of rice flour mixed with sugar.

I said I'd make it, even though I didn't know how to. I figured to myself, "Some one will come and help me." [Laughs.] That was how I thought I'd do it!

So I just said, "Yes, I'll make it."

Well, just while I was away, her relatives gave Dayu Resi to someone else in marriage. She was still a virgin, my future wife. She was forced to marry a kinsman of hers. He already had one wife. He took her without even an engagement period. He took her and she was angry. I can't tell you how angry she was. She herself was hot in her heart. She had stayed in his house only a month, and then she left him and went home.

Later she told me, "Only *one* time, he came to me. He said he had to come in to my room to look for a chisel, and that's why I opened the door."

Well, in spite of that, I still wanted to marry her. We were a good match. So when she came back I moved in with her, and we were like a married couple [but they had not yet been officially, ritually married].

Then she got pregnant, and I wanted to marry her.

But she didn't want to.

Second Act: Going to Karangasem and Learning the Ritual of Tooth-Filing

So I just went away from Batuan.

I went to Karangasem. I walked the whole way. I took with me the picture I told you about, the one made of bark paper, to pay for my trip. [This was the first painting Togog ever made. See Chapter 6.]

I went by way of Klungkung. I walked very fast and got there quickly. When I got to Klungkung I went to the market and offered it for sale. Someone bought it for three *rupiah*. I had priced it at five, and she offered three, but I just let her have it for that. So that I'd have money for the trip. It was a lot of money, three *rupiah*.

A *spice* trader bought it! [rather than, as would be the case today, a dealer in paintings]. I thought that she must have thought it was very good or she wouldn't have bought it like that!

So now I had some money for the trip, and I went on eastward.

When I got to Karangasem, Budakling—my Pedanda's spiritual mentor *(nabé)* is from there, from Gria Ageng in Budakling—I went to find Gria Ageng, asking for directions as I went. When I got there, I went in.

"Hello! Dé! Where did you come from?" he said, speaking down.

"I came from Batuan, Tu," I said respectfully. "I'm the grandchild of the *pedanda* who did his spiritual studies here."

Beh! They were kind to me! *Beh!* It happened that it was good for them that I came to stay because that house was empty. There were just the two *pedanda*s [husband and wife]. There weren't any boys or men there. They'd all left. One had become a judge. They all had high positions elsewhere. High status.

So I stayed and worked for them there. I husked their rice, and in the mornings I went to the fields to get food for the pigs.

Beh! I can't tell you how hard I worked. I wanted to distract my mind from my troubles. If I had stayed at home I'd have felt very confused. So I worked hard.

There were lots of girls there, and they didn't know that I had a girl at home. They didn't know that I had a girlfriend back home and about the badness, the trouble, and the pregnancy. I kept it a secret. They thrust themselves at me. There were six of them—all very young—visiting there.

One of the girls there, named Dayu Madé Gud, said to me: "Dé, Dé, Madé, you have all these 'older sisters' here, and also 'younger sisters.' Of all of these which one would you like? If you are interested in having a girl, I'll help you!" That's what Dayu Madé Gud said. One morning she had told me to make some shampoo for her, to gather up some *dadap* leaves and cut them up with *kemiri* nuts. And I brought them to her. She was inside the house, and I gave her the shampoo through the window. That's when she said that about whether I had any desire for one of the girls. Besides, the older people, the ones who owned the *gria* there, would have liked it if I could have married one of those girls and lived there, because their house was empty. All their sons had left to find work in distant places; they weren't even in Bali. I didn't have any desire for those girls as I already had a sweetheart at home.

So then, once I had learned how to do the ritual of tooth-filing *(masangih)*, I went to Ujungsri with the Pedanda, to help him. He had nine to do there.

The Pedanda called me to him and said, "Dé, Dé! Dé, Dé Jelantik!" That's the name they called me by there [Jelantik is the name of Togog's clan]. "Come with me and I'll teach you how to file teeth" [speaking down].

"Yes," I said. I always spoke in high words to him *(basa)*. So we went. Someone came from there to take us there. It was called Ujungsri, in Karangasem. The place was utterly desolate. The house was far from any other houses. The other houses were far to the north and west of the rice fields. It was way at the end of the area. We were to do the tooth-filing there.

So we set to work with the ceremony, to file the teeth. There were nine people to be done. And they didn't give us anything to eat from morning until noon. I turned and looked at the kitchen, and there was no one cooking there.

"*Bah!* I'll die of hunger," I thought.

And the Pedanda just kept on right there next to me.

"Do it this way!" he'd say, and he'd take my hand. "Don't do it like that! Hold the file like this, so you won't make a mistake and hit the lips. Like this, like this!"

But it was already twelve o'clock, as we say now, and there was no one there helping to prepare the food.

"What kind of a festival is this? What's going on?" I thought. There were only a few offerings there on the *balé dangin,* just four *wanci*-dishes of them.

My hunger got greater and greater, and I thought I couldn't work any more. They hadn't given us anything except coffee and one bunch of bananas, and we ate them all up. The sun was already moving towards the west when a bicycle came up bringing the food. They had *bought* it, the food, complete dinners. It was all laid out for us, plenty of it!

I thought, "*Beh!* This is the way they do things here. It's easy for them to just buy the food!"

And then they gave the Pedanda a lot of money, 1,700 *képéng* for each one whose teeth were filed. After that, the three of us brought it all home, and I was given 1,200 *képéng* and a piece of cloth.

That's what I got for learning how to file teeth.

In Budakling they gave me some money and also some cloth, and I took that money and I bought a shirt, a head cloth, and a shawl because it was the cold season then. I was there a long time, and the work was very hard. I had to thresh the rice with mortar and pestle, and I had to gather food for the pigs. I had never done that sort of work in Batuan. Whatever they asked me to do, I made myself do, even pounding the rice.

Third Act: Dayu Resi Is Pregnant; Return to Batuan and Marriage

After a while, my future wife back here in Batuan was very big with the child, and a telephone call came to Budakling telling me to return to Batuan. [The use of a telephone indicates the involvement of the colonial government, as those offices were the only ones with telephones at the time. Probably someone from the Batuan noble house with connections with the Dutch used the phone.]

This is what they told me: "Dé, Dé, Madé, they say that you can't stay here now. The government has ordered you to go home!"

So the next morning I left. I had left home because even though she was pregnant I wanted to marry her, but she didn't want me. That's why I left her. So now I began to walk home. I went straight south to Manggis. It was absolutely empty country, just a *jaka* forest and no one in sight. I sang songs to myself to make myself brave. I had right on my side. I looked around carefully all the time for people with evil in their hearts. I thought if I saw someone like that, I would hide. I passed that area and then came to the region east of Klungkung, still far from Klungkung to the southeast near the sea, and there were nothing but cactus plants along the road—cactuses to the north, cactuses to the south, nothing but cactus. There weren't even any coconut palms, just cactus and thorny bushes.

Suddenly someone appeared right behind me, "Jero! Jero! Stop!"

I paused and said, "What do you want?"

"Where do you come from?" he asked [politely].

"From Batuan" [politely too].

"Where were you just coming from now?"

"I just came from over there, from Karangasem."

"Well, what were you doing there?"

"Well," I answered to make him think that I was bad and tough: "It was like this. The people back home in Batuan were angry with me because they knew I had stolen something. One day I passed a crowd of ten of them who were hoeing. When I came near they came towards me. They didn't say anything but I knew they were angry. So I ran away. I went to Badung to Ida Bagus Tantra's place where I learned the martial arts *(pencak)*. When I was good at it, I heard that there was a man, a commoner named Guntur in Peguyangan, who was very good at *pencak,* so I went there for a while, and then I heard that over in Karangasem there was a man who was especially good at *pencak,* and that's why I went there, to learn some more."

"Did you take lessons from him?"

"Yes, I sure did!" I said. Those words seemed to come out of my mouth as if some strange wind had put them there, as if my lips were moving like a shadow puppet's.

Then he asked, "What are you carrying?"

"I've got a sarong, a shirt, 1,200 *képéng,* and also two and a half in silver money. That's what they gave me when I did some tooth-filing ceremonies."

He then spoke in a much more respectful manner, "Oh yes, Ratu, if it were not that you were a Brahmana and like my own head *(tendas titiang),* I would have demanded all that you have!"

He was carrying two pots of oil hanging from either end

of a long club made of *uyung* wood over his shoulders. I thought to myself, "If he attacks me with that club, I'll get him with my knife. It has blades on both sides. If he tries anything with that club, I'll not let him near me." That's why I had such a firm voice with no trace of fear in it. So then he told me who he was.

"Begging your pardon, Ratu, my name is Selam Ketimun from Sasak. [Sasak are a people in Lombok. The name Selam comes from the word Islam, so this is a Moslem man from Lombok.] I am very unfortunate. At home I have two wives and four children. I was working on a ship, but I walked away with their money—a million it was. That's why I came here. I'm just staying right here by this road. I get my food from anyone who passes—whatever I can get—or with my loot I get the people around here to go and buy food for me. Every day the police come by looking for me, so I just lie down in among the cactuses and hide. I'm suffering because I never see my wife or my children because I gave in to my greediness."

Just then we passed a peddler sitting on the road with one leg stretched out, selling betel-chewing materials. She had a jug of water next to her but was apparently selling nothing else.

So then the thief tried to sell her some drugs: "Here, buy these drugs! I've got medicine for aching bones, medicine for skin infections, medicine for stomach troubles, and here is some specially fine honey [considered a medicine in Bali]." He held out to her the skin infection salve because the peddler had an infection on her leg.

"Oh, let me look at the skin medicine! I have an infection on my foot. Please look at my leg," she said.

So he stopped and said to me, "Wait a minute for me."

"Oh, I'll just walk on slowly," I said. So I walked on, and as soon as I was out of sight I broke into a run.

Togog makes three statements to the thief, all of which seem to have been intended to convince him that he is *sakti*. First he says that he is an accomplished *pencak* fighter. This martial art discipline always entails mystical technique as well as athletic skill. He then tells the thief that he is carrying a lot of money—with the notion that the thief will think that if he's so bold as to boast of how much he's carrying, he must be very tough. Last, he tells him that he has just been tooth-filing. Togog's son told me that any person competent to do the ritual of tooth-filing has to be *sakti*. The people lying there having their teeth filed are especially vulnerable to sorcery because their minds are all caught up in what is being done to them, and so they need the strong mystical protection of the tooth-filer himself.

I ran as hard as I could. I was afraid that once we were alone he'd try to rob me, and what would I do then? I ran as far as Kusamba, and only when I got there did I slow down. But I was still walking very fast. I came to the turn where the road goes west, and there are a lot of thorny bushes that are quite high right there. I was walking very fast when all of a sudden right near me was a man carrying a big knife.

"Jero! Jero! Stop!" he cried out to me.

"*Badah!* Now I'm in real trouble!" I thought to myself. His knife was razor sharp, and it looked as if he'd just been cutting down those tough bushes.

"Jero, please stop! Why are you running like that?" he said.

"I was running away from a man all dressed in black with black pants, black shirt, and black hat."

"Why were you running from him?"

"He didn't look like a friend to me."

"*Beh!* You were very lucky! . . . What are you carrying?"

"I have 1,200 *képéng!*"

"*Beh!* You were really lucky! Yesterday a man was attacked by him. He was transporting sweet palm wine worth 175, and *bantal* cakes, which sell for 10 each. He's a highway robber, that man dressed in black pants, black shirt, and black hat. He hides right there where you were. Anyone who comes by there he throws down among the cactus and robs. The police are looking for him." That's what he said. "*Beh!* You are very, very lucky! Good luck on the rest of your trip!" [Togog laughs heartily.]

So then I walked on until I came to the area just east of Klungkung. Ratu! Was I thirsty! I can't tell you how thirsty! And all the way there, coming from the north, there were many streams, but they were dry. There they have peddlers selling pitchers of water. For one *képéng* you could drink as much as you wanted to. But because I was running just ahead of that man I hadn't wanted to stop and buy water.

Then I saw a man picking coconuts—it was still east of Klungkung, still really far from the town. I thought to myself, "*Bah!* What'll I do? If I don't make myself bold, my stomach will burst from the heat and the thirst! If I just try and bear it what will I be like when I arrive home? If I arrive home at all! I should ask help from that man, and if he won't give me a young coconut, then I'll buy it from him."

So I went up to him. He was up in a coconut tree in the middle of a field. "Jero! Jero! You up there, please help me. Bestow *(icén)* a coconut on me!" I said [in respectful words], and then I added [speaking down], "Give me one!" I asked him like that, in two different ways. If you speak to a commoner and you use the term "bestow *(icén)*," that's not right, but if it's a noble, you should say "bestow."

"Hey! Where've you come from?" he said politely. "Where are you coming from?"

"I'm from Batuan" [also politely].

"Where were you coming from now?"

"I just came from Budakling—I was there a long time."

"Ratu! Oh, Ratu, Your Highness *(tendas titiang)*. Oh, Ratu, are you an aristocrat?"

"Yes, I am a Brahmana from Batuan, and I have kinsmen there."

"*Bah!* Well, Your Highness *(tendas titiang)*, what might it be that you desire?" he said [very respectfully].

"Oh, break off a young coconut for me" I answered [in low words].

The above passage is a good example of how Balinese negotiate relative rank in a situation of uncertainty. As Togog explains, since he does not know what status the stranger up in the tree holds, he at first addresses him in both the high and the low register terms for "give." The stranger's question "Where are you coming from?" is the conventional greeting. The answer may be quite vague, but Togog deliberately chooses to tell him specifically that he has come from Budakling, which automatically informs the stranger that he must be a Brahmana, and the stranger immediately catches on and addresses him as "Ratu" and "*tendas titiang*" (lit. "my head," which I translate as "Your Highness") both of which are very respectful terms of address appropriate to a Brahmana. In the end Togog knows that the low register is appropriate for him and the high register for the stranger.

So he brought me down a young coconut, and then cut it in two for me so that I could get the milk from it.

"Take this with you, so that when you need a drink along the way, you can drink this," he said [with great respect].

So I carried it along with me, until I got close to Klungkung and I didn't need it anymore because now there were many food sellers. I threw it away then and walked on.

There weren't any cars in those days. Only the government people had cars. So, to make my story short, by night I was in Samprangan [just east of Gianyar]. It was very late at night, and I couldn't walk any more towards home. I just couldn't. So then I looked for a place to spend the night, and there was the home of a man who had once come and stayed overnight here in Batuan.

I knocked on his door and called out, "Grandpa! Grandpa!"

"Who's there?"

"Your grandson, Grandpa, from Batuan!" I said boldly.

"Yes, well, where're you coming from now?"

"I've been in Budakling, Grandpa," I said.

"Well, welcome! Come on in!"

Well, he had only one little house *(balé)*, the size of six posts only [about 15 by 10 feet at the most], with an inner room made of woven bamboo walls. And he said, "You can stay here, I'll make you some rice porridge."

"No, don't bother. I just finished eating," I said. "Don't go to any trouble!"

I was surprised to see that he was wearing a huge gold ring, a gold ring. He was too old a man to wear a gold ring, and I guessed that he wore it to attract the young woman who was with him, for young women always desire gold. She was very young and she was caressing him as if they were married, you know.

So there I was lying just outside their room, and they were inside fooling around and rustling. I couldn't sleep, as if it were daytime. I said to myself, "*Bah!* I can't sleep!" It was still late at night, what you call today four o'clock.

"Grandpa! Grandpa! I'm leaving, Grandpa!" So then I started walking home again. I'd been walking for two days, but my fatigue had left me completely.

When I got home here no one else had yet been told to take her in marriage, my present wife. So I went to Gria Pacung.

The reason I went there was that from the beginning, you know, from the time she was young, I had always wanted to marry her. I had always showed that openly, and we never did anything bad. I was always over at her house. I'd help with the cooking. I did all sorts of things for them.

Then, that time when I went to Badung to help the Pedanda, and while I was there, her parents gave her in marriage to a kinsman in order to prevent her from marrying me. [The phrase I have translated as "to prevent her from marrying me" was actually *pang ten nglintang meriki*, or "so that she would not cross over to here."] They kidnapped her *(mejuk)*. They forced her.

When I heard the news in Badung that I had lost her, I cried. I grieved for myself because it hadn't happened the way I wanted it to. When I went to sleep my pillow was soaking wet with my tears. I felt so very sad.

Those of my generation, if they can marry a virgin, they are so thankful, so happy for at least a month, kissing and loving, feeling for at least a month as if immortal. But she [my future wife] was no longer a virgin because she had been forced to marry her kinsman. She was less than a month in his house. He already had a wife. And she was right for me. But her parents did not think I was right for her, thought she should marry only a kinsman. After she was with him a month she went back to her home, and then I took her there and she became pregnant—and I made her pregnant. The reason I went east [to Budakling] was that she still didn't want to marry me.

Fourth Act: The Child Is Refused by the Clan-Temple Group

When I got home again [from Budakling], her relatives forced her to marry me. I wanted to marry her, but here in my family they would not accept the baby. They called the child a bastard *(panak bebinjat)*.

Togog's son explained to me that the baby was considered a bastard, not because he had been conceived before there had been a wedding ritual *(masakapan)*, nor because of some special Brahmana purity, but rather because it was not really clear who the father was. The clan of Brahmana Buda in Batuan had to defend itself from the possibility that a child with outside paternity was to be included in it. This was similar to the threatened expulsion of Togog himself from the clan, described below, in that in both cases a threat existed that in future generations there would be an alien or polluted soul reincarnating himself in his descendants.

And then, in order that the child would not have trouble when it grew up among my relatives, I did as my Po Ketut had done before, as I told you already, when he got a girl from the same *gria* pregnant. He took the child to Pangsan [see Chapter 2]. I did the same thing as he had done, looked for someone to take the child so that he would not grow up here.

So I was in a defiled state *(letuh)* much like I had been once long before when I was gambling.

Flashback: How Togog Had Been Defiled and Nearly Expelled from his Clan Temple

The way I became defiled when I was gambling was this. I was slapped [in the face] by a Satria boy while gambling. We were playing *papincer.* Do you know, Nyonya, how to play *papincer?* If the white side comes up, the person on the east wins, not the west. So then when the east wins the west pays.

Togog demonstrated his point with a coin daubed with white lime on one side. In *papincer,* one set of players bets that the white side of the coin will come up, while the other ones bet on the plain side. At each throw the bettor who places the first bet gets paid off first by his counterpart on the opposing side. If you place your bet late, and are not recognized, you won't be paid off. The argument described came about because of a disagreement as to who placed the first bet. Togog thought he had placed the first bet and should have been paid off first. The others thought his bet was made later and therefore he should receive no money.

I was gambling and I placed my bet on the west. I bet only one coin. Others were betting three, two, five. And then I won, but I wasn't given my winnings whereas the others were given theirs—one was given four, another one got five. No one had said that I had put mine down after them, and I had had a strong hunch that I was going to win. The other fellow took his winning portion, and then I asked, "Is he the only one who's getting paid off?" And everyone was still, didn't say anything. I said, "If you don't give me my winnings, for the rest of your life you'll always lose!" Rightfully, the first one who puts down money should get paid first, and then the second one. So that's what I said, "For the rest of your life, you'll just keep losing!"

This is a very serious curse that Togog was attempting to place on his fellow gambler. Perhaps he felt empowered mystically to make it stick. In any case, the dispute was caused in part by Togog's own carelessness, as he hadn't made sure that everyone knew he'd placed his bet first. And it was aggravated by the intensity of Togog's desire to win, indicated by his saying that he had had a hunch that he would win.

And then suddenly—I didn't see it coming—I was slapped, *peng!*—right here, *plak!*—not too hard, not hard. And then I said nothing.

A portion of the story was lost here, in changing the cassette. Togog told how his kinsmen felt that he had been so insulted, so polluted *(letuh)* by this slap on the face, that they wanted to expel him from the family temple, their *mrajan,* and by extension from the clan temple, the Pura Panataran. Such an act would mean that Togog would no longer be a Brahmana, but demoted to Satria.

He went to an older member of a further branch of the family, Ida Bagus Wayan Duduk, who advised him to find out from a *pedanda* what sort of ritual could free him from the *letuh,* or else sometime in the future the group might turn him out. He went first to the *pedanda* of Batuan and then to Pedanda Kerta in Gria Kaliungu, Badung. He thought he was about eleven or twelve years old at the time.

Who exactly among his kinsmen were eager to have him expelled from the temple is not clear. He implied that it was everyone in the whole clan, since all of them came to his final ceremony to absolve him of the defilement. However, the members of his own houseyard must have been strongly involved, because the actual ceremony was in his own houseyard temple. His father was dead at the time. His father's two older brothers refused to go with him to visit a *pedanda* to find a way out, so they were clearly against him. His own older brother, too, was not interested in helping him. His father's brothers and his own brother had an economic interest in excluding him from their group.

So I went to ask advice of the Pedanda Kerta in Badung. He was a judge *(kerta)* there, and I respectfully requested him to tell me what was the right thing to do.

Who went with me there? My mother's brother, named Ida Bagus Ketut Jelantik, and also Ida Bagus Wayan Duduk, whom I called "Uncle Yan" because he had married the younger sister of my father.

Note that these two intermediaries are people who do not belong to the family temple to which membership descends through the male line: the first, Togog's mother's brother; and the other, his father's sister's husband, Duduk. The latter man, in particular, was respected because he had been close to Pedanda Istri during her lifetime and then became a companion of the new *pedanda* in the family, Pedanda Madé Jelantik, Togog's father's half-brother, whom Togog often assisted.

The ones who should have gone with me [his closest paternal relatives], who didn't want to talk to me, who just wanted to expel me, were the two brothers of my father. One was called Ida Bagus Wayan Dupa, and the other was named Ida Bagus Ketut Raja, and I called them both "Uncle" or "Po." When I asked them to go and they didn't want to go with me, I said to my father's brothers: "Don't you want to go with me, Po Yan, Po Ketut? If you don't want to go with me, if you don't want to accompany me in trying to find the right thing to do about being slapped by a Satria, then that means that you are throwing me out of the family! Yes, that's just the way it is. If you want to break off with me, I'll break off with you."

In the end neither of them went with me, and forever after that, until both of them died, I never went to any of their ceremonies. I didn't want to. If they didn't like me, why should I lower myself to go to them? That's how I felt. So when they had ceremonies—for instance, a tooth-filing—I wouldn't go there. That was the beginning of the problem—they didn't want to help me, they were ready to lower me down to a Satria's rank.

So I went to ask for advice in Kaliungu, Badung, with the two people accompanying me. This is what Pedanda Kerta said [speaking down]: "What we here in Badung think is the right thing to do might be different from what is done in Gianyar. You should go first to Gianyar and ask what is right to do, and then come and tell me what they said."

That's how my friendship with Pedanda Kerta in Badung began and my getting stories from him [recounted in Chapter 3]. From that time on, I went often to the *gria* in Badung, often slept over there, and they always gave me good things to eat and he would tell stories. He liked to tell stories, and the *gria* was often empty, so he was glad when I came to visit.

So, then I went to Gianyar with the Prabekel and the Punggawa. In Gianyar we met with the judge (*hakim,* Ind.). And he said that there was no need to do anything because I was still very young. He said [in the respectful way]: "For someone like you, whether you have done wrong or right, you do not need to do anything. There is no proper thing for you to do because you are still very little. However, if you want to do a *prayascita* ceremony, you can, but if you don't it won't matter." [A *prayascita* ceremony is addressed to one's ancestors to ask forgiveness for some major infringement (such as here, allowing himself to have been slapped on the head). Togog and his grandfather decided to hold such a ceremony, as recounted below.]

The Satria of Gianyar come to my *gria* for their holy water, *tirta*. And still today the Pedanda in Sukawati [Togog's father's half-brother] goes to Gianyar to perform the rituals at their *patirtan*. And the Cokordas from faraway come to him too, even from Bangli. They come from Gianyar to Sukawati. I used to help him with the rituals. [The judge *(hakim)* in Gianyar was evidently a Satria, probably from the royal house of Gianyar, and also, since he was called a *hakim* (a Malay word), he was probably part of the colonial government.]

I wanted to act carefully so that it would all be clear. The judgment in Gianyar was that there wasn't any problem because I was still young. A young person is not fined, can't be in the wrong or in the right. So I said to the judge in Gianyar, respectfully,

"Yes, well now this is what I think: it is not that I won't accept your judgment, but I must go to Pedanda Kerta in Badung to ask his advice first."

And he answered, "Well, yes, that's all right." Also respectfully.

So the next day I went alone there to Badung. I didn't go with anyone. No one was with me. When I arrived, some people before me were leaving, and they had brought the Pedanda a lot of money and he was knocking it on the table. The *képéng* in a tight roll had all stuck together. He didn't need the money. He gave me about 25 *képéng*. Then I told him what the big judge in Gianyar had said.

"This is what the judge in Gianyar said." I spoke respectfully.

"Oh, well, that's good. You are near in caste to that Satria. You are like his head. Since he was so bold with you, certainly he will be punished in the future." And indeed later on he became very sick, unspeakably ill. The seed had sprouted. [The Pedanda was echoing an oft-repeated metaphor that the Brahmana is the head while the Satria is the body. And another common notion that some unseen being will punish the slapper.]

"Well, now, what do you think you should do?" asked the Pedanda [speaking down].

"Well, this is what I think, Ratu Pedanda. I would like you to come to Batuan to perform the ceremony to cleanse me of this defilement. It is very near the time of the yearly ritual, the *odalan,* of our clan temple [Pura Panataran]."

"Yes, I'll come back home then," said the Pedanda.

So then, to make my story short, I went to the clan temple and asked my kinsmen, respectfully: "This is how I want to set things right. If I do this will I still be polluted *(kasepungan)?*"

"No, if you do everything the court said, it will be all over. Why should we still have bad feelings? Now go and work on the offerings," the head of the clan-temple group *(klian)* answered [speaking down to Togog as a younger person of the same Brahmana clan].

Then I said, "Well, now tell all my kinsmen that I'll pay for the whole annual temple ritual *(odalan)*. They can do the work, but I'll provide all the materials. Whatever is needed, leave it to me. Whatever it costs, I'll take care of it. All the meat, all the rice, leave that to me. And then at the time of the *odalan* I'll have a *prayascita* ceremony. And the Pedanda from Badung will come to perform it." That's what I said to all my kinsmen.

Well, the Pedanda Kerta from Denpasar came here for the ceremony in my family temple. There were two *pedanda* here and also the one from Badung was here in our houseyard, sitting up on our *balé dangin.*

At the time of an *odalan* in a clan temple, the subsidiary family temples of the group all have similar ceremonies at the same time. These houseyard rituals are not usually carried out by a *pedanda.*

I invited all my relatives—including those from Badung and Pliatan. Really, even the ones from Pliatan came. So then, when the ritual was over, I could tell that they accepted me because they all were willing to eat my offerings after my ceremony. Some ate just a little, some a lot, but they all went there, to the *balé dangin* to take some food. Some just took a few sweets as a sign that they accepted me.

Eating offerings after they have been proffered to certain deities (called *surud* or *lungsuran*) is an act of subservience to those particular deities. If Togog had been still polluted *(letuh)* in regard to the gods of the family temple and therefore degraded in status, then anyone who ate the offerings would themselves be degraded to Togog's level.

In a much later interview, I asked Togog how it could be that a boy of twelve could pay for all these rituals as if he had an adult's resources. And he said it all came from his Grandfather Gria, who paid for both the *odalan* and the *prayascita*.

I also asked Togog whether the slapping event happened before he took the trip to the coffee plantations in the mountains, recounted in Chapter 2, when he repeatedly said that the reason he had gone to harvest coffee was to free himself from the passion for gambling. He said yes, and that the reason for his trying to give up gambling was that gambling had brought about the slap and in turn had resulted in no end of ritual and social trouble for him.

Fifth Act: The Death of the Baby

Well, I've finished telling you about that. Now I'll go back to the little baby, yes?

Togog's son considered that the connection between the difficulty Togog had with his kin over the baby and the event recounted just above was merely one of mental association. Togog had been seriously defiled by the gambling incident, but it had occurred and been cleared up some years before Togog's involvement with his wife-to-be. In the incident with the baby, no one was in fact defiled. The associative link may not have been defilement, as Togog told it, but that he was in trouble again with his kin group.

So, when all my kinsmen wanted me to send the baby far away from here, we took it to Sibang. I went there with the baby and my wife. She stayed there [about a month] and I went back and forth. The baby was placed with the younger brother of my mother's father, Uncle Putu, who was living in Sibang but had no children. He had married a woman from Sibang and brought her to Batuan, but she wasn't happy in Batuan, so he went home with her and built a house on a dry field next to the rice fields. So that's where we went.

After about a month there in Sibang, I was about to go home to Batuan, and my Uncle Putu asked me to sell a fighting cock in Batuan for him: "Take a fighting cock with you to Batuan to sell. There's someone here who'll sell you one to resell there."

"Where is the one who'll sell me a cock?"

"To the north there," and he took me there. When I came into his yard I was amazed to see that it had a gate on the east, a gate on the west, and a gate on the north—because he was a thief. [He had many doors so he could escape quickly if someone came to his house after him.] I didn't know at all that my Uncle Putu was going to tell me to do something like that.

"Is it true, Bapané, you want to sell that cock?" I asked him [in low speech]. "There's someone in Batuan who has asked me to get him one."

"Yes, indeed," he said. "I'll sell it anywhere except around here. The reason is that when I go to cockfights, I meet everyone from around here, so I'd meet the same rooster." [The implication was that the man was selling stolen roosters. It isn't clear whether or not Togog bought a cock from him.]

That night when I went to sleep, I had two purses with money in them. One I tied in my head scarf, the other in the pocket of my shirt. The one I put under my pillow. And I hung my shirt up. In the shirt I had not only money but also some gold coins to be made into a ring. In the morning I looked for my shirt and it wasn't there. That man must have been the mother of thieves! That man who asked me to buy his fighting cock! I was naked above the waist. People would think I was a crazy man going along the road with no shirt on.

Now there was a man there in Sibang named I Pangkur. He was learning how to make pictures, but his pictures were in a different style from mine. He'd paint a single dancing figure on a sheet—a *baris* or a *jauk*.

A man named I Sibang of Pangkur was listed as an artist on the Pita Maha membership list. (On Pita Maha, see Chapter 6.) Drawings like these of a single dancer against a white background were the style of Badung (Denpasar) and Ubud, but not Batuan. In Batuan they painted scenes rather than single figures and filled in the backgrounds with foliage, a mode that in the 1980s they called *pemandangan* (Ind.), or naturalistic scenes. (See H. Geertz, *Images of Power* [1994].)

And when I was in Sibang, I was already working hard at making pictures, so I thought I'd go to Badung and take a few pictures with me to sell. But I wasn't wearing a shirt. I put my purse in my head scarf. I walked from Sibang to Badung—a long, long way. When I got to Badung I bought a shirt and put it right on. So then I went home to Batuan. And then the next day I went back again to Sibang.

Along the way to Sibang, just about at the open field near Kadiri [near Singapadu], the rain began to fall fiercely and there was lightning. I took shelter in a temple in the rice fields, up on a *balé* where they put all the offerings. I took shelter there to wait for the rain to subside so I could go on to see my wife and child. I wasn't in a hurry because it wasn't yet time for the ritual. I was just going to see the child. So I sat there a while, cooling off in that place for the offerings. And then—*beh!*—there was a thunderclap! *Taaarrrr!* I thought I was dead. And it was now almost nightfall. How was I going to find the way? I was on the edge of a deep river lined by thorny *pandanus*. It was hard to find a way through, so first I went west to look for a path. The water was high, above my head, and running very fast. I couldn't cross the river.

"*Peh!* Maybe I can find the way over here . . . maybe if I went farther west . . . ," I thought. So then I went along north, kept going north. Then I found a ladder, a long ladder. Whoever owned that ladder must have been somewhere else looking after his fields—maybe. I thought I'd use it. There wasn't anyone in sight. The owner must have been off looking at his property faraway. If that ladder hadn't been there, I wouldn't have been able to cross. It was a good long ladder. So I went over the river on it.

It was late at night when I finally got there. I told them how I'd lost my shirt, and I told them how I had had to cross that river.

Well, concerning the child, the Pedanda there had asked for him.

My Uncle Putu said [in familiar speech], "This is the request of the Pedanda."

I answered [politely]: "Well, Po, if the Pedanda would like him, I'm willing. The reason I'm willing is that I should not become too attached to the child, since they won't let me raise a bastard *(bebinjat)* there at home. Before, when the child had not yet been born, I wanted to marry her, but she didn't want to. Who was in the wrong?" That's what I said.

"Well now, it is good to hear your words, Po Putu, especially after all the good things you've already done for me. Yes, give him the child. Later, when he's adult, if he remembers me, tell him to come back to me in Batuan."

So we took the child there to Gria Dalem in Sibang. The *pedanda* there was going to raise him as a servant *(parekan)*. *Beh!* After about fifteen days, I went back again to see the child. *Beh!* Hell! Hell! *(Neraka! Neraka!)* To hear that little baby cry! They said that the child hadn't been properly cared for! They just left him to lie there alone, that little child. He could hardly stand up yet and they said that when he cried they put pepper in the eyes! How terribly sad I felt! A little child like that can't do bad things, a child who can barely crawl. And to punish him with pepper in the eyes! It would burn them horribly. Well, I had given the child to them, so that he would have a place. But I didn't just give him to them—they had asked for him!

Then the child died [after about a month in the *gria*]. And they came here to Batuan to tell me. And right soon after that the Pedanda began to be afflicted *(ngrabéda)* [by the spirit of the dead child]. So then someone came and asked me to go there and get my child because he, the

Pedanda, was terribly afflicted. [Apparently, what Togog meant by "go and get the child" was for him to go and perform the requisite rituals (the cremation followed by the *nyekah* ceremony) to free the child's soul from his body. Both Togog's money and his authority for carrying out the ritual were being requested.]

Five times, six times they came looking for me to go there and get the child. But why should I go and get the child? They tried all sorts of things to persuade me to come, but I would not come. After all, I had given him the child because he had asked for him *(kidih)*. Why should I go back there again and get him? The child's spirit was afflicting the Pedanda. They said that the afflicting was being done by the Barong as a service *(ayah)* to the child's spirit. That *barong* was very powerful *(tenget)*. [The *barong* was normally kept within the *gria,* probably in its houseyard temple. While rare, it does happen that a *barong* has its ritual home in a Brahmana house.]

The Pedanda was in the wrong, doing what he had done to the child. The child had done nothing wrong. The child was asking to be cremated and to have the *nyekah* ceremony. Later the word came that they were going to do the *nyekah* ceremony for the child and wanted me to go, but I wouldn't go because it was already all over and I told them that. And I told my Po Putu that. It wasn't right that I go and visit the child in the *gria*. It wouldn't be right for me to provide the offerings for the ceremonies to try to make things right again. It would have been different if I had raised the child myself, if he were still my child.

So after that, after we had that experience, I went back to making pictures, and to accompanying the Pedanda of Sukawati in performing rituals. That was steady work. At that time my wife was with the little baby. She felt as if she was being punished, because she was in Sibang and it had not yet been possible to do any of the necessary ceremonies for the marriage. Because of that, it was as if I were still a bachelor. That's the way it was at that time.

After the baby died, Togog was married formally and his wife was accepted by his ancestors into the family temple. They had a child soon after that, Dayu Putu Gambar, named Putu because she was the first legitimate child, and Gambar or "picture" because picture making was Togog's new occupation.

The Family Dispute over Rice Land

The tangled events of a protracted argument within a family may reveal important perennial ties and strains. The ones recounted here extended back several generations before Togog's birth, reached a climax during his life, and were finally settled in the 1980s.

When I was in Batuan there were such legal cases in process in nearly every family I knew. They had been stimulated, in part, by the presence of the Indonesian court system, which offered the promise (often illusory) of ultimate settlement of all claims on land. The difficulty of achieving settlement lay in the absence of adequate written records of landownership and the reliance on oral testimony.

When the Dutch set up their colony in 1908, one of their first projects was to establish a system of taxation on arable land, accompanied by extensive registration of its ownership. Before that time oral arrangements reached in meetings of the *banjar* communities were supplemented by appeal to the power of local princes (whose personal claims to the land often trumped those of the commoners). The Dutch introduced not only a system of registration of land but also a juridical system to reconcile conflicting claims. However, in practice, even today, although registration of land may be formally in the name of one person, at his death the papers (or often *lontar*) are usually not updated, out of respect to the deceased owner. In many cases the land has been given in security on a loan, still unrepaid, and the owner has long relinquished claim to the harvests from the land. Several generations can go by before such a pawn arrangement has been settled and ownership can become unclear.

Before the Dutch arrived, land disputes were taken first to the *banjar* meeting, and then to the local prince. During Togog's lifetime, the system was an unstable mixture of the two—the former oral consensual system and the new written legal apparatus—a situation that encouraged all sorts of machinations, just and unjust.

It never became clear to me how many or which parcels of land were involved in this case. Togog says below that "in the beginning there was a lot of land, perhaps twenty-five pieces." The time when the family had twenty-five pieces of land may have been when Togog's father's father, Ida Pedanda Wayan Jelantik, was alive, which was in the first quarter of the twentieth century, or it may have been even several generations before that. According to the family genealogy, the first Pedanda Buda in Batuan moved there from Budakling seven generations before Togog was born. Presumably, when the *pedanda* was set up in Batuan, he was supported by the local royal house (who needed him for important rituals), and the raja provided the priest with plenty of rice land and house land.

These pieces of land formerly owned by Togog's ancestors were scattered all over the region, some as far away as Ubud. In the days, some generations past, when the family was well off, it all may have added up to five hectares, as Togog says. By the time Togog was born and his grandfather, the old *pedanda,* was dying, almost all of it had been sold or pawned away. Togog's father's father's brother, the man Togog called "my Grandfather," had inherited some of it when Togog was a boy, along with half of the family houseyard. (See, for all these protagonists, the kin chart in Chapter 1, figure 4.)

The story begins with the cremation of the old Pedanda Wayan Jelantik, Togog's paternal grandfather, which occurred when Togog was probably about five years old, at a time when the family had no land to sell to pay for funeral expenses. *Pedanda* are supposed to be cremated right after death, and not, as was usual for most people, buried for a period while the family collects the funds needed for the cremation rituals. This often means that the corpse of a *pedanda* is kept lying in state on the *balé gedé* for months, with daily offerings placed before it.

Balinese cremations are extremely expensive, and typically a family will sell some of its rice land to cover the expenses. There may be no legal bill of sale, but rather all parties make an oral agreement witnessed in a *banjar* meeting. Or, perhaps more frequently than outright sale, the family may borrow money against the security of a plot of land, a transaction sometimes referred to as *plais,* in which the moneylender gets full use of the land and all its products until the money is repaid.

While a *pedanda*'s commoner clients pay for some of the costs of his or her cremation, and perform much of the manual labor, most of the costs, including feeding all the workers every day during the long months of preparation, must be carried by the family. In this case the family had few resources left. Togog's Grandfather Gria, the deceased's brother, might have been expected to help shoulder the costs of his brother's cremation, but for reasons I never found out was excused from that obligation. Togog's own father was already dead, and Togog's older brother was still alive but sickly and poor and living next door, and apparently did not play a large part in the cremation preparations. This meant that the widow, the old Pedanda Istri, had to find the money and food elsewhere. She got some materials from Grandfather Gria, who participated in the ceremonies on behalf of his recently deceased young daughter; but most of the money that Pedanda Istri obtained she borrowed from him. And that loan became the heart of the controversy.

Togog's Grandfather Gria himself borrowed that money against his own land, which he had inherited. This arrangement, however, was not just a business transaction. Because the plot of land had originally been owned by his brother, the deceased *pedanda* (or by his father), these personages, even though dead, still had a claim of sorts on it. Inheritance of land is not just the passing down of property from one generation to the next, but rather part of a complex reciprocal process that never ends, in which the younger generations continually pay homage to, and actually assist, the deceased generations. A cremation and a *nyekah* are rituals on behalf of the dead person, to free him from mortal ties. Until after the whole series of mortuary rites is over, the deceased is still around, and is apt to be easily angered if the family does not seem to want to do the rituals, as a result causing illness and other disasters. Togog's Grandfather must have been well aware of these possibilities, but because of his own personal *sakti,* felt himself able to fight against them as well as against his brother's wife, the Pedanda Istri.

The first two "acts" concern the dispute over money between Togog's Grandfather Gria and the Pedanda Istri. The second dispute began many years later, here recounted as the third through fifth acts, and is between Togog and a cousin who was the widow of Togog's deceased elder brother. Togog considered it to be somehow a continuation of the first quarrel.

As I have mentioned in the Introduction, I had great difficulties in figuring this one out because there are major silences in Togog's account. Other people may have had quite different views on the case, but all I have is what I was told from the point of view of Togog and his son, Gedé.

First Act. 1920s: The Cremation of Pedanda Wayan Jelantik

As I told you, I was born in a *balé* on the eastern side of our courtyard.

Here Togog is setting out part of the case that he was his Grandfather's proper heir consisting of the facts that his Grandfather wanted him to be born in his own *balé* and that Togog's mother was helped in the childbirth, not by her mother-in-law, but by the wife of his Grandfather. (See Chapter 1.)

Now when my grandfather the Pedanda [Ida Pedanda Wayan Jelantik, Togog's father's father] died, they laid out his body on the *balé dangin.*

Here in Gria Gedé all the land had been sold or pawned. The one who did the selling and pawning for her [because a *pedanda* can't buy and sell or go places to do so] was a man named Mangku Regut, from Jeleka. He was very sly.

When she asked him, "Go back to that person and borrow some more money," he'd go and get, say, fifteen and only give her five. The Pedanda Istri would just sit there. She was a woman and she didn't know how to read and write.

Oh, he was very sly and he was very rich. Before that my family [Gria Gedé, meaning his father's mother, the female Pedanda, and her husband's brother, the man Togog calls "my Grandfather"] had about five hectares of rice land and a lot of dry land, and besides that a lot of sloping grassy land.

Then his wife, my grandmother, the Pedanda Istri, wanted to have the cremation ritual. But because there wasn't enough money for the cremation, she allowed my Grandfather, Ida Bagus Kakiang Gria, to cremate his daughter at the same time. [This would oblige Togog's Grandfather Gria to contribute to the cremation costs. This daughter had just died (see Chapter 1).]

He borrowed some money against his rice fields, and since he was cremating his daughter along with my grandfather, the Pedanda, he gave my grandmother sixty pieces of money. He also gave her a huge tree for the firewood for the cremation.

But my grandmother, the Pedanda Istri, still didn't have enough money, so she asked Ida Bagus Kakiang Gria to lend her some. So he borrowed some more money against another piece of rice land, seventy-five pieces of money, and lent it to her.

My Grandfather often said to me, "If I had been arranging this cremation myself, I wouldn't have had to spend so much" [meaning that the Pedanda Istri couldn't handle money sensibly]. She was very careless in spending everything. My own father had been careless too, and had used up everything.

Now years later my Grandfather wanted her to pay back his loan so that he could get his rice fields out of pawn. But my grandmother, the Pedanda Istri, didn't give him the money she owed him. He asked for it repeatedly but she still didn't pay him.

Second Act. 1930: The Court Case between Togog's Grandfather and the Pedanda Istri

So, finally, he took his case to the government in Gianyar. I was still very little and I didn't know anything about the court case. I remember he'd go away and then I'd ask him, "Where were you just now?"

"In Gianyar." That's all he'd say. So I knew nothing about the trial.

Then the judge called both of them there, my grandmother the Pedanda Istri and my Grandfather. The judge asked her [in very high Balinese, because she was a *pedanda*], "How is it that a *pedanda* who was lent money a long time ago can't repay it?" And she answered: "I'll pay it back in a month. I have to find the money first."

So then she had promised to pay it back in a month. But months passed and she still had not paid it, and they called her in again to the court.

"Well, Ratu, you said you were going to repay your loan. Why haven't you? Since you haven't given it back, you are guilty. You must cleanse yourself of the guilt by going to Tampak Siring and bathing in the holy water there, and then going to the sea and bathing again. This is because you are guilty of breaking a promise to the government."

She said she'd try to find a way to pay the money back, and she went to Tampak Siring and bathed in the holy water. She walked all the way there, because there were no cars in those days. My Po Yan went with her.

This was Ida Bagus Wayan Duduk, husband of one of Togog's father's younger sisters, and thus a son-in-law to the Pedanda Istri. This is the same man who advised Togog when he was in trouble with his temple group because of the slap in the gambling argument. By this time Duduk had moved to Sukawati to live with and assist Ida Pedanda Madé Jelantik.

And she went to the sea too. But after that she still couldn't pay him.

So then my Grandfather went back again to the judge in Gianyar. First, however, he went to the Déwa Agung Regen [probably the regent of Gianyar], and the Déwa Agung Regen said to him [in low Balinese]: "Now, Grandfather, go on over to the judge's office. I'll phone them from here." So my Grandfather went over to the office, and there had been a call from the Puri.

The judge said to him, "How come it's been so long since I spoke to her right here? Why did you keep silent? Why didn't you come here sooner?" [in low Balinese].

So then they sent down a verdict and still she couldn't pay. [The word for verdict is *ponés* from the Dutch *vonnis*, "judgment, verdict, sentence." The document in question is still available, and is dated 1930, when Togog was about twelve to fifteen years old.]

The Pedanda Istri said, "What can I do? I don't even have enough to eat sometimes." She had no one to look after her money matters for her. She didn't know anything—how to work, how to get her retainers to bring her contributions. And my own mother was able to make only a penny or two, selling food to eat. Sometimes she didn't have enough to feed me.

So then the judge told the Pedanda Istri, "If you don't pay up in one month, we will seize all your property and auction it off to pay the debt."

So it came about that the Punggawa came here to

Batuan along with an auctioneer. They put all the pavilions in the western side of the houseyard up for sale.

They set the price on the *balé dangin* at thirty-five, and the *balé sianganti* they valued at just fifteen, because it was old and the wood was rotten. The *balé gedong* was worth seventy. That's all she had, the three buildings.

What Togog called a *balé sianganti* has a high platform (higher than the other ones in the houseyard), an open front area, and a rear closed-in room with thatched walls and nine posts holding up the roof. It was the one in which Togog lived most of his life, and where we were sitting during the telling of these stories. In 1930, the time of the suit, it was nearly in ruins. It was later rebuilt anew in 1937 by some of the *sisia* of the family.

Most of the buyers came from Banjar Babakan [a *banjar* of Sukawati, just to the south of Batuan]. No one came from our village, with the exception of the Prabekel's representative, Anak Agung Bubur, his younger brother. I overheard the Punggawa and the auctioneer say, "This will all together bring in fourteen pieces of money." The *balé dangin* had a leaky roof. The *balé gedong* and the *balé sianganti* both were still standing, but they were in very poor condition too. The total for all the buildings and so on was seventy pieces of money. No one wanted to bid more than seventy. The people who wanted to buy parts of it were from Babakan in Sukawati. They went away, and in one month they were going to take all the buildings apart. They noted down all the prices.

So then that evening I went to Sukawati, to tell my Pedanda [Pedanda Madé Jelantik]. I was good friends with Ida Bagus Wayan Duduk.

"What have you come for, so unexpectedly in the evening like this?" asked my Po Yan [Ida Bagus Wayan Duduk].

"There's something I have to talk with you about. They are going to take our *balé* apart and sell them!"

"What do you mean, take them apart?" He hadn't heard anything about it, nor had my Pedanda. ["My Pedanda" here is the same one Togog later often accompanied on rituals, Ida Pedanda Madé Jelantik. He would have been about twenty-five in 1935, and about seventy-five in 1985. He was a *pedanda* already in 1931, I calculate on the basis of other evidence.]

They didn't even know how poor we were. So I told them all about it and then my Uncle Yan said, "If they do that to the *gria* in Batuan, we will all be shamed before the whole village." And then he added: "This is what you should do. Go to your Grandfather and ask him to stop demanding the money. He loves you very much. No one except you could ask him to do that, but if you don't your house will be destroyed, for sure. Now go back home, and ask your Grandfather not to make them tear it all down. But speak to him very humbly and politely."

I said: "I don't know how to say it to him. Tell me what I should say, Po Yan."

"What do you mean, you don't know how to say it? Here's what you should tell him." And he told me what to say. "Say this and this and this. If he doesn't trust you, he won't trust anyone. He loves you more than anyone in the world."

And my Pedanda said, "Yes, that's what you must do. I can't give you any money. I couldn't lend you seventy pieces of money, not even twenty-five." I agreed to do it. After all, my Pedanda was like my own head [to be respected in the same way].

So I went home, and as soon as I got there, I went over to the eastern part of the courtyard, and I said to my Grandfather: "Now, there's something I want to talk with you about, Grandfather. If you go on asking for your property back, you are asking for what you already own. If our home is torn down, I will be here [with you], but where will my older brother sleep? And don't you have any pity, Grandfather, for my mother? If you insist on going on demanding your money back, I will leave this house. If you, Grandfather, have love for me, you won't do that. But, as I am still young, I can go anywhere to live."

So then he gave in. He accepted what I said. He said: "Well, it's like this. I love you so much I would do anything for you. If you stay here with me, I'll give you all you need. I have done what I have done because I thought it was right for you. After all, you were born here, not over there on the west side of the courtyard.

"I'll tell you now what my father the Pedanda said to me, before you were born, when your mother was carrying you in her womb. He said, 'Don't do anything to harm this baby that is about to be born, because I am going to return after my death into his body.' That's what my father said to me, and that's why I have placed my bet on you [he used the word *metoh,* "to place the central bet in a cockfight"]. I don't want to be left dangling. Now if you stay here after I die, if you can make a few offerings for me, I'll be contented. And if you can't afford to make them, just cremate me, that's enough. Now, tell me what it is you want me to do and I'll do it for you."

The intimate and forceful moral ties between generations, and between land and human lives, are vividly evident in this statement by Togog's Grandfather Gria. He says that Togog's great-grandfather, the Pedanda, had intended to return after his death to be reincarnated in Togog's body. He also says that Togog is to use the produce of the rice land in question to pay for the mortuary rituals—both at cremation and at a later ceremony called the *nyekah*—needed to finally release his Grandfather's soul from worldly suffering. As long as these rites are postponed, the dead soul continues to linger miserably around the surviving family members and can not reincarnate. Togog's son explained a phrase that Togog used to describe this limbo, "to be left dangling" *(glantingin),* as referring to a passage in the Adiparwa text that tells of the sage Warabrata being tormented in the other world, after his death but before his cremation and his *nyekah* rituals have been performed for him by his descendants. Warabrata was hung by his feet from a bamboo tree while a red rat chewed on the tree trunk, and when the tree fell, Warabrata dropped into the abyss below. This happened because his son Jaratkaru had no offspring who could have performed those rituals. Grandfather Gria, whose only child died young, says that he is gambling *(metoh)* on Togog doing these rituals.

The land produces foodstuffs (especially rice and coconut products) with which to make offerings and to feed the numerous people who devote months of work to the ritual. The conflicts among kinsmen may be about the use of these foodstuffs for offerings. The history of a particular plot of rice land—of who has worked it and to whom its harvest is given—thus has a pressing spiritual and moral dimension.

"Well, if that's so, then we have to go right now to see the Perbekel and tell him not to pull the *balé* down. And later, if it is not torn down, my grandmother the Pedanda Istri will repay you little by little," I said.

So first I went by myself over to the Puri to see the Perbekel. He was sorry for us and he told me: "The best thing would be for your grandmother the Pedanda Istri to hand over everything she has to Ida Bagus Kompiang Gria, to give him all the rights to the land she has, whether it is in pawn completely or not. Then that land can be sold, and with the money much of that debt can be paid." That's what he said in the Puri.

So then I went to look for my Grandfather and when I brought him to the Perbekel, he said: "Whatever my grandson here says is alright with me. I'm getting old now. He is the one on whom I want to hang my fate [i.e., to take care of my cremation]. There's no one else. And I've placed my bet on him. Because he was born in my house." That's what my Grandfather said.

The Perbekel said: "Well, this is what I think you should do, Grandfather. You should accept everything that the Pedanda Istri has, so that you own it all."

"Alright, I'll do that, provided my grandson here is witness to it."

So then we went to Gianyar. And there my grandmother, the Pedanda Istri, said she would turn over everything she had to him. And my Grandfather accepted it.

But he never put my name on the papers. And I never knew that till much later.

Now about my older brother. He couldn't be persuaded not to marry the woman he did, that woman who is now in Sukawati.

Togog is shifting now to begin the account of the subsequent land dispute between himself and his older brother's wife, "that woman who is now in Sukawati," Dayu Dudung. He suggested at another time that no one in his family had wanted his brother to marry the girl, a daughter of one of Togog's father's older brothers, who may have grown up in the houseyard just on the other side of the north wall of theirs. According to Togog, both his Grandfather Gria and Pedanda Istri, the head of the family, had been particularly against the marriage, perhaps because of their enmity toward her father, but Togog's brother went through with it anyway.

I once brought him another girl, a Dayu from Sibang, a young girl. She happened to be visiting in Gria Pacung, and I went to her and brought her here. She was standing right outside the front door.

She said, "I don't think he wants to have me."

And I said, "No, my older brother doesn't have a girl yet, and he asked me to help him." Her name was Dayu Nyoman from Sibang.

"Well then, if that's how it is, I believe you," she said.

I had made an agreement with my brother: "You stay home here, and I'll go and bring the girl here to you, Beli, that Dayu Nyoman that's visiting right now in Gria Pacung. You'll have to believe me."

So then I went up there to the north and got the girl and brought her back, and she waited out front. But *then* he wasn't at home! *Badah!* [Laughs.] He wasn't there! *Badah!*

"He doesn't want her," I said to myself, and I took the girl back again. Now that Dayu has become a *pedanda istri.*

So after that my older brother took the wife he has now and wasn't ever at home.

So sometime later, my grandmother, the Pedanda Istri, died. She had been living in the *balé dangin,* and it was all falling down. It was turning into dust. No one took care of it. So I went to my Grandfather and said: "Grandfather! Grandfather! The Pedanda Istri lived there a long time in the *balé dangin,* and if you will agree, I want to use it for the cremation ceremony right away.

"Well, just use that *balé* the way it is. In the future you can fix it up."

So I just built a temporary *balé* for the ceremonies. [The cremation of Pedanda Istri was performed in 1938, as recorded by Mead and Bateson.] And much later [in 1974, see Chapter 4] I built the present one.

Little by little I repaid the pawns on my rice land. I got three pieces back, adding up to about a hectare. But then I had to use that land for money for the cremation.

Third Act. 1950s: Dayu Dudung Is Sent Out of Togog's Home

Now, a long time later when my older brother died, he left us his widow, Dayu Nyoman Dudung [to support]. But we sent her home to her brother's house [that of Ida Bagus Ketut Diding, just north of Togog's houseyard], and we announced in the *banjar* meeting that we relinquished all obligations to her.

There had been a case here in our *banjar* of a woman who, after her husband died, was sent home, and she made no complaint. Because I knew about that case, I never thought that Dayu Nyoman Dudung would do anything, and I never changed the names on the papers concerning the land.

Widows of men in a household are entitled to lifetime support from the family of their husbands. However, it is also permissible for a family to send a widow back to her original family, and to announce in the *banjar* meeting that *"Tiang suud ngundulné,"* "We are no longer governing her." In this case, apparently, there had been a long-standing argument between Togog's older brother and Grandfather Gria over a plot of land, in which Dudung had energetically participated. Togog's older brother and his wife Dudung had no surviving child who could have defended her, but after her husband's death she nevertheless continued to claim the land.

Dayu Dudung, angered at being expelled from her mother-in-law's home (and source of income), refused to pay the *banjar* dues that were levied on her directly now that she was not part of Togog's houseyard. Apparently Dudung also had bad relations with her own kin, even with her brother in the houseyard next door to Togog's, who did not want her. At about that point, their cousin, Ida Bagus Nyoman Oka, the son of Pedanda Madé Jelantik in Sukawati, decided to take her into his own home in Sukawati, and support her. But she kept up her fight for the plot of land from Sukawati.

To explain how it was that Togog had the authority to refuse his brother's wife the land she claimed and therefore the sustenance she needed, Togog had to go back in time and tell how it was that the *banjar* accepted his side of the story.

Flashback. 1940s: Togog's Grandfather Names Him as His Heir

Now, when my Grandfather got older, I took care of all his property, and I wanted to borrow some money on it. It was Japanese time, and with the Japanese money I couldn't get more than 10,000 *rupiah* on it. But Dayu Nyoman Dudung, together with my own mother, went to the Perbekel and blocked me from borrowing on that land. They were allies now [where formerly they had been enemies]. When they went to the Perbekel, he told me to go and get my Grandfather. [The Perbekel at the time was Anak Agung Gedé Alit, who was in office in 1942.] I brought him there, and the Perbekel said to him: "Well, Grandfather, this Gus Dé here [Togog] wants to borrow some money on your land. Will you permit it?"

And he answered, "My grandson knows how to read [Balinese script]. None of the others know how to read. Who else should I let take care of these things?"

"Well, in that case, I'll let him pawn the land." So then those two women couldn't say anything more to me.

Another time the Camat [Cok Agung Payangan] came to me and said: "I want to buy that grassland of yours on the edge of the ravine to put a government building on. That land over on the right, southwest of Peninjoan."

That was land we owned. But when the government [*pemerintah,* Ind.] makes such a request it's not right for me to say no. I didn't want to get in wrong with the government. So they gave me a little money for it, 90 *ringgit.* It wasn't like today when if the government requests you can say no. I was afraid of the government. So I sold it to them. [Use of the words *camat* and *pemerintah* suggests that this event occurred after 1950, when the government was the Indonesian Republic and these terms came into circulation.]

"The *pedanda* will permit it." I said. But then when I was about to sell it, my mother stopped the sale. She went with her daughter-in-law [Dayu Dudung] to the Puri and wouldn't let the sale go through. My mother said: "I won't allow the sale. The land belongs to me." That's what she said. She went to the Puri and she wouldn't allow it to be sold.

There are three conflicting authorities ruling over

the ownership of the land: first, the Batuan Puri (one of whose members was, until the 1960s, also the representative of the Indonesian government); second, the *banjar,* the local village community; and third, the court system, to which the claimant, Togog's brother's wife, then turned and won.

Fourth Act. 1959: A Settlement

Now then, many years later when all the old people were dead, Dayu Nyoman Dudung brought suit against me, claiming that she was the rightful heir to that land. I lost the case because my name was not on the papers. So after we lost the case, she gave the property to Ida Bagus Nyoman Oka. All the land was given over to him in the settlement. I thought it was right and proper. That was the morally right thing to do.

The final settlement, explained Togog's son, was made in 1959. The court decreed that Ida Bagus Nyoman Oka, Togog's nephew and son of Pedanda Madé Jelantik, the Pedanda whom Togog had assisted for many years (and head of the family with whom Dudung had been living), would take the land and apply some of its produce to support Dudung throughout her old age, and the rest of the income from the land would be used for repairs on the family temple.

But now, today [Jan. 2, 1986], Dayu Nyoman Dudung is living in Sukawati with my Pedanda and his son Ida Bagus Nyoman Oka. Now all the rice fields have been sold. In the beginning there was a lot of land, maybe twenty-five pieces.

I now let my oldest son take care of our land. I don't know much about these money matters now. I just live quietly off my painting. It's enough to live on. Sometimes I have to borrow a little, but I can pay it back in a month. Thanks to God's blessings.

When we lost the land suit, I thought at first of appealing the verdict, of going to Jakarta, but my son wouldn't let me. [Togog's son said he told his father that if he wanted to go on with the suit for his sake, as the heir he wouldn't want him to do it, and besides it would cost too much.] I had thought that if I won the appeal I would sell the land and divide up the money among the five people who claimed it. [For "divide up" Togog used the word *tréstésang,* "to scatter into many pieces, like drops in a stream of water falling on a stone."]

My other land had all gone to pay for the cremations of my older brother and my grandmother, the Pedanda Istri. When I did those cremations [probably the ones in 1938] most of the costs came from those lands I had inherited. At the time I did those cremations my work was selling well. Foreigners liked it. I didn't get a lot of money, though. Once I had 800 *rupiah*—it was when the value of money was much higher than today. I had to go to the bank in Denpasar to get the money. Most of it was from Tuan "Nurwelak" of Baturiti. I made a picture of people fighting *pencak.* I've never fought *pencak* myself, but I watched it a lot when I was in Jabarana. I didn't want to learn *pencak* myself, because I was afraid I'd grow overbold *(bregah).* They did it with knives, long knives, which they kept in sheaths along their legs. And now some do *pencak* with clubs. I made a picture showing that. The reason I was doing well then was that there weren't very many other painters. At the time of my mother's *ngasti* ceremony there were no other painters.

A few weeks after the above was taped, in 1986, the old lady Dayu Dudung died. The issue then arose as to who would pay for her burial and cremation. She was no longer living in Batuan, and she had never made a clean break with the *banjar,* nor had she paid her regular dues, which meant that she had accumulated a large debt to the *banjar.* So the *banjar* met and stated that it would not pay for her funeral expenses, and that whoever did so would have to repay her debts to the *banjar.* So then, at her death, Togog and his son, as her closest kin, decided to take on the cost of her funeral rituals, as well as payment of the debts to the *banjar.* With that, the case was considered closed.

Six Painting

The Creation of a New Kind of Painting

The Creation of a New Kind of Painting • Starting to Paint • Selling • The Anthropologists • Making a Temple Painting in Tourist Style • Painting in Togog's Life

The beginnings of painting in the genre that Togog developed were directly tied to the coming to Bali of foreigners and their desire for paintings made by Balinese in Western format. This was also true for Togog's start. His paintings were made expressly and solely for money. The foreigners were their only buyers, and when the Europeans left Bali during the Japanese occupation nearly all such work ceased.

Togog's anecdotes about his experiences with the strangers are pervaded with uncertainties about their intentions and acts. His relationships with them had a dimension new to him, since they all involved what were for Togog large quantities of money and in an unfamiliar currency, that of the colonial Dutch East Indies, the *rupiah*. He had been accustomed to buying and selling, gambling and snacking with iron *képéng* coins, and now he was being given heavy silver coins with which he could buy expensive clothing. (See, for instance, in Chapter 2, the story about spending *rupiah* for a new sarong.) Also confusing for Togog were the languages of these encounters, Malay and Dutch.

Two European artists who settled in Ubud in the late 1920s appear in Togog's stories, the German Walter Spies and the Dutchman Rudolf Bonnet. These men have been rightly credited, both by Togog and by scholars, for suggesting the making of "modern" paintings to young Balinese, and also for promoting and even selling them. However, other evidence, even here within Togog's tales, shows that Balinese crafting of other kinds of objects, such as wood carvings and silver jewelry, especially for foreign purchase had already been long customary in Bali before the arrival of Spies and Bonnet.

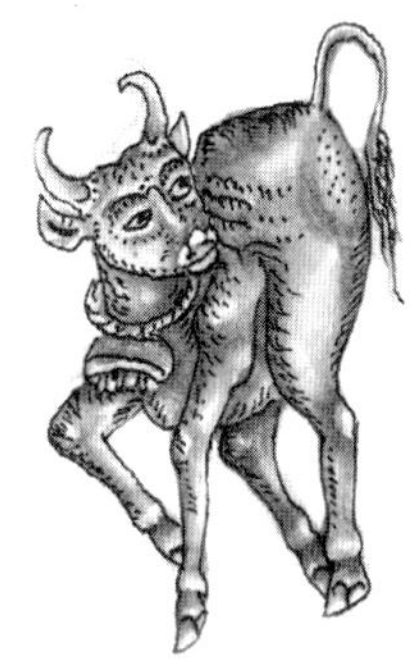

Spies and Bonnet, as Togog tells us below, bought the first of the new kind of Balinese paintings and also arranged that other foreigners in Ubud would see them, including Spies' frequent guests who rented several small houses from him. But soon the Balinese artists also took their wares to the shops that had been selling wood carvings to tourists in Denpasar, Klungkung, and on the road in Mas and even in Batuan. They also adapted their own food-selling peddling practices, not only carrying their own works and those by others to stores but also taking them door to door inside the only hotel in Bali, in Denpasar, to government rest houses in the mountains, and to the homes of the more permanent expatriates.

Several other westerners soon joined the commerce: two young German brothers named Neuhaus opened up a souvenir stall on the beach at Sanur; and a Dutch journalist named Houboldt developed a wholesale business, buying paintings in Bali and selling them to Jakarta shops. Chinese souvenir shops in Denpasar and Singaraja also picked up a few.

In Batuan, a peddling family from a big commoner clan in the roadside *banjar* of Dentiyis led the marketing effort. A couple of them, I Nyoman Patera and I Ketut Ngendon, made paintings before Togog. The latter was also an imaginative entrepreneur, organizing dance programs at Batuan's Pura Désa where he also sold carvings and paintings.[1] Several of his kin specialized in peddling them. Among these were Wayan Gobag, who figures in one of Togog's tales below, and also, later, some younger ones, Nyoman Ada, Wayan Senter, and Wayan Regug. The latter two men opened large and lucrative art shops on the road in the 1970s.

One of Batuan's Brahmana peddlers, Ida Bagus Bon, had set up a shack by the road to sell souvenirs probably as early as 1930. One of Togog's relatives, known by the foreigners as Ida Bagus Buda, was selling wood carvings (and possibly a painting or two) there before Togog himself started.

The wares sold in these various commercial outlets were almost all as Covarrubias described: crude and mechanically imitative. By 1933, says Covarrubias, "the modern [paintings] sold at the lobby of the Bali Hotel were coarse, hastily made, and with a sad poverty of subject-matter."[2]

In response to this rapid emergence of a market for works of inferior quality, Spies and Bonnet decided to invent an institution through which the best Balinese painters would be encouraged to work towards a "fine-art" ideal. They set up a shop next to the newly built Museum Bali in 1933, where the best pictures were sold. In 1936 they organized an artists' cooperative where materials could be bought and set up juries to select the best pictures for exhibition and sale. It was given a Balinese name, Pita Maha, and Balinese officers were chosen, though throughout its brief life it was actually run by a foreign advisor. Togog talks about the establishment of Pita Maha below.

Bonnet was particularly active in Pita Maha and organized a series of exhibitions of the new paintings and carvings outside Bali—in Dutch art clubs in Surabaya, Yogyakarta, Bandung, and Batavia (Jakarta). The first ones were held in 1934 in Batavia, 1936 in Yogya and Bandung, the latter with a catalog written by Bonnet. Balinese work, both traditional and modern, was also displayed at the 1937 Paris World's Fair. Government prizes for the best paintings were also awarded. Bonnet made an extensive collection of these paintings from the outset, a collection that was later divided between the art museum Bonnet established in Ubud (the Museum Puri Lukisan) and the Museum voor Volkenkunde in Leiden. All of this promotion had as its aim the raising of the painters' own standards for techniques and materials used.

It was within this complex social situation that Togog first made contact with the art-loving foreigners. Other Balinese had done so before him. Togog mentions meeting—and seeing the paintings of—Dewa Gedé (later known as Anak Agung Gedé) Sobrat and Gusti Nyoman Lempad from Ubud, Ida Bagus Madé (Poléng) from Padang Tegal, and, in Batuan, I Patera, I Ketut Ngendon, and a man from Togog's own family, a wood-carver named Ida Bagus Buda.[3] Togog tells the stories of his travels as though he were always alone, but the records (of purchases by Mead and Bateson) show that he was usually accompanied by kin and friends from Batuan. Although Spies and Bonnet certainly early singled out Togog as a promising artist, and Togog threw himself enthusiastically into his new work and became an important leader in Batuan, nonetheless he must be understood as a member of a small group entering an already existing but new tourist-oriented world.

Starting to Paint

First Meetings with the Foreigners in Ubud

It is difficult to date exactly when it was that Togog first met Spies and Bonnet. My best guess is 1933, one or two years after others had begun and most of the social and commercial institutions of tourist art in Bali were already established.[4] Togog would have been around twenty years old at the time. This was the same period when he married and had his first child, the one who died. It is also the period when he was just beginning his work as a ritual expert. Thus the stories of Togog's starting to paint are closely intertwined with those about his starting a family and regularly performing rituals as an occupation.

I was a little unsteady in my heart. Even though we had a lot of property—rice fields, and also gold and jewels, I was looking for some steady work of my own. So that's why I was going around here and there. I was still gambling, but I was also strong on singing *kidung* and *kekawin.* Wherever I heard there were people who knew about them, I'd go there to learn. I wanted something for the future. I learned how to interpret the calendar for people [pointing out the auspicious days and the bad], and I learned also how to measure out a houseyard [where to place the gate, houses *(balé),* and family temple] following the *lontar* Asta Kusala and the Asta Gumi. I've been doing that all my life.

I was looking for things to do, because I was confused in my heart because I had no work for the future. I thought of making walls of woven bamboo strips for my *balé.* I figured out how to make them by myself. No one taught me how to plait bamboo. I studied a flat woven basket and copied it for the weaving of the walls of my house. My neighbors were all really amazed because I wove all the walls and hid them away. When they were finished, I put up the whole thing in one day. So people thought I was unusually clever in weaving. I did many kinds of work, and I had many friends, and no one ever spoke angry words to me.

Now, because I was so extremely confused and overwhelmed by gambling, I decided by myself to change my ways and give up the bad. I needed work, to earn a living and to take care of my future.

My Grandfather had a wind chime, and I sold it to Tuan Bonnet. I got to know him well. It was a long walk to Ubud, but even when it was nighttime I'd walk back to Batuan again. There were no cars in those days to ride in.

I had heard that there were tourists in Ubud, living there. There weren't any in Batuan, just the Chinese who sold medicines and oils. I remember watching the little children running away in fear from that Chinese. So now when I heard that there were foreigners in Ubud, I thought I would take that wind chime to sell to them. So I screwed up my courage to go up and look for the foreigners.

I went to my Grandfather and said: "Grandfather! How about selling the wind chime?"

I took the wind chime and a kris handle that was very old. I found it under the eaves in my house. It might have been made from the tusk of some sea animal. It looked cracked all over, but it wasn't broken.

When I got to the *tuan*'s, he asked me where I was from, and I said, "From Batuan."

"Well, stay here, Ratu, and work, make pictures," he said. "Yes, sometime I will make pictures," I said.

Well, he bought the wind chime, and was I happy! But he didn't want the kris handle.

Then Tuan Bonnet instructed me: "Don't sell this sort of thing, Ida Bagus. Learn how to make pictures instead!"

"But if I wanted to make a picture, where could I get some paper?" There was nowhere in Batuan where you could get paper. And it was hard to get to Badung because there weren't any cars then, or very rarely. So then I said: "Well, someday I'll study drawing, Tuan. Right now I'm still uncertain."

So, to make a long story short, after he bought that wind chime, I went home—dancing like Délem because my heart was so happy. I was very, very happy because I had never had a silver coin *(rupiah)* before. I took it and threw it against a rock, harder and harder, to make it ring out. I was so happy to hear that sound.

So the next day, or a couple of days later, I wanted very much to get some more money like that, so I found a flat wooden board. I took it home and carved on it the picture of a heron with a crab. I knew that story from the Tantri, I knew that song a little, and I knew the story. Someone had told me the story. That's why I could make a picture of the bird with the priest's headdress. I carved it. I worked on it five days and four nights. In the evening I polished it, because I was so eager to get another coin.

The story of the heron and the crab was a favorite one with Togog, who continued to paint it throughout his life. It is about a heron that deceived some fish into trusting him to take them in his beak to another pond, by dressing up as a *pedanda* and claiming that he was fasting, who then carried the fish away, ate them, and came back for more. The crab, suspecting something, grabbed onto the heron's neck, forced him to fly to the other pond, and found out his secret and then killed him. The story was appealing to Togog, as it was about an immoral *pedanda*. (See also his story of another deceitful priest in H. Geertz, *Images of Power* [1994], pp. 22–23.) Togog may have thought this an appropriate topic for foreign taste if he had seen an earlier rendering of this subject by the Ubud area painter, Ida Bagus Madé Poléng, which Bonnet had in his collection by 1932 and may have hung on his wall.[5]

So when I was finished, I took it up there. I took the carving in bone too, even though it wasn't finished. When I got to the *tuan*'s house, he seemed to be laughing at me. I thought it was because I had come so far but only brought goods to sell worth one penny and the cost of coming there would equal that. So the trip would be for nothing. I thought that was why he was laughing at me.

"*Peh!* Ida Bagus, I told you to draw pictures."

"Well, I could get a picture done in about ten days. But give me the materials for making them, please, Tuan."

"From now on, Ida Bagus, come and work here, right here below me. No one will bother you here."

"*Pah,* maybe I'll come here tomorrow, Tuan—but I'm not sure."

He bought my carving for one *rupiah* like the other one. There were a lot of people at his house, come to get medicine from him, from the Ubud area. Someone sent him a dinner, with twelve sticks of *saté,* because they were so grateful to him. There were people there with cuts, with boils, that the Balinese healers *(balian)* couldn't cure.

Because I was there so often, he gave me medicine too when I needed it. Once I had a sore throat from singing *kekawin* too long. It was very bad, and I couldn't talk. My throat seemed hard. Then he gave me some medicine—it was a kind of oil mixed with water, and he told me to rinse my mouth out with it. But I forgot and almost swallowed it right down. *"Eh eee!"* he said and ran and stopped me from swallowing it, and then I spit it out. After a while the sore throat was gone, and it was because the *tuan* had made it well.

Peh! There were many people there! It made me feel a little embarrassed. Especially when the Cokorda Agung came by. [At that time Bonnet lived in a *balé* which had been built for Walter Spies right outside the wall of Puri Saren Kauh, next to a small pond. The Cok Agung who came visiting was Cok Agung Lingsir from Puri Saren Kangin.]

Now he bought the picture on wood for one *rupiah,* and I was extremely happy in my heart. Now I still had the kris handle. I said to myself: *"Peh,* where can I sell this one for another *rupiah*? Then I'll have two *rupiah*." So I took it to the house of Tuan Tepis, but he wasn't at home. [Tuan Tepis was the name the people of Batuan gave Walter Spies.]

Three days later I went there again, and I was told that there was a foreign woman living west of Ubud, in Sayan. [This was Jane Belo.] The one who told me had sold something to her, said she liked statues, and even liked statues by people who were just learning. They called her Nyonya Méng ["the Foreign Lady with the Cats"]. The fellow said, "Just go there, Tu!" So I quickly did, since Tuan Tepis wasn't there. So I went straight north and then west, way out in the middle of the rice fields where there weren't any people. When I arrived there were a lot of foreigners there, three of them. I was glad.

And there was a man there from Batuan, named I Wayan Gobag, from Dentiyis. [Gobag was a wood-carver, a cousin of I Patra and I Ngendon, both of whom had started making paintings on paper just before Togog.] He was there selling wood carvings, and when I met him it was already afternoon. He was there already. The Nyonya was busy talking with her guests and couldn't talk to me.

I said to Wayan Gobag: "Hello, Wayan! What are you doing here?" I spoke nicely to him like that [in low words, but addressing him as Wayan is respectful].

"Hello! Let's go home together later!" he said respectfully.

"All right," I said. So after a while the guests looked at my thing that I had brought, and one offered me one *rupiah* for the kris handle. I was very happy. Today if you offered me 50,000 *rupiah* I wouldn't sell it. But at that time, I didn't know anything about how expensive good, old things are, and I was happy with what I got from the *nyonya* in Sayan. After that I sold other things, precious stones and rings, whatever I could find to sell.

That day I Wayan Gobag had sold a lot, but I didn't look carefully at how much money he got. He had sold a carving of a woman pounding rice. It was made of *bentawas* wood [a kind of hardwood tree, white in color], not like the wood they use now, which is very good. So by then it was late afternoon, and we went home.

On our way home, south of Sayan and west of the place where there are a lot of bushes, where it is very desolate and lonely, we came to a place where there wasn't anyone on the road, and there was only a little bunch of houses far away.

"Da Bagus, Da Bagus!" he cried out.

"Yes?"

"I beg you, Da Bagus; don't kill me right here. Don't kill me, just take my money!" That's what he said.

Beh! What could I think, I really thought my heart would drop away.

"*Beh!* What do you mean by saying that, Wayan? What can you be thinking of, Wayan? Don't talk like that to me. You should talk about other things with me. Don't talk like that to me!"

"That's what I thought!"

"Well, don't! It seems as though you think I want your money, Wayan. But I don't want it. I came up here just to learn. At home I'm not lacking enough to eat. It's the opposite. I have only to ask my Grandfather for something and he gives me anything I want. The reason I went up there selling was to try to reform myself, so I would no longer act so stupidly that even little children were scolding me. That's how miserable I had become, and I went there so I'd no longer be like that."

"Well, don't be angry at me," he said. And we walked along some more. He had a knife and so did I. I didn't dare go on a trip like that without a knife. But now we kept a good distance between us, at least two arms' lengths. It was very dark by the time we got home.

The First Drawings

Now after I got home, I started to work again. I asked my Pedanda for some *ulantaga* paper. [This was the *pedanda* from Gria Taman in Sukawati whom Togog often assisted. *Ulantaga* paper was a paper made of thin sheets of bark, used for writing on in cremation ceremonies.] He gave it to me because I often worked there helping him paint masks. He gave me a piece a meter square in size, and I cut it into four parts.

I scritch-scratched my first picture on it with a pencil. It was an astrological calendar *(pralintangan)* that told you which day had what in it, with the god for each day and the demon for that day and a sign for days when you should plant rice. I copied it from a *lontar.* I found one in Gria Pacung, and I copied it to learn how to make it, all of that stuff about the days. I worked hard on it.

The second one was a *palindon* of the twelve months, all on one sheet. Both had dark figures on a white background, unlike the next pictures he made with black backgrounds, using Chinese (Indian) ink. One like these is in the Bateson-Mead collection, but has no illustrative figures on it. For these first two, Togog did not yet have Chinese ink, but used the juice of a *nagasari* fruit. He describes how to make it below.

So now I had made two pictures, but I didn't yet know about selling them. So I went up to Dentiyis to find out. I went by myself and looked at the pictures there [in the house of I Patra].

They told me to take it up to Ubud. So then when I was finished I went up, and the *tuan* looked at it and said: "You're very able! Why didn't you want to make pictures before this?"

"Well, I didn't have any paper. Where could I get any paper?" I said. "I asked for this paper from my Pedanda. Now it looks as though you like my picture. Please give me some paper."

"Well, you won't be without paper from now on," said the *tuan.* "Now this other picture, take it to Tuan Tepis. Perhaps he will buy it." That's what Tuan Bonnet said.

He bought only one and told me to take the other to Tuan Tepis [Walter Spies]. He hoped that Tuan Tepis would continue to buy my pictures. So then I went there to Tuan Tepis' house.

At that time, I was nearly the only one making pictures. There was Dé Sobrat, who was working at Tuan Tepis' house, but no one else. Ida Bagus Madé [Poléng] at that time had not yet gone there—but I was already going there often. Once or twice I met Gusti Lempad there, but he wasn't bringing a lot of pictures there as I was. So I took the second picture there to Tuan Tepis' house, and outside the house sat Nak Agung Dé Sobrat, working. And Tuan Spies said to me, "Well, how long did it take you to make that picture, Da Bagus?"

"It took me twenty days," I said.

And Tuan Tepis said, "Well, you ought to learn how to draw."

"But what can I use for paper and ink? I don't have any."

"*Beh,* Da Bagus, you know Tuan Bonnet—he'll give you the materials," said Tuan Tepis. So then he bought the picture for three *rupiah. Beh!* That money was in coins, cents and ten-cent pieces. So it was a whole lot of money. The bundle was as big as a coconut. A lot of people saw me selling those pictures and getting the money. They might have thought it was more than it was, all big coins instead of the pennies and dimes. When I got home people asked me where I got all the money, and I told them that someone bought my pictures. Since that time, many other painters have sprouted.

The *tuan* gave me paper, and it was a meter in size, and I cut it into four. I made one picture first. I worked on it for twenty days and four nights, working on top of the flat side of a wooden serving dish *(wanci).* I didn't have a table like this one then. When I was finished drawing it, I made some ink. I didn't know where to buy ink, and I was too shy to ask for some from the *tuan,* and I didn't meet him anyway. That's why I made some ink at home. I got some *nagasari* fruit, and I made a little cotton yarn and I burned it, and as it was burning, covered it with a coconut shell.

Then I collected the black ashes, ground them up with glue, and that took a very long time. That was my ink.

I didn't know yet that you could buy ink in Badung. So when the picture was finished I took it up to the *tuan,* and he looked at it, and said, "*Pah,* this is wrong here, this is wrong there!" he said. So that's why I say he was like my teacher. So then he bought the picture for one *rupiah,* and I was very happy and I went home.[6] So after that I kept on bringing him pictures. I thought after a while I would try colors. And in my heart grew up *(mentik)* the desire to make them good. So then he gave me some colors, but I also used some Balinese colors, because I had the equipment to make the Balinese colors. So, to make the story short, I brought him a picture that was in color.

"What's this here? You have to make this better!" he said. That's why I consider him a teacher. He told me how to change it, to make it better, to add white on top, for instance, and to put yellow in. I worked on that one a long time, maybe twelve days, but the money was all right. So then, when it was finished, he didn't buy it but sold it for me.

Once he said, "Come here in seven days, Ida Bagus!" Because some of his guests were coming in seven days. In fact I went there in seven days and found the guests there. And he talked with the guests. I couldn't understand his talk about how much the price should be for the things. The guest asked the *tuan,* how much? and he said, "Here, ask the Ida Bagus here."

But I just left it to the *tuan* to put a price on it.

"Whatever you think is right, *tuan,*" I said, because I didn't know anything about the prices of things.

"Ida Bagus, how much do you think this should be? —just say," he said.

I thought, well, I had worked on it this many days, and I thought that I should get paid at least a *talén* [one-fourth of a *rupiah*] a day. I didn't think that was so much. If I put too high a price on it, they wouldn't want to buy it, and I'd lose, and so would the buyer. Both would lose. So then I calculated the price so that I got a *talén* a day. In those days if you did manual labor as a *kuli* working on the road, you'd get a *talén* a day. So then I gave the price and after the guest gave me the money, I showed it to the *tuan.*

"This is what he gave me." But the *tuan* didn't want any money. He was very honest.

Tuan Bonnet was more honest *(jujur)* than Tuan Pandy. [Togog here shifts time frame from the 1930s to the 1940s. Jimmy Pandy, an Indonesian from Surabaya, set up an art shop in Sanur in the late 1930s or mid-1940s. Togog explains below what he meant by "honest" here—taking no profit for oneself.] When I took a picture to Tuan Pandy, he'd take it right away, and give me the money—for instance, if I gave him a price of 25 he'd pay it right then and there. Later on, when a guest came, he'd sell it for more. That's how he was with me. I didn't think that was honest [because he took a profit himself]. It was different with Tuan Bonnet—he didn't want to take a profit. With him everything was out in the open.

Once when we were playing the *gamelan* in the Balé of Banjar Tengah [in Batuan], I noticed pictures hanging up high near the roof. They were of shadow-puppet figures from the Ramayana. When I didn't have anything to do, I'd go there and look at the pictures. It was the story of the death of Kumbakarna. At that time I already knew the story. It was the work of the Pedanda Gria Pacung, but from the time when he was still young, not yet a *pedanda.* Ida Bagus Ketut Kantung was his name. I wanted to copy them, for they were very, very good. They were exactly like the *wayang* puppets. So I decided to study their proportions very carefully, to memorize the distances: from the nose to the forehead so much, from the end of the nose to the lower jaw so much, from the end of the nose to the ear so much. I learned them by heart.

Togog later commented that the pictures on the *balé banjar* were large and square, colored in Balinese paints, with no black lines on them. He said the man who had made them died in the 1930s, so they might have been made much earlier.

Then I heard that there were some *wayang* figures in Cangi. "If you want to make *wayang* figures, Ratu, there are some very good ones in Cangi," someone said.

So I went there the next day. I took a blowpipe, borrowed from someone in Gria Pacung, and I got there before noon. I would say that I was hunting birds with my blowpipe. So I got there [to Pura Ganggangan, in Cangi] and went in.

There they were, sure enough, high up on the place where they put the god-figures, on a *balé*. There were two *balé* like that. They were very high. Ida Sanghyang Surya, the sun, was exactly in the center of the sky, and so there was no one around. So I climbed up there. I thought that if anyone found me there I would say that a bird had flown up there. I'd hit it with my dart and it had flown there. That's what my idea was. But in fact I went up there to learn the proportions.

I brought paper with me and a pencil. So I leaned against a post and copied and no one came and saw me. I liked those pictures, and when I got home I tried scratching out a drawing, but I couldn't get them right.

So I went back to the first picture, the one in the *balé* of Banjar Tengah, and did a picture of the capture of Kumbakarna, with colors.

I thought to myself, "I can make these."

But when this practice work was finished, I didn't know yet about how to sell them. Someone came by from Puaya, a cloth merchant, and she asked me to lend it to her, and I did. She never returned it, even to today. I went there to get it, but she always put me off with excuses.

Foreign Patrons

Now Tuan Bonnet and Tuan Tepis, the two of them, said to me: "Ida Bagus! We're going to enter your work in a contest! Go over to Tuan Tepis' house and work there. Give him some things!" I brought them a small picture. I had gone there to ask for some colors. Both of them had colors.

Well, Tuan Tepis opened up his cupboard: "Which ones would you like, Ida Bagus?" There were paints piled up two hand-spans high. He had paints in three different places. Ones that he was finished with.

"Take home whichever ones you want, Ida Bagus!" he said. I opened the cupboard. I'll show you what the old paints looked like.

When he said this, Togog went inside his room and brought out a box of the old paints, tubes of tempera paint. He still had some that Spies had given him with labels from Rembrandt paints, Apeldoorn, Holland: cobalt blue, ultramarine, burnt sienna, green, burnt umber, ivory, yellow, ochre, cadmium red.

So Tuan Bonnet told me to go to Tuan Tepis' house, and he had some paper there. I don't know who owned it. Tuan Tepis said: "Here, Ida Bagus, is what you need for the order for a picture. It's the same order that Tuan Bonnet talked about. Take this paper home and make the picture. Make any picture you want, but use colors."

The paper was about a meter and a half, or maybe a meter and a quarter, in length, plus a little. He said it to me and to Ida Bagus Madé Wija. Ida Bagus Wija had been told to go there, too, because he had done good work and because he was looking for orders too.

Here Togog went on to relate his experience carrying this roll of paper home to Batuan with Ida Bagus Wija, being threatened by rain and using his sorcerer's spell for keeping the rain away. I have placed that anecdote in Chapter 4.

Now back to Tuan Tepis. He told me to make a set of twelve little pictures of Rangda, each picture within a circle, about the size of a *rupiah*. He told me to put the picture inside the circle, which wasn't bigger than two fingers wide. The sheet of paper had straight lines drawn on it, dividing up the paper into boxes. There must have been about a hundred sheets of that paper. He told me to draw the Rangda inside the circle without touching the lines—that was the difficulty, and besides at that time I didn't know how to draw very well. I didn't know the proportions of *wayang* figures very well, and even less how to draw a human being.

So then Tuan Tepis set out to teach me, "If you work here, Ida Bagus, I'll teach you, but don't get angry if I correct you."

"Oh no, I won't. It's very important to me to learn how to draw figures," I said. So I worked there. And Anak Agung Kadé [Déwa Madé Cukit from Puri Batuan] was working with me. But I didn't pay much attention to him. And so then one day the Tuan said to me: "Ida Bagus, tomorrow you'll stay here alone in my house and work. Here's the key." The key was to the cupboard where he kept his paints. He was going out somewhere, and he was leaving the key to the cupboard with me.

"But be careful, don't lose it," he said.

And so then I went there early in the morning, together with Anak Agung Kadé Cukit.

"I'm going away, but I'll be back tomorrow," the *tuan* had said. So the two of us went to work there. Anak Agung Kadé Cukit is the father of my son's wife. I don't remember whether he was there to work or whether he brought things to sell. So I was working there, and he was in another place a little distance away. When it came time to go home, we went home together. Whoever finished first waited for the other.

It happened that day that I'd left home without eating. I had left very early in the morning—if you use a clock, at four a.m. When you leave at four, you are at Mas by dawn. So then I was working and working all day, and then it was time to go home, and no one had given us anything to eat. I had a burning pain in my stomach. There was water there, plenty of it, for there was a pond of clean water there. But neither of us had had anything to eat, and we were feeling very weak, could hardly talk because we were so hungry.

"*Peh!* What'll we do?" we said to one another. "We'd better just go home. It's almost sunset, and no one has given us anything to eat."

So when we left, we didn't say good-bye or anything to the cook. And I carefully took the key with me. We got as far as Ubud [from Campuan], and there in the space in front of the palace, there was a *baris* dance. They were practicing the *baris,* and we met Anak Agung Ngurah there [the secretary to the district head from the Batuan Puri]. He was a clerk in the Punggawa's office there in Ubud. When we met him, he was coming from the east and we were coming from the west. That was a good thing. When we met, he said, "Hey, what are you doing here at this hour?" He said it to me, not to Anak Agung Kadé Cukit [who was the nephew of Anak Agung Ngurah], so I answered that we'd been working in Campuan there.

The Anak Agung spoke down to Togog. Customarily a Satria (Anak Agung) when addressing a Brahmana, even a young one, should use high Balinese and address him as Ratu, but as Togog reports it, the direction of respect is reversed here. I asked Togog why this was so, and he said that it was because the Anak Agung was high in the government and had authority over him.

And then he said, "Did you have anything to eat yet?"

But I was embarrassed, and I said, politely, "Yes, Ratu, we ate already." But from my voice he knew that I was weak from hunger. I was so weak from not eating all day. [Togog laughs.] Well, he knew, and he said: "Ah, you're just saying that. I don't believe you." And then he took my hand, "Come with me this way," he said.

"*Peh!* Aren't you going to watch the dance?" I asked. I had already seen that at the dance performance there was no one selling food, only one stand selling betel chew, but no one selling rice.

He yanked at me, "Come on over to my house, come on."

"Yes, well, I'm with Anak Agung here," I said. And so the two of us went with him. When we got to his house, he whispered something to someone in the house, and now they went to get some rice with cooked eel in a dish. I murmured to Anak Agung Kadé, "He knew that we hadn't eaten all day!"

In a moment it was cooked. They had a kerosene stove there. And then he gave us a meal, and after a while we began to feel better. He said to us: "Even though you said you had already eaten, I didn't believe you. You looked just like a tree with yellow wilting leaves, so I didn't believe you."

So then I said, respectfully, "Yes, the truth was that I had left home this morning without eating anything, and the *tuan* didn't give us anything to eat."

And he said, "Maybe he was held up on the way home."

So then we spent the night there. We slept there, and in the morning we went back to the *tuan*'s house. When we saw Tuan Tepis, he said: "What happened, why didn't you stay here overnight? I told you to stay here, even if I wasn't here."

"Oh, it was like this, Tuan, we hadn't eaten all day, and we thought we'd go down to the palace courtyard and buy something to eat, and then we were going to come back here."

"What!" he exclaimed, and then he asked his servant *(jongos),* "Didn't you give Ida Bagus any food?"

And the servant said, "You didn't tell me to feed them, Tuan."

Pah! He was angry. Tuan Tepis scolded him very angrily.

"Well, from now on, Déwa Ketut, if it is after twelve o'clock, if it gets to be one o'clock, give them some food. No matter whether I didn't say anything to you, you must feed them. These painters were working here all day, and it was time to eat, so you should have fed them." Like that, he scolded him for a long time.

"Well, that's all right, don't say any more," I said respectfully. *Pah!* He [the servant] went away without saying any more, he was so angry. So then I worked there, and after that he'd bring me coffee, sometimes even twice or three times.

So I worked there a long time at Tuan Tepis' house, together with Nak Agung Kadé, until we finished the job.

There was another painter there working, Anak Agung Madé Sobrat. And one day Tuan Guru from Buleleng ["Mr. Teacher from Buleleng"] came and talked with Tuan Tepis, and then Tuan Tepis said to me: "Ida Bagus, make as good a picture as you can. This *tuan* here will pay for it. He wants to enter it in a contest." There was a contest for the best pictures in Bali. Whoever won would get a lot of money. The losers would get a little. It went according to numbers—first, second, third—like that. The Tuan Guru came from Buleleng. [The "Tuan Guru from Buleleng" was probably the Dutch supervisor of schools who promoted art education in the schools through competitions. At that time the Dutch capital of Bali was in Singaraja, Buleleng.]

And just then the Cokorda came in, the Cokorda who married the Dutchwoman [really a Frenchwoman], the one who was living in Payangan. They said he had a child there too. So he came in and he said to me, "Gus, make a very good picture for that *tuan* from Buleleng." The *tuan* from Buleleng had gone by then. "The *tuan* from Buleleng will promote your painting, but he said that the work has to be handwork. You're not allowed to copy other pictures. That's what the government has said. I'm going to support you in the competition, Ida Bagus, so make your pictures very good."

So then I drew a picture after he had said that, and in came Tuan Tepis while I was still doing the pencil drawing. He picked up a red pencil, and he drew on my picture, *kocok cok cok,* right over my drawing. And then he just went out. I couldn't understand. What should I do?

"*Bah!* I don't know how to do it—he didn't tell me how—he just left. *Peh,* this isn't clear!" And so I took another piece of paper. And it was only, as we say today, a half-hour later, and he came in again. He came in and he laughed and laughed.

"What are you doing, Ida Bagus? Where did you put the other picture?"

"Here it is," I said.

"Didn't you understand what you did wrong?"

"No," I said, and so then he explained to me how I had drawn it wrong.

"*Pah!* Do it this way. I'll show you what you did wrong. When you draw the calf of a leg of a girl, a beautiful girl like they say you have here in Bali, it should be shaped like a petal, not like that. Draw the curve like a petal. The one you drew looks like a pillar of a rice barn!" [Togog laughed here.]

I was very grateful to hear this. And then he took a book of pictures and showed it to me: "Here, look through this, Ida Bagus!" There were pictures of ears, of legs, and I could see what the proportions were. When you draw an arm, don't make it too long. When you do legs and feet, don't make it too long between the heel and the toes. All of that was in the book.

Badah! That was the kind of lesson he gave me. He didn't miss anything. If I was careless, he would correct it. He even showed me how to draw the muscles and sinews on an arm, so that the arm would look alive, not dead. If an arm is dead you can't see the muscles, he told me. That's why I consider him my teacher. A person who is not your teacher won't pay close attention to you. Well, to tell the story faster, he must have taught me four or five times, really often. He would come and look very carefully at my picture, and then one day he said: "Ida Bagus, tomorrow I'm going away with a foreign visitor. I'm going to Buleleng. Now you stay here in the house, and here is the key to the cupboard." He gave me the key.

"Yes, Tuan, tomorrow while you are gone, I'll go home and work at home. I have paints at home."

"Ah! Well, Ida Bagus, whatever you need, take any paints you need, from the cupboard."

"I don't need anything except yellow and red," I said.

"Well, take them; whatever you need, just take the tubes. These are ones I don't need anymore. I'm not going to need these anymore," he said. At that time, it was not like today—someone today might have taken twenty tubes home. But at that time it was different. I thought that I didn't need so many, and that's why I only asked for two. I took two tubes home, and I would be coming back there soon again.

I'd get up very early in the morning, and when I got there I'd clean up my workplace. And then he'd put the book near me. He had many books, some of them were very thick and full of everything. The book I used was as thick as a hand-span. If I did something incorrectly he'd show it to me in the book, and I'd copy it. Or else he'd show me a picture in the newspaper.

Now then, one day Tuan Tepis said to me: "Ida Bagus, when something happens I'll tell you. When something happens, soon, within six months or so, you will be lucky. I'll tell you about it then. The news may be good, or it may be bad. They may have powerful weapons or they may not. And they will come here and tell you. Now I want to tell you, Ida Bagus, don't believe anything they say, even if they say you will get rich. Don't believe them. In short, think about what I am saying. The reason I asked you to make these pictures of the Rangda, Ida Bagus, if the pictures sell well, you won't be lacking in money, Ida Bagus, because I knew you liked to learn. I'm telling you now. Now someone from the government told me to tell you the meaning of the Rangda. Now, for instance, if there were Balinese people whom I would address as *'beli'* ["older brother"], I would say to them, 'Listen, *beli,* there are people in Bali who eat human beings; here is a picture of someone eating a child. That's wrong isn't it? And here's a picture of someone eating a sick person, that takes strength. Now, older brother, if you want to act like that, that is wrong, that is wrong. If you want to do the right thing, make a ceremony, a great ceremony. If you want to act like the person in this picture, this is what will happen.' That's what

I'm going to write on the pictures, and then I'm going to throw them out of an airplane, the pictures that you have made, Ida Bagus. Like this, swish! They'll fall down to the ground, and the people there will learn. Yes, I'm going to release these from an airplane."

I didn't dare ask him any questions about it. That's all he told me. So I kept on working on it.

This whole episode is puzzling to me, and asking Togog and his son later did not help to clarify it. Perhaps Togog mixed up talk he had heard in 1939 about the war threatening to come with his own confusion about what the foreigners were asking him to do. However, Spies was not in Bali during most of 1939, since he was first in Dutch prison (on a charge of having sexual relations with boys under sixteen), and as soon as the war broke out in Europe he was put in prison camp in Sumatra as an enemy alien because he was German. The painting with the Rangda figures in circles was apparently the one entered in the contest in Buleleng.

A long time later they were going to organize the Pita Maha group, and I heard that the *tuan* wanted us to come to a meeting. [Pita Maha, the artist's cooperative, was organized in January 1936.] There were about 150 of us. From Badung, the only one I knew was Gusti Deblog. And there were many from Klungkung. In the beginning there were just myself and Anak Agung Dé Sobrat. There weren't any others yet.

Now, if I went there with a picture to give to the *tuan,* someone would grab it and borrow it and copy it, for sure. Well, by that time there were many people who made pictures.

So then we all got together there, and they were going to make a place for Pita Maha in Mas where the big central field is today. They had collected all of the building materials. The man whom the *tuan* most trusted was Ida Bagus Putu Taman, and it was going to be put north of his place, a museum like they have now in Ubud. But then there was some shifty business by that man. I didn't know what he did, but the money was gone, and it was over.

So then they decided to have it in Ubud, to build a building there, and they were looking for a name for it, and Ida Cokorda decided to call it Pita Maha. *Pita* means "desire." *Maha* means "fire"; thus, if your desire is not lighted you won't do anything. If you want to cut down a tree and you don't have fire in your arms, you can't cut it down. That's why they named it Pita Maha.

So then we were all photographed by Tuan Tepis. That's when I first got to know Tuan Tepis. And after that I often went to Ubud, whenever I had finished something to sell.

And then once one of the guests was going to take a bath, and Tuan Tepis had just finished bathing. And I was about to go home when the *tuan* took a book and said, "Here, Ida Bagus, you should know about this." It was a big book, "Here, look at this." There was a picture of a wire fence with posts leaning every which way, and behind it were sandbags, all piled up. And in between the sandbags there were guns. Three big guns.

So then I asked, "Where is this?" I forget . . . he said that the Japanese were about to come. In the picture the fence was broken down. That's what he said.

Now, that book I used to study the pictures, I looked at them, because they were right next to me. And then the *tuan* went out to eat.

And just then, two foreigners came by, a man and a woman. Now there were two paths by the place where I worked; one path went to the south and the other went to the north. The one path went down to the water. Now these two people, I didn't see them, because I was facing west. Here was I, and here was the path. So then the woman and the man went down the path to bathe.

And their son came down after them. He was still young. Now when he was right by me, he put down his wallet, right up among the papers and books there. And then he went on down the path to bathe. I didn't much notice, because I was hunched over my work—it was very important, you know. So I didn't pay attention. I didn't hear when he put the wallet there.

Then, after they finished bathing, they went up again, the three of them, and I just glanced at them because I was working so hard. I was trying hard to get that prize. [Laughs.] It was a big prize. So the three of them went up there, and then I heard the sound of a car honking. So the three of them went up, and then they went away.

But the wallet was left behind. It was a very fat wallet, and there was money sticking out of it. The sheaf of money sticking out was as thick as my finger. So after a while, when I was tired, I stood up to stretch, and just then I saw it—in between all those books.

"Hey, what's this? They left this behind," I thought. So then I put some paper over it, so that it wouldn't be seen. I was going to go home soon. Then I realized that the foreigners had gone away—that was when the car honked. So then I covered it with paper. I thought they'd come back for it in a minute, but it got to be late afternoon, and they still hadn't come back.

So then I thought, "*Beh!* What'll I do about this money? Should I move it, or leave it there? Should I take it, or not?" and then I thought, "*Beh!* No, that wouldn't be good. If I don't take it . . . He lost it. When he realizes it he won't remember where he put it. . . . This is really lost money. I should take it. . . . But this is the *tuan*'s place, and he owns these things."

That's the way the war was going in my heart. It lasted as long as it takes to cook a potful of rice, that battle in my mind, whether I would take it or not take it.

"If I take it I could buy five rice fields, or even more. It looks as if that wallet is just full of money. It's just stuffed with money. If I had five rice-fields . . ."

But then a whisper came to me, "Don't steal"—it was my spirit guardian *(kawi)*, my protector *(widi)*. "If you steal, your grandchildren or even your children will be punished."

"Now, what you should do is leave this, and when they come back and ask for it, give it to them, and they'll give you a reward. Yes, that's the best thing." That's what I thought within my embattled heart, staring at that money.

So then, I thought: "I'll go home now. I'll hide the money here and think about it at home." So then I put the money inside the cupboard where the paints were kept and hid it underneath the paints. So then I went home. But my heart was beating very fast from the struggle within me.

When I got to the square in front of the Ubud *puri*, there was no one there. There was an epidemic, and at least a thousand people had died, thirteen one day. *Aduh!* It was still and quiet. There was no one even walking in the road. All the way to Pliaten I didn't see anyone. I just kept on walking, but I was very scared. And then I was by the graveyard of Ubud, the one to the west and south. And then I passed the square at Pliatan, and as I came up from the west, there wasn't a single person there. So then I went on south through Pliatan, and I saw one person, out fishing for eel in the rice field with a lamp. But no one else. Everyone was afraid because of the epidemic.

I passed the marketplace at twilight and there was just one old man there. He was carrying peanuts. So I bought some peanuts. I asked him, "Where are all the peddlers?"

"Eh, so many people have died, thirteen one day, nine another day, four, then five, for so many days. Now no one dares come out here and sell." That's how I found out. I felt as if it were hell! It was a hellish situation for everyone. So I went on my way. It wasn't until I was just north of Mas that my heart began to feel easier.

Well, to get on with my story, the next day I went back to the *tuan*'s house. And while I was working, the *tuan* arrived. He had planned to be gone for two days, but now he had come home sooner. So I was there working, crouched over my drawing. I had just finished drinking the coffee his servant had given me.

So then he came in. It was a little after noon. And he just sat down—*ted!*—on the chair beside me. Just plopped down like that. I didn't dare greet him, and he didn't say anything. I just kept on working quietly. So then his guest came in, and sat down with his head hanging. So then I thought to myself: "If you don't make yourself greet the *tuan,* you will be in the wrong. It's proper for you to say something first, because he left you in charge of his house temporarily. It's as if it were your own house and as if the *tuan* were the guest. If you aren't polite you'll be in the wrong." That's how I was trying to think it out. So then I said: "What happened, Tuan? Did you get what you were looking for?"

"Pah!" he said suddenly. "Ida Bagus, you can't imagine! I'm so sorry about this friend of mine here!"

The guest was sitting north of me on the *balé dauh,* just about a hand-span away. The *tuan* was sitting across from me.

"*Peh,* you can't imagine, Ida Bagus! My guest here was about to buy something, an antique, in Buleleng, for 250 *rupiah,* and he had already taken the thing and then he was going to pay. But when he looked in his pocket he didn't have any money. There was just a handkerchief in his pocket—he'd thought it was his wallet. *Pah!* My heart is breaking!"

"*Peh!* If that's the trouble, that money is here, left behind with me!" I said. I felt free again. Well, then he sat up again suddenly! [Laughs.]

"Well, yesterday, here you had gone down to bathe, and the son came down after him, and he just put his wallet down here. I moved it, I thought it over, and I thought that since you weren't going to be home last night, I'd better put it somewhere." [Here Togog used familiar speech, unlike his usual report of how he addressed Tuan Spies.]

Well, then he said, "Where did you put it, Ida Bagus?"

"Here in among the paints!" And after I had told him, he was so happy. And so then I took it and gave it to him. "Here it is," I said.

"Did you count it up, Ida Bagus?"

"No! Why should I count it up?" Well, then the *tuan* told me how much it was, two and a half million. That's how much money.

"Well, no matter how much it was, Tuan, I wouldn't want it whether it was a lot of money or only a little, I wouldn't want it. If you behave properly at base, you won't need to beg and you will always be provided for."

"*Beh!* You are very good, Ida Bagus." And then the son stood up and went to get me a handkerchief and a shirt and some fruits. He gave them to me. He was very happy, very grateful. But whether he gave me a little or a lot, what I most wanted was to be allowed to continue to work there. So then they went away again, laughing, and I stayed and worked. And a little later the father came in and gave me some money, a *rupiah.*

"Don't do that," I said because he'd already given me something.

"Well, I'm so happy, Ida Bagus. This is all I can give you now, for that money was not my money. It belonged to the government. I was asked to buy some things for the government. I have to go back now, but when I come again, if you aren't here at Tuan Spies' house, I'll look for you at your home."

"Yes, whatever you say, Tuan. I just wanted to do what was right," I said.

Sometime later, I finished those twelve pictures, and the Tuan from Buleleng came again. Because they were now finished. He looked them over, and he corrected them in places, told me to fix them up. When they were all done, then he made some more improvements. Then he checked them all again, and said they were all right. Then he said to me, "Now in seven days I'll come here again, and I'm certain I'll have a prize for you from my chief." Nowadays I'd dare to ask, but at that time I didn't. Wherever he told me he came from, I couldn't go there anyway. So then I went home again and seven days later I went back to Ubud. When I got there, the *tuan* had just arrived.

"Hello!" said the teacher *tuan*. "You've had bad luck, Ida Bagus!" he said. "Your work lost, Ida Bagus, lost to someone from Buleleng. It would have been different if I had been working along with the jury. I defended you for a long time, but they weren't convinced by me. The painter from Buleleng had taken another picture of a Rangda, a small one, and then he'd traced it with a pen, so that it looked like handwork. That's how he beat you, Ida Bagus. Even though you lost, Ida Bagus, don't be sad. It was your region that lost, not you. The government estimated that your region is one of grade 5 roads, while Buleleng is one of grade 1 roads [i.e., Gianyar is backcountry, whereas Buleleng is modernized]. If it wasn't for that you would have won the first prize. But, anyway, they gave the same amount of prize money to the first and the second prizes. So that second prize is just as good as first prize. The money is just the same. I tried to explain to the government [juror], 'How can you give a first prize to this one who just copied a picture, while this other was done by hand?' That's what I said to him. And he answered: 'It might have been a copy of another picture, but I have no proof of that. It's clear that it was done by hand, that both of them were done by hand, but that region where this picture comes from, that's backcountry out there where that Ida Bagus lives.'" [Apparently the government official thought that the judges were biased toward North Bali (Buleleng), thinking it more cosmopolitan than South Bali.]

So then he said to me: "Don't worry about it too much! Don't be sad. Even though you got second prize, the money is enough. There is a lot of money, and also a shirt and a handkerchief."

The prize was 22 silver *ringgit*. Both got 22. The *tuan guru* from Buleleng brought the letter, and then he said that there had been twelve people entered in the contest, and only two people were given prizes. "So, if you want to know who got the third prize, you got that one too—you got the third prize as well," he said, laughing.

And then the Cokorda came in [the one from Ubud who lived in Payangan with a foreign wife], and he said, "What's going on?" and he talked to them. He'd brought some guests with him. So he said, "It was like this, and like this, and like this."

So then the Cokorda said to me, speaking down, "Don't be sad, Ida Bagus, I was there too, and I too tried to persuade the juror, but he wasn't convinced by me. He gave the prize to the one from Buleleng because Buleleng is the number one place—the houses are number one, and the roads are number one—and that was the reason the government gave him the number one prize. Ida Bagus, you live in a region counted as number five. If they had raised up the roads here to number two, you would have gotten the first prize. But they gave you the money. Did the *tuan* give you the money?" Both of us got 22 *ringgit*. So then he counted out the money to me, and *peh,* I was astounded. That was real silver money that clinked when you hit it. [Laughs.] So then all my sadness disappeared from my heart, and I was happy. I owed all that to Tuan Bonnet and Tuan Spies.

So then they gave me the 22 *ringgit*—they were big coins—and also a shirt and a handkerchief. And in addition they let me pick out some paints. I took all that home, but I just took four tubes of paint, just the important ones.

Selling

I went often to Dentiyis, to I Senter's house, that is the house now lived in by I Senter. It was the home of his father, Nyoman Patra. He was the one who first knew about Badung. I went to Badung with him.

At his house I met I Ngendon, who knew how to make

pictures. So I watched him draw, and I looked at his pictures, and I thought that I could make some like those. I'd stay there all day, watching very carefully.

In the very beginning I gave my pictures to I Senter to sell. He was just learning about how to sell pictures. Do you know I Senter, the one who has a shop, the one that is farthest east and north? When he was first learning how to sell he was poor as hell. His father paid no attention to him, exactly like mine. So I would give some pictures to him, and sometimes he'd pay me for them and sometimes not until several days later. He'd pay me for the pictures only from time to time. That was before I knew very clearly how to go to Badung to sell them.

Then, after a long time like that, I met another man from Dentiyis named Nyoman Ada and he told me about where to go in Badung to sell pictures to tourists. So I forced myself to feel indifferent and carried some pictures there.

I went to the hotel where the tourists were. In those days they let you go right in to where they stayed. There were no guards, neither on the east side nor on the west. So I went right in, and no one stopped me, no one said anything to me. Even though there were a lot of clothes being dried right there by the side of the path, I resisted the desire to steal them. I made the bad thoughts leave my heart.

I took my pictures into the room of a *tuan*. He was standing by a table, and I was at one side. I came in looking for him, and his child was standing there too. So I handed him my picture, saying, "Would you like to buy this thing, Tuan?" And just then a huge dog came from the other side and jumped up to bite my hand as I held it out. Well, the child grabbed the dog by the collar and hit the dog over and over, so that the dog couldn't bite my hand. I was just protected by my spirit guardian *(widié)*. That dog was very big, and there were two of them, as high as this. They weren't bred here in Bali, that's certain. So the child grabbed the dog and took it out. And then I went out. It was very dark that night, like hell *(neraka)*. I don't remember whether or not I sold the picture.

Another time, forty tourists came all at once to the hotel in Badung to stay three days. So one of them took my pictures to keep overnight and to pay the next day: "The one that my wife likes I'll buy tomorrow," he said. There were two pictures, one by me and one by my friend. He took them into the inner room. Well, the next day when I went to get the money, the *tuan* counted out the money and handed it to my friend, who thought it was his thing that he'd bought, that he'd liked. So, since he didn't put the money in my hand, I didn't say anything. He took it, and he was very happy. It was about ten *rupiah,* in silver. So he went out and was far away, buying something, probably thinking to himself, "What will I buy?" But just a little later after he left, I was still sitting there outside the *tuan*'s door, just sitting there, and he who took the money had gone away. Just then, the servant came out carrying a picture and gave it to me. "Here's your picture," he said.

"*Bah!* This is not my picture. Why are you giving it to me?"

"Is it the picture by the man with you? Who was that?"

"*Beh!* He's gone already!"

So then, the *tuan* was very angry, because he had bought my picture and given the money to the other painter.

"Well, go and get that man!" he said to his servant. So then we went looking for him. *Beh!* There are a lot of people in Badung, and it was far to the market and there weren't any cars then—cars were very rare because only those in the government had them. I ran and the servant went on his bike, and we found him in the market.

"Yan, Yan! You have to give that money back to the foreigner. Come on back there with me. He told me to go hunting for you," I said. I spoke like a crazy person.

"All right, let's go." So we went back there. Some of the money was already gone, since he'd bought something to eat.

So then the servant said, "That thing was the one belonging to this Wayan here. It was the picture of this Wayan here that the foreigner liked, so give the money to him." He simply gave the money back. I didn't understand the language they were speaking [Malay] very much—even now I'd like to learn it a little more.

Another time I had a small picture, and a foreigner came by and I offered it to him. I was standing by the edge of his *balé* and offering it to him.

"How much is it?" he asked.

"Five *rupiah,*" I said. And then he said, "*Sri gulden* [three guilders]." I didn't understand him, thought he meant "three *rupiah.*" I didn't understand him, so I shook my head and went away. I would have been willing to sell it for two *rupiah,* but since I didn't understand what he said I went away. So then one of my friends who had been watching came up to me and said, "*Bah,* Ida Bagus, I'll buy your picture, Ratu, I'll buy it for two *rupiah.*" So I wanted to and he gave me two *rupiah.* "Okay, take it," I said. And then I went on to the north, while he went back in where the *tuan* was. Later on my friend said to me, "The thing that you sold me, I got three *rupiah* for it." [Laughs.] He made a *rupiah* on it. So then when I got home here in the north [in Batuan] there was a woman, the mother of Si Alit, Gusti Alit Oka, who said to me: "*Peh,* what were you doing, Ratu? How come you gave away something worth two *rupiah* for three *rupiah?*"

"*Peh,* Biangé, I didn't understand what he said."

"*Peh,* that was a very easy way for that man to earn a *rupiah!*"

These last two stories about confusions in talk about money are good examples of the linguistic difficulties encountered by painters who couldn't speak Malay. The tourists' servant spoke only Malay, and may have come from Java.

Nyoman Ada told me where Tuan Dobol lived. [Tuan Dobol was a Dutch journalist named Houboldt who also bought Balinese paintings for sale in shops in Batavia.] His house was near the crossroads in the center of Badung on the road going east-west, on the north side of it. So I went there to sell a wood carving by Ida Bagus Wayan Duduk. The statue was of the story of Ida Betara Sanghyang Ratih being devoured by Kala Rau. He had his mouth around her feet.

Another time Togog told me that he once took a half-finished statue by a Batuan wood-carver, Déwa Putu Kebes, finished it and sold it to Houboldt. It was of Anoman.

It was already night when I got to Badung, but I knew of a place to sleep. So I went first to the Pedanda [in Gria Kaliungu, in Denpasar] and said to him, respectfully, "I'd like to stay here later, Ratu."

"Yes, come here and stay! I haven't seen you in a long time!" Speaking down.

"I've been busy learning how to make pictures, Tu."

"Well, come here later tonight—I won't lock the front door."

So then I went to sell the statue that night.

When I got to the foreigner's house, I offered him the statue to him to buy. The *tuan* was standing outside his room. When I held it out to him, he took my hand and wanted to draw me inside to talk. When we were inside, it was already late at night, and then he offered one *rupiah* for the statue. I didn't dare give it to him for that because the man who made it had told me not to sell it for less than three *rupiah.* I had some pictures of mine with me, but he didn't want them.

"Tomorrow I'll look at your pictures carefully, because it is too dark now, and I'll see which I like best."

Well, now he was looking at me. I understood his language a little, even though I'd never been in school, but because of all my brash roaming around I'd picked up a little. So then the foreigner said to me, "It would be best, Ida Bagus, if you slept here. Don't look for another place to sleep."

But I had already promised to go to Gria Kaliungu to sleep, and they had left the door unlocked for me. And I was afraid not to.

He kept hold of my hand, wanting to pull me inside so that I would sleep there with him, and maybe he would buy the things in the morning. I knew that even if he didn't buy them in the morning he'd give me a tip anyway, for sleeping with him. Now, I already knew what sort of a man this foreigner was. [Houboldt was known by everyone to be a homosexual.] Even though I could understand only a little of his talk. And I didn't want to [sleep with him].

And because I had promised to go to the *gria* I said: "No, Tuan, I already have a place to sleep tonight. Don't be angry with me, because I was told to stay there by my *pedanda*." So he let my hand go. I was going to go there again the next day to see if he might buy the things.

Once I had a very good thing to sell [Togog used the word *barang,* or "thing," here meaning a picture to sell, as was customary speech in Batuan], but no matter where I took it I couldn't sell it, because it was very big. Finally I sold it and was paid the money. I forget where I sold it but I remember when I got the money. It was on the road to Ubud, just north of here, in Blahtanah. I sat right down by the side of the road there and laid out the money in stacks to count it. It was a lot of money. A lot of people from here heard about it, and that's why it happened that so many artisans *(tukang)* sprouted up here, like I Jata, who had been a wayang puppet maker, first. He had a school, teaching puppet making, in the *balé* of the temple, Pura Dalem Jungut south of here.

Togog and his son later told me more about selling this very big picture. When Bonnet left Bali in 1943 to go into a Japanese prison camp, he gave Togog a letter of introduction to Jimmy Pandy, an Indonesian interior designer who had recently set up a new shop in Sanur. Togog continued to bring pictures to Pandy after the Japanese occupation was over. The incident of counting his money on the road must have occurred in the 1950s. Togog took some pictures down to Pandy, where he would leave them, but Pandy would not pay for them until he had sold them.

In this case, a week after Togog left the painting in Sanur, an American came to Batuan looking for Togog. The American said that he'd been looking for Togog for a month, but that people in Batuan had said he was dead or gone away. When the American finally found him, Togog told him that he had just finished a picture that was at Pandy's gallery. The two went down to Sanur together on the American's very large motorcycle. Togog remembered riding on the back and being very frightened.

When they got to Sanur, Togog went in by himself to persuade Pandy to give him the picture back. Pandy didn't want to give it to him and made all sorts of excuses because he didn't want to lose the sale. But in the end Togog got the picture. Then he and the American rode up to Denpasar to withdraw money from the bank to pay for the picture. The American told Togog not to wait for him, but to take the picture up to Ubud where the American was staying in Puri Ubud. He told him to roll the picture up, but Togog didn't have the tools with which to take it off its frame, so he carried it back to Batuan. There he rolled it up and walked on to Ubud. On the road just north of Belahtanah, the American came along, took the picture from him and gave him the money. It was about 900,000 *rupiah,* all in tens and fives. Togog said he sat down by the side of the road and counted it right there.

Another time Togog told me that once he heard there were some tourists living in Baturiti in a government rest house there and he took a picture to sell to them. His cousin, Ida Bagus Ceta, another painter a little younger than Togog, went with him. They walked from early morning till after dark to get there, up in the mountains. They stayed overnight with a man from Klungkung named Pan Ratep who was living there because he had been exiled from his village for making a forbidden marriage. They found the tourists, but they didn't want to buy his picture, asking him instead to make a picture of someone doing the *pencak* martial arts dance. So he went home, made twelve more pictures, bought some betel-chewing supplies to give to Pan Ratep in payment for staying overnight, and set forth alone. When he got there, Pan Ratep wasn't there, there was no place to stay, so he walked home again.

The Anthropologists

Margaret Mead and Gregory Bateson arrived in Bali on March 25, 1936, to begin a study of "Balinese character." They stayed for the first few months in one of Walter Spies' guest houses. From the second day of their stay in Bali, painters came to their door to sell their works, as was their custom with visiting foreigners. Some of these may have been from Batuan. On the evening of April 22, 1936, Bonnet showed them his collection of the new Balinese paintings. The next morning Bateson and Mead decided to study them as a possible source of information about the personalities of the Balinese. Soon after that they began to purchase paintings, each time recording the full name of the painter, the date of purchase, plus further notes on each picture. They began, even while in Ubud, asking each painter to tell the story he had illustrated in his picture, and continued that practice throughout the time they were in Bali. Bateson and Mead chose to focus on the painters of Batuan, since that village, unlike Ubud, was still untouched by foreign presences. They moved up to their field site in the mountains, the village of Bayung Gedé, on June 8, 1936; then, a year later, on July 27, 1937, they relocated to Batuan, where they stayed off and on until March 16, 1938, when they left for New Guinea. They returned to Bali on an unplanned visit in February and March 1939.

By the time they moved to Batuan, Mead and Bateson had come to know Togog well and asked him to be their assistant in correctly identifying the maker of each painting they bought. They also asked him to recount and illustrate his dreams, and conducted a variety of psychological tests on the painters, some of which are described below.[7]

In Togog's following anecdotes, he does not mention meeting Bateson and Mead in Ubud, although Bateson's records of pictures bought shows that he visited them there at least seven times in late May and June, 1936.

In the Mountain Village Bayung Gedé

Sometime after that Tuan Bayung [this was the name the people of Batuan gave Gregory Bateson, after the village in the mountains where he and Margaret Mead lived for a year] came here. He was living in Bayung with his wife. And he came here, and said: "Well, Ida Bagus, I want you to make me a picture of your dreams. [These are the dream paintings described in Appendix 1. Bateson did not make this request until he had moved to Batuan.] If you can't make your dreams, make anything else you want. That's what he said. So I made the picture. First I drew the outline in pencil. It was almost finished, still about half done. But when it was just that way, just in pencil, he came and saw it and said: "That's good just like that, don't do any more. I'll buy it now." And he didn't want me to finish it.

Bateson bought several unfinished drawings from the painters from Batuan and Ubud. I believe he was trying to study the drawing process, and also to get samples of preliminary sketches, which he considered more spontaneous and expressive than finished works.

Tuan Bayung asked me, "How much is this one, Ida Bagus?"

I said, "This is one *rupiah,* Tuan." And he just paid it! He didn't look at it closely because we had known each other so long. I had been going up there to Bayung and bringing pictures, and Madé [Kalér, the Batesons' Balinese research assistant] would accept them and later give them to the *tuan.* He'd just ask how many pictures did you bring, and then he'd ask, "How much is this one?" The *tuan* would give me the money. He was a steady customer. And because he was a steady customer I never raised the price. That's why today I'm so poor. I'm different from other people who, when someone likes their work, raise the prices. But I always think of the future [of a friendship].

When I went to Bayung, I could take a bus, but there was only one bus there. It would leave at four o'clock. I'd have to catch the bus at Sukawati—it was going to Buleleng, but I would get off up on the high place overlooking Lake Batur. I got off. I intended to get off to the south of Kintomani, but I forgot the way. So I went along asking my way to their house. I was on a very lonely path through the dry fields. It was very far, and finally I got near their house. Usually when you get there you come in from the north, but that time I had gone around and come in from the east.

Well, I gave them my pictures. They were very good foreigners. I can't tell you how good they were. They gave me something to eat, and they gave me medicine when I had a fever. They gave me a pill and my fever went away. So now, there I was, and they gave me some money.

Another time, a relative from Sakah was very sick with malaria and hadn't eaten for a week, and Togog, remembering the medicine that Nyonya Bayung had given him for malaria, went up to Bayung and asked for some of these pills to give to her. They did, and she got better.

Once they gave me 80 *rupiah* [for a large collection of pictures and carvings by Togog and by some of his friends]. The other times I had stayed overnight there, but there was a ritual back at home, so I thought I'd better go home. I was worried. But when I set out, there was no bus. It was troublesome. I might have stayed overnight, and I hadn't slept for a day, because of the worry about my home.

So it was already night when I left there, and I got to the open fields filled with corn. And I ran through the corn as fast as I could so that I wouldn't be seen by the owner. The *tuan* had given me a check. He wanted me to take the check to Badung, in the bank there. So I ran. Three times I ran as fast as I could. When I was tired, I went slowly, and then I'd go fast again, and then slow again. And I came to the end of the cornfield, where the road was, but there still was no bus. So I stopped in a *warung* on the south side of the road.

It was going to rain, and the girl in the *warung* asked me, politely: "Where are you from, Jero? Come and sit here."

So I went in, and there was her father, sleeping there, and the daughter was all dressed up, with powder on her face. The powder was not like what we have now. It was made of ground-up rice. She was a young woman and was all dressed up, looking at herself in a mirror. I sat there and she was talking with her father. I wasn't paying much attention to their talk because I was listening for the bus. And then her father went down into the field to look at the corn plants.

"Wait here, Tu, I'm going to watch over my corn—it's almost eaten up by the monkeys. My daughter here will keep you company." So then the two of us were there alone, and I asked, speaking down: "Your father just said that he was going to a reading performance *(mabasan)* in Bangli. Is he strong enough to walk there? Is there something to ride on to Bangli?"

She reached over and pinched my thigh and said, politely: "*Pah!* You're very bright, Tu! My father can fly!" she said. "It's almost night now, and he's gone already."

"If your father can fly, Yan, can you fly too?"

"No, I've never studied how to, Tu."

Togog, I think, intends to imply that the woman knew a great deal of sorcerer's lore *(désti),* and had *sakti* competence, and he narrowly escaped her clutches. Perhaps he felt particularly vulnerable because he was carrying a lot of money, or perhaps he wanted to imply that he himself was *sakti* enough to protect himself.

Just after that the bus came.

"I'm leaving now, here's the bus," I said.

"Yes, yes, good-bye," she said.

So when the bus came I waved to it, but it didn't stop, and went right on. Now what was I going to do? I was worried. It was past sunset. I was carrying a lot of money, and I was afraid I would lose it. "*Beh!* What'll I do?" I thought. So I just walked from there. It was very far, many kilometers. I felt as if I was all used up. I was almost out of breath, and my feet were tired. I got to Samprangan, east of Gianyar, and it was very late at night. What could I do? I couldn't go any farther that night. I just kept on walking without paying any attention. I came to the house of someone I knew, and I walked into the yard. It was empty, and I called out, "Kak! Kak! Kak!"

"Who's there?" The old man got up, and then he said, "Hello! It's your holiness! *(tendas tiang)!*"

"It's like this, Kak! I'm in trouble. I'd like to sleep here tonight. I can't get home tonight."

"Yes, of course you can sleep here! I'm on the south side." He had just one small *balé,* with six posts, with the northern part of it screened off. That's where he put me. And I noticed that he had a very valuable ring on. I thought that was strange. So then, as was proper, he offered me something to eat, but I said, "I already ate something before."

I was very tired because I hadn't slept for twenty-four hours. He was sleeping with a girl, a young girl. It could only have been that she wanted to have that ring. The old man was living alone, but he had that girl. And they were playing around together, the two of them. To make the story short, some time later, when I told someone that I'd stayed overnight with the old man and they said: "Did you meet that young girl who comes to him? She loves jewelry," he said.

The reason I know for certain about that young girl is that the man who told me was an Anak Agung from Puri Samplangan. I happened to be there for a cremation. That *puri* was like my own home. This time they had asked me to climb up on the funeral tower and do the ritual. It had nine levels, so I was up very high. And while up there, I sang *kekawin* too. That's when I learned about her.

So then I went on home, and just west of Samplangan I caught a bus. It was coming from Buleleng. The one who owned the bus was a Chinese named Nyoman Cingkang, from Sukawati. I knew him well because I often went there to gamble with the Chinese. So finally I got home.

Whenever I went up to Bayung, I had to take the path through the fields, and there were no trees there, and I ran. I ran so that no one would meet me. One doesn't know whether everyone is honest or not. In the mountains a lot of people knew I had money, and I was still quite small then.

In Batuan

Tuan Bayung [Bateson] and I were close friends. So I was the first one he looked for in Batuan. He wanted to build a *balé* in my place.

"Ida Bagus, I want to come and live here. What would you think if I built you a *bale?* I want to live there about a year, but then after about one year, I'll go home to my country and all the things here, and the *balé,* you can have.

Well, there were a lot of people in my place. There were all my younger siblings, but mainly I was worried about our *sisia.* We had a lot of *sisia* here, and whenever I told them to do something for me they would. If I had wanted I could have gotten a lot of money, but I was worried about the *sisia*. There was going to be a big cremation here, and there would be many *sisia* here in the *gria*, especially at the time of the *ngaskara* [ceremony before the cremation]. And they would often come to our houseyard temple, to give offerings to the *pedanda*.

This was the cremation of the Pedanda Istri, to which Togog refers in Chapter 5. Togog told me later that they were worried about having a foreign woman living there, since there would be many offerings, not to mention the dead body, and she might not know some of the very important dangers of pollution that she could bring about—if, for instance, she was menstruating and went too near the corpse, of if she accidently stepped or leaned over the offerings.

So now if the *tuan* and his wife lived here, it wouldn't be good, and the *sisia* would complain. That's why I didn't dare, wasn't free to let the *tuan* live here. So I told him that he could stay in the place of my "older brother," Gus Wayan Truwi. He was *perbekel*. I told them to go there. He was right for them—he wanted for nothing, had enough rice and money. And besides he is very honest, and he would do whatever the *tuan* wanted him to do.

So my "brother" Wayan said, "Yes, Tuan, build your house here." So then they measured out *(sikut)* the house of the *tuan*. He put up a *balé dauh*, with nine pillars, a long one, like this *balé dauh* that we are in. Nine pillars is pretty big. So they built it there, and then they moved in. Now by that time I no longer had any desire to steal, although I thought that the *tuan* might leave a lot of things around.

So then he would ask many questions. He was going to write a book. He asked people, for instance, "What does *sanga* mean?"

Here it's the custom for people to go and visit guests. Whether old or young, they liked to visit the guests, and so the *tuan* would ask everyone who came to visit him, "Please draw me a picture of a rhinoceros." And he would give a gift in exchange, a shirt or a handkerchief. So people were drawing pictures of rhinos, and some drew it in the form of a lion and wrote on the drawing and gave it to the *tuan*. He gave them some money, but I don't know how much.

So then he asked me to draw a picture of a rhinoceros: "Ida Bagus, draw me a picture of a rhinoceros."

"That's a smart thing to tell me to do, *tuan!* [Togog meant this ironically.] I don't know what a rhino looks like!" I said, "If I looked in the *lontar*, I could find a description of a rhino written there, but now I don't know how to draw a rhino." He thought that was good, and they went out and looked in their box of pictures.

"You're very good, Ida Bagus, very smart, because you said that you didn't know. Here's someone who just brought me a picture of a rhino, but it is a picture of a lion, not a rhino."

And then he showed me something and asked, "What's this?" He showed me the horn and fang. That's like its blood here. I didn't know at that time how valuable the horn and tooth of a rhinoceros are. If you grind them into powder, you can used them as medicine. The blood can also be used as medicine. The rhino was killed in Karangasem, and they brought it here, with some of the meat.

Contrary to what Togog thought, the rhino had not been killed in Karangasem. Bateson and Mead knew that rhinoceros is considered the most valuable of offerings in Bali and had obtained the horn of a rhino at the Surabaya Zoo and brought it as an offering to the Raja of Karangasem, who was having a major mortuary ceremony in August 1937.[8] I would guess that Bateson asked his guests to draw pictures of rhinoceroses to elicit fantasies from them, since the rhinoceros is not indigenous to Bali. Togog told me that when everyone finished their pictures of the rhinoceros, Bateson took their photographs holding them up.

I didn't ask for any of it because I didn't know what you could do with rhinoceros horn.

So then he showed me a picture of a rhinoceros with a very shiny horn. And he said: "*Peh,* Ida Bagus, you're very smart, not to try to draw a picture. That's not wrong. See here: this one did a picture of a rhino as a lion, with many sharp teeth. That's what he did," he said. He had about fifteen people who made pictures of rhinos, and he gave them each a gift.

So then, another time, the *tuan* showed us nine pieces of yarn and told us to take some and then to tell us what we might make with the yarn. Some people took two, some took three. And then he'd ask them what they could make with those three: for instance, a sarong, a scarf, and a sash, with the three colors. And then he'd write it down. He said: "Now, Ida Bagus, do as the others are doing. The gift *(persén)* is the same." At that time there wasn't any money. So then I took a piece of yarn—a single, white one.

"Why, Ida Bagus, you've taken only one. What can you make with just one?"

"That's all I want," I said. "I'll stand with this one."

"Well now, Ida Bagus, you've taken just the one piece of yarn. Later I'll take a picture of you."

And I told him, "Tuan, with this one piece of yarn I'd make a *wayang* figure of Anoman, who is white. I'd use it to make Anoman."

He wrote that down. And I added, "I could also make Ida Sanghyang Cintia, because you only need one color, white, for that." And he wrote that down. And then he said, "*Pih!* You know all about Ida Sanghyang Cintia!" [About Cintia, see my Afterword.]

"Yes, because I've studied the *lontar* that I have at home. But if you ask me more about it, I don't dare tell you. If you want to ask more, Tuan, ask those people who know about these things. if you want to know about ceremonies, ask those people. I don't want to tell you wrong things."

"That's good," he said. "With one piece of yarn you could do many things."

Making a Temple Painting in Tourist Painting Style

This painting (fig. 23) is one of two made for the *pura désa* of the village of Peguyungan in Badung, whose members were largely clients of Togog's Brahmana house. More details of this picture are given in Appendix 2. The two are the only paintings ever made by Togog for ritual use.

It was the time of a cremation here. The people from Peguyungan came to serve here, and they stayed overnight. I was working on a picture of a witch *(rangda)*. The Bendésa of Peguyungan saw it here. He was amazed at how good it was.

The cremation Togog mentions was for the second wife of Togog's father, the mother of the Pedanda in Sukawati, Togog's half-brother. The commoners of Peguyungan are traditional clients *(sisia)* of Togog's family.

"If I move to the south its eyes seem to follow me—that picture you made. If I move to the north and sit still, that *rangda* stays still too. Sometime I would like you to make one for us, your servants from the West, if it pleases you, Ratu."

So three days later they came here again, bringing materials, the white cotton cloth. They also brought me coconuts and rice. They said, "If you need money for materials for the work, please come and ask us, Ratu."

I was going to use Balinese paint, so I went to buy glue and other things to make the paint with and some *atal* [a kind of yellow clay] for the yellow in a Chinese store in Badung. It cost 11 *rupiah*—but he had asked for much more than that. I bargained four times: "9 *rupiah?*" "No." "10?" "No." I needed a lot of yellow for that painting, so finally we settled. [Togog uses yellow for an undercoat.]

"Yes, you come here a great deal and you make me feel embarrassed [to set too high a price]. So take it for twelve. If I give it to you for less than that I lose money." That's what the Chinese said.

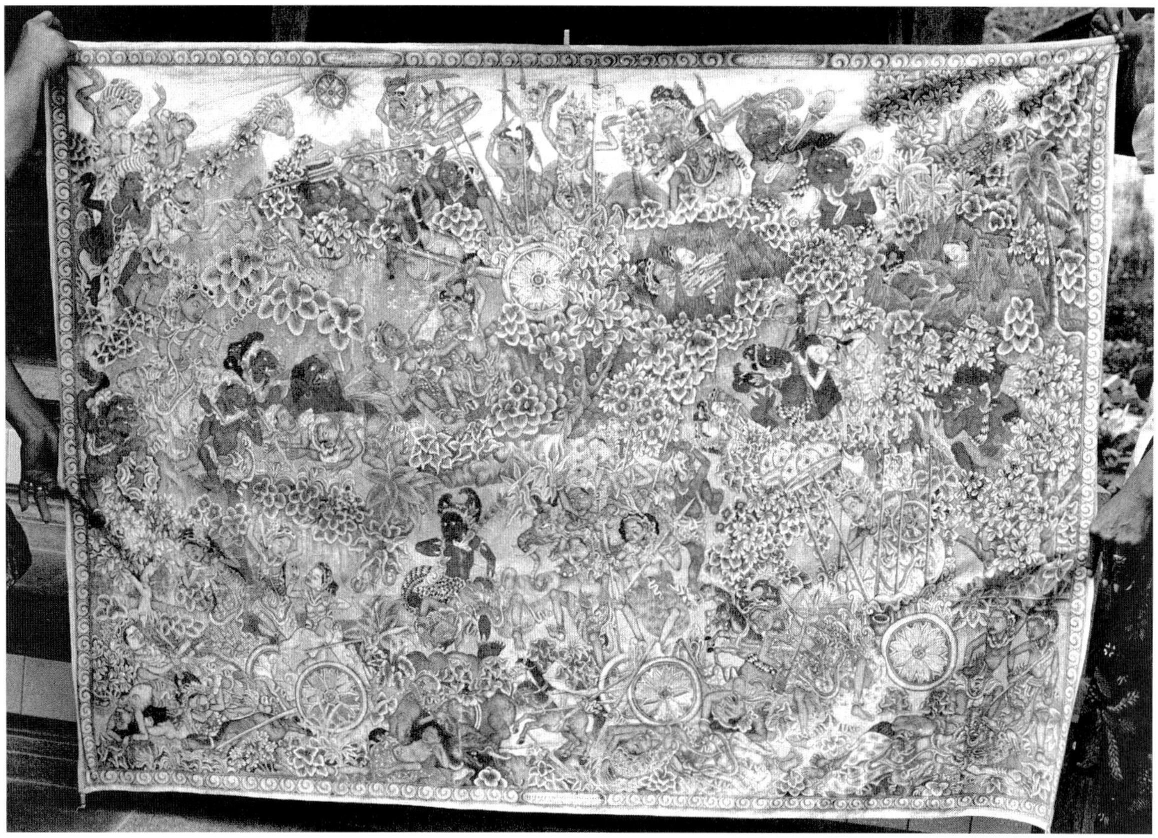

Figure 23. *The Bratayudha: The War between the Korawa and the Pandawa.* Painting by Ida Bagus Madé Togog, c. 1946.

So I went to Peguyungan to get 12 *rupiah,* but they didn't have enough. I said to the Bendésa: "Uncle [Togog uses the term *Po* for "uncle," as a polite way to address an older commoner], I need some money to buy materials. I need about fifteen, to buy glue and other things.'

"Alright, Ratu, take the money over there, take the money that has numbers on it. He had a whole basket of money. I took the money. It was silver *rupiah.* I took fifteen. I was on the *balé dauh* where the baskets were.

"Take the money."

"There are fifteen here," I said. He didn't watch me as I took the money. It was the money of the Kas Désa [village funds]. So then I took the money to Badung and bought those things so that I could finish the picture. I bought everything I needed. In the end I spent about fifteen on materials, because the glue was so expensive.

The first part of the story about eleven or twelve *rupiah* and not having enough doesn't seem to fit with this price of fifteen, but there were other things he needed, other colors, paintbrushes.

I never asked them for money for myself, to buy a shirt, for instance. A long time later someone gossiped that I had taken 250 *rupiah,* but they said it secretly. Then someone came to me and said, "Ratu, they said you took 250 *ru-*

piah." In fact I hadn't asked for a cent. This was something from another village said to one of my neighbors, who told me. I said: "Well, if you think that, you ought to ask the Bendésa directly. Did you ask him? That's just gossip of the road. Did Po Madé Bendésa say anything like that? That's just gossip." I didn't lie. If I had to buy something I told him how much it was. If I had ten to spend and I had two left, I might spend that for food for the trip."

Painting in Togog's Life

What was "painting"—which brought me to Togog in the first place—in the mind of Togog himself? How integrated was the painting craft with his inner life? Judging from the surface of his stories, painting was a trivial peripheral activity, more connected to money earning, peddling, and so on, than with tapping into significant levels of his inner life or to expressing deep concerns shared with most of his fellow Balinese of the sort that westerners demand of "art."

Togog's painting was market-driven from first to last, as he has told us. Yet, while he does not say it directly, he suggests that there was something else guiding his brush at times, not merely an imagination teeming with images and associations, the riches of his lived life, but also what his village mates might rather describe as *taksu,* or even *sakti* or "spiritual mastery."

I have already discussed some of Togog's paintings in my *Images of Power,* where many that he made in the later 1930s are also reproduced.[9] There I also explored the other Balinese painters of his time, in both Batuan and Ubud. I pointed out that the genre conventions of the form and content of paintings made for purchase by foreigners were new in Bali at that time. Although their European buyers had their own orienting tastes and preconceptions about the nature of Balinese culture, the painters of Batuan did not yet fully understand those buyers' desires and drew instead on their own imaginations for much of the content of the new pictures. This was particularly true of Togog.

Since the newly emerging genre was a hybrid or fusion of conventions and expectations deriving from both the Western and the Balinese painting traditions, the content and meanings of the paintings were likewise bicultural. The subject matter most desired by purchasers of tourist art were images of traditional daily life in Bali. But many of the Batuan painters, especially Togog, chose not to paint only pictures of farmers and fishermen and women carrying offerings on their heads, but instead used the opportunity to illustrate episodes from well-known stories of heroes and demons, which they often placed in a setting of the same ordinary village activities of the sort romantically admired by their buyers. Togog, too, from the outset to the end of his life, often depicted the tourist-pleasing subject matter of everyday life in Bali, of rural scenes and ritual spectacles.[10]

Tourist paintings, as a genre, are deliberately shallow and easily enjoyable, corresponding to the expectations that tourists bring to their travels, and their desire for a privileged and pleasurable skimming over the surface of other people's lives. The difficulties, disasters, and confusions of "real life" have little place in tourist paintings.

The most important characteristic of these new sorts of paintings—especially from the point of view of the Balinese craftsmen—is their insulation from ritual and social life. Creation exclusively for sale, and for customers who were foreign visitors not participating in the everyday engagements with the gods and other spiritual beings, was entirely novel at the time. All of the other arts in Bali are both strongly context-sensitive and complexly collaborative. They are in fact hard to comprehend except as elements in ensemble arts and as parts of community rituals.[11]

This detachment from other activities, concerns, and people had an important impact on the nature of the pictures in the long run. And yet, from the outset, Togog—perhaps unknowingly—resisted some of that trivializing pressure and used the act of painting to explore profound cultural themes, most particularly those of sorcery and healing. He did this through organizing his pictures around stories of bewitchment, combat, and victory through magical means. When speaking with me about his own paintings, Togog always forefronted the stories illustrated, narratives that to him rendered the pictures meaningful.

Togog made only two paintings that were intended to be hung in the sacred precincts of a temple. These are the ones described above that he made for the village temple of Peguyungan. They are not to be touched except by the temple priest or others who have been ritually cleansed. When he spoke about these two pictures, he did not speak about the subject matter, which is the main difference between these and the tourist paintings. The temple congregation had asked him to paint two stories from the high Indic epics—the Adiparwa and the Bratayuddha—as suitable subject matters for a *pura désa,* having to do with the high gods. The villagers, most of whom were ritual clients of Togog's Brahmana house, asked him for the story of "Garuda in search of *amerta,* the elixir of life" and the story of "the death of Salya."

The first, the Garuda story, is a tale of the highest gods, since Garuda is one of the closest protectors of the god Wisnu. In the tale that Togog told me he made for the temple (not illustrated), Garuda is the son of a famous master of *sakti,* Begawan Kasiapa, who goes up to the abode of the gods and steals a cup of *amerta* from Wisnu the god. Catching him in the act of carrying away the *amerta,* Betara Wisnu stops Garuda and says, "I'll give you anything you ask for if you return the *amerta!*" Garuda answers, "*Peh!* How can you command me to ask you for something since I am more *sakti* than you?" Betara Wisnu submits, and then asks Garuda instead to go everywhere with him from then on, and Garuda agrees.

The second Peguyungan painting (fig. 23) is about the death, not only of Salya as requested, but of the other followers of the five Pandawa brothers. All the characters in the Bratayudha war are quasi deities in the Balinese view. As Togog painted the war between the Pandawa and their cousins the Korawa, the fighting is witnessed by two other holy masters of *sakti,* Begawan Narada and Begawan Krépa.

Although the subject matter of these two paintings has much in common with that of Togog's tourist paintings, these two are stories of a higher seriousness. Most of Togog's story pictures derive from more homey folktales and the tales cycled in the popular plays of the *arja* and the *gambuh.* However, more elevated subject matter is not the only important difference between Togog's temple paintings and his tourist paintings. The former are much more carefully done. Clearly, he was attempting to make these two pictures the best he had ever made, and he succeeded.

Details of the Bratayudha painting are presented in Appendix 2. They illuminate the complexity of Togog's compositional task, and the ingeniousness with which he handled it. What seems striking to me is the way the artist intertwined the various events of the war to produce an even, general appearance. Looked at as a whole, the Bratayudha picture presents a homogeneous surface with no foreground–background layering.

The painting is unusual in Togog's corpus in that here he does not use the device of setting off each element with black shading, darkest next to the figure and fading away from it. This is a common device in Batuan paintings, and can be seen in Togog's earliest pictures as well as his last. In the Bratayudha painting, however, the lines around each image are delicate, and most figures stand against a small grayish or cream-colored clearing in the foliage. Here he uses color rather than heavy lines to distinguish foreground from background.

The Bratayudha story was known to Togog primarily through shadow plays. His figures in this painting exhibit their shadow-puppet ancestry in their clothing. However, they are not in *wayang* poses but in vigorous dance postures; they are much more rounded and have much more supple postures than those of Kamasan artists whose style is usual in temple hangings. The many corpses strewn around the battlefield are especially realistic. The vigor of the figures, the intricacy of the whole, and the adroit use of color as a design element make this painting perhaps Togog's best.

The painting must have been done soon after Togog began painting in color, in tempera paints on prepared cloth. His major shift in technique (and, to a certain extent, style) came when he moved from paper to cloth, and from black-and-white ink and pen to tempera colors and paintbrush. This must have occurred right after the end of the Japanese occupation in 1945, when Dutch administrators and travelers returned and began again to buy paintings, and when shopkeepers in Denpasar began to stock supplies for the artists. Cloth and tempera, several painters told me, meant being able to erase mistakes and paint over them, a feat impossible with ink on paper. Cloth also permitted the making of paintings in much larger formats, with multiple figures spread over a wide expanse.

The use of cloth and color had been taught to Togog and others by Walter Spies and Rudolf Bonnet in the 1930s. They supplied the materials, because they were not commercially available to the Balinese. In a few cases they gave the young men masonite boards (which Spies himself used sometimes). But for the most part, before the war, the young painters stayed with ink and watercolor on paper because they could buy them in the shops.[12]

Bonnet also taught his protégés how to draw human figures that were anatomically correct with shadows indicating rounding. Togog experimented with this sort of naturalism from time to time to the end of his life, but the peak of his efforts resides in the Bratayudha painting.[13] The picture that his village clients exclaimed over, of a *rangda* whose eyes seem to follow you around, must have been another successful experiment in naturalism. Subsequent paintings never reached that level.

Although the Bratayudha picture is sacred, it too is a crossover in that he brought the new techniques into temple painting. In both kinds of paintings, Togog constantly chose to depict moments in narratives about issues of *sakti*. These popular stories provided him with characters, acts, and strings of consequences, each of which could set up possibilities for associations beyond their surface meaning—analogies, metaphors, and ironies, which the maker or the viewer may bring to a painting. And all of these acts of interpretation are based on religious premises that seem undoubtable to him—premises and extrapolations that themselves have profound meaning. The paintings, just like Togog's tales about himself and his life, have to be understood as complex products of contradictory conceptions of what life is about.

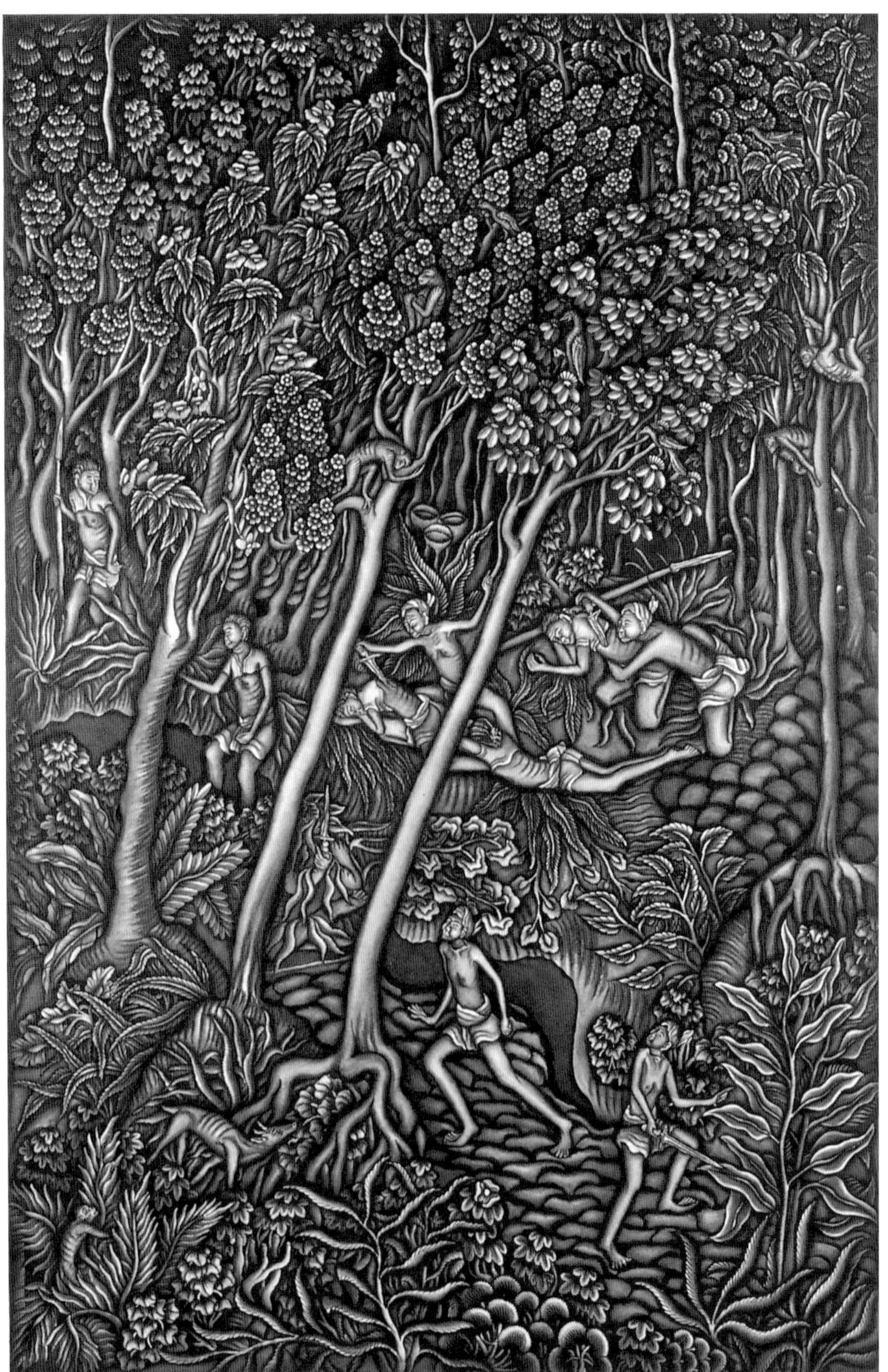

Figure 24. *The Story of Amad and Mohamed Killing the Men in Iron Armor.* Painting by Ida Bagus Madé Togog, 1939.

Afterword A Charmed Life

In person-centered narratives the problem of perspective, the relativity of the speaker's point of view, is both urgent and obvious. Togog tells you all about himself from the position of that self alone and how it felt—for him—to come gradually into consciousness within a family of Brahmana Buda in a lowland village in colonial times in Bali. The related problem of selective omissions constantly arises. There are many matters about which Togog does not tell us, either because he doesn't know or care about them—as, for instance, trance or violent killing, both of which are quite common in Bali—or because he is reticent, as is the case in matters relating to the nature of his spiritual protectors.

And yet, despite awareness of these issues of particularity and omission, some readers will still persistently ask the text to reveal "what it is to be 'Balinese.'" That question, entailing many logical and practical difficulties, naturally springs to the mind of any reader raised in a cultural tradition that assumes ethnicity is both homogeneous and psychologically central. Similar questions, such as "How is Togog like or unlike other Balinese?" or "How is Togog like or unlike Americans?" also assume that there is some sort of essential "Balineseness" that could be a suitable object of study.

For me, better inquiries would be of the sort "How would other Balinese make sense of Togog's stories?" or "What do other Balinese 'know' that helps them interpret what Togog has said?" It has been in the spirit of this latter kind of question that I have framed my commentaries on Togog's recitals, seeking to avoid assumptions of cultural uniformity and consensus. This kind of cultural contextualization is, to me, the indispensable primary step toward interpreting a personal text such as this. Basing my readings first on Balinese commentaries on this text, such as those of Togog's son, and second on my knowledge of Balinese ideas and practices, enables the conjectural filling in of conventionally suppressed information, of the omissions and ellipses to which every Balinese is accustomed.

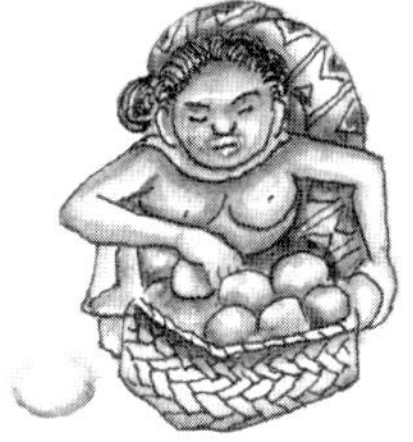

Direct Balinese commentary must, however, be supplemented with less certain insights or guesses drawn from the foreign researcher's experience of puzzling through other conversations and events in Bali like, for instance, learning the constraints and suggestions built into local genre conventions for storytelling. A final source of help has been the cumulated scholarly writings about aspects of Balinese culture that enable all sorts of comparisons to be made. These last two sources must be constantly and critically reexamined, for they are directed by foreign rather than Balinese interests and assumptions.

Thus, in my commentaries I have been mainly occupied, not with making generalizations about "all human beings" or "Balinese people" or even "Balinese culture," but rather with comprehending what Togog had to say about issues he himself raised. A quite different approach to reading Togog's words would be to reverse that stance and look to see what light the text might shine on questions raised by scholars, notably by those writing Bali's history. Although in practice they inform and enrich one another, these two directions of interpretation must be kept separate conceptually, because they involve different logics, procedures, and goals. The first, the particularizing stance of the commentaries, looks inward towards Togog's own personal experiences, towards his own conceptions, and ultimately towards his inner life, while the second, the generalizing stance, looks outward towards the other people in his world, towards other people's ideas and categories, and ultimately towards all the circumstances that structured his and their lives. The first brings public and historical materials to bear on the understanding of a specific life, whereas the second turns towards the understanding of those public and historical materials themselves.

I have used Togog's life as a stepping-off place for research oriented around one scholarly puzzle that has preoccupied me throughout my other work. This is the study of the nature, purposes, and meanings of Balinese religious beliefs and practices. Figuring out what Togog assumed that I—or any other audience—already knew about such elements in his experiences has taught me much about the larger verities by which he and his companions lived.

I started out in 1981 holding the standard view scholars of the time had of Balinese religion—the assumption that the driving aim of most of their rituals was to bring about cosmic harmony coupled with social order, and that the Balinese felt such constant equilibrating would result in agricultural fertility, bodily health, and political peace. I also believed that the Balinese lived in fear of demonic evil beings. Both ideas turned out to be misleading, if not false.

Listening to Togog made me realize that many such assumptions about the nature of Balinese religion in the scholarly and popular literature are seriously incomplete. I have set forth those ideas at length in *The Life of a Balinese Temple* (2004), in which I contrast the Hindu Dharma theology current in Bali of the 1980s with the theologies implicit in Balinese temple rituals and in *balian* healers' diagnoses for understanding trouble. I am sure that if I had asked him directly about the meanings of his rituals, Togog would have echoed the Hindu Dharma theology that permeated his son's and everyone else's discourses. His stories, however, implied something quite different: that what might be called "sorcery" or "witchcraft" lies at the core of Balinese notions about the purpose of rituals and the nature of Balinese deities and spirits. When I began talking with Togog, I already knew that fears of witchcraft were to be found in Bali, but I did not yet know how pervasive they are in everyday life—how every illness, every lack or excess of rainfall, every personal disaster is scrutinized for its probable source in malevolent neighbors or kin, including the recently deceased. I gradually came to realize that sorcery in Bali entails that the victim recognize his suffering as the result of an intentional act by a human working in concert with *niskala,* or intangible beings, the powerful godly, demonic, and ancestral agents of human well-being and suffering.[1]

Togog does not stress or dramatize sorcery in his anecdotes but takes it for granted. For instance, in one of his earliest memories, the very place where he sleeps has been cursed so that any weak person who sleeps there is plagued with sickness. The assumption is that the illness was caused by a specific but unknown enemy of someone in the family, but when Togog first becomes sick, the *balian* does not try to confront the malefactor directly but strengthens Togog's own defenses against the sorcerer's attack. The means by which the enemy was able to attack Togog does not become clear until many years later when the *balé gedé* he slept on was torn down and a hidden burnt place on a wood pillar was discovered, suggesting that the intended victim was not Togog, but the *pedanda* for whom the *balé* had been built long ago. Who the sorcerer could have been was by then unguessable.

Another example in which the (unmentioned) cause of trouble was witchcraft is the deep cut made by the blade of a fighting cock that Togog suffered while watching a cockfight in the temple. It is understood not to be an accident but a sorcerer's attack that must be warded off by anti-sorcery spells wielded by two powerful neighborhood healers.

The everyday quality of witchcraft accusations is demonstrated by the casualness of the talk of the *balian* whom Togog consults about the terrifying ghostly beast that stopped him in the night on the way home from gambling. The healer names all the local sorcerers who might have been able to assume the form of a frightening animal and determines that none of them were afflicting Togog. The *balian*'s conclusion is that the apparition of a huge, shining white calf did not intend harm to Togog but came instead to protect him from something ahead on his path. It was, he said, Togog's personal protector, what he referred to as his *ilon,* and it was probably a manifestation of one of his own dead kin.

A more direct but just as everyday instance is Togog's youthful peddling trip to Sanur, which climaxes in his nearly being made sick or killed through eating a neighbor's gift of food that contained a "poison" aimed at his host. He learns from whom he can obtain a similar death-dealing substance and goes to get it to sell to an adult acquaintance who wants to do away with a woman in his own village, some distance away. Togog reports this transaction as merely a profitable deal, associated in his mind with his trade in candlenuts, and he makes no comment on any moral implications it may have had for him.

Togog tells of his work as a ritual specialist in the same mundane, practical-minded terms. He is concerned mainly with his own personal interests and risks, with his own discomfort and disgust, and sometimes with achieving recognition for his prowess as a singer. For Togog, "religion" (if he had a word like it) would be a range of everyday practices with pragmatic goals.

Even the risks are everyday matters, although they are not threats from natural forces, but rather from personalized *niskala* beings intent on punishment, revenge, or other immediate satisfaction. Togog's courage in confronting such perils is demonstrated in the first chapters. He displays it when hunting bats in the night at the temple near the graveyard, the Pura Dalem; when his friends panic, he laughs. This may have been the bravado of a small boy's ignorance, but I believe it was based rather on a growing sense of his own sources of strength in the face of sorcery.

Underpinning the Balinese notion of sorcery and healing is a cluster of concepts touching on *sakti,* the idea that some human beings are able to do what nonhuman deities and spirits can do—cause human suffering, death and life, and also to bring about personal well-being and prosperity. A number of these people, whom I have termed "masters of *sakti,*" appear in Togog's stories.[2] All the healers he speaks of are masters of *sakti* in various degrees of competence, as is Togog's own grandfather. Another master of *sakti* is I Jana, the old man who gave Togog his first palm-leaf manuscript, a sorcerer's manual called "Candra Bérawa." Jana turns up again much later, during the rebuilding of the temple next to the Triwangsa cemetery and burning ground, when he is thought to have tested out his own *sakti* by maliciously putting out the fire the workers were using to bake bricks. He is described as pitting his own *sakti* powers against those of the Triwangsa pedanda.[3]

Anyone who is *sakti* (or who is associated with a master of *sakti*) is protected to some degree, and the implicit message of Togog's stories of escape from danger is that he is always protected. In his tale of being blocked by a ghostly white calf in the dead of night, he calls his protector his *ilon*—but he doesn't elaborate on who that might be. I believe that he considered himself surrounded by the spirits of his forefathers, *sakti* Brahmana priests, especially those recently deceased. These intangible beings not only guard him at all times but also can, if crossed, unleash angry punishments, as for instance when they allowed Togog to be hit on the side of the head by a person of lesser title while gambling.

As Togog suggests, his *ilon,* his protectors, were always around him and always at work. The earliest mention is the near miss of a falling tile that might have killed him. Soon after, his foot is prevented from stepping on the sharpened bamboo stakes surrounding a coconut tree from which he was stealing. Later there is the more dramatic story of a malaria-plagued trip to Bali's mountain areas for wage work and his rather miraculous return home and final healing. As Togog matures, his stories shift to tell of his own assiduous cultivation of personal spiritual abilities, or *sakti,* through study and through acquiring and caring for talismans like his kris and coins.

It was Togog's pervasive sense of growing spiritual strength that led me to title this book *Tales from a Charmed Life.* I could have picked a number of other adjectives (such as "Brahmana" or "ordinary" or "extraordinary" or "courageous" or "traditional" or "bicultural"). The term "charmed" has obvious drawbacks. In English its earlier meanings, as with near synonyms such as "bewitched" and "enchanted," have been eroded, and now "charmed" belongs in vocabularies of "attractiveness" and "chance." And yet, I liked its older implications of protection against the perilous world of powerful "supernatural" beings.

But Togog is no different from other Balinese in having a "charmed" life. In fact, one might say that all Balinese—certainly not just Brahmana—assume that they have spiritual protectors. Togog is different from many Balinese in that he is a Brahmana ritual specialist, and in that he assumes his task in the world is to help others in their engagements with their own unseen protectors.

A sense of balance on the issue of how ordinary Togog was might be gained through study of other Balinese autobiographies. The foremost one, distinguished by the quality of analysis made by the anthropologist who recorded it, was that of a healer, a *balian* called "Jero Tapakan," who recounted to Linda Connor how she attained her abilities to serve as a spirit medium. Connor has shown how Jero's stories of her own life were given their form through echoing the manner of folktales, and how the conviction that she had several powerful spiritual protectors ran through all of Jero's accounts.[4]

There are other autobiographies in which their tellers were not spiritual professionals yet nonetheless convey a similar sense of the omnipresence of unseen guardians. Dr. Anak Agung Madé Djelantik titled his life story *The Birthmark: Memoirs of a Balinese*

Prince, to stress his own certainty that he was protected from birth, and he quotes a seer, or *balian,* as saying about him as a child that he was "destined to meet many dangers in his life, but he will always survive unscathed."[5] A study of the biography of "a modern Balinese," I Nengah Metra, and other such narratives by Adrian Vickers, concluded that

> stories linking the world as it is perceived by the senses *(sekala)* and the world beyond the senses *(niskala)* are common in Balinese biography and autobiography. Embedded in the narrative of Metra's modernity is the same kind of basis of identity which characterizes stories of coming to power or being granted boons by the gods as characterize the narratives of healers *(balian)*. . . . These same senses of rectitude and formation of self pervade various forms of Balinese biography and autobiography. The intervention of what we Westerners might call 'magical' forces are part of an interplay between outside agents, such as gods, owners of the ground and 'invisible people,' and actions of persons in creating the correct emotional states.[6]

Complicating any study of Balinese sorcery—including an interpretation of Togog's words—is the powerful taboo against speaking openly about any threat or suspicion of threat from witchcraft.

An example of the secrecy surrounding the acts of a master of *sakti* is Togog's picture of "The Story of Amad and Mohamed Killing the Men in Iron Armor" (fig. 24). Painted in 1939 and purchased by Gregory Bateson, it was given its title by Bateson. The title forefronts the two heroes, Amad and Mohammad, but the real protagonist of the picture is their father, who is meditating and gathering *sakti,* nearly covered with tropical vegetation, at the mouth of a cave. He is almost completely hidden in the center of the picture, and yet it is his actions that drive the picture's action. He is behind the center tree, and all you can see of him is a hand holding an upright dagger. The story, recounted at length in my *Images of Power* (1994),[7] concerns two brothers who incur the wrath of the king; they flee to the forest to find their father, who helps them by giving them two daggers with which they defeat the entire army of the king. The *sakti* father is able to focus and relay his powers through the daggers. The painting emphasizes the Balinese point that concealment is crucial to the gaining and wielding of *sakti.*[8]

Togog's stories themselves demonstrate his careful indirection in speaking of such matters. He uses allusion, metaphor, allegorical narrative, and euphemism in his talk—ways of speaking that must all be "read" for their underlying message. An example is Togog's report of a conversation with a woman who runs a coffee shop he stopped at when hiking down from the mountain village where he had just sold a load of pictures to Gregory Bateson. Carrying a lot of cash, Togog was on the alert against robbery, so when her father left, saying that he was going to Bangli some distance away, he asked the woman how her father was going to get there. When the woman said that her father could fly there, Togog took that as a warning that the father, and possibly the woman herself, were capable of felling and robbing him through witchcraft. Without further discussion, he fled as fast as he could. The conventionalized way of speaking, characterized by indirection, as engaged in by Togog and the coffee-shop woman, fits well with Balinese ideas about sorcery.

Some more of the complexity—social and intellectual—surrounding issues of sorcery shows up in Togog's account of the death of his first child and his revenge by killing the *pedanda* who had neglected the baby. The avenging agent is not a human sorcerer but the dead child himself with the aid of a spirit inhabiting the Barong costume that was housed in the *pedanda*'s own compound. A similar collaborative act of sorcery between humans and *niskala* beings is shown by Linda Connor in her report on the séance of the *balian* Jero Tapakan. The spirit of a dead boy undertakes to kill his murderer, but with the express consent of his living relatives.[9]

Another kind of complication of acts of magic is presented in Togog's story of rain dispelling to protect his art paper, where he is not entirely sure which ancestral spirits have aided him. He said he asked the ancestor of his companion to prevent the rain from falling. But the next day, when Togog is caught in a blinding thunderstorm while bathing in the river, he believes that the storm is punishment from his own ancestral guardians for his frivolous use of his knowledge of sorcery. He had gained that knowledge of rain prevention from the *lontar* book that had been given him in childhood by the local sorcerer and *balian* I Jana. He said that the book, the "Candra Bérawa," tells the story of the legendary sorcerers Begawan Mpu Bhrada and Begawan Mpu Bahula and contains all their mantras and instructions for the rituals involved in witchcraft. Rain magic and witchcraft against enemies use mantra and offerings and involve asking for the aid and blessing of *niskala* beings. By inference, these "magical" practices are the same as the acts of a priest at a cremation or at temple worship.

In a similar situation in his work as a ritual expert, Togog implied that if he took any wrong step he would be in danger of being punished by his own guardians. The story he told is of incurring the punishment of a heavy sick headache because he had worked on the carving of a wooden cremation bull for some clients without their giving him a *santun* offering—a set of foodstuffs that the Brahmana ritual expert takes home to place on the shrine of his own ancestral beings. Thus he had allowed his clients to ignore his own guardian spirit, the main source of his capacity to help them.

From these examples it is clear that my use of the term "sorcery" in speaking of Balinese matters must be understood in a larger sense than the usual English notion of it and its related notions of witchcraft and magic. Balinese notions of *désti* and *sakti,* which are often translated as "black magic," involve engagement with *niskala* beings of all kinds, including the highest deities, and this engagement itself is of many sorts, including worship and propitiation. The conceptual distinction between "magic" and "religion" that is culturally specific to European thinking as developed within and after the Protestant Reformation is not appropriate to Balinese thought. Within the framework of post-Reformation thought, actions labeled "witchcraft" and "sorcery" are narrowly defined as working automatically through the manipulation of some general force, and are confined in their aims to personal and practical gains. They are considered to be mere by-beliefs—peripheral to central "religious" activities and beliefs.

In contrast, I have conjectured that all Togog's ritual practices and the premises on which they are based are of a single piece with worship of the highest gods as well as with dealing with sorcery attacks on family and neighbors. I believe that in the thought and practice of at least most Balinese there are no important distinctions drawn among deities, demons, ancestors, and lesser spiritual beings, that they merge together in everyday experience.

The high deities are worshiped in temples. Togog rarely mentions temple worship in his stories. Many of the rituals that the *pedanda* he assists performs are in temples, but they are not his own. The *pura désa* of Batuan to which I have devoted another book was Togog's community temple until the 1960s, but it plays only a small part in his stories. The incident of the cockfight accident took place there, but it had more to do with witchcraft than with the high gods. It was only coincidental that it took place inside the temple. Togog's wound was brought about by some human evil-wisher working with the collaboration of some *niskala* being, and it could be cured only through the efforts of another human being with similar spiritual connections. In the story of diverting rain from his roll of new art paper, he seems to draw no line between "ancestral spirits" and "gods." At one point Togog says that he prayed to "Sanghyang Embang," suggesting the name of a deity (unknown to me). But soon after that he says clearly that he had prayed to Madé's ancestors *(luhur)*.

Although Togog rarely mentions the high gods in his stories, they have great importance for him and show up often in his paintings. Important examples are his many paintings of the highest deity, Sanghyang Cintia (also called, more recently by the Hindu Dharma theologians, Sanghyang Widi Wasa, a translation of "God Almighty" and "Allah Akbar"). One of these pictures of Sanghyang Cintia is reproduced at the beginning of this book (fig. 1). During our interviews in 1983, a similar but rather clumsy tempera painting hung on his wall. Several times he pointed to it and said that it would make a great cover for our book. Sanghyang Cintia was the subject of one of Togog's earliest drawings, done in 1934. It was reproduced in a book by Miguel Covarrubias, *Island of Bali,* in 1936. Covarrubias stayed with Walter Spies from January through March 1934 and probably purchased it then. Covarrubias titled the picture "The Balinese Cosmos: The World Turtle, Bedawang, and the Supreme Being, Tintiya," perhaps because Togog had told him that the turtle stood for the world, but certainly Togog had not used the phrase "the Balinese cosmos."[10]

After Togog's death, I visited his son again and asked him about the picture of Sanghyang Cintia that still hung on their wall. Ida Bagus Gedé said that it had been adapted from an image *(rerajahan)* drawn in ink on a burial shroud *(kajang)* of a Brahmana, of the sort that Togog often prepared for his clients.[11] Togog's son added that, strictly speaking, the painting diverges from a proper image for a *kajang.* He showed me an actual *kajang* drawing in which the central figure is not that of Sanghyang Cintia, but rather a human Brahmana, the person being cremated. The most important of Togog's modifications from the usual *rerajahan,* said his son, was the substitution of the image of the highest god, Sanghyang Cintia, for the human being that stands at the center of any burial shroud. Togog had made some other changes as well. A *kajang* drawing is simple ink lines on a white cloth, but the first one he made, the one he sold to Covarrubias, had a black background, and the snakes were drawn with shadings to make them look rounded, in the style of Batuan tourist paintings of the time. Besides, Togog left out of the picture the scriptural writings that are a necessary part of a shroud as they are the equivalent of the priest's mantra. Gedé added that the elaborate headdresses and necklaces on the snakes have no theological meaning and were put there for the purpose of adding *seni,* or artistry. Togog had taken a powerful and dangerous image and modified it so as to defuse its efficacy in ritual and make it into a pretty painting, derived from but free of actual engagement with the *niskala* being it portrays.

I asked Togog's son what was the meaning of this drawing for Togog and why had he thought that it should be in his book? He said that the central figure was Sanghyang Widi Wasa (the younger man's preferred name for Sanghyang Cintia).[12] The turtle stands for the earth, and it is the throne for Sanghyang Widi Wasa, said Gedé. When the turtle moves, there is an earthquake, and the two snakes are there to keep it steady. They have no names and are sometimes misidentified as the two *niskala* beings, Basukih and Taksada. At other times they are wrongly thought to be the two snakes in the story of the origin of the world from the Indic scripture, the Adiparwa. But this is a mistake; the images on the funeral shrouds, he said, are not depictions of characters from the

Adiparwa, but of human beings, and they were drawn first for the Balinese by Ida Pedanda Sakti Wau Rau, the bringer of orthodox Hinduism to Bali and the ancestor of all Brahmana, to help each human spirit in his transformation from human being into *luhur,* or ancestral being.

Gedé said that the picture of Sanghyang Cintia gave his father a feeling of peace and safety, and he wanted to give this feeling to others. Of course, he said, to make it potent, to "bring it to life," would require the addition of the proper mantra in Balinese script around it, as well as the appropriate rituals. Gedé said that the state of peace and safety is achieved through a balance between the forces of *darma* and *adarma* (of which a rough translation might be moral and immoral action, or as Christians might have it, good versus evil), symbolized by the snakes holding the turtle steady. The struggle goes on at two levels—that of the *buana agung* (the world) and that of the *buana alit* (the inner self of every person). The *mudra* position of the hands of Sanghyang Widi Wasa stands for unity both among people and within one's own heart. This stress on psychic and moral equilibrium and the metaphorical comparisons between inner and social peace are characteristic of the late-twentieth-century theology of the Hindu Dharma movement to which Togog's son and most of his contemporaries adhere. But I believe that here Gedé was misrepresenting the nature of his father's convictions.

It is not that the high gods were not of great importance to Togog, but rather that he experienced them at a distance, as manifestations—more abstract but not more powerful—of the same beings that he felt around him at every moment in his life. Togog used various terms in his anecdotes, referring to his spiritual guardian(s) as *ilon, kawi,* and *widi.* These are all terms that other people could employ to refer to one of the high deities. Nonetheless, whenever Togog mentioned his *ilon* or *widi,* his primary referent was probably some particular personal ancestral figure. I have no doubt that Gedé was right in saying that the picture of Sanghyang Cintia gave his father "a feeling of peace and safety"—but I do doubt the reasons he gave. I saw no evidence in Togog's own talks with me that the hand gestures, or *mudra,* "stood for" anything other than a mode of communication with the *niskala* beings. Nor, in any of Togog's talk about moral issues, did he speak of *darma* and *adarma* or of harmony. For Togog, I think, *niskala* beings were personalized individuals, sensible of particular acts of humans and unpredictable in their responses to them; they were not ways of speaking about some abstract "force." For him, Sanghyang Cintia was a transmutation of his own immediate deceased kin.

In the course of recounting tales of his life, Togog gave hints of the nature of his actual experience of his rituals, hints that other Balinese would find intelligible in the ways I have suggested. His Balinese auditors would also know that their traditions are so varied and rich in possibilities that the version that Togog lived by was only one of a number of different options. An adequate understanding of the other facets of Bali's complex religious life by scholars would require the study of a number of other personal histories of lived religious experience in Bali, with close attention to the day-to-day dilemmas and choices that are only partially described in the discourses of Bali's theologians.

Togog and I together have created a text with many potentialities. I have given some of my interpretations and extrapolations of this text, and I have followed up with my own research some of the many hints that he threw out concerning matters of importance to him and to other Balinese. No doubt others would learn other kinds of things from Togog's stories and use them for springboards to other kinds of research.

Each reader brings different knowledge and concerns to the act of reading or hearing, and in so doing creates a new, more complete "text." Providing new contexts for interpretation, whether Balinese or Western or some mixture of these, is the reader's share in these complex collaborations.

For instance, Togog's tales could tell us much about Bali during its colonial period—the time of coming of age of Togog and his generation. His laughingly reported confusions in his encounters with foreigners—from the black man who wanted to swap his blowgun for a toy pistol to his misunderstandings about Dutch money—illuminate the processes of commercialization, monetization, and ongoing and changing authority structures. It was not a "simpler" world than that of the 1980s of the time of telling, but one with different kinds of complexities.

Another important thread that winds its way through these stories is the image of "self" that Togog invokes. Does he assume a central identity that carries him through all the vicissitudes of his experience? Who is the "I" in his stories? Telling anecdotes about oneself necessarily produces several images of oneself, the person to whom others speak, the one with various intentions who makes choices, the one who lives within a variety of social networks that are brought into play in the course of the story; but these images do not necessarily cohere into a single personage. In Togog's paintings of his dreams, he placed a similar self-portrait within each picture, an objectifying move. Is he likewise objectifying his self in some of his anecdotes? In his other paintings, those of the big sorcerers and the tales of heroes in the *gambuh* narratives, perhaps the painter was alluding to an imagined self with mystical powers. Answers to these questions can be found only through knowledge of the various ways in which Balinese have conceptualized—or made metaphors about—"selves," and through making detailed comparisons of other Balinese acts of self-presentation. One must keep in mind that these texts were always primarily performances, told to an audience that was understood to expect to be pleased, thrilled, improved, edified, and above all, amused. But who was Togog's audience, to him? He seems to have spoken little of the "foreigner talk" in which, for instance, his son is fluent. He provided few of the explanations or defenses that would be due a hearer with a different sense of the world; he appears to have had little sense of himself as "a Balinese." My own gut feeling about these performances is that they were directed, not at me as an inquisitive but ignorant American, but rather at some imagined Balinese listener, someone much like himself.

Last, an issue that profoundly puzzles me is the nature of the moral framework (or frameworks) that guided Togog throughout his life. The stories in Chapter 1 about stealing peanuts and bananas seem to be mainly about Togog's inner struggles to behave morally and not to steal. He also places the fishing expeditions of Chapter 2 within a similar struggle, as distractions both from his desire to gamble and from his disappointments in gambling. Yet it seems to me that the effort to achieve an ethical life, as Togog reports it, is best understood within the context of a very different conception of self-improvement, that of working toward a high level of *sakti,* an amoral kind of competency that resolves everyday exigencies. The two perspectives do not conflict but are different; but which one was more important to Togog I leave to others to decide. He speaks of his study of singing *kekawin* and *kidung* songs as motivated by a need for moral guidance, but it never became clear to me how that might work. Further, if my interpretation of his religious ideas, centering on engagement with humanlike, unpredictable *niskala* beings, is correct, then he would have found few ethical teachings in his ritual practices. Again, further studies of other Balinese lives, supplemented with knowledge of how other Balinese might interpret them, could give some insight.

Ida Bagus Madé Togog of Banjar Gria, Désa Batuan, has taught me much about his sense of his world, his manners of thinking and feeling, in all their particularities. At the same time he has taught me much about the cultural and historical circumstances within which he spoke and lived. I hope he will now do the same for others.

Appendix 1: The Dream Pictures (1937–1938)

In Gregory Bateson's field notes recorded on August 24, 1937, he asked Togog to make pictures of his dreams accompanied by their narratives. The first of the dream pictures were dated August 26, 1937, and Togog continued to bring more to Bateson steadily through March 11, 1938, with one last narrative dictated a year later, on March 16, 1939. At the outset, Togog dictated directly to Bateson, who went over them (sometimes a year later) with his assistant, Madé Kalér. After that Togog told his stories directly to Kalér. They did not ask for associations, except in a few cases when Bateson had instructed Kalér to ask Togog to tell him what he had done the day before that was connected with the dream. Kalér's transcriptions are a little fuller, and he, unlike Bateson, added punctuation. Bateson's, however, are remarkably clear—he had a good ear—and sometimes he added an explanatory comment of his own or Togog's. During 1937–1938, Togog illustrated and dictated forty-nine dreams, illustrating most of them with two pictures, and a few with only one or three. A high proportion of these dreams seem to have been about with what might be called issues of *sakti*—*léyak, tonya, detia,* and *balian.* In the first four months, nineteen out of thirty-four were of this sort, while in the last four months, until Mead and Bateson left Bali in March 1938, out of fourteen dreams, only three might fall into this category.

A few of the dreams have to do with sex—eight out of the forty-nine. In a number of the dreams issues of the use of language registers dominate, and in at least two of them this is central, where a person is accused of using "rude" or, better, "careless" speech to someone higher on the respect scale.

What is striking about all of the dreams is their everyday tone and content. Even the sorcerers and frightening spirits seem to have an everyday quality to them. These narratives and pictures were organized, or "elaborated," in the Freudian sense. The process of preparing them for Bateson's consumption required that Togog's memory of each dream be modified, first so that it "made sense" to him, and second so that it could be made "representable" in narrative and in picture. There are occasional, but rare, comments indicating that Togog was still confused or uncertain about what happened in the dream.

These accounts of the dreams are somewhat smoothed out as a result of the circumstances of their telling. In many cases, Togog postponed presenting Bateson with the pictures for several weeks, so that he could give him many at once. The dream pictures fall into only eight of these bunches, nine including the 1939 pictures.

The pictures are, for the most part, carefully composed so as to present a pleasant pictorial composition. They clearly fall within the genre of Balinese tourist art and not that of, for instance, Kamasan hangings, both in the use of space and in the roundedness of the figures. The "naturalism" of the tourist paintings makes it possible to locate these dreams in everyday life. Togog's invention of placing himself, the dreamer, in every picture solved an important problem of how to represent a dream. The use of the black background, which had already been developed in other pictures by him, also helped to forefront the main dream material, and allowed him to select key scenery to depict and to leave out any other kinds of background information. Each picture presents a separate "scene" in the narrative, much as Togog's story-pictures do. The texts of the dreams, as Togog dictated them, are often largely in the form of dialogues, in the same manner as his reminiscences and his traditional tales.

This everyday quality allows a cultural analysis of the dreams, for they make sense within the contexts of Balinese cultural presuppositions and common activities and also within Togog's own presuppositions about figuration and image making. For instance, Togog's first reported dream is one of picking flowers from a tree—this is an almost daily task of boys and girls in a Brahmana household and is described in some of his tales. Ritual tasks, especially the making of offerings, are often represented. The first few months of dreams came during an intense ceremonial season of cremations, which were then followed by a series of life-cycle rituals in every household that had a cremation. Togog's second reported dream was about a cremation.[1]

Everyday life activities of the dreams include fishing, fondling girls, children crying, washing hair, hunting birds with a blowpipe, hoeing, putting dogs on ropes, dogs barking, encounters with snakes, riding on cows, cutting firewood, studying *lontar,* being bitten by a centipede, theft, women making and carrying offerings, peddlers selling food, building a new altar out of old bricks, and helping a woman find her child.

I have written about the dream pictures in my *Images of Power* (H. Geertz 1994:85, 89–94) and presented five of Togog's dreams (90–93, 119). In that book I was interested in documenting the concern of the Batuan painters in the 1930s with issues of *sakti,* and therefore I selected those of Togog's dreams which dealt with "sorcery, violence, conflict, terror and the involvement with spiritual beings." I observed that it is not only Togog's paintings that show a preoccupation with spiritual mastery, but sometimes also his dreams, and that the paintings of this sort were made at the same time as he had similar dreams.[2]

Here, to balance those selected for the book, I have chosen five dreams that are not mainly concerned with *sakti,* but rather with more mundane issues. As before, the titles were composed by me only for the purpose of quick identification.

A Dream of Polite Speech (Dream 12, November 27, 1937)

SCENE 1 (fig. 25)

I was first walking in the place called Tegallinggah [a haunted field in Batuan; see Chap. 1]—there was a person in the field, just one person.

"How come you're alone here?" I said [speaking down].

"Alone here!" Why do you talk so rudely to me!" he said [speaking down]. "Don't you know how to ask politely 'who's here'?"

"I'm a Brahmana. That's how I speak," I said.

And then he sicced the dog on me. I ran here and there—almost was bitten—I felt as though I hardly touched the ground as I ran. There was someone up above me running too, and I called to him, "Come here to this tree!"

SCENE 2 (fig. 26)

"Hey! Why are you running here with me, Beli Kadé?" I said. [It was Beli Kadé Londos, a neighbor.] But then I couldn't see him any more—he'd disappeared.

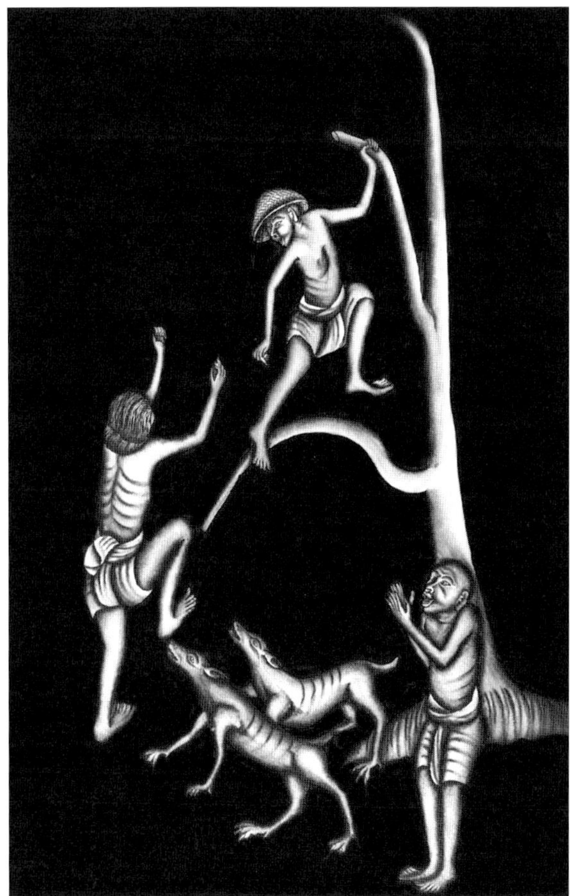

Figure 25. A dream of polite speech, scene 1

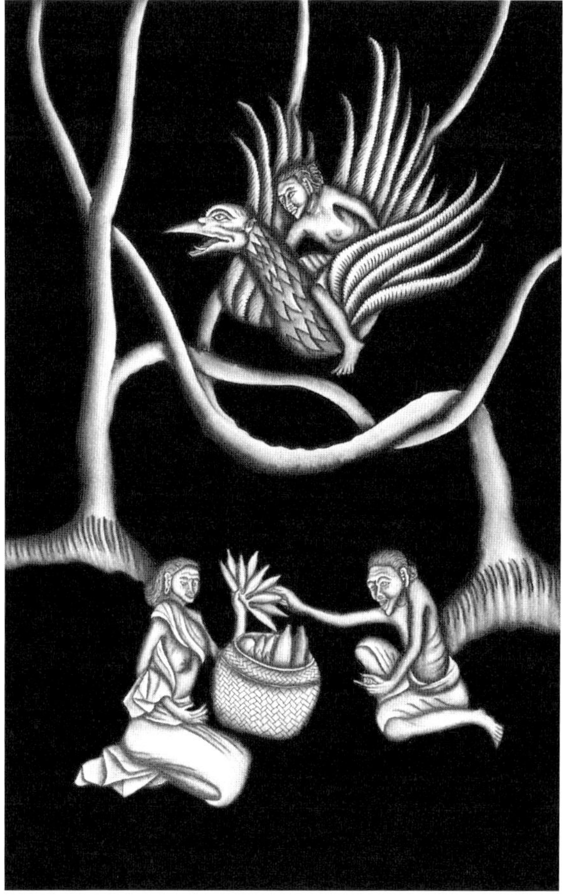

Figure 26. A dream of polite speech, scene 2

"Where did that dog go?" That's all. Then I sat down, and turned my head towards the side. There was a peddler beside me.

So then I was riding on a bird, flying. I laughed. Where am I going? I felt as if I was above, on the branch of a tree maybe. I was very afraid. Where was I going riding this bird? Where was he going to land?

I woke with a start and I opened my eyes and it was morning.

A Dream of Gathering Firewood (Dream 16, November 27, 1937)

SCENE 1 (fig. 27)

I was speaking in a low voice with my wife, "*Beh!* It's almost Galungan. What can we put in the fire to cook the sweets? We don't have even a little firewood! I'll go and look for some firewood." [Galungan is an important festival in which everyone makes offerings containing cakes and fruit and then serves them to guests over the next few days.]

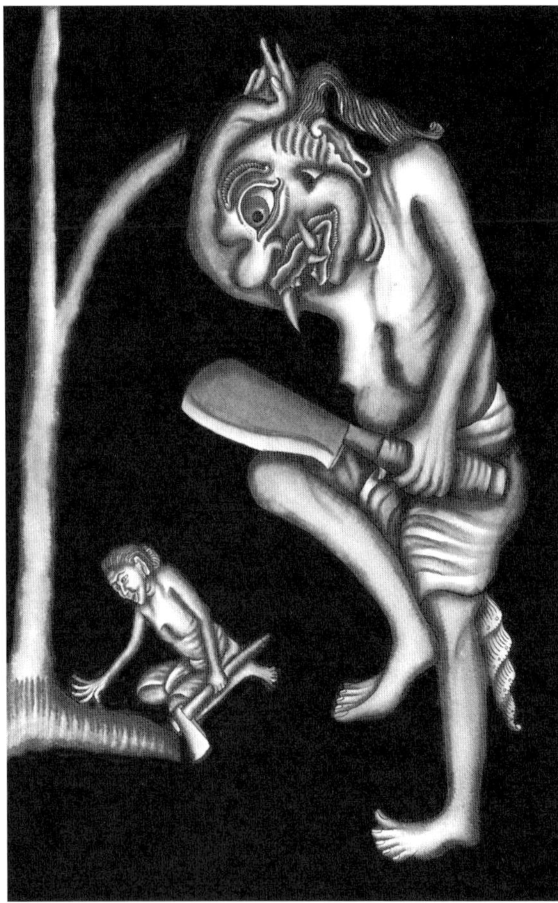

Figure 27. A dream of gathering firewood, scene 1

I was gathering firewood in the ravine. There was a *boni* tree there, old and worn out, with no leaves.

"*Beh!* Here's some firewood! I'll gather those branches together. Ah, now I'll dig up the roots." So then I chopped it up. Then it was nightfall. It got very dark [even though it was daytime]. I couldn't see to chop. So then I heard the sound of a *raksasa* [ogre].

"*Beh!* Who's chopping up my firewood? I'll slice his head off!"

Beh! My terror was great. I didn't dare look to either side. I didn't dare.

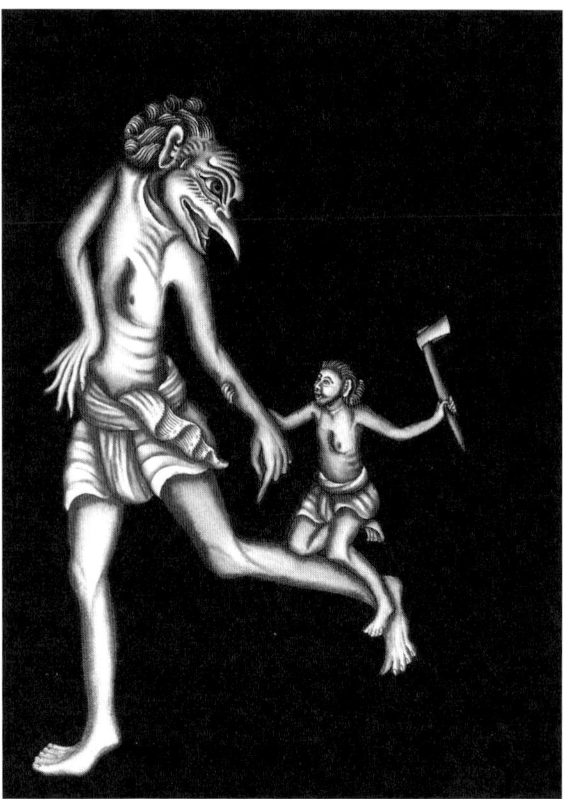

Figure 28. A dream of gathering firewood, scene 2

SCENE 2 (fig. 28)

"It must be the spirit *(tonya)* of the tree. Even if I stay still she'll bite off my head. I'll fight against her—whatever happens!

So then I turned. "I'll use my ax," I said. I grabbed her hands and stepped on her feet. "It was you who was doing that just now! That frightened me!" [speaking down].

But I couldn't free my hand. It was as if it was stuck there.

I pinched myself and woke up.

In the first picture, the *rakṣasa* is in the *buta nawasari* dance position, which usually means that she is about

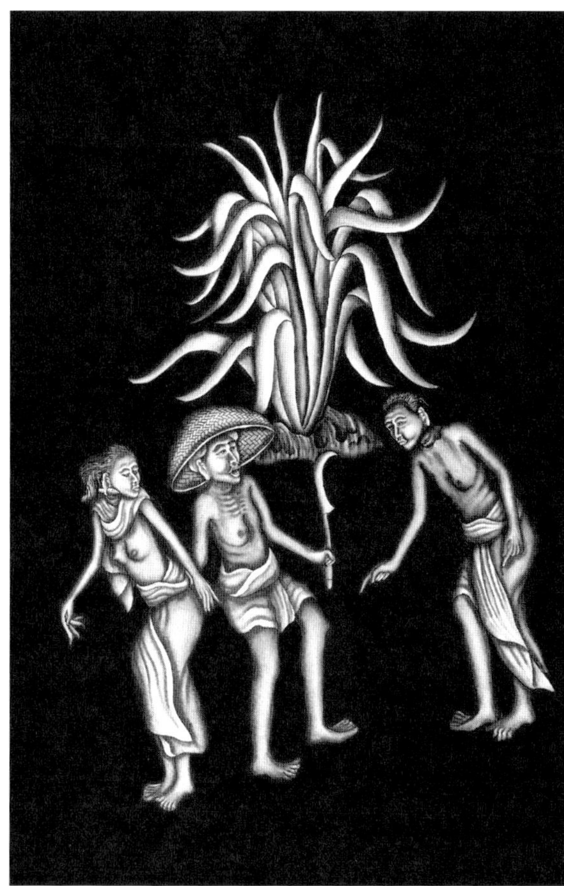

Figure 29. A dream about a girl, scene 1

to do something, here possibly to attack. Note also that the *raksasa* in the two pictures are different.

A Dream about a Girl (Dream 26, January 4, 1938)

Bateson asked Togog to tell him what he had done in the daytime before this dream.

In the evening I had been talking with my Grandmother. "I'll just go over and look at the yam crop in the west field. I'll just go there a moment," I said. So I went there, and there were some people there cutting down the grass, a whole lot of women.

SCENE 1 (fig. 29)

In the dream, I was in the west field. "Nang! Nang!" I said. [Nang is a term of address for a commoner man.]

"Who are you, walking up and down there?" [said the old man, in coarse, disrespectful language].

"That's terribly rude speech! I'm an Ida Bagus!"

The old man said, "Who says I'm rude?"

"I'm really angry! I'm going to take your daughter there!" His daughter was there, next to a red pepper bush.

"Come on home now, it's after sunset" [said the old man to his daughter].

It was a man I know from Puaya. [Puaya is a commoner *banjar* just south of Batuan.]

"What do you mean go home! I'm not yet tired of looking at your daughter. Go on home and after a while I'll come and visit you there."

"If you visit me there, I'll stab you. I'm looking for a son-in-law to be my *sentana*."

A *sentana* is a man who marries into a clan, takes on the clan deities, and gives up his own, so that his children will continue the genealogical line of the wife. As the girl was a commoner, Togog could not become a commoner. If he took a commoner wife, she would be raised to his status, but she would be cut off from her own family's gods.

"Well go and look for a *sentana,* but I'll burn up your house if you do that!"

SCENE 2 (fig. 30)

I went there after them. I got to the end of the western fields. There were dogs running after me. I just discovered that there were dogs running after me. And the house was indeed burning up.

"What's this? I didn't put that house on fire. I just wanted to talk with his daughter, and he didn't want me to."

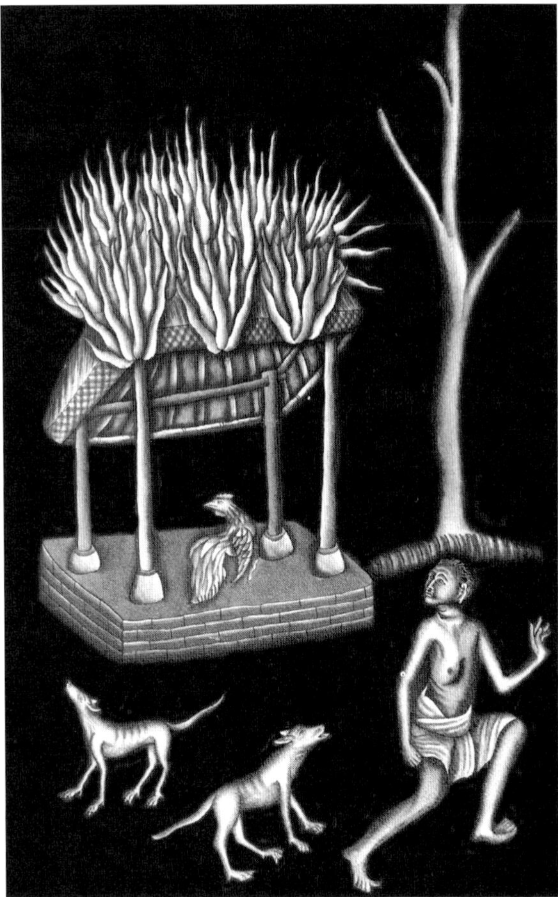

Figure 30. A dream about a girl, scene 2

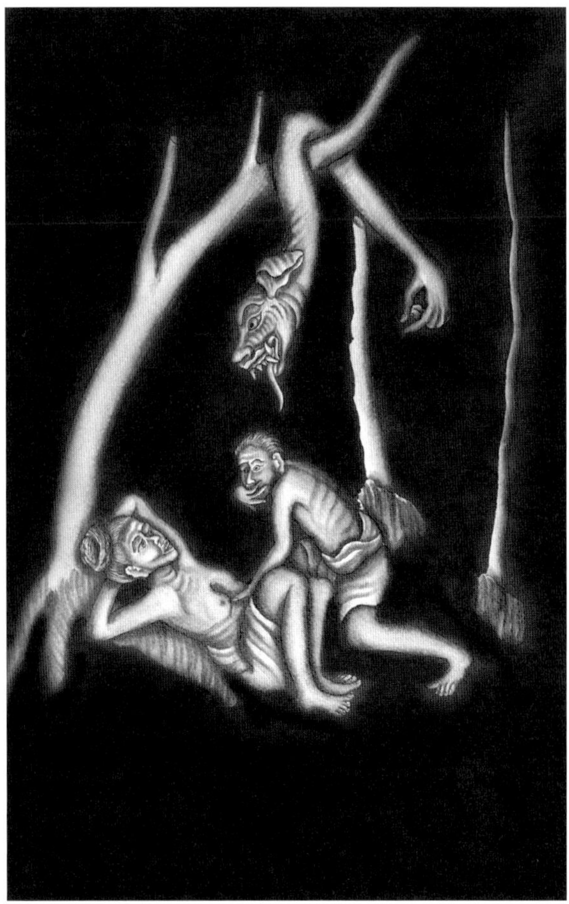

Figure 31. A dream of healing, scene 1

I saw a chicken there, next to the huge fire. "Oh how great that fire is! How can I help him? How can I help when I don't belong to this *banjar*? I'll just go home," I said.

So then it was morning and I woke up.

A Dream of Healing (Dream 32, January 4, 1938)

Bateson asked Togog what happened the day before he dreamed. This was his answer.

In the evening just before [the dream] I had gone down to Sukawati to look in on my older brother. There I met a healer *(balian)* carrying medicine. When I came home from Sukawati it was already dark. I was looking all around [i.e., he was afraid] because I was alone on the road.

SCENE 1 (fig. 31)

So then, that night, "It would be hard if I were a *balian,*" I said to myself. "In the night people would look for me, in the morning too. I couldn't do anything about it." So then I saw a person who seemed to be sick. "What's happening? I don't know what the matter is." Under a tree, leaning.

"Oh! Oh! *(Aduh! Aduh!),*" said the sick person.

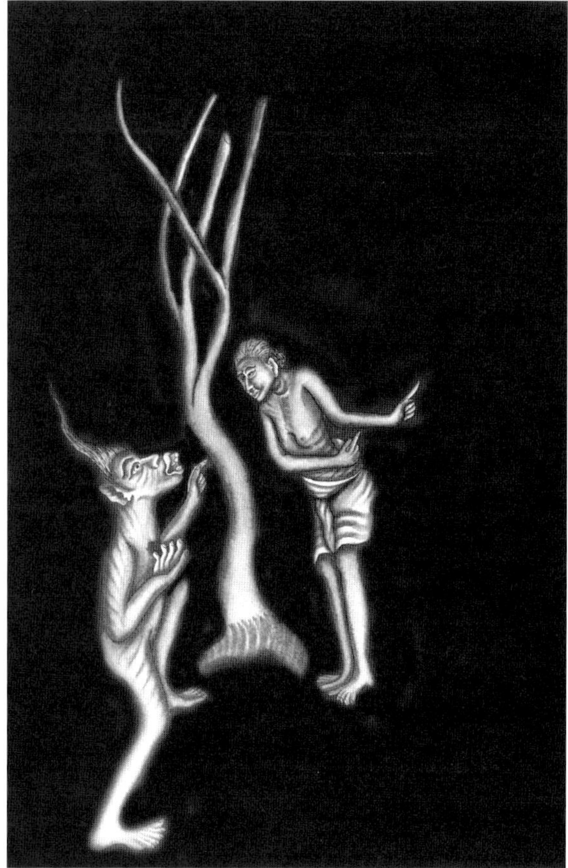

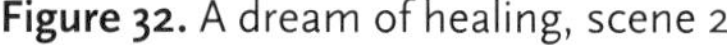
Figure 32. A dream of healing, scene 2

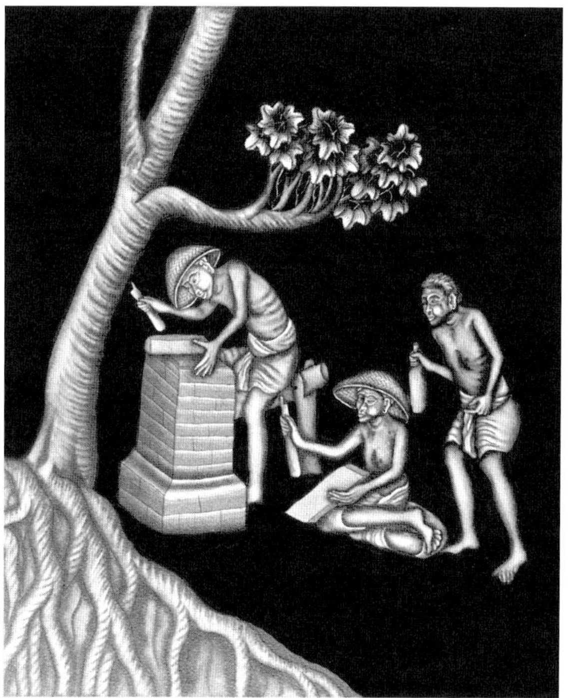

Figure 33. A dream of building an altar, scene 1

"Here I just became a *balian* and I just came out and found someone like this," I mumbled to myself. So I said a mantra over her, and "*Beh!* She says she's better. Really I don't know anything." I said a mantra over her. Up above her there was a fearful being on the branch of the tree, hanging there, like a hand.

"Well, whatever I said, it has helped her, the person was sick and is now well. She'll remember."

SCENE 2 (fig. 32)

Later the person got up and walked somewhere, and I didn't see the sick one anymore. Then I saw there was someone following me, and I turned around. "That's a demon named Cerungcung," I mumbled to myself.

"Please give me two coins," said the being.

"Over there to the east, you'll find the money," I said.

A Dream of Building an Altar (Dream 40, February 26, 1938)

SCENE 1 (fig. 33)

"Here's a house all falling down," said my older brother Ayan, muttering to himself. "[We can use the bricks] to

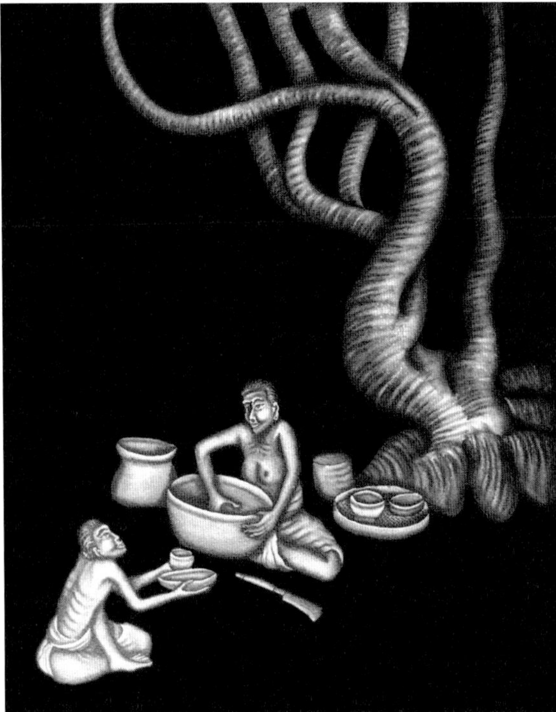

Figure 34. A dream of building an altar, scene 2

make the altar for the guardian of the houseyard *(pangijeng umahé),*" said my older brother Ayan. [Ayan is short for Wayan. The man is not Togog's older brother, but his cousin, also termed "older brother."]

"That would be good," said I. "The stones."

"We'll get I Rawuh [a commoner client of theirs] and tell him to build the altar, so there will be the two of you, Togog."

So then we were working on it. And after, he brought some rice wine.

SCENE 2 (fig. 34)

When he brought the rice wine, I asked for some bananas and *nangka* fruit. "It's to feed the workers, here in the empty house." My brother Ayan called me then to make *lawar* at home.

"But the house is empty," I said.

"We'll meet there, and make a little at home," I said.

"Yes, we can do that," said my older brother Ayan.

"Give me a little too," I said.

Appendix 2: The Temple Paintings

Two important paintings by Togog, very large in scale and on cloth, both ambitious and masterfully executed, are those he made for the villagers of Peguyungan to hang in their village temple, the Pura Désa, as recounted in Chapter 6. I date these around 1946. Togog told me when we went to Peguyungan that he had made these pictures during "the Dutch time" and before he was married. That would have been about 1932 or 1933, if not earlier, but we may have misunderstood one another, or perhaps his memory failed him. He could have made them during the Dutch colonial period, but if so it would have to have been during the brief return of the Dutch after the Japanese occupation between 1946 and 1950. I say this partly on stylistic grounds, but mainly in regard to the materials used: the paintings are done in tempera paints on prepared cotton cloth. As Togog related, he bought the tempera paints for them in Denpasar, but I do not believe these were on sale there until after 1946. As Togog himself said, before that time he was given his paints by Spies or Bonnet, and so would not have had to go to Denpasar for them. Besides, paintings were not made on cloth in the 1930s (with the exception of several by Sobrat, who got the cloth from Spies). During the Japanese occupation there was no cloth to be obtained anywhere, even for clothing. Stylistically, these two pictures show considerable experience and agility, especially in the depiction of figures and in composition. Compared to his paintings of the 1930s, these are much larger and more complex — so much so that they could be considered a new kind of painting for Togog.

One of the paintings tells the story of how Garuda freed his mother from her bondage to the thousand snake children of her co-wife through stealing the *amerta,* or life-giving elixir, owned by the high gods.

The other, reproduced as figure 23 in Chapter 6, is of the Bratayudha War. It is an *ulon* or *tabing,* a rough square hanging that could be placed against the wooden headboard of the raised bed or table on which offerings are placed. The picture in no way resembles those of the village of Kamasan, which are the usual temple paintings. Kamasan paintings generally have a plain, light-colored background against which the figures stand out clearly.[1] Togog, in contrast, has filled up most of his intervening space with foliage.

The Bratayudha is a tale of a horrible war in which young and noble boys are cut down in tragic, gory battle. It is a war in which the enemies are cousins and fellow soldiers are brothers and fathers and sons, a war in which the grieving wives and mothers are present, one who takes an oath to drink the blood of her enemy and wash her hair in it, while another commits suicide with a dagger on hearing of the death of her lover. Terror and grief are vividly expressed. Two cremations in the upper-righthand corner of the picture (fig. 23) demonstrate the spiritual meaning of these noble deaths.

Of the several people with whom I talked about this painting, with my photographs of it in hand, ev-

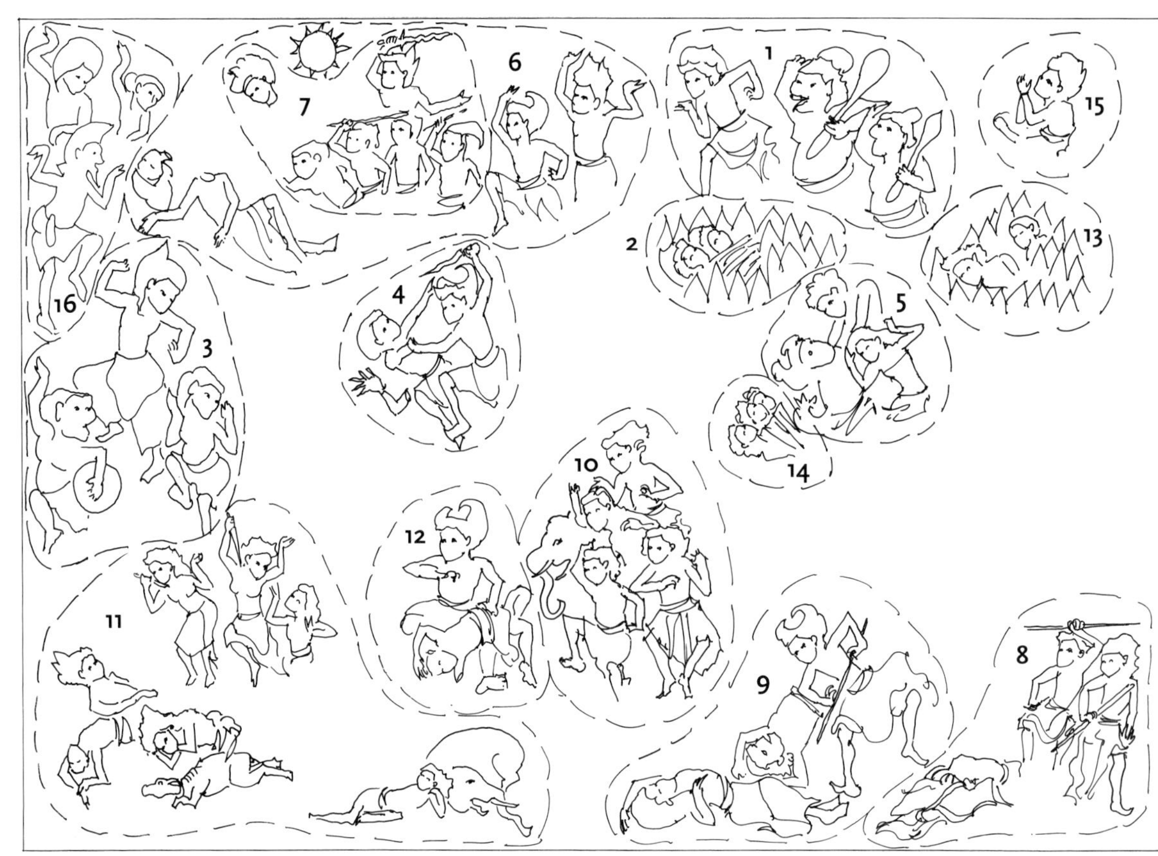

Figure 35. Diagram of figure 23, *The Bratayudha: The War between the Korawa and the Pandawa.*

eryone stressed the dangerous nature of the story, and the necessity of getting the details right when telling or picturing it. The last episode is particularly perilous to represent, and is rarely presented in shadow plays. A noted shadow puppeteer had recently been killed in an automobile accident the night upon which he had performed the last episode in the Bratayudha War: the death of Duryodana, leader of the Korawa. Duryodana had died of leg wounds, and so did the *dalang*. The episode is read and interpreted in *mabasan* performances of the classic literary text, so everyone knows that it is the climax of the story. Togog, they all thought, was spiritually protected enough to dare to paint the Bratayudha (although he, too, omitted the death of Duryadana).

As Togog related the story to me it had a powerful framework of elapsing time. The war lasted for eighteen days, and each of the many incidents is linked to the day it happened. The days are numbered in a reverse countdown order: seventeen days before the end, two days before the end, the day before the end. Each event has a killer and a killed, and each killer himself is destined to be killed.

This poignant representation of time is not at all

1. Abimanyu, the son of Arjuna, one of the five chiefs of the Pandawas, going to war. Right behind him stand the two godly protectors of the Pandawa, Malén (Twalén) and his son Merdah. Abimanyu was later killed by Jayaderata, who was then killed by Arjuna in episode 6.
2. Abimanyu's cremation, accompanied by his wife *(mesatia)*.
3. Duryodana, chief of the Korawas, watching the battles, flanked by his followers and the two godly protectors of the Korawas, Délem and Sangut.
4. Buriserawa, the son of Salya, of the Korawa, being killed by Satyaka, the son of Kresna, after Arjuna had shot off his arm with an arrow.
5. Bima of the Pandawa, strangles Dursasana. Next to Bima is his wife, Diah, who before the battle swore to wash her hair in Dursasana's blood. Bima is about to drink Dursasana's blood.
6. After Abimanyu's death (in episode 1), Arjuna vows to kill Jayaderata before nightfall or else commit suicide *(mesatia)* with his four brothers. Jayaderata hears of Arjuna's vow and does not venture out until dark, but he is fooled by Kresna, who throws his discus to cover the sun. Jayaderata thinks it is nightfall, emerges from hiding, and Arjuna's arrow cuts off his head.
7. The death of Ida Begawan Drona. Only Drona's head is visible, flying through the air at the top. When Ida Begawan Drona hears of the death of his nephew Jayaderata, and then of his son Aswatama, he faints and then is killed by Drestajumena, who cuts off Drona's head.
8. Arjuna and Kresna kill the snake in human clothes, Dworalika, who is the warrior of Karna from the Korawa side.
9. Then Arjuna kills Karna and his guard.
10. Darmawangsa (Yudistira) sets off on his elephant to kill Salya. (I did not identify the Pandawa hero in chariot just below him in the center of the picture, dressed in an orange sarong.)
11. Salya's cremation and his wife's suicide *(satia)*. The picture shows Salya's body in a heap of corpses and his dead horse. Another group of bodies lies to the right of them, with a dead elephant.
12. Bima killing Sakuni
13. The cremation of Gatotkaca, son of Bima, with his mother beside him *(satia)*.
14. The bodies of three Pandawa heroes, Wresongka, Utara, and Suweta, being readied for cremation.
15. Begawan Narada, overlooking the battle.
16. Begawan Krépa with his servant Baru, overlooking the battle.

depicted in the picture (see fig. 23 and 35). The battles are scattered over the hanging, and several of them are interwoven with one another, set out on the canvas not in their sequence in the story but in terms of some sort of pictorial logic. The foci of the viewer's attention are distributed fairly evenly, with only a few sequential juxtapositions.[2] Togog had done large dispersed compositions of this sort before, but this is much larger and more ambitious than any other I have seen.

When I spoke with Togog about this painting he was about seventy years old, and he felt he had to check up on the names of the characters and to prepare some notes before telling me the story. Even with that, he left much out, and I had to consult with his friend Déwa Ketut Baru and a shadow puppeteer from Sukawati, I Wayan Wija. The results of these consultations are summarized in figure 35, keeping to the order in which Togog recited the story to me. Some uncertainties remain as to who is who on the canvas, and, I'm sure, some errors, either on my part or on Togog's.

When Togog was working on the painting, he must have been very familiar with the shadow-play version

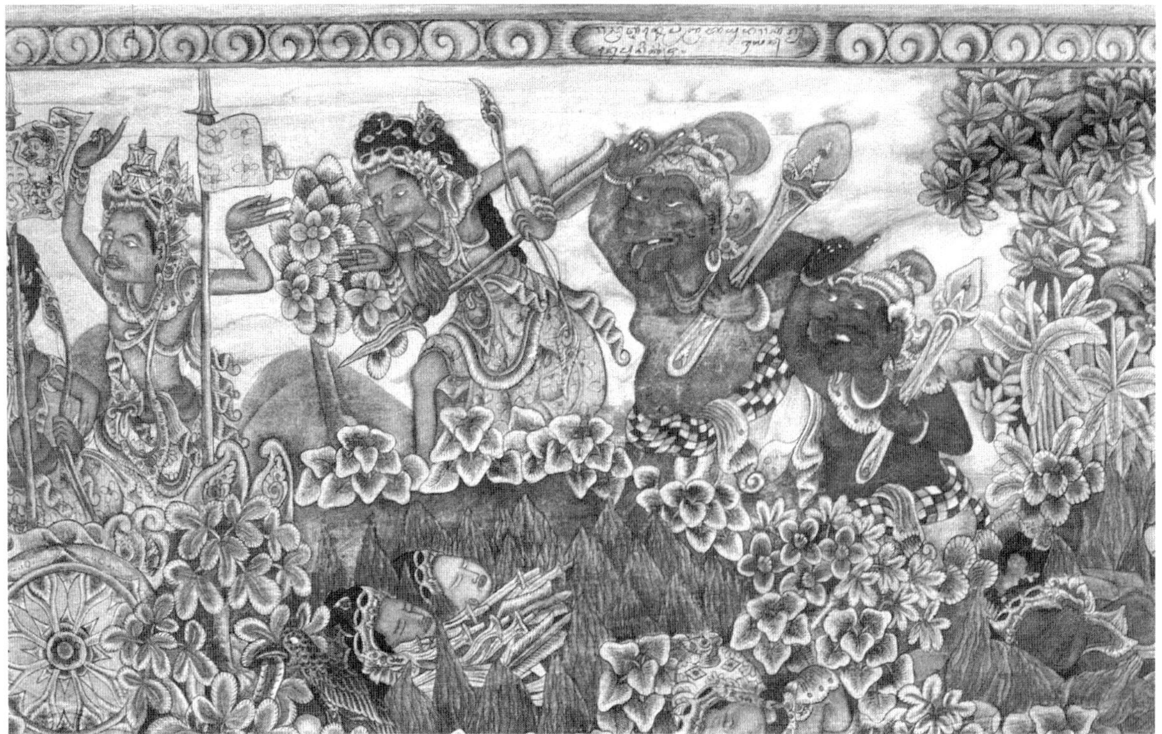

Figure 36. Detail of figure 23, *The Bratayudha: The War between the Korawa and the Pandawa.* Scene 1: Abimanyu, the son of Arjuna, ready to attack, with Malén and Merdah behind him. Malén is the larger figure behind Abimanyu, and Merdah, his son, stands below him. At left, with greenish skin, is Kresna, incarnation of the god Wisnu and charioteer of Arjuna. Scene 2: The cremation of Abimanyu and his wife. A wife is expected to accompany her husband in the cremation. This act of suicide is called *satia,* a term Togog also used for Arjuna's threat to kill himself if he could not kill Jayaderata before nightfall (scene 6).

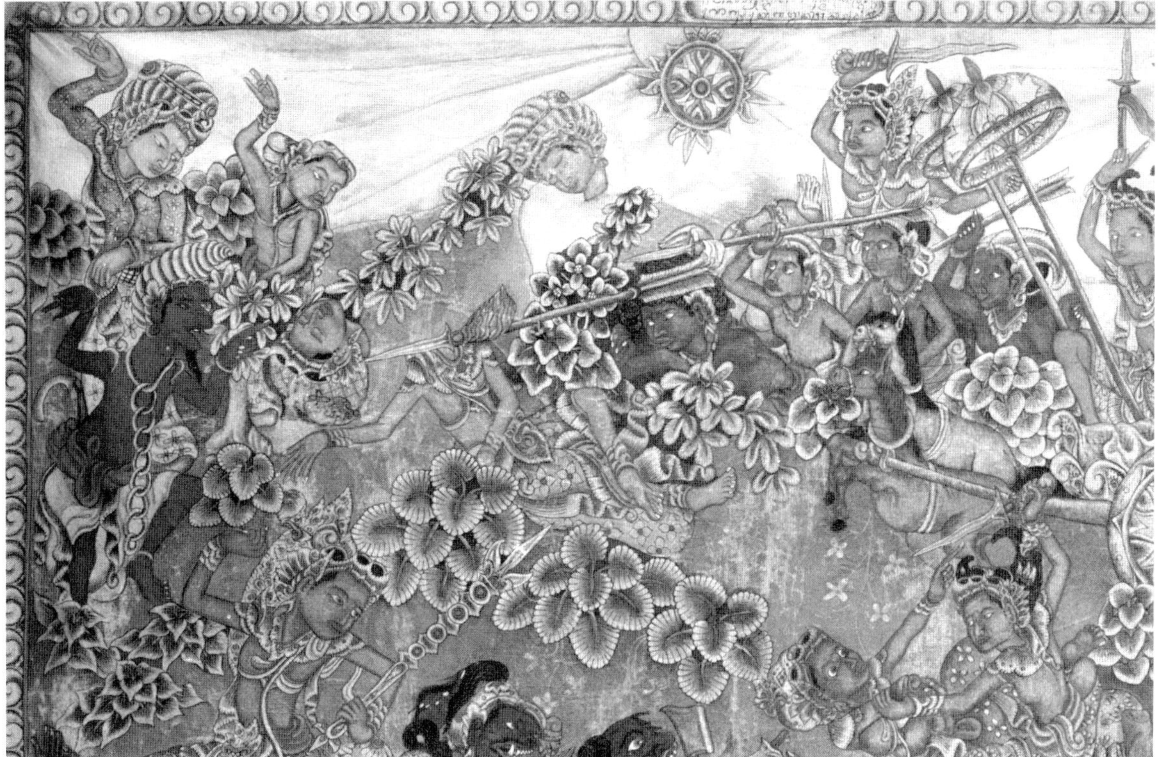

Figure 37. Detail of figure 23, *The Bratayudha: The War between the Korawa and the Pandawa.* Scene 6: The covering of the sun with Karna's discus and the death of Jayaderata. Jayaderata's body is in the center of this detail, with his head being cut off by Arjuna's arrow. Scene 7: The death of Drona. Drona's turbaned head is top center, and his killer is at the right, waving a sword. Scene 16: *(left)* The holy man Begawan Krépa, watching the battle. In front of Begawan Krépa is an unidentified follower, and below him is Baru, servant to Begawan Krépa.

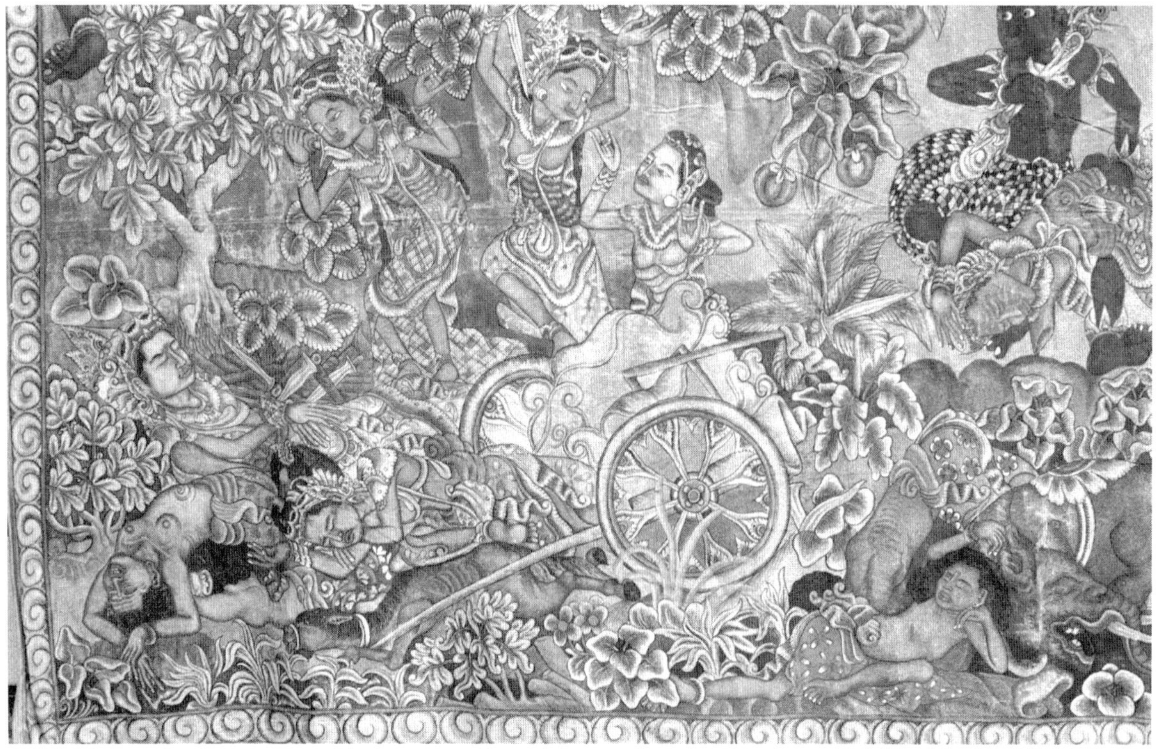

Figure 38. Detail of figure 23, *The Bratayudha: The War between the Korawa and the Pandawa.* Scene 11: The death of Salya and the suicide of his wife Satyawati. Salya is apparently the figure with closed eyes and hands crossed on his body, with a few flames to the right of him. His wife is shown in two poses: one above him, looking at his body; the other turned toward a woman of the court who is beseeching her not to kill herself.

of the Bratayudha. Each character has the particular clothing and ornaments assigned it in the shadow play. The stories of this great battle, and the events leading up to it and after it, are many. They are not usually combined in the way Togog has put them together for this painting, but only a few episodes are selected by a shadow master for a night's performance.

The order on the canvas has nothing to do with the sequence of the episodes. The Pandawa are mainly on the right side facing toward the Korawa, who are mainly on the left. Each set of heroes is accompanied by *sakti* servants (the *penasar:* Malén and Merdah on the Pandawa side; Baru, Dalem, and Sangut on the Korawa side) and by various *raksasa* ogre-warriors. There are three holy men, marked by their white turbans, along the top of the picture: Begawan Narada (upper-righthand corner), Begawan Krépa (upper-lefthand corner), and Begawan Drona (only his head is shown, which has just been cut off).

A number of the characters appear several times on the canvas, participating in different episodes; for instance, Arjuna with Kresna appears in two places, and Arjuna by himself in a third, and Bima appears twice.

The death of Salya and the suicide of his wife out of grief was an episode often presented in shadow plays, for it was a favorite among the audiences, who responded perhaps sentimentally to the despair of his wife. Salya, though assumed to be an enemy of the Pandawa, was secretly on their side, and in fact at one point prevented the death of Arjuna. Here Togog has given careful attention to the horror of his death.

These temple paintings are instructive crossovers. They take highly conventional tourist-art techniques and adapt them to traditional forms to make a new sacred art. However, Togog never followed up on this enterprise. There are other examples of contemporary temple paintings to be found in various parts of Bali. Some from Batuan are illustrated in my *The Life of a Balinese Temple* (2004).[3] But of all the ones I have seen, this one is unique in its forcefulness and naturalism.

Notes

Introduction

1. A number of Togog's paintings from the 1930s are reproduced in my *Images of Power* (1994), where I have discussed them in detail, and in Hohn (1997), who also reproduces works from the 1970s, when Togog had shifted with the market to making large paintings in color. For reproductions of Togog's paintings see Bakker (1985: ill. 15, 18, 56); Bateson and Mead (1942:74, 134); Covarrubias (1956:7); Djelantik (1986: ill. 8); Galestin (1962:85–86); *Donald Friend's Bali* (1990:24); C. Geertz (1980:117); H. Geertz (1994:12, 20–22, 53, 78, 82, 90–93, 115–119); Haks et al (1999:45); Hohn (1997:60–66, 68); Kam (1993:89–92); Lueras (1987:116–117); *Museum Puri Lukisan* (1999:50, 51, 73). Major collections containing Togog's works include the Bateson and Mead Collection, Lois Bateson; the Margaret Mead Collection in the United States Library of Congress Manuscript Division; the Tropen Museum, Amsterdam; the Rijksmuseeum der Volkenkunde, Leiden; and the Puri Lukisan, Ubud, Bali.

2. H. Geertz (1994 and 2004).

3. Bateson and Mead left Bali on March 16, 1938, for Australia and New Guinea and returned to Bali in February and March 1939, when they collected a few more materials from Togog and other artists.

4. See Bateson (1973) and Bateson and Mead (1942). Two pictures by Togog are reproduced in the latter book on pages 74 and 134; several photographs of Togog with his young family can be found on page 225.

5. See Vickers (1989:205; 1986) for graceful portraits of Togog.

6. See H. Geertz (2004) for a detailed history of Batuan, including the circumstances of those killings, obtained from other participants.

7. Balinese titles are highly varied, and I make no attempt to describe them here. See Geertz and Geertz (1975) and C. Geertz (1973) for details.

8. See Geertz and Geertz (1975) for a study of Balinese kin terms.

9. In the Gianyar dialect of Balinese, the final -a in most words is pronounced as -o, as in *Ido* for *Ida* ("he," "she," or "you" in the highest register) or *grio* for *gria* ("house" in the highest register). I've changed these to conform with standard spelling, according to the major Balinese dictionary, *Kamus Bali-Indonesia* (1978/1989).

Chapter 1: Childhood Memories

1. See, for further interpretation of the key ideas involved in notions of *sakti,* H. Geertz (1994, 2004).

2. What I call "clan" here is given many names in Bali —*dadia, panataran, pemaksan,* among others. These same terms may also indicate an associated temple. They may refer either to small, strictly kinship-defined groupings or to larger groupings of several kin groups. See Geertz and Geertz (1975).

3. See Geertz and Geertz (1975) for a systematic account of Balinese kin terms.

4. Connor (1986).

5. See also H. Geertz (2004).

Chapter 2: Wanderings, Gambling, Friendships

1. See Eiseman (1989: vol. 2, 158–159) for an explanation of *dauh.*

Chapter 3: Learning

1. See Eiseman (1989).

2. For an extended study of *gambuh* in the 1930s, see DeZoete and Spies (1973: chap. 4). The photographs are probably from Batuan.

3. See Vickers (1986).

Chapter 4: Performing Rituals

1. See H. Geertz (2004).

Chapter 6: Painting

1. See H. Geertz (1994) for an extended discussion of this history and of Ngendon's work. See also Bonnet (1936, 1953 [?], 1961); Galestin (1962); Haks et al. (1999); Hohn (1997); Rhodius and Darling (1980), Vickers (1989).

2. Covarrubias (1956:189).

3. Studies of twentieth-century Balinese paintings can be found in the Bibliography. See especially Bakker (1985), Bonnet (1953 [?]), Djelantik (1986), Hohn (1997), Holt (1967), and Vickers (1989).

4. The most reliable Western sources for calculating dates in the early history of Balinese tourist paintings are the various articles by Bonnet (1936, 1953?, and 1961) and the small book by Galestin (1962). The last is a catalog of an exhibition of Bonnet's collection of Balinese paintings, the ones now in the Rijksuniversiteit voor Volkenkunde in Leiden. Galestin consulted with Bonnet in identifying and dating these pictures. Aside from a few small drawings by schoolboys in Tampaksiring found by Bonnet in 1929 when he was living there, the first dated pictures surviving in collections were made by the Ubud youths Sobrat and his cousin Meregeg, whom Bonnet and Spies supported and trained for the year 1931–1932, and are dated 1931.

5. Galestin (1962:46). See Hohn (1997:66) for a picture by Togog of the story of the heron who pretended to be a *pedanda* in order to catch fish, made in 1985.

6. An illustration of this picture is in H. Geertz (1994:12).

7. Some of these dreams, with their texts, are given in Appendix 1, and others can be found in H. Geertz (1994).

8. See Mershon (1971: pt. 3) and Vickers (1991).

9. See H. Geertz (1994) for a number of Togog's paintings made in the 1930s. For other published paintings by Togog of different periods, see those listed in Introduction, n. 1.

10. For examples of these daily-life pictures, see Kam (1993:89) and C. Geertz (1980:117) for paintings of cremations with the focus on all the preparatory work, made in the 1970s. Many of Togog's story pictures are set within panoramas of daily life, for instance, the painting reproduced in Hohn (1997:60–61) that is titled "Life on the Coast" but in fact is an episode from the Amad story-cycle, showing the moment when the Princess of Beregedab, after seducing Amad, stole the objects that contained his *sakti*.

11. See H. Geertz (2004).

12. Dating the Peguyungan paintings is difficult. Togog told me he made them "in the Dutch time," but his story of buying the colors in a Denpasar store indicates it would have to have happened after 1946. The Dutch returned to power in Bali in 1948, staying until 1950, so the picture could have been made then. Two other published paintings by Togog, large and in color, have been given much too early dates. These are both in the Museum Puri Lukisan in Ubud; *Museum Puri Lukisan* (1999:50, 51) In the catalog, they are dated 1932, but for stylistic and color reasons they must have been made in 1939 or 1940. One is painted on hardboard, the other on plywood, materials that Togog could only have obtained from Spies, Bonnet, or their later representative in Pita Maha, Maria v.d. Sleen van Wessem. One, "The Idiot Belog who became King," is listed as having been purchased by van Wessem in 1940, in an exhibition catalog (Bonnet 1961: entry 276). She later gave it to the Museum Puri Lukisan, and probably also donated the other misdated picture by Togog on page 51 of the Museum Puri Lukisan catalog.

13. An example of Bonnet's attempt to teach Togog how to draw a figure can be found in H. Geertz (1994:12). Togog tried to show perspective in a picture of a receding path between trees, reproduced in Hohn (1997:60). He even tried doing a self-portrait, which can be found in the Manuscript Division of the U.S. Library of Congress.

Afterword

1. See H. Geertz (1994, 2004).

2. H. Geertz (1994: chap. 5).

3. In the 1980s Jana's descendants were active in a religio-political group advancing the claim of the Paseks to using their own priest in place of a *pedanda*.

4. Connor (1986).

5. Djelantik (1997).

6. Vickers (2000:99–100).

7. H. Geertz (1994:52) The names "Amad" and "Mohammad" mark the story's ancestry in a cycle of stories borrowed from one of the neighboring Islamic islands.

8. Vickers (1990) describes a similar picture, also of the Amad tale, in which Togog first painted in images of the gods of the directions overseeing the action, but a year or so later painted over them deliberately to conceal them from public view.

9. Connor (1986:126–130).

10. Covarrubias (1956:7). See also Williams (1994:75).

11. Hooykaas (1980) has reproduced a number of these human figures made for funeral shrouds. (See, e.g., the one on p. 21.)

12. The image of Sanghyang Cintia that Togog drew is the same as that carved at the top of the altar called the Padmasana, which stands in Batuan's village temple (the Pura Désa). The Padmasana is an altar that was introduced into the temple in the late 1920s for the Brahmana to pray at during village-wide rituals held there. Brahmana may not worship at any of the other altars in the village temple, because they are the seats of lesser gods or ancestors of lower humans. Togog may have been quite impressed with that new carving, enough to use it in his 1934 drawing. A photograph of the figure on the Batuan *padmasana* may be found in H. Geertz (2004).

Appendix 1: The Dream Pictures (1937–1938)

1. The second picture of Dream 2 appears in Bateson and Mead (1942:75, no. 6). There Bateson gives the translation of the text and an analysis. One thing that he does not take into account in his interpretation is that Togog was a cremation specialist, and so it is not at all certain that the *banjar* that is reluctant to help him with the fire and just stares at him working is his own *banjar*. In the text Togog says, in Bateson's translation, "I mumbled to myself," but the word is *nglemek*, which means to perform a certain ritual connected with cremation. (See Togog's account, perhaps of the very experience upon which the dream draws, in Chapter 4.) Bateson makes a big point of the fact that Togog placed himself low in the picture, below the *banjar* people, and thinks that Togog was very status-anxious, "because he had broken a serious caste rule in stealing the wife of another Brahman." According to Togog's own story about his marriage, it was not exactly "stealing," and his trouble with his "caste" was not about the marriage but about their "illegitimate" child.

2. Geertz (1994:126n7).

Appendix 2: The Temple Paintings

1. See Forge (1978) for a discussion of Kamasan paintings.

2. For a similar scattered nonlinear layout, see in H. Geertz (1994) the picture of the story of the two sisters, Bawang and Kesuna, by Togog's cousin, Tibah, (pp. 50–51).

3. H. Geertz (2004).

Glossary

Adé Short for Madé, the birth-order name for second-born sibling.
Agus Short for Bagus, title for a Brahmana male.
Alit Little, often part of a name or nickname.
ageng, agung, gedé Large, in the lower to higher registers.
agung See *ageng.*
anak Person.
anak alit Child.
anak bebinjat Child born outside of ritual marriage.
Anak Agung Title of a noble person high in the government.
anak lingsir (1) Elderly person; (2) priest.
anak sakti Sorcerer, person of high spiritual powers.
arja A popular kind of dance-drama.
astra, hastra Child born outside of ritual marriage.
Atu Short for Ratu, a term of address for a high-status person.
ayah, ngayah To serve a higher person or being.
baca, maca To read. See also *papacan.*
Bagus Abbreviated term of address for male Brahmana.
Bagus Alit Abbreviated term of address for young male Brahmana.
balé Pavilion or building.
balé agung High-register term for *balé gedé.*
balé dangin Pavilion on east side of houseyard.
balé dauh Pavilion on west side of houseyard.
bale gedé Pavilion in center of houseyard.
balé gedong or ***balé metén*** Pavilion that has a closed-in room.
balé kulkul High pavilion with a signal drum.
balé piasan Pavilion in a temple.
balé sianganti Pavilion with a high platform and rear enclosed room.
balian Healer, sorcerer.
banjar (1) Subgroup of *désa;* (2) neighborhood.
bapa Father in low register; respectful title for commonor man.
basa (1) Language; (2) to speak politely.
basan, mabasan Performance of reading classical texts.
beli Older brother; term of address for a man older than oneself of the same rank and generation; husband.
bendésa Village leader in charge of the temple called *pura désa.*
betel Leaf of a pepper plant used as one ingredient in betel chewing, taken together with areca nut and *gambir* (a substance made from a leaf) and lime.
Biang (1) Mother in high register; (2) title for a noblewoman.
Brahmana A category of titled people, those with the title of Ida Bagus or Dayu.
Brahmana Buda A sect-like clan of Brahmana.
Brahmana Siwa Another sect-like clan of Brahmana.
cai You, in lowest register, familar or insulting.
canang An offering consisting of materials for a betel-chew plus flowers.
cang I or me, in lowest register, familiar or insulting.
Cokorda A title within the Satria category.
dadia (1) A clan temple; (2) clan.
dalang Shadow-play puppeteer.
dangin East.
darsana A kind of prayer.
dauh Traditional unit of time of which there are twelve in twenty-four hours.
Dayu Title for a female Brahmana.
Dé Short for Madé, birth-order title for second-born.
Délem A character in the shadow play.
désa (1) Ritual work group of temple called *pura désa;* (2) village.

Désak Title for a Satria female.
désti Sorcerer's lore.
Déwa Title for a Satria male.
druwé See *dué.*
dué, druwé To be owned by someone, in upper register.
dueg Learned, clever, cunning, mastery of *sakti.*
gambuh A kind of dance-drama.
gamelan Traditional Balinese orchestra.
gedé See *ageng.*
geguritan A kind of song.
gending A kind of song, melody.
gria A house, in high register, of a Brahmana family.
guna Magical means used by a sorcerer to hurt someone.
Gus Short for Bagus.
Gus Alit Short for Bagus Alit.
Gusti Title for someone in the Wesia category.
ida (1) Title of respect; (2) you, when addressing a Brahmana.
Ida Ayu Title of a Brahmana woman, usually shortened to Dayu.
Ida Bagus Title of Brahmana male.
ilon (1) To protect or care for someone; (2) protector.
indik Moral content or burden of a song or story.
istri Woman or female, in high register.
jaba Commoner.
jero (1) Inner, interior; (2) home of a noble.
Jero Polite title used to address someone whose title you don't know, respectful title for a commoner.
jero gedé Home of highest noble in area.
jogéd A kind of dance performance.
jotan A dish of food sent to neighbors or friends at the time of a family ritual.
juru Artisan.
juru paca A reader in papacan.
juru surat Clerk or secretary.
kak Grandpa, from *pekak,* in low register.
kakiang Grandfather, in high register.
karang Houseyard.
kasepung, kasepungan To be lowered in status, polluted.
kasiluman To be transformed from one body into another.
kaula Commoner.
kawi (1) Classical languages (Old Javanese, Old Balinese); (2) spiritual protector, god.
kekawin A kind of classical poem or song.
képéng A penny in traditional coins.
kerta Judge, court.
Ketut Birth-order name for fourth-born.
kidung A kind of classical poem or song.
klian Head of a group.
kobokan (1) Half a coconut shell, used as a measure or dish; (2) gambling game played with coins.
Kompiang Birth-order name for noble firstborn sibling, equivalent of Wayan and Putu.
kulkul Signal drum.
lawar Feast dish made of chopped vegetables, meats, and spices.
leteh, letuh Polluted.
léyak Demonic form taken by a sorcerer or witch; a witch.
léyak gundul Bald-headed demonic form taken by a sorcerer.
lontar Book made of palm-leaf strips with Balinese letters scratched on it.
lukat, penglukatan A ritual for purification.
lungsuran Leftovers from someone's meal, opposite of *sukla.*
luur, luhur, leluur God or ancestor.
mabak To interpret, from *babak,* to open up.
mabasa To read, translate, and interpret a text, from *basa,* language.
maca To read aloud, from *baca,* to read.
Madé Birth-order name for a second-born sibling.
Mangku Term of address for a temple priest. See *pamangku.*
masanin To translate.
mémé Mother in low-register, familiar term of address, and self-reference for commoner woman.
mrajan Family temple of a Brahmana or Satria.
mutus, putus (1) To complete or end; (2) ritual for finalizing a ritual sequence.
nak Short form of *anak.*
nak lingsir, or ***anak lingsir*** Polite term for *pedanda,* literally "old person."
neraka Hell.
niskala Invisible and intangible, sometimes used as short term for *niskala* beings or spirits.
nunas (1) To request, in high register; (2) to pray.
nunas pengelukatan To pray for purification.

nyekah A kind of mortuary ritual.
nyikut See *sikut.*
Nyoman Birth-order name for third-born sibling.
nyonya Term of address for a foreign female.
odalan Calendrical festival of a temple.
oton Birthday.
pamangku Temple priest.
panesan Hot, vulnerable to sorcery.
papacan A performance of reading classical texts.
parekan Servant, client.
patut Proper, right, appropriate.
pawintenan Personal ritual for purification; see *winten.*
pedanda Brahmana priest.
pedanda istri Brahmana female priest.
pekak Grandfather, commoner.
penglukatan See *lukat.*
perbekel, prabekel Dutch-appointed local official.
Po Term of address for father or uncle, short for *bapa,* pronounced in Gianyar fashion.
prabekel See *perbekel.*
prasutri A sacred dance, also called the *rejang.*
prayascita A ritual addressed to ancestral beings.
Punggawa A Balinese colonial official who is head of a region.
pura Temple.
Pura Dalem Temple next to the graveyard and cremating field.
Pura Désa Temple of the village.
Pura Panataran Temple of a clan.
puri Noble house, palace.
Putu Birth-order name for a noble first-born sibling, equivalent of Wayan.
racun Poison, both material and mystical.
rangda A mask of an old woman sorceress.
Ratu Address title for noble person.
Ratu Aji Address title for a nobleman who has children.
rejang A sacred dance, also called the *prasutri.*
resi Practicioner of mystical arts, master of *sakti.*
ringgit A coin worth two and a half *rupiah.*
rupiah A unit of money first established by the Dutch in the colonial time.
saged Ability, magical competence; synonym for *sakti.*
sakti Personal mystical power over others via spirits and deities.
santun, sesantun Basketful of food substances given in payment to a ritual performer.
sastra Holy writings, literature.
Satria Category of status titles of nobles, including such titles as Déwa, Cokorda, and Gusti.
sawah Floodable rice field.
sengker, penyengkeran (1) Wall or boundary; (2) type of prayer that places a protective wall around a person.
sesantun See *santun.*
sikut, nyikut Ritual measuring procedure for the layout of a new building or courtyard.
simbuh Saliva mixed with betel juice used as a medication.
sisia Ritual client of a priest or healer.
subak (1) set of rice fields linked to one source of water; (2) organization of owners of a set of rice fields.
sukla Untouched, pure. See *lungsuran.*
suku Penny.
tegal Dry field.
tenget Haunted by spirits and deities; spiritually powerful, usually referring to places or objects.
tiang, titiang I, in high register.
tirta Holy water.
titiang See *tiang.*
tonya A spirit, usually of a natural feature of the landscape.
Tu Short for Ratu.
tuan Mister, lord, respected foreigner (male).
tukang Artisan.
tukang banten Ritual expert, female.
Tut, Tuté Short for Ketut.
ulaka Brahmana ritual expert, male.
uug To be destroyed.
warung Coffee or wine shop.
Waséng A cycle of songs.
Wayan Birth-order name for the firstborn of a set of siblings.
wayang Shadow play.
wayang lemah A shadow play performed in daylight without shadows.
wayang wong Dance based on a shadow play.
widi Protector.
winten, pawintenan Ritual to purify and prepare a ritual expert.
Wo Address term for an uncle.

Bibliography

Bakker, Wim. 1985. *Bali Verbeeld.* Delft: Volkenkundig Museum Nusantara.

Bateson, Gregory. 1973. "Style, Grace and Information in Primitive Art." In *Primitive Art and Society,* ed. Anthony Forge. London: Oxford University Press.

Bateson, Gregory, and Margaret Mead. 1942. *Balinese Character: A Photographic Analysis.* New York: New York Academy of Sciences.

Bonnet, Rudolf. 1936. "Beeldende Kunst in Gianjar." *Djawa* 16.

———. 1953(?). "A New Era, A New Art." In *Bali: Cults and Customs,* ed. R. Goris. Djakarta: Republic of Indonesia.

———. 1961. *De Kunst van Bali/Verleden en heden.* Den Haag: Haags Gemeentemuseum.

Connor, Linda. 1979. "Corpse Abuse and Trance in Bali: The Cultural Mediation of Aggression." *Mankind* 12:104–108.

———. 1986. "A Balinese Trance Séance" and "Jero on Jero: 'A Balinese Trance Séance Observed.'" In Linda Connor, Patsy Asch, and Timothy Asch, *Jero Tapakan: Balinese Healer—An Ethnographic Film Monograph.* Cambridge: Cambridge University Press.

Covarrubias, Miguel. 1956. *Island of Bali.* New York: Knopf.

DeZoete, Beryl, and Walter Spies. 1973/1938. *Dance and Drama in Bali.* London: Oxford University Press.

Djelantik, A. A. M. 1986. *Balinese Paintings.* Singapore: Oxford University Press.

———. 1997. *The Birthmark. Memoirs of a Balinese Prince.* Singapore: Periplus Editions.

Donald Friend's Bali. 1990. Exh. cat. Sydney: Art Gallery of New South Wales.

Eiseman, Fred B., Jr. 1989. *Bali: Sekala and Niskala.* 2 vols. Berkeley, CA: Periplus Editions.

Forge, Anthony. 1978. *Balinese Traditional Paintings.* Sydney: The Australian Museum.

Galestin, Th. P. 1962. *Hedendaagse Kunst van Bali.* Utrecht: Centraal Museum.

Geertz, Clifford. 1973. "Person, Time, and Conduct in Bali." In *The Interpretation of Cultures.* New York: Basic Books.

———. 1980. *Negara: The Theatre State in Nineteenth-Century Bali.* Princeton, NJ: Princeton University Press.

Geertz, Hildred. 1992. "A Theatre of Cruelty: The Contexts of a Topéng Performance." In *State and Society in Bali: Historical, Textual and Anthropological Approaches,* ed. Hildred Geertz. Leiden: KITLV Press.

———. 1994. *Images of Power: Balinese Paintings Made for Gregory Bateson and Margaret Mead.* Honolulu: University of Hawai'i Press.

———. 2004. *The Life of a Balinese Temple: Artistry, Imagination, and History in a Peasant Village.* Honolulu: University of Hawai'i Press.

Geertz, Hildred, and Clifford Geertz. 1975. *Kinship in Bali.* Chicago: University of Chicago Press.

Haks, F., et al. 1999. *Pre-War Balinese Modernists 1928–1942: An Additional Page in Art-History.* Haarlem: Ars et Animato.

Hohn, Klaus D. 1997. *Reflections of Faith: The History of Painting in Batuan, 1834–1994.* Wijk en Aalburg, Netherlands: Pictures Publishers Art Books.

Holt, Claire. 1967. *Art in Indonesia: Continuities and Change.* Ithaca, NY: Cornell University Press.

Hooykaas, C. 1980. *Drawings of Balinese Sorcery.* Leiden: E. J. Brill.

Kam, Garrett. 1993. *Perceptions of Paradise: Images of Bali in the Arts.* Bali: Yayasan Dharma Seni Museum Neka.

Kamus Bali-Indonesia. 1978/1989. Denpasar: Dinas Pendidikan Dasar, Propinsi DATI I BALI.

Lueras, Leonard. 1987. *Bali: The Ultimate Island.* Singapore: Times Editions.

Mershon, Katharane Edson. 1971. *Seven Plus Seven: Mysterious Life-Rituals in Bali.* New York: Vantage Press.

Museum Puri Lukisan. 1999. Ubud, Bali: Yayasan Rathna Warta.

Resink, Th. A. 1961. *De Kunst van Bali: Verleden en Heden.* The Hague: Haags Gemeentemuseum.

Rhodius, Hans, and John Darling. 1980. *Walter Spies and Balinese Art.* Amsterdam: Tropical Museum.

Vickers, Adrian. 1986. "The Desiring Prince: A Study of the Kidung Malat as Text." Ph.D. diss., University of Sydney.

———. 1989. *Bali: A Paradise Created.* Victoria: Penguin Books of Australia.

———. 1990. "The Amad Story by Ida Bagus Made Togog." In *Donald Friend's Bali.* Exh. cat. Sydney: Art Gallery of New South Wales.

———. 1991. "Ritual Written: The Song of the Ligya, or the Killing of the Rhinoceros." In *State and Society in Bali,* ed. Hildred Geertz. Leiden: KITLV Press.

———. 2000. "I Nengah Metra 1902–1946: Thoughts on the Biography of a Modern Balinese." In *To Change Bali: Essays in Honour of I Gusti Ngurah Bagus,* ed. Adrian Vickers, I Nyoman Darma Putra, and Michele Ford. Den Pasar, Bali: Bali Post.

Williams, Adriana. 1994. *Covarrubias.* Austin: University of Texas Press.

Index

Boldface numbers refer to illustrations.

art materials: cloth, 205; dating paintings by availability of, 148, 225, 234n12; ink, 184–185, paints, 186, 201–202; paper, 136–137, 182, 184; table, 148; *ulantaga* paper, 183–184

balé dangin, 24, 25, 62; construction of, 150–154
Balinese language: plurals, ix; registers, ix, 9–10; roots and affixes, ix. *See also* kinship terms; language etiquette; titles, honorific
Bateson, Gregory, 75, 157, 211, 217, 235n1 (app. 1)
Bateson, Gregory and Margaret Mead, 2, 4, 6, 83, 99, 175, 180, 197–201, 233n3 (intro.); Library of Congress archives, 2; their painting collection, 2
Batuan: description of, 13–14; map of, **28–29** (fig. 7)
Belo, Jane, 183
Bonnet, Rudolf, 6, 7, 179–182, 184–185, 186, 205, 234n4, 234n13
books *(lontar),* 14–15, 21, 71–72; copying, 89–90, 113; reading and translating, 85–86; as talismanic objects, 120–121. *See also* literary readings
Brahmana: Brahmana Buda, 14–15; Brahmana Siwa, 14–15, 86; clans, 13, 15; demotion to Satria, 164–167; and ritual clients *(sisia),* 14, 46, 83–84, 136, 199–200; as ritual specialists, 13–14, 86
Brahmana role in carving ritual objects, 135–136. *See also* ritual work
Brahmana women's work, 49

calendar, 20, 87–88, 152; Pawukon year, 19; Togog's picture of, 184. *See also* time
Calon Arang, 97–98
"charmed," 15, 210
clan organization, 15, 156, 233n2 (chap. 1)
client relationships of Brahmana, 73, 83–84, 136
clothing, 49, 55, 59, 129; as object of envy, 146
cockfights, 20, 38–39, 147, 150; as offerings, 94; play fights, 49. *See also* gambling
coins, as talismanic objects, 145–150. *See also* currencies; money
colonial social relationships, 47, 81–83
Connor, Linda, 210, 212
construction: in a dream, 223–224; of household pavilion *(balé dangin),* 150–154; rituals *(sikut),* 140–145; of temple, 142–145, **144** (fig. 22)
corpse-abuse *(ngarap),* 132
court cases. *See* legal disputes
Covarrubias, Miguel, 180, 213
cremation. *See* mortuary rites; rituals: cremation
currencies, 22, 46, 55, 179; confusion over, 55, 195. *See also* coins; money

dances: *arja,* 23, 99, 107–108; Calon Arang, 97–98; *gambuh,* 23, 82, 94–95, **96** (fig. 21), 97, 107; *jogéd,* 75; ritual *(prasutri),* 20, 93–94, **95** (fig. 20)
dancing, 96–97
Déwa Ketut Baru, **3** (fig. 2)
Djelantik, Dr. A. A. M., 210–211
drawings, Togog's: of childhood scenes, **42** (fig. 15), **89** (fig. 18), **92** (fig. 19), **144** (fig. 22); of dance performances, **95–96** (figs. 20 and 21); of houseyard layout, **26–27** (figs. 5 and 6); of sites in Batuan, **30** (fig. 8), **32** (fig. 9), **35** (fig. 10); of temples, **36–40** (figs. 11 to 14). *See also* paintings, Togog's
dreams, Togog's, 197, 217–224, 235n1 (app. 1); pictures of, **219–224** (figs. 25 to 34)

economic situation, 1920s and 1930s, 45–47, 77–78
Eiseman, Fred B., Jr., 233n1 (chap. 2)

fate *(karma),* 104–105, 107, 111
foreigners, 41–43, 47, 88, 179–201; anthropologists, 197–201; "foreigner talk," 7, 215

Galestin, Th. P., 234n4
gambling: cricket fights, 22; declared

illegal, 72, 73; dispute during, 164, 167; games, 59, 70–71, 74, **89** (fig. 18), 90, 164; as obsession, 60–61, 72–73, 76; winnings, 74. *See also* cockfights
gamelan orchestra: instruments, 90; playing, 93–94, **95** (fig. 20), **96** (fig. 21)
genealogy: of Brahmana clans, 14, 21; Togog's, 14, 16, **17** (fig. 4), 18
George, Kenneth, vii
God *(Tuhan),* 104, 106; and *niskala* beings, 105. *See also* fate; *niskala* beings; Sanghyang Cintia; spirits
Gordon, Karen, vii

healers *(balian),* 18, 24–25, 39, 61–63, 71, 147–149; kinds of, 121
healing. *See* healers *(balian);* illness
Hooykaas, C., 235n11
Houboldt, 180, 195–196
household, definition of, 15
houseyard layout, **25–27** (fig. 5, fig. 6)
houseyard, social composition of, 15–16, 155–169

illegitimacy, 51, 163–164, 235n1 (app. 1)
illness: cured by foreign medicine, 198; in a dream, 222–223; pervasiveness of, 45, 191; prevented by ritual dance *(prasutri),* 93; due to ritual misstep, 134–135; due to sorcery, 20–22, 24–25, 60–65. *See also* healers *(balian)*
inheritance, 100, 155–177

karma. See fate
kawi (language), 85
kinship terms, 16; use for non-relatives, 10

Lake, Alison, vii
language etiquette, 76–77, 162, 187; in a dream, 218. *See also* Balinese language
Leeman, Albert, 6
legal disputes: debt, 169–175; inheritance, 100; land-tenure, 169–177
literacy, 85–86, 88, 96
literary readings *(mabasan),* 85–86, 124–125, 129
literature, Balinese. *See* books *(lontar)*
lontar. See books

Madé Poleng, Ida Bagus, 180
Malay/Indonesian (language), 47, 195
map of Bali, **48** (fig. 16)
marriage: affairs, 58; elopement, 54; rules and practices, 15, 155–169, 221
martial arts *(pencak),* 60, 160–161; Togog's picture of, 177
mask-making, 88, 89, 91, 92, **92** (fig. 19)
Mead, Margaret. *See* Bateson, Gregory and Margaret Mead
medicine, 62, 63, 161, 182, 198. *See also* sorcery: chewed betel nut *(simbuh)* as counteragent
methods of interviewing, 4–7
monetary system, colonial, 46. *See also* currencies; taxes
money: cash, 46–47; found jewels, 138; gambling winnings, 74; and magic, 60, 67–68; ritual earnings, 124; used in ritual, 58. *See also* coins; currencies; monetary system, colonial
moral philosophy *(indik):* moral framework, 215–216; moral sayings *(tutur),* 128; in stories and songs, 85, 101, 108, 109, 111, 116–117
mortuary rites *(nyekah):* expense of, 177; need for, 168–169, 171, 174. *See also* rituals: cremation
Museum Bali, 180
Museum Puri Lukisan, 180, 234n12
Neuhaus, Hans and Rolf, 180
Ngendon, I Ketut, 180
niskala beings, 98, 105, 209–216; as audience for art, 99; at crossroads, 126; fear of, 41; kinds of, 120. *See also* God *(Tuhan);* spirits

objects, sacred. *See* talismanic objects
offerings, 18, 102, 103; kinds of, 135–136, 158; to protect a religious practitioner *(santun),* 18, 124, 135
opium, 131

painting god-figures, 135
painting: modern Balinese (1929–1938), 179–193; (1940–1970), 196–197, 205; Batuan style, 1; as bicultural, 203; for foreigners, 1; Togog's role in development of, 1
paintings, Togog's: content of, 203–205; made for temple, 201–205, **202** (fig. 23), 225–231, **226–230** (figs. 35 to 38); of a plowing race, **53** (fig. 17); pricing of, 185, 198; proportions in, 185–186, 189, 234n13; reproduced and collected, 233n1 (intro.); sale of, 150, 158, 167–168, 177, 179–180, 193–197; of Sanghyang Cintia, **x** (fig. 1); of the Story of Amad and Mohamed Killing the Men in Iron Armor, **206** (fig. 24), 211. *See also* art materials: dating paintings by availability of; dreams, Togog's
Pandy, Jimmy, 185, 196
Pita Maha, 180, 190, 234n12
pollution *(kesepung, letuh),* 77, 164–167, 200. *See also* purification
poverty, 45, 78; and *karma,* 107; and wealth, 106
priests *(pedanda),* 13–14
purification, 60, 61; of building materials, 153; to end gambling, 76;

through story-telling, 100. *See also* pollution

rain-dispelling rituals, 136–140, 145–146, 212
religion, Balinese, 208–214
religious expertise, 85–86, 119–154; as esoteric knowledge, 54, 98, 112
ritual calendar. *See* calendar
ritual work, 86–87, 119–120; carving a cremation bull, 134–135. *See also* dancing; mask-making; painting god-figures; singing
rituals: cleansing of corpses, 131–132, 133; construction *(sikut),* 140–145; cremation, 80, 83–84, 126–128, 133; prayers to local deity, 60–61, 67–68, 128; rain-dispelling, 136–140, 145–146, 212; tooth-filing *(masangih),* 113, 114, 130–131, 159–160. *See also* literary readings; mortuary rites; ritual work

sakti: concept of, 209–210, 233n1 (chap. 1); contained in talismanic objects, 145; masters of, 14–15, 21–22, 142, 204; as personal potency, 171; possessed by Brahmana, 88, 119; possessed by sorcerers, 143–144; its power to heal, 24; proof of possession of, 147–148, 161; secrecy about, 211–213
Sanghyang Cintia, **x** (fig. 1), 213–214, 235n12
Satria, 13; and Brahmana, 164–166
Shanklin, Eugenia, vii
singing, 108–116. *See also* songs
skull, discovery of possibly prehistoric, 143
Sobrat, Anak Agung Gedé, 180, 184
Socolow, Elizabeth Anne, vii
songs: *geguritan,* 99, 109–111; *kekawin,* 85, 91, **92** (fig. 19), 115, 132; *kidung,* 109–115; *tandak,* 95; *waséng,* 95–96. *See also* singing
sorcery, 208–214; chewed betel nut *(simbuh)* as counteragent, 24, 39, 122; described in *lontar,* 121; fear of, 54; motivated by envy, 146; motivated by revenge, 69–70; protection against, 142, 144; sorcerers in animal forms, 71–72, 93; versus countersorcery, 136. *See also* illness: due to sorcery; *sakti;* spirits
Spies, Walter, 2, 6, 7, 179–193, 205, 213
spirits: ancestral *(leluur),* 18–19, 139; guardian, 72, 81, 191, 194, 210, 214; kinds of, 71–72; local *(tonya),* 67–68, 69–70, 93, 138; of uncremated dead, 168–169, 174. See also *niskala* beings
stealing, 55, 191–192
stories: of Amad and Mohamed Killing the Men in Iron Armor, **206** (fig. 24), 211, 235n7; of Batur Taskara, 111; of the Frog Prince, 108; of the Greedy Man, 106–107; of Koripané ring Daha, 23; of the Poor Man and the Rich Man, 101–105; of the Poor Man's Offerings, 105–106; of the Three Fish, 110–111
story-telling, 69–70, 98–99, 109–110, 125–126, 138; through dance, 94–96; moral philosophy in, 106, 108; as purificatory, 94, 100; through songs, 109

talismanic objects, 14, 119–122, 135–136, 138, 139, 140, 145–150, 151–152
taxes, 81–83, 169
temple painting of Bratayudha, 225–231, **226–227** (fig. 35), **228** (fig. 36), **229** (fig. 37), **230** (fig. 38)
temples: clan temple (Pura Penataran Brahmana Buda), **36** (fig. 11), 36–37; temple construction, 142–145, **144** (fig. 22); temple of death (Pura Dalem Jungut), 39, **40** (fig. 14); temple of the sea (Pura Segara), 34; village temple (Pura Désa), 37–38, **37–38** (figs. 12 and 13), 235n12
tenget, 25. See also *sakti*
terms of address. *See* kinship terms; titles, honorific
time *(dauh),* 60
titles, honorific, ix, 9–10, 77
Togog, pictures of, **3–4** (figs. 2 and 3)
translation: of Balinese classical language, 85, 96, 112; of Togog's words, 8–10

van Wessem, Maria v.d. Sleen, 234n12
Vickers, Adrian, vii, 6, 96, 113, 132, 211, 235n8

witchcraft. *See* sorcery: versus countersorcery
wood carving, for tourists, 55, 68
work, 22, 45–46, 68; agricultural exchange labor, 52; as *klian,* 36–37; assisting priests, 122–131; caring for a bull, 30–31; —pigs, 31; fishing, 67–69, **92** (fig. 19), 93; versus gambling, 181; gathering flowers, 55–56; in government offices, 46; guarding fields, 78–80; —a government office, 83; harvesting chili peppers, 56; —coffee, 57–58; making coconut oil, 67; peddling, 20, 56, 63–64, 66; picking coconuts, 23, 32, 51; —candlenuts, 63, 66; —mangos, 33, 34–35; planting, 59; plowing, 52; raising crickets, 22; —ducks, 80; sawing, 81; share-cropping, 73; stonecutting, 54; trapping birds, 21–22; wage-labor, 56–60; weeding, 80. *See also* ritual work

About the Authors

Hildred Geertz has spent much of her career seeking a deep and nuanced understanding of Bali. This volume, like her two previous works—*Images of Power* (1994) and *Life of a Balinese Temple* (2004)—moves from specific objects, in this case recorded texts, to their contexts, and finally to Balinese life as a whole. The result is an insightful and revealing view of Balinese culture.

In her thirty years of teaching at Princeton University's Anthropology Department, Geertz taught courses in art and anthropology, social theory, and fieldwork methods. She was department chair for five years and is now professor emeritus.

Ida Bagus Madé Togog was an important innovator in Balinese art in the twentieth century. Both an artist and ritual specialist, he played a significant role in the history of Balinese ethnography. In the 1930s, Togog came under the influence of expatriate artists Walter Spies and Rudolf Bonnet, emerging as a major representative of the Batuan style of painting. He was central to Margaret Mead and Gregory Bateson's pioneering studies of "Balinese character," and over the course of his career spoke with other scholars about his life and work. His paintings remained highly sought after in the market of fine tourist art until his death in 1989.

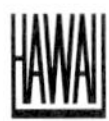

Production Notes for Geertz / TALES FROM A CHARMED LIFE
Cover and interior design by April Leidig-Higgins
Text in Monotype Garamond and Scala Sans; display type in Tarazana Wide
Composition by Copperline Book Services, Inc.
Printing and binding by Thomson-Shore, Inc.
Printed on 70# Fortune Matte, 540 ppi